T0367217

THE I TATTI
RENAISSANCE LIBRARY

James Hankins, General Editor

BEMBO

HISTORY OF VENICE

VOLUME I

ITRL 28

PIETRO BEMBO

✦ ✦ ✦

HISTORY OF VENICE

VOLUME I · BOOKS I–IV

EDITED AND TRANSLATED BY

ROBERT W. ULERY, JR.

THE I TATTI RENAISSANCE LIBRARY

HARVARD UNIVERSITY PRESS

CAMBRIDGE, MASSACHUSETTS

LONDON, ENGLAND

2007

Series design by Dean Bornstein

Library of Congress Cataloging-in-Publication Data

Bembo, Pietro, 1470–1547.
[Historiae Venetae libri XII. English & Latin]
History of Venice / Pietro Bembo ; edited and translated by Robert W. Ulery, Jr.
p.   cm. — (The I Tatti Renaissance library ; 28)
English and Latin.
Includes bibliographical references and index.
ISBN 978-0-674-02283-6 (cloth : alk. paper)
1. Venice (Italy) — History — 697–1508.   I. Ulery, Robert W.   II. Title.
DG677.A2B413 2007
945'.3103 — dc22   2007009602

Contents

ॐঃঃॐ

Book II (1493–95)   78

Book III (1495–1497)   166

Introduction

※❦❧

In the troubled years of the early part of the sixteenth century, the government of Venice sought to preserve the reputation of the Republic through the appointment of an official historian.[1] In 1485 Marco Antonio Coccio, called Sabellico (1436–1506), presented to the government a work it had not commissioned, namely, his *Rerum Venetarum ab urbe condita libri*, which in thirty-three books traced Venetian history from the foundation of the city to the present. Sabellico's work first came off the press in 1487, and, as its title suggests, he drew inspiration from and modeled his work on the history of ancient Rome by Livy. Sabellico subsequently published, in 1491, an edition of Livy with textual commentary. Sabellico exemplifies how under the impetus of contemporary political events the philological interests of the fifteenth century could lead to the production of history in imitation of a Roman model.[2] When the Venetian government decided early in 1516 to commission someone to carry the work forward from 1487, it chose a member of the Venetian nobility, the young Andrea Navagero, who had already written Latin poetry and prose for private and public purposes.[3] Navagero worked from 1516 until 1529, producing a first draft in ten books; but during a diplomatic mission to France he fell ill and before dying ordered that the draft be burned. The authorities thus looked to find a suitable man to replace Navagero who might begin anew to write a history of Venice from 1487 onward. Their choice fell upon Pietro Bembo (1470–1547).[4]

Born in Venice on 20 May 1470 of a noble family and a prominent father, Bernardo, Bembo was educated in Venice. In addition to the rich culture of that city he had the advantage of his father's extraordinary library. Pietro's education was intended to prepare

the young noble for a life of participation in governing the affairs of Venice, but that life did not attract him as strongly as the literary world. He wrote poetry, in Latin and in the vernacular, and accompanied his father on diplomatic missions to Florence (1478–80) and Rome (1487–88); on his return from the latter city he decided to continue his education rather than enter political life. In 1492 he went south to study Greek with the Byzantine émigré Constantine Lascaris in Messina, returning in 1494 when King Charles of France threatened to invade Italy. Aldus Manutius printed in 1496 his first published work, a Latin prose dialogue called *Aetna*, describing his ascent of Mt. Etna in 1493.[5] He continued his study of philosophy at the University of Padua and later in Ferrara, when his father worked there in 1497–99. In Ferrara he began the project of a prose dialogue in the vernacular on the subject of love, *Gli Asolani* (The People of Asolo). Returning to Venice in 1500, he ran for minor offices unsuccessfully, then occupied himself with philosophy, theology and vernacular love poetry with a circle of friends. Further visits to Rome and Ferrara ensued in 1501–03, including an affair with Lucrezia Borgia; but he had begun to consider an ecclesiastical career, deciding ultimately to pursue that vocation after more failed attempts at electoral office in Venice. In 1504 he had prepared for publication a philological work on Latin poets, *De corruptis poetarum locis* (On Corrupted Passages in the Poets), also written at Ferrara; this would be a first draft of what was finally published in 1530 as the Latin dialogue *De Virgilii Culice et Terentii fabulis* (On the Gnat of Virgil and the Plays of Terence). He also began to edit vernacular texts (Petrarch and Dante) for the printer Aldus, attempting to restore the purity of their original Tuscan after the changes made in the fifteenth century, and setting the two poets on the same level as the Latin classics. At the same time, his revision of the language of his *Asolani* led him to lay the foundations for his great work on the vernacular, the *Prose della volgar lingua* (Prose in the Vernacular

Tongue). *Gli Asolani* appeared in 1505. The next year Bembo transferred to the court of Urbino in search of an ecclesiastical position. While in Urbino, he wrote a Latin dialogue about the duke and duchess and composed his *Prose della volgar lingua*.

In 1512 he moved to Rome with his friends Giuliano de' Medici and Jacopo Sadoleto, and found a new patron in the archbishop of Salerno, Federico Fregoso. After publishing in 1513 a defense of his choice of Cicero as the model for writing Latin, the short treatise *De imitatione* (On Imitation), he was appointed secretary to the newly elected Pope Leo X (Giovanni de' Medici).[6] His work involved the writing of papal correspondence in Latin and diplomatic missions, and he was able to continue his association with the learned community in Rome. From 1519 on, he lived increasingly on a family property in Padua where he installed the woman with whom he had fallen in love in 1513 (Ambrogina Faustina della Torre, known as la Morosina) and who later bore him three children (Lucilio, Torquato, and Elena).

Pope Leo died in 1521, and Bembo devoted himself to literary work, publishing the *Prose della volgar lingua* at last in 1525 to great acclaim. His argument for the Tuscan of Dante and Petrarch and Boccaccio as the model for vernacular prose sparked intense discussion. He was working to form a new literary society on the basis of his ideas, and he republished his own works at the end of the decade (1530). Pope Clement VII awarded him a Paduan benefice, and it was then that the Venetian authorities asked him to become their historian and librarian. The librarian duties were undertaken for him by his friend Ramusio, and he occupied himself with the writing of the history from 1530 until 1544, during which period he survived an assassination attempt, attacks on his literary dominance, the deaths of la Morosina and their son Lucilio, and changes in the papal court; he was named to the College of Cardinals in 1539 by Pope Paul III. He lived then in Rome until taking up a bishopric in Gubbio in 1543, where he finished

the *History* as far as the accession of Leo X in 1513. He then translated the work into the vernacular. He died of an illness at the beginning of 1547, and the *History* was submitted to the Venetian authorities by his executors after his death.

The censorship of the work in 1548, by the *Riformatori* in Padua, was said to be motivated by concern for living persons and their families, but also involved political opinions, national pride, and diplomatic sagacity.[7] The recommended cuts were then discussed and deliberated in the Council of Ten. The changes were made in both the Latin and Italian versions, with some alteration of the Italian on stylistic grounds, changes that were later reversed in part by subsequent editors. The uncensored Latin version was subsequently lost, but the Italian autograph emerged from Venetian archives and was published in 1790, allowing a comparison of the two versions that will be noted where appropriate in the translation below.

For the composition of the *History* Bembo accumulated historical materials such as the papers of Luigi da Porto (1485–1529) of Vicenza, which included his *Lettere storiche*, of use to Bembo for events of 1509–10.[8] He was able to draw upon official documents as well as the oral tradition for these events of the recent past, in addition to works by Bernardo Giustinian, *De origine urbis Venetiarum rebusque a Venetis gestis libri XV*; Pietro Marcello, *De vitis principum et gestis Venetorum*; a summary by Giampiero Stella; a chronicle of Andrea Navagero; the *Historia general y natural de las Indias* of Oviedo for the digression on Columbus' voyages of discovery; and Marin Sanudo's *Cronache*.[9]

The work, in twelve books of 9–10,000 words each (Book VII is half again as long), is largely taken up with the first phase of the Italian Wars (1494–1513). A second focus is provided by the conflict with the Turks in the East, while domestic events in Venice receive ever decreasing space as external affairs become increasingly complex. Book I covers the years 1487–1493, with a detailed ac-

count of the war against Sigismund in the Tyrol, the persuading of Caterina Cornaro by her brother to cede the island of Cyprus to Venice, the visit of the Holy Roman Emperor Frederick to Italy, and changes in the voting mechanism in the Venetian Great Council; it ends with the deaths of Lorenzo de' Medici and Pope Innocent VIII. Book II (1493–95) contains the account of the invasion of Italy by King Charles VIII of France, his progress to Naples and back, the Battle of Fornovo, and Charles's return to France. Book III (1495–97) is divided between Venice's involvement with King Ferrandino of Naples and the conflict with the Florentines for Pisa, along with the machinations of Ludovico and Maximilian I. The Pisan conflict continues in Book IV (1497–99), which includes the death of Charles VIII, the beginning of troubles with the Turkish sultan Bayazid II, and the invasion of the Piedmont by the French under King Louis XII. Book V (1499–1501) is dominated by the struggles against the Turks in Dalmatia and Greece, ending with the death of Doge Agostino Barbarigo.

Book VI (1501–1504) begins with a long digression on the voyages of Columbus to the New World and of the Portuguese to the East and continues to recount the conflict with the Turks, resolved by a peace treaty; the troubles caused in Romagna by Cesare Borgia result in his downfall; Pope Alexander VI dies, as does his successor Pius III, succeeded by Julius II. Book VII (1504–1509) leads through a variety of conflicts to the League of Cambrai, ending with the defeat of the Venetians at the Adda (Agnadello). The events in Italy of 1509 take up both Books VIII and IX: Venice regains some of what she lost to the League, ending Book VIII with the retaking of Padua; more towns are regained in Book IX, which ends with the defeat of a Venetian fleet in the Po by Alfonso d'Este. Book X (1510) continues the story of the Venetians' conflict with Maximilian and with Alfonso d'Este; Julius II lifts the excommunication of Venice, but the Republic suffers more losses to France and Maximilian. The struggle to control towns in northern

Italy continues through Book XI (1510–1511). Book XII (1511–1513) describes the conflict and truce with Maximilian in Carnia and Friuli; a Holy League is formed against the French and the Battle of Ravenna is fought; the French are driven from Piedmont, and the Medici return to Florence. The work ends with the excommunication of the King of France, the death of Julius II, and the election of Leo X.

In modern times Bembo's Latin poetry and his importance in shaping the vernacular have overshadowed his historical work. Francesco Guicciardini's fame as an historian has quite eclipsed that of Bembo. As a source, moreover, Bembo has suffered by comparison with the great richness of primary material offered by Marin Sanudo in his *Diarii*. Finally, his work is found wanting by the standards of modern scientific history. Eric Cochrane, in *Historians and Historiography in the Italian Renaissance*, disparages the attitude that Bembo took toward his task.[10] According to Cochrane, "Bembo felt no vocation for history, which, as he protested to the Senate, he had 'never had the slightest thought of writing'; and he had always remained 'very distant from public life and from those actions that form the material of history.'" But the words Cochrane quotes may be interpreted otherwise in their context: Bembo's initial response to the idea of the appointment by Venice's Council of Ten, expressed in a letter not to the Senate but to his friend Giambattista Ramusio, the secretary of the Council, on 21 June 1529.[11]

> First, I thank their Lordships for having thought to select me for this enterprise, which I truly regard as the most difficult one in literary studies generally, both for style, which must be learned and pure and very rich, and for prudence, which is the foundation of good history and happens not to be required so much in other genres. Second, I tell you that I am rather removed from that life and those public activities

which are in large measure the material of history; both by personal choice, in that I have dedicated myself to study, and by my role in the Church, which separates me from them. In addition, in the many kinds of writing to which I have at times put my hand and produced some work, I never had a thought of wanting to write history. And again, I tell you that I am now far advanced in years and an old man. And this would be a task, if not for a young man, at least for one of an age still green, not white. For one must write about events of many years, of many kinds, and of great diversity, and involving great labor, first in having to collect them, and then in portraying and depicting them on paper in such a way that they may provide both utility and delight. Besides, I have gone into retirement, as you know; and to turn from it would doubtless be both troublesome and burdensome to me. For this reason I beg you and press you to ask their Lordships to leave me to furnish the remainder of the life before me with the studies to which I have become accustomed and which are the sweetest to me; this I shall receive as a most grateful gift at their hands. However, if they do not accept my excuse, and wish me to pledge to bear this burden, I do not feel able to deny my homeland something she wishes of me; for I love her as much as do those same Lordships, who are taking this under their care.

This is a very elegant response, but it is not necessary to take it as a sincere attempt to avoid the assignment; initial refusals and demurrals were a regular part of patron-client negotiations. Moreover, in the marshalling of arguments, Bembo's letter displays the very qualities required of the historian, makes the authorities aware that they are imposing a burden upon him, and protects him against any charge of overweening authorial ambition against which the resulting history might be measured. These arguments

concerning the difficulties of the task are further detailed in the proem of the *History* (see 1.1).

Cochrane regards as even more unfortunate than his lack of motivation his decision "to compensate for this disadvantage by reducing history largely to a matter of language."[12] One may say rather that he treated the project as an essentially literary enterprise rather than as an opportunity to do original historical research (Cochrane details the materials that would have been available to Bembo had he chosen the latter tack). In this literary approach he was being as self-consciously "classical" as in his linguistic choices. That is to say, he took on the Livian role of shaping available accounts in a convincing literary form. If we ask "Convincing to whom?" the answer in the first instance is the Venetian Senate and governing elite generally; the evidence, however, is that the work did not satisfy them until some revisions were made after his death (again, Cochrane gives a summary and the bibliography; the revisions are very slight in comparison with the bulk of the work). But we should note as well that a larger European audience is implied by the choice of Latin as the language of composition, just as the choice of publishing it almost simultaneously in Italian implies an Italian audience wider than the educated elite. Bembo set himself the task of creating a literary representation of Venetian history that not only reflected the image the Venetian elite had of itself, but also aimed to shape the view that the rest of Europe would take of Venice's ethos and her role in the history of the period between the end of the war with Ferrara and the death of Pope Julius II.[13]

This is how he described his task in a letter to Oviedo in 1538: "My homeland and this Republic [have] some years ago now given me the task of writing in Latin the history of its affairs." "Its affairs" (*le cose sue*) are of course the *res Venetae*, the affairs of Venice (the title of the work also appears in the editions as *Historia rerum Venetarum*), a phrase parallel with the classical *res Romanae*;

throughout the work he refers to the political entity of Venice as the *Respublica,* and the phrase also suggests *res gestae,* the achievements of that Republic.

Despite its status as official history, Bembo's *History* is not wholly free of the personal voice. Some of the insertions of the first person in Bembo's narrative appear to be as Cochrane characterizes them, deliberate attempts to increase our sense of him as a contemporary of the events and personally involved in them in some way.[14] Other instances seem almost inadvertent. For example, in the midst of his account of the Pisa campaign, Bembo slips in this lament (4.46): "It is tiresome for me to go through the minor points of the war. Who can read every last detail without aversion, especially if, as in most cases, the reader is only looking to reach the conclusions as soon as may be? But I think that people will readily forgive me when they realize that my chief aim in this historical labor is to avoid the appearance of passing over in silence the public deeds of my fellow citizens as if they had no importance." Here he seems to anticipate the sentiments of Guicciardini's translator, Sidney Alexander, who justified his cutting a passage of the historian's account by recalling "the dilemma of the prisoner who chose the galleys rather than freedom at the price of reading *in minutiae* Guicciardini's account of the Pisan campaign."[15]

Though Bembo is rightly known as the foremost Ciceronian of his day, the principal models for these histories are Caesar and Livy — there being no Ciceronian history to serve as model, and Livian historiography having been the model of his predecessor Sabellico. In several instances (6.1, 10.49, and 78) in the twelve books he refers to his work as *commentarii,* which is of course the term for the work of Caesar he imitated. But the Livian model predominates, as even the battle descriptions do not match the clarity and economy of Caesar's *commentarii.* The two classical historians he chose to imitate are of course part of the classical heri-

tage of all Italians, but there is also a particular connection with Venice: Caesar was responsible for bringing the cities of the Po valley into the empire as a part of Italy; and Livy was a native of Padua. Bembo's practice of imitation is illuminated by this note of the biographer in the 1729 edition of the *Opere*: "It is said by his servants that when he wanted to compose something, he would take the author whom he wished to imitate and would read him and diligently observe him for several days, to refresh, I believe, the scent of his style." But Bembo's practice of immersion was in fact useful for more than the style; and in the first book Bembo appears to have made a great effort to match the historiographical procedures of Livy. This was an effort largely abandoned in the later books, as he sought to bring the very complex history of those times to some conclusion as his own life ended.

As for the Ciceronian traits of style, at least some of the criticisms leveled at Bembo's *History*, notably by Justus Lipsius, are exaggerated. Lipsius made his harsh criticisms in his *Notae ad primum librum Politicorum* (Notes to the First Book of the *Politics*),[16] and in greater detail in a letter to Janus Dousa. In the former he claims to find the narrative style flat or frigid; he speaks of verbal affectations, excessive limitation to Ciceronian and Caesarian usage, awkward periphrases to avoid new terminology, the pretension of Roman republican terminology for the Venetian present reality, and even outright errors of Latinity. Of all these he gives a number of examples, some of them false or misleading, in the letter to Dousa.[17] For instance, he says that the Venetian Senate is always called *patres conscripti*. There are four instances (6.22, 7.15, 8.58, 10.5) where Bembo refers to senators as *patres conscripti* (two of them in speeches), but he regularly calls them just *patres*; and it was not Bembo's fault that Venice's principal deliberative body had begun to call itself the Senate in the fifteenth century, in imitation of classical Rome.

In addition to the example of *patres conscripti*, the following usages are not accurately represented by Lipsius. Bembo regularly refers to Venice as *urbs*, but only as a physical entity; far more frequent are *civitas* for the citizenry, and *res publica* for the political entity, the state. *Venetiae* is used instead of *urbs* whenever there might be a confusion with Rome. Since *urbs* is customarily reserved for Venice, he tends to call all other cities *oppida*, and towns are *municipia*, with small places denoted as *vici* or *pagi*; but he is not perfectly consistent. Dates are infrequent, and always given *ab urbe condita*, from the foundation of Venice. Military terminology is fairly clear, with *imperator* reserved for the captain-general, not all generals, as Lipsius charged (his example of Contarini in 3.28–29 is due to a misreading); *praefectus* (also used for the governor or rector of a town), *tribunus*, and *centurio* are used for captain, colonel, and constable, respectively; a *legatus* may be either an ambassador or a *proveditore*, i.e., the officer sent by the Venetians to oversee their hired commanders or *condottieri*. The term *rex* is used, as expected, for the kings of France, Spain, England, and the Holy Roman Empire, as well as for the Turkish sultan; but the lords of Italian city-states are variously called *duces* or *principes* or *obtinentes*, aside from one reference to the *regina* of Urbino; Bembo does use *regnum* for the various realms. For the Turks, Bembo tends to use *Turca* as the substantive, *Thracum* (genitive) or *Thracius* as a modifier, carefully distinguishing between people, who have a nationality, and things, which only belong to them; both terms were widely used in humanist Latin. Lipsius says that second declension genitive endings are used for some fourth declension nouns, but only one example can be found: 3.3 *nihil tumulti*, possibly a Sallustian usage; the objection to *neminem* for *nullam* (9.17 *neminem unam*) seems unjustified considering the usage of Livy; and the use of *veritus* with the dative is also found in Caesar and the *Ciris* and Apuleius. Lipsius' strictures about periphrases for such things as

"falcons," "sables," and "wethers" will seem to most readers justified; likewise perhaps the occasional coinages: *prooppidum* (sub-
urb), *prodominus* (visdomino), *proimperator* (deputy captain-general), *proordines* (irregular recruits?).

The use of pagan Roman terminology for Christian Roman
faith and practice may be as disconcerting to the modern reader as
it was to Lipsius. But Bembo's usage seems rather restrained in
this work.[18] He refers to nuns as *sacrae virgines*; saints are *dii* in two
instances (4.47, 12.58), in another *numina* (7.72). Cardinals are always *cardinales*, never *senatores*, a word Bembo reserves for individual senators outside of the context of Senate meetings. Excommunication is expressed by the Latin for banishment, *aqua et igni
interdictio*, but in a later book (11.56) it is more fully defined. The
Deity is regularly *di immortales*, but sometimes *Deus* (*Optimus
Maximus*); the Church of Rome and the Papal States are *Respublica
Romana*. Ecclesiastical buildings are variously named *sacellum*,
fanum, *templum*, and *aedes*. A monastery is a *sacerdotum collegium*, a
convent *sacrarum virginum collegium* (11.73); but at 11.20 we find
societas monachorum. The public prayers and solemn processions
made at Venice in times of trouble are generally *supplicationes*.

The sentence structures in which these terms are presented are
fully elaborated in the Ciceronian and Livian mode; in many instances there is artful variation with shorter sentences. Bembo
passes frequently between past and historical present tense in his
narration. Chronology is extremely vague, both within years (only
some 60 instances of a precise day) and between them. The geog-
raphy of battles and travel is often quite imprecise, as well. One
hesitates to say whether this is in imitation of classical historiography. There is a marked increase in the rhetorical effectiveness of
Bembo's Latin idiom whenever there is occasion for the creation
or reproduction of a speech, or the challenge of describing something that would have been outside the experience of a Cicero or a
Livy. These are the parts of Bembo's *Historia Veneta* that impress

and delight the reader most greatly. It is hoped that the ready availability of a Latin text and translation of it will enable readers to form a true judgment of its style, to place this work in the tradition of Neo-Latin prose writing, and to see this piece of Venice's history through Bembo's eyes and pen.

I gratefully acknowledge the support of Wake Forest University through the R. J. Reynolds Research Leave program (2003–2004), which granted me a year in which to work on Bembo's text and the translation, and I am thankful to my colleagues for their encouragement. Colleagues in several places were quick to respond to my queries, in particular Patricia Osmond and Dennis Romano; the remarkable website of Roberto Damiani, <condottieridiventura.it>, was of invaluable assistance in many details. John Monfasani kindly read my introductory remarks, and James Hankins as editor gave me useful counsel. I am especially indebted to Martin Davies, the associate editor for the series, who made manifold improvements to the style and accuracy of the translation. I should like to dedicate this volume to my parents.

R.W.U.

Winston-Salem, North Carolina

January 2007

NOTES

1. See Felix Gilbert, "Biondo, Sabellico, and the Beginnings of Venetian Official Historiography," in J. G. Rowe and W. H. Stockdale, eds., *Florilegium Historiale: Essays Presented to Wallace K. Ferguson* (Toronto, 1971), pp. 275–93.

2. For his work on the text of Livy, see A. H. Macdonald in *Catalogus Translationum et Commentariorum*, vol. 2 (Washington, D.C., 1971), pp. 336–37; for his biography, see vol. 4 (1980), pp. 347–48 (where it is wrongly implied that he was the official historiographer), and further bibliography in vol. 7 (1992), pp. 231–32. See also Eric Cochrane, *Histo-*

rians and Historiography in the Italian Renaissance (Chicago and London, 1981), pp. 227–28.

3. Paolo Margaroli, "Introduzione" to Marino Sanudo, *I Diarii (1496–1533): Pagine scelte* (Vicenza, 1997), p. 13; for the biography, see Louis Gabriel Michaud and Joseph Fr. Michaud, *Biographie universelle ancienne et moderne*, 2nd ed., 45 vols. (Paris, 1870–73), 30: 247.

4. See Carlo Dionisotti, "Bembo, Pietro," in *Dizionario biografico degli italiani* 8 (Rome, 1966), pp. 133–151, the authoritative biography from which much of the following is drawn.

5. Published in the I Tatti Renaissance Library in the translation of Betty Radice: Pietro Bembo, *Lyric Poetry. Etna*, ed. and tr. Mary P. Chatfield (Cambridge, Mass., 2005).

6. Published in the I Tatti series in *Ciceronian Controversies*, ed. JoAnn DellaNeva and Brian Duvick (Cambridge, Mass., 2007).

7. Carlo Lagomaggiore, *L'Istoria Viniziana di M. Pietro Bembo*. Estratto dal *Nuovo archivio veneto* 7–9 (1904–1907) (Venice, 1905), pp. 208–218; see E. Teza, "Correzioni alla Istoria veneziana di Pietro Bembo proposte dal Consiglio dei Dieci nel 1548," *Annali delle università toscane* 18 (1888): 75–93.

8. Cecil H. Clough, "The Library of Bernardo and of Pietro Bembo," *Book Collector* 33 (1984): 305–31, esp. 308–09.

9. Mario Santoro, *Pietro Bembo* (Naples, 1937), pp. 122–123, and Lagomaggiore (above, n. 7), both cited by Cochrane (above, n. 2), pp. 228–31 and n. 55.

10. Cochrane, *Historians*, p. 229.

11. Translated from the Italian, found in vol. 3 of his *Opera* (Venice, 1729), p. 121.

12. Cochrane, *Historians*, p. 229.

13. See also Santoro, *Bembo*, pp. 123–126.

14. Cochrane, *Historians*, p. 230.

15. *The History of Italy* (New York and London, 1969), p. 138.

16. Justus Lipsius, *Opera omnia postremum ab ipso aucta et recensita*, 4 vols. (Versailles, 1675), 4: 219.

17. *Epistularum Centuriae II. Miscellanea*, LVII (*Opera omnia* 2.1: 177–9).

18. Izora Scott, in her *Controversies over the Imitation of Cicero in the Renaissance* (New York, 1910; repr. 1991), p. 23, misquotes Jacob Burckhardt as criticizing Bembo's *Venetian History* in this regard, but he was referring generally to "pedants" of the period; see his *Civilization of Italy in the Renaissance* (London, 1929), p. 254.

✦ The Republic of Venice, ca. 1500. ✦

Dotted line indicates borders of the Republic and its possessions.

Moldavia

Wallachia

Black

Sea

OTTOMAN

Constantinople ● ●Scutari

Sea of Marmara

E M P I R E

●Thessaloniki

Aegean

Sea

Gulf of
Arta

Euboea

Lepanto
✕

●Athens

to Genoa

Methoni ● ●Coron

●Monemvasia
Cape Malea

Rhodes
to Knights
of St. John

Sea of Crete

Crete
to Venice

RY

gno

razzo

fkada

lonia

Zante

E A

OTTOMAN EMPIRE

Cyprus
to Venice

0   100 miles

HISTORY OF VENICE

LIBER PRIMUS

1 Urbis Venetae res annorum quattuor et quadraginta scribere aggredior, non iudicio aut quod ita mihi libuerit, sed quodam quasi fato vel certe casu. Nam cum Andrea Naugerio, cui haec publice cura tradita fuerat, in legatione Gallica vita functo, decemviri a me collegii decreto petiissent, ut, quando is moriens sua scripta comburi iussit, ipse ea in re atque munere patriae meam opem requirenti ne deessem, pudore verecundiaque recusandi ad variam atque multiplicem, quodque vere possum dicere, multo maxime operosam scriptionem me contuli, annos natus sexaginta; ut, nisi reipublicae exstaret postulatio, merito me homines reprehendant id aetatis ausum tantum onus sustinere; bella enim plurima propeque continentia atque maxima, cum ab Italiae, Germaniae, Galliae, Hispaniae populis et regibus, tum a Turcarum imperatoribus excitata, vel terra vel mari gesta, sunt scribenda; quorum quodque iustum totius historiae volumen atque separatum posse conficere, quam uno omnia comprehendi atque contineri, nemo non dixerit. Multa praeterea domi vel senatus consulta, vel leges, vel iudicia illustria, vel novi magistratus, multi hospitio reges liberaliter accepti, multi honores dis immortalibus habiti, multae prodigiorum domi forisque praedictiones, tempestatum ac siderum mirae vicissitudines, huius temporis memoriam exemplis innumerabilibus referserunt; quae colligere et mandare litteris nec amantis otium animi est, nec minimae industriae.

2 Sed nihil est profecto tam arduum, quin id patriae caritas exsuperet, apud eos viros praesertim qui, praeclara in urbe geniti atque

BOOK I

I am setting myself to write an account of 44 years of Venetian 1
history, not by my own choice or because I want to, but the outcome of a kind of destiny, as it were, or at any rate of chance.
Andrea Navagero had been officially entrusted with the task,[1] but
when he died on a diplomatic mission to France, asking as his dying wish for his writings to be burnt, the Council of Ten sought
my aid in the matter of this public service and requested me by
formal decree not to fail my country. I should have felt ashamed
and embarrassed to refuse, and so at the age of 60 I turned to a
sort of writing that is varied and many-faceted and (I can truly
say) far and away the most difficult to accomplish: were it not for
the request of the Republic,[2] people might well criticize me for
daring to take on such a burden at that age. What I have to de-
scribe are a great number of almost continuous major wars provoked not just by the peoples and kings of Italy, Germany, France,
and Spain, but by the leaders of the Turks too, waged on land and
sea alike. No one will deny that each of them could fill a complete
and separate volume of an entire history rather than being included and embraced all together in a single volume. And on the
home front there are in addition many decrees of the senate, many
laws, famous trials, new magistracies, many kings generously and
hospitably welcomed, many acts of divine worship, many predic-
tions of prodigies at home and abroad, amazing vicissitudes of
storms and stars, that have filled the history of this period with ex-
emplary incidents beyond number. Collecting these and committing them to writing is not for a leisure-loving spirit, and it re-
quires no small industry.

But there is indeed nothing so difficult that love of country can- 2
not overcome it, especially for those men born in a famous city

optima in republica educati, suae civitatis temperationem institu-
taque adamaverunt. Ita qui rebus tot atque tantis complectendis
numquam sponte curam et cogitationem adhibuissem—mihi
enim post Romanos labores, bonae tandem valetudini, quam penitus amiseram, restituto, paterna in villa fundi Patavini maiorem
anni partem requiescenti, satis erat pascere levioribus tractandis
artibus animum—voluntate meorum civium perspecta, facile ad-
ducor ut nihil mihi refugiendum putem, dum eorum studiis satis-
faciam. Ab illorum igitur commentariorum fine quos Marcus
Antonius conscripsit exorsus, quo ab fine decemviris placuit ut initium scribendi facerem, continuato rerum filo, historiam ad hoc
diei, si vita suppetet, perducam; tot enim, quot supra dixi, anni inter illius scripta atque hoc tempus intercesserunt. Ac eo sane tempore quo in statu esset, quam haberet faciem respublica, satis est
ab illo demonstratum; quae, bello Ferrariensi confecto foederi-
busque initis, plus biennium soluta oneribus civitate et pacato imperio est usa.

3   Idem autem posthaec et publicae quietis et Sabellici librorum
finis fuit; pacemque illam et tranquillitatem reipublicae bellum statim Raeticum excepit; neque ei profuit, quod suo se in otii capto
iam portu magna perseverantia continuisset. Eius belli levissima de
causa initium hoc fuit. Erat nonnullarum cum Raetorum et Nori-
corum, tum earum terrae Germaniae gentium quae sunt his fini-
timae, dux atque princeps Sigismundus Federici Romanorum imperatoris frater, homo non malus, sed qui facile malis hominibus
crederet. Ei cum senatu Veneto iam inde a maioribus orta necessi-
tudo intercedebat. Itaque vetusta consuetudine homines mercaturae dediti omnibus ex reipublicae municipiorum vicinitatibus eius
ad oppida libere commeabant; mercatumque imprimis celebrem,
apud Beurenses quotannis fieri solitum, stato tempore pete-

and raised in the finest Republic who have come to love the character and institutions of their community. Of my own accord I
should never have given serious consideration to covering matters
of such complexity and importance. After my labors in Rome I
was at last restored to good health, which I had wholly lost, and I
relaxed for the greater part of the year at the ancestral villa on my
Paduan estate, content to nourish my spirit in the cultivation of
the less serious arts. But now that the wishes of my fellow citizens
are apparent, I am readily persuaded that I must shirk no toil till I
have satisfied their desires. Starting from the end of the records
written by Marcantonio Sabellico,[3] accordingly, a point of depar-   1486
ture fixed by the Council of Ten, I shall bring the history down to
the present day in a continuous narrative of events, if life allows,
the 44 years I mentioned above having elapsed between his work
and the present. Sabellico certainly gave a clear picture of the Republic's situation and aspect at that time. At the conclusion of the
War of Ferrara[4] and with treaties in place, she enjoyed for more
than two years a state free of financial burdens and an empire at
peace.

Yet after that, the peace of the populace and Sabellico's book   3
came to an end at the same time. The period of the Republic's   1487
peace and tranquillity was followed immediately by war in the
Tyrol. The pains that the Republic took to keep herself in the harbor of peace she had just reached were of no avail. The war began
for the most trivial of reasons. The leader and prince of a number
of nations, not only Tyroleans and Carinthians but also those on
German territory bordering them,[5] was Sigismund, the cousin of
the Holy Roman Emperor Frederick: not a bad man, but one who
too easily put his trust in those who were. He happened to have a
connection with the Venetian Senate that went back to his ancestors, and so by ancient custom those engaged in commerce traveled freely to his towns from all over the Veneto. In particular they
used to attend at regular intervals a busy fair that was held every

bant. Id cum anno post urbem conditam millesimo sexagesimo sexto fecissent, Sigismundi iussu, ipso in mercatu ad quem fide publica venerant, comprehensi suis cum rebus custodiaeque sunt traditi.

4 Et iam antea Sigismundi operae[1] nostros homines, qui argenti fodinas in Alpibus exercebant, fugatos conductis iure gentium secturis et cuniculis deturbaverant; eosque cuniculos, quod essent ipsorum vicis et municipiis vicini, vi atque armis parvo negotio possidebant. Eius rei causam quaerentibus dictitabant Sigismundi clientelas, quae in imperio Veneto essent in Benaci lacus ripa, suis e finibus expelli; de qua tamen controversia, iactari pridem coepta, per interpretes ab utrisque amice disceptabatur.

5 Itaque, cum eos qui ex reipublicae municipiis ad ipsorum mercatum vere inito venerant in vincula coniecissent, omnibus ex eorum oppidis atque agris, tum ex Lepontiis et Helvetiis coacto iam milite apud Tridentum, Germani hominum numero ad decem milia — id enim agere constituerant — Gaudentio Amasiano duce in Veronensium fines impetum faciunt. Germanos autem illos diximus, quando nunc quidem omnes eae ab Alpibus nationes compluresque aliae uno nomine Germani appellantur. Flumen est Athesis, ex Arbona monte profluens, quod duobus auctum fluminibus Tridentum fertur Alpesque reliquas dirimens vallem plerumque angustam efficit Veronam usque, quam etiam intersecat. Eius fluminis laevam ingressi ripam Germani, ac quindecim milibus passuum confectis, oppidi Rovereti, in Alpium angustiis laxiore paulo atque apertiore loco positi, suburbanis aedificiis direptis, pugna etiam cum praesidiariis militibus commissa, defenso

year at Bolzano. When they did this in the 1066th year of the foundation of Venice, they and their goods were seized by order of 1487 Sigismund and they were taken into custody at the very fair to which they had come under safe-conduct.

At an earlier stage, hired hands of Sigismund had put to flight 4 our men working silver mines in the Alps, driving them from the quarries and tunnels leased under the law of nations and taking possession of the tunnels by force of arms with little difficulty, since the tunnels were near their own towns and villages. To those who inquired why, they asserted that dependants of Sigismund who were in the Venetian domain on the shores of Lake Garda were being expelled from their lands. This dispute, however, had long been the object of frank discussion and there continued to be amicable debate on the matter by the representatives of both sides.

After the Germans had thrown into prison those who had 5 come from the Venetian towns to their market at the beginning of spring, they gathered soldiers in the neighborhood of Trento from all over their towns and countryside, and from the people of Ticino and Graubünden besides, to the number of about 10,000 men. Then, as a deliberate act, they attacked the territory of Verona under the leadership of Gaudenz von Matsch. (I call them "Germans" because at least at the present time the peoples of the Alps, and several others besides, are all known by that name.) There is a river called the Adige which rises on Mount Arbona[6] and swollen by two other rivers reaches Trento; cutting through the other Alps it forms a generally narrow valley as far as Verona, through the middle of which it runs. The Germans gathered on the east bank of the river, and after a march of fifteen miles reached Rovereto, a town occupying a rather more spacious and open site in the defiles of the Alps. There they looted the buildings on the outskirts and actually joined battle with the soldiers of the garrison, turning to plunder and destruction as the town de-

municipio ad praedam et populationem sese convertunt; eaque facta in vicinos oppido pagos tumultuose militem recipiunt.

6   Hac re nuntiata, senatus decrevit ut et veterani milites qui in Carnis et Taurisanis quique in Gallia hiemaverant omnes ilico Veronam convenirent, et delectu statim habito novi milites conscriberentur; creatisque ad id confestim legatis Petro Diedo, Veronae praefecto, Hieronymo Marcello dat negotium, ut ex usu reipublicae bellum administrent. Iulium etiam Caesarem, qui regnum in Camertibus obtinebat, copiarum reipublicae imperatorem, accersitum ex Umbria eodem contendere magnis itineribus iubet.

7   Interea Germani, ad oppugnationem Rovereti iis quae bello essent usui celerrime comparatis, et castris ad oppidum positis, tormentorum vi, quibus maxime abundat ea natio, muros quatere atque deicere instituunt. Id cum plures dies labore non intermisso fecissent ac magnam murorum partem aperuissent, neque Venetus imperator, qui iam eo venerat, propter Germanorum magnum numerum repellere hostem posset, saepe oppugnare omni missilium telorum genere scalisque ad murum positis adorti, saepe cum clade repulsi, postremo oppidum capiunt.

8   Eis in oppugnationibus unum eorum teli genus maxime oppidanos terruit; de quo propter novitatem praetereundum non videtur. Pilas ferreas non magnopere cohaerentes, picis atque bituminis plenas, igne incluso tormentis muralibus impellebant. Eae pilae muro impactae infringebantur ac plures in partes dispergebantur; quibus ex singulis ignis prosiliebat acri cum flamma sic, ut quaeque earum pars quantumvis parva hominem corriperet; pice autem illisa retinebantur, ne excuti neve reici possent. Ita fiebat ut neque in muro consistendi, neque quae opus essent administrandi,

fended itself, whereupon they withdrew their soldiers in disarray into the countryside around the town.

When this news reached the Senate, it decreed that all the vet-   6
erans who had wintered in Friuli, the March of Treviso, and Lombardy should assemble at Verona forthwith, and that an immediate levy should be held and new soldiers recruited. Pietro Diedo, the governor of Verona, and Girolamo Marcello were at once appointed proveditors for the purpose and given the task of conducting the war according to the usual practice of the Republic.[7] Giulio Cesare Varano too, the lord of Camerino and captaingeneral of the Republic's forces, was summoned from Umbria and ordered to head for the same place by forced marches.

The Germans, meanwhile, very quickly gathered together mate-   7
rial to use in a military attack on Rovereto, and pitched their camp outside the town. They then began to make the walls shake and fall down with a barrage of their artillery, something that that nation has in great abundance. This went on for several days with no let-up of effort, and a large part of the walls were breached. In the meantime the Venetian captain-general arrived but was unable to repel the enemy on account of the great number of Germans. The latter frequently returned to the attack with all kinds of missiles and siege-ladders set against the walls, and though often repulsed with great slaughter, they at last seized the town.

In these assaults one sort of weapon above all terrified the   8
townspeople, and in view of its novelty it is well worth describing here. Iron balls, not specially solid and filled with tar and pitch, were set alight inside and hurled from siege catapults. These balls would break up on impact with the walls and explode into many different fragments, from each of which fire and acrid flames sprang out, so that every particle, however small, would set a person on fire. Being smeared with pitch, they stuck so fast that they could be neither shaken off nor brushed aside. The result was that the soldiers had no opportunity to take up position on the wall,

neque se defendendi militibus facultas daretur. Quod ubi semel atque iterum est animadversum, culcitras centonesque quos habere poterant aquis immergebant, eosque pinnis et fenestris ex quibus propugnarent interponebant. Iis neque pix adhaerescere neque ignis nocere propter humorem poterat. Ita se tandem, compluribus suorum ante absumptis, praemunire ac tueri didicerunt.

9   Sed capto oppido, ut diximus, Nicolaus Priolus praetor et milites qui, ad defendendum municipium per Alpium crepidines missi, hostem circumfusum et sedentem fefellerant suaque virtute ac fortitudine eorum impetum ad eam diem sustinuerant, in arcem se recipiunt. Veneti, qui omnino in se longe maius quam initio crediderant excitatum bellum viderent, neque in Camerte quantum oportebat industriae virtutisque agnoscerent, a Roberto Severinate petunt ut imperium totius belli una cum Camerte administrandi, magna opinione civitatis sibi delatum, laeto animo accipiat et, quo celerius fieri potest, suis cum militibus et liberis, claris bello adolescentibus, viae se det atque in Raeticum Alpesque contendat.

10   Robertus, qui, posteaquam Innocentius pontifex maximus eum missum fecit, in agrum Patavinum se contulerat atque ibi apud oppidum Citadellam, quod ei una cum urbanis aedibus cumque amoenissimo ac peramplo apud Veronam fundo et villa in Ferrariensis belli exitu senatus dono dedit, sine imperio, sine stipendio complures menses commoratus, aegre se suosque milites aluerat, illam ipsam sibi occasionem suae vel amplificandae vel omnino retinendae dignitatis dari votis omnibus cupiebat. Itaque, accepto peropportune imperio, ad bellum proficiscitur. Eo cum venit, modo in spe, modo in metu Veneti saepe fuerunt; saepe Marte ambiguo, levibus proeliis est certatum. Ponte etiam navibus impo-

carry out vital tasks, or defend themselves. When this was observed to happen again and again, they took whatever cushions and blankets they could find and soaked them in water, placing them all along the battlements and windows from which they were fighting. Being wet, the pitch would not stick to them, nor were they damaged by fire. So in the end, after losing a good many men, they learned how to safeguard and protect themselves.

The commander Niccolò Priuli and the soldiers who had been sent along the base of the Alps to defend the place had escaped the clutches of the enemy as it lay in siege all around the town and by their valor and strength had withstood their onslaught up to that point. But once the town had been taken, as I said, they retreated into the citadel. The Venetians realized that they were involved in a war very much more serious than they had imagined at the outset, and they did not find in Varano the energy and courage that there should be.[8] They accordingly asked Roberto da Sanseverino if he was willing to take on overall command of the conduct of the war alongside Varano, a command offered him because of the high opinion that the citizenry had of him, and with all possible speed to take to the road with his soldiers and his sons (young men distinguished in war), and to make for Tyrol and the Alps.

Following his discharge by Pope Innocent VIII, Sanseverino had moved to the Paduan countryside. He stayed there for several months near the town of Cittadella (which the Senate had given him at the conclusion of the War of Ferrara, along with a palazzo in Venice and a fine and extensive estate and villa near Verona), without a command and without pay, supporting his troops and himself with difficulty. His every prayer was to be given just such a chance of advancing, or at least maintaining, his position. So he accepted this very timely command and set out for the war. At the time he arrived there, the mood of the Venetians frequently alternated between hope and fear, and the fighting was often conducted by skirmishing, with no decisive outcome. He also linked

9

10

sito, ut et copiae transmitti et commeatus ex altera fluminis regione supportari facile possent, utramque ripam coniunxit.

11   Eodem quoque tempore Germanorum militum centuriae aliquot, in Vicentinos et Feltrinos saltus atque in Carnorum fines repente immissae, plus terroris quam periculi intulerunt, propterea quod Hieronymus Saornianus, summo in Foroiuliensibus natus loco, cuius proavus Federicus ob singulare atque praeclarum in rempublicam studium et civitate ab ea et iure comitiorum donatus fuerat, cum suis clientibus et agrestium manu, quam celeriter coegerat atque armaverat, superatis Alpium quae adiri non consueverant iugis, illos omnia vastantes ac depopulantes a tergo aggressus, ita fregit atque concidit, ut nonnulli timore incitati e montium in quibus erant cacuminibus rupibusque fugientes se praecipitaverunt. Qua de re gratiae illi a senatu actae militesque tercentum attributi; quos Hieronymus Iacobo fratri habendos permisit, cum ipse pacatae ac civili sese vitae quam militari mallet tradere. Sed dum reliqua sic, ut dixi, agerentur, Rovereti arce muralibus tormentis prope diruta, praetor quique cum eo erant milites deditionem faciunt.

12   Et iam summa aestas praeterierat, cum veteris exempli res utrumque exercitum spectaculo haud magnopere cruento tenuit. Erat Germanorum numero iuvenis acer et fortis Georgius Sonnembergius, claro loco natus, qui turmae equitum praeerat; ad hunc cum esset allatum Antonium Mariam Severinatem, imperatoris filium, inter suos iactavisse, si ex hostium copia egregius vir quispiam equestri pugna congredi velit, se cum illo decertaturum

the two banks of the river by constructing a pontoon bridge so as
to send troops across and transport supplies easily from the other
side.

At the same time several companies of German soldiers also   11
suddenly erupted into the valleys of Vicenza and Feltre and as far
as the borders of Friuli, though they brought more fear than danger, thanks to Girolamo Savorgnan. Savorgnan was a man born
into the highest nobility of Friuli, whose great-grandfather
Federico had been granted Venetian citizenship and noble status
for his singular and extraordinary devotion to the Republic.[9] With
his dependants and a band of country folk that he had quickly collected and armed, Savorgnan scaled the Alpine heights (which
they generally never went near) and attacked the Germans from
the rear as they were plundering and laying waste to all about. He
so crushed and slaughtered the Germans that a number of them
threw themselves in panic from the peaks and cliffs of the mountains where they were as they fled. For this he received a formal
vote of thanks from the Senate and was assigned 300 soldiers.
These Girolamo entrusted to his brother Giacomo's keeping, since
he preferred the peaceful life of a civilian to that of a military man.
But while these other events were taking place in the manner I
have described, the citadel of Rovereto was all but destroyed by
the siege-artillery and the commander [Priuli] and the soldiers
with him surrendered.

The height of summer had now passed when an episode recall-   12
ing bygone days gripped both armies with a relatively bloodless
spectacle. Among the Germans was one Georg Sonnenberg,[10] an
energetic and brave young man of distinguished birth who commanded a squadron of cavalry. He got word that Antonio Maria
da Sanseverino, the captain-general's son, had boasted among his
own people that if some enemy champion was prepared to meet
him in mounted combat, he would fight it out with him and
would show for his part how far the Italians excelled the Germans

proque sua parte ostensurum quantum belli gloria Itali Germanos
antecellant, mittit ad Venetos tubicinem, qui Antonio denuntiet se
paratum esse certaminis fortunam experiri. Remissus ad Georgium, tubicen refert expectari cupide illum ab Antonio. Itaque die
dicta clausum in campum atque ad id comparatum, aequo inter
bina castra spatio, diversa ex parte uterque armatus atque adorna-
tus sese intulit; et parva interiecta mora, citatis equis concurrunt.
Antonius hastam in Germani pectus infringit; thorax aegre hastae
impetum sustinet. Tum vero equus Antonii, iam incitatior neque
sat habilis contineri, in trabales campi munitiones ita impegit, ut
iis perfractis atque disiectis, ipso humi prolapso, Antonius se eice-
ret. Itaque pedes ex equite factus, ubi hostem in equo iam conver-
sum, districto in se gladio venientem videt, post tignum, trabibus
repagulisque sustinendis solo fixum, sese continet. Ita Germanum,
assultantem atque ictus de superiore loco adigentem, districto item
gladio, repellebat, quaque ipsum poterat appetebat; nam equum
lege prius dicta ferire Antonius non poterat.

13   Sed dum crebris ictibus acriter uterque rem gerit neque quantum vult proficit—propterea quod galea, thorace, ceterisque ferreis
indumentis totum paene corpus protegebatur—Antonius ira-
cundiae plenus, quod iniquam subire dimicationem cogeretur,
seque ipse tacite incendens hosti cupidius ferienti, impetu facto,
gladium aufert. Ille ab ephippiis ferra quam gerebat abrepta clava
pro gladio utitur. Tum vero clara ad Germanum voce, "Quid tu
autem," inquit Antonius, "me cogis unum cum duobus depugnare,
quorum alteri lex, alteri aliena arma sunt praesidio? Si vir es,
aequo Marte manum consere." Ita Germanus, existimationem
hominum veritus et magno praeterea animo, equo et ipse desilit;

in military prowess. Georg sent the Venetians a trumpeter to announce to Antonio his readiness to try his luck in the contest. On his return the trumpeter reported that Antonio eagerly awaited him. So on the appointed day, into an enclosed field prepared for the purpose, equidistant between the two camps, each made his entrance armed and ready from opposite directions, and after a brief delay, they spurred on their horses and dashed together. Antonio broke his lance against the German's chest, the breastplate barely withstanding its impact. But then his horse, more excited now and difficult to control, dashed against the wooden guardrails of the field, breaking and scattering the timbers. The horse itself collapsed on the ground, and Antonio leaped off. Thus transformed from knight to foot soldier, when he saw his enemy turned about on his horse and coming toward him with drawn sword, he kept himself behind a post fixed in the ground to support the beams and barriers. In this manner, with his own sword drawn, Antonio managed to fend off the German's attack as he rained down blows from above, and himself tried to go for him in any way he could — it was a condition agreed beforehand that he could not strike the horse.

The blows came thick and fast but neither was making any 13 headway, because almost all of their bodies was protected by helmets and breastplates and the rest of the heavy armor. In anger at being forced to take part in the unequal struggle, and silently enraged at the enemy as he struck with ever fiercer blows, Antonio rushed at him and knocked away his sword. The German seized the ironclad club that he carried in his saddlebags and used it in place of the sword. Then Antonio said to the German in a loud voice: "Why do you force me to fight it out single-handed against two opponents — one of them protected by the rules of engagement, the other by his foreign weapons? If you are a man, join battle in fair fight." So the German likewise leaped down from his horse, for fear of what men might think, yet with great spirit too.

comprehensique statim inter sese atque arcte diu luctati, ambo concidunt. Erant utrisque magna et procera corpora et vires corporibus pares. Germano tamen cadenti paulum superincubuit Antonius; sed eius dexterum bracchium a sinistro Germani humero atque adeo armorum corporisque pondere sic premebatur, ut eo uti non posset. Tum Germanus, impedito atque implicito Antonio, ipse manu dextera liber, abrepta sica quae femori Antonii erat alligata, nates ei convulnerat; ea tantum corporis parte sua illum tegumenta non munierant. Vulnere Antonius accepto, cum omnino nullam defendendi sese viam sibi reliquam et facultatem videret, sicaeque aciem Germanus ictu altero atque tertio adegisset, "Vince," inquiens, "quando ita voluit fortuna; casu enim, non virtute vincis," gloriam certaminis hosti dedit; quem quidem victor magno apud se honore plures dies ad exercitum habuit curatoque vulnere, donis etiam additis, ad patrem remisit.

14   Posthaec, paucis interiectis diebus, cum Germani insolentius atque laxius vagarentur Venetique eos adoriri ex insidiis statuissent, re ab hostibus per exploratores cognita, ipsi in hostium insidias inciderunt. Ita excepti a pluribus pauciores, conglobati virtute atque armis se tuebantur fortiterque proeliabantur; ex quibus Robertus modo voce imperatoris curam, modo manu militis operam praestabat. Verum crescente hostium multitudine circumsaeptus, iam iamque tenebatur, cum Antonius filius id conspicatus (non enim longe aberat) in confertissimam hostium aciem se iniecit, fortissimeque pugnans aciemque submovens, patri se recipiendi facultatem praebuit; ipse in hostium potestatem venit. Reliqui fugati, paucis captis atque interfectis, se in castra receperunt.

They at once took to grappling with one other, and after lengthy wrestling at close quarters both fell to the ground. Each had a large and tall physique, and strength to match. As the German fell, however, Antonio got on top of him slightly, but his right arm was hampered by the German's left shoulder and even more by the weight of his weapons and body, with the result that he could not use his arm. Now that Antonio was stuck and tangled up, while the German had his right hand free, he seized a dagger strapped to Antonio's thigh and stabbed him hard in the buttocks, the only part of his body not protected by armor. After taking this wound, Antonio saw that there was absolutely no way left of defending himself, or any chance to do so. When the German had driven in the dagger a second and third time, he yielded the glory of the contest to his enemy with the words "Win, then, since Fortune would have it so: for chance, not strength, has given you the victory." For several days, indeed, the victor kept Antonio by him at the camp with every mark of honor, and when the wound was healed returned him to his father, even sending gifts as well.

A few days after that, the Venetians decided to ambush the   14 Germans, who had taken to roaming about in an arrogant and carefree fashion, but enemy spies discovered the plan, and the Germans themselves fell upon their enemy's ambush. Outnumbered as they were in this situation, the Venetians massed together and defended themselves with spirit and arms, putting up a brave fight. Among them Roberto da Sanseverino displayed now a commander's authority by his words, now the physical effort of a soldier. But surrounded by growing numbers of the enemy, he was just on the point of being taken when his son Antonio, who was close by and saw it happening, plunged into the thick of the enemy. By dint of stalwart fighting he drove the line back and gave his father the chance to retreat, while he himself came into the enemy's power. A few of the Venetians were captured and killed, and the rest were put to flight and retired to their camp.

15   Neque multo post Camers in febriculam incidit; eoque Veronam delato, rerum et totius belli administratio in Robertum incu-
buit. Germani autem cum inopia commeatus adducti, qui segniter
subministrabatur, tum stipendii fide non servata indignabundi, palam ad seditionem incitabantur; cuius rei periculum eorum praefecti veriti indutias ab imperatore Veneto petierunt. Saepius re iactata, non impetratis indutiis, nocte intempesta Rovereti arcem
incendunt; et prima luce, conclamatis vasis, omni cum exercitu
abeunt. Mirum id Venetis videri; neque satis credere hostem
abeundi consilio discessisse; itaque timere insidias, quas etiam essent experti. Sed ubi illos longius profectos ab exploratoribus cognoverunt, Rovereti oppidum recipiunt.

16   Interim Robertus, certior factus omnes hostium copias domum
discessisse — auxerat enim eam rem atque affinxerat multa rumor;
sibi autem miles, ex Ravennati et Piceno et Umbria per eos dies
accersitus, animum addiderat — statuit ulterius progredi Triden-
tumque ipsum, si res processerit, obsidere, ut qui ultro ac sine
causa bellum Venetis intulissent scirent atque cognoscerent bellum
gerere in eorum finibus et posse Venetos et audere.

17   Eo consilio cum legatis communicato, Lucas Pisanus, aetate
iam gravior, quem senatus Petro Diedo submiserat atque illum ad
praefecturam Veronensem reverti iusserat, existimare sese inquit e
republica non esse tantam rem eo tempore aggredi, primum quod
credibile non esset Germanorum exercitum, quem ipsi florentissi-
mum paulo ante vidissent, ita iam in ultimas Germaniae terrae latebras se abdidisse, ut non modo revocari atque restitui, sed etiam
adaugeri paucis diebus non possit in tam promptis ad arma cap-

Not long afterwards Varano contracted a slight fever, and with   15
him taken to Verona, the conduct of business and of the whole
war fell to Roberto. But the Germans were being moved to open
mutiny both by lack of supplies, which were slow in coming
through, and by their anger that the promise of pay was not being
kept. Alarmed at this eventuality, their leaders asked the Venetian
captain-general for a truce. After much discussion and no truce
granted, they set fire to the citadel of Rovereto in the dead of
night. At dawn they gave the order to strike camp and departed
with their whole army. This took the Venetians by surprise; not
being quite able to believe that the enemy meant to leave for good,
they feared an ambush, something they had actually experienced.
But when they discovered from scouts that the Germans really
had moved away, they took back the town of Rovereto.

Meanwhile Roberto learned that all the enemy troops had left   16
for home—rumor had exaggerated the actual state of affairs with
many false reports, and soldiers summoned in the interim from
the area of Ravenna, the Marches, and Umbria had fortified his
courage—and so he decided to proceed further and besiege Trento
itself, if things went well, so that those who had attacked Venice
without provocation or pretext should come to realize that the Venetians had the ability and the daring to wage war in their territory.

When the plan was communicated to the proveditors, Luca   17
Pisani, by then somewhat advanced in years (the Senate had sent
him to replace Pietro Diedo, ordering the latter to return to the
governorship of Verona), said that in his opinion it was not in the
Republic's interest to attempt such a major undertaking for the
time being. In the first place, it was unlikely that the German
army, whose great effectiveness they had just seen for themselves,
had now so hidden itself away in the furthest recesses of the land
of Germany that it could not be recalled and reconstituted, and
even enlarged in the space of a few days from a populace so ready

19

ienda populis, tantoque in periculo municipium ad gentes Italas continendas opportunissimum amittendi; deinde quod, si tum reipublicae ad hostem repellendum copiarum satis fuit — quamquam quis eum reppulit? sua ipse sponte se recepit — sed sit omnino repulsus, ad inferendum tamen bellum, atque in hostium fines irrumpendum obsidionesque ducendas, id ipsum non suffecturum, praesertim cum existimandum sit omnem Germaniam, ne tantum dedecus admittatur, eo conventuram viresque suas in communem utilitatem explicaturam; postremo quod, si offensum in aliquo sit, non esset receptui locus circumventis ab hoste undique mediis in Alpium iugis; tum itinerum angustias esse pertimescendas, quas evadere vix pacati possent. Praestare autem reipublicae bellum quoquo modo confecisse, dum oneribus extraordinariis finis imponatur, quam spe melioris victoriae[2] ipsam periclitari civesque conflictari tributorum conferendorum quotidie causa. Defessam civitatem bello Ferrariensi otium inglorium laboribus paulo etiam honestioribus certoque cum fructu praeponere, nedum ambiguis et periculosis praeferat. "Haec mea quidem," inquit, "est sententia; qui fortasse, vel meo vitio vel etiam senectutis, omnia timeo. Vos consulite, et quod optimum factu est, id sequamur."

18   Tum Marcellus, facto a collega silentio, in hunc est modum locutus: nihil sibi dubitationis dari, si ea ita essent, quemadmodum Pisanus dixisset, quin sit ab invadendis hostium finibus Tridentique oppugnatione abstinendum. Quae enim eius regionis pars, quod municipium tanti essent, ut cum eiusmodi conflatione belli totiusque Germaniae irritatione consensuque comparetur? Verum habere se rem, suo quidem iudicio, longe secus. Nam neque Ger-

to take up arms and so much at risk of losing the town best placed to hold back the peoples of Italy. Second, even if the Republic had at present enough troops to drive the enemy away — though who had driven them away? they had retreated of their own accord — but even granting that they had been repelled, all the same for carrying the war to the enemy, invading their territory, and setting sieges, that in itself would not be enough, especially since they must expect that all Germany would converge on that spot and exert its strength for the common good rather than suffer such disgrace. If, finally, they should run into difficulties at any point, there would be no place to retreat to, once they were surrounded on all sides by the enemy in the middle of the Alps. And then the narrowness of the passes was much to be feared, which it was difficult enough to negotiate even in peacetime. It was better for the Republic to bring the war to some sort of conclusion, as long as it brought to an end the extraordinarily burdensome costs of war, than for her to remain in danger in the hope of a greater victory while her citizens engaged in a daily struggle to find the money. A citizenry worn out by the War of Ferrara preferred an inglorious peace to further struggle, even if that were slightly more honorable and accompanied by a sure benefit; and all the more would they prefer it to a struggle that was uncertain and risky. "That at any rate is my opinion," he said, "though perhaps some defect of character, or just old age, makes me worry about things in general: you must consider the matter yourselves, and let us find the best course of action to follow."

When his colleague fell silent, Girolamo Marcello spoke as follows: if matters were as Pisani had stated, he had not the slightest doubt that they should hold off from invading enemy territory and attacking Trento. What stretch of land in those parts, what city was so valuable that it could be compared with igniting a war of this sort, with provoking and uniting the whole of Germany? But the situation, at least in his opinion, was quite different. It was not

18

manorum copias sua se sponte dissipavisse, sed cum rei frumentariae inopia coactas, tum stipendio non persoluto egentes despe-
rantesque domum quemque suam revertisse; neque qui collectam
iam manum prospereque agentem commeatu supportando alere
stipendiisque repraesentandis retinere, ne diffugeret, non potuerit,
eum novo conficiendo exercitui stipem alimentaque subministratu-
rum; multo enim facilius contineri stantia, quam lapsa prostra-
taque sublevari.

19   Neque vero esse verendum conventuram contra Venetos Germaniam, quos amicos semper habuerit, ut Sigismundi rebus auxilio sit, qui nullo reliquorum principum consilio, nulla ipse lacessi-
tus iniuria bellum reipublicae intulerit; praesertim cum Federicus
imperator, eius frater, neque pecunia neque milite neque ulla eum
re omnino iuverit, prae seque potius tulerit id se numquam bellum
probavisse. Qui a suis negligatur, eum ab alienis exterisque hominibus auxilia impetraturum credere, cuius tandem esset timoris?
Quod si dicatur non iam quidem Sigismundi aut alicuius privatim
causa Germanos principes ad arma capienda conspiraturos, sed
plane sua, ne Tridento capto Venetis aditus pateat ad sese, responderi posse complura esse in Alpibus reipublicae oppida, diversis
acquisita adiectaque imperio tempestatibus; quibus ex oppidis
Germaniae populi adeantur; ab his ipsis non longinquam locis Fel-
triam, Belunium quamque in Carnis Cividalem appellant; complura praeterea itinera vicis et castellis munita, cum hoc in Alpium
ad orientem solem tractu, tum vero etiam in Brixianorum finibus
ad Moernam atque Licates; in Bergomatium Sebini lacus fauces
vallemque universam Triumpilinorum, quique ad Lepontios La-
riumque lacum saltus atque angustiae pertinent; neque tamen ullo

true that the German forces had dispersed of their own accord: each had made his own way home in desperate need under the compulsion of lack of food and a failure to be paid. Nor would someone who was unable to feed an already assembled and successful band of men by bringing in provisions, and unable to keep them from deserting by paying wages in ready cash, be likely to supply the money and food for putting a new army together. It was much easier to hold together whatever was still standing than to raise what had fallen on the ground.

Nor indeed (he continued) need they fear that Germany would 19 unite against the Venetians, whom it had always considered friends, in order to promote Sigismund's interests, Sigismund having made war on the Republic without consulting the other princes and unprovoked by any injustice: all the more so because his cousin the Emperor Frederick had given him absolutely no help with money or soldiers or in any other respect, but had instead made it clear that he had never approved of the war. To believe that someone ignored by his own people would get help from strangers and foreigners was an unreal fear. If it should be said that the German princes would agree to go to war simply for their own sake and not for the sake of Sigismund or any particular individual, in case the capture of Trento should give the Venetians a means of attacking them, one could reply that there were plenty of towns in the Alps that Venice had at various times acquired and added to her dominion from which the peoples of Germany could be approached — not far from their present position there were Feltre, Belluno, and the place in Friuli called Cividale. There were besides a number of routes protected by villages and forts, not only in that stretch of the Alps towards the east but also in the territory of Brescia at Moerna and Lodrone,[11] and in the territory of Bergamo, the mouth of the Lago d'Iseo and the whole Val Trompia, and the valleys and passes that extend to Graubünden and Lake Como. At no time had the German princes acted in

tempore Germanos principes conspiravisse eis ab oppidis atque finibus repellendi Venetos causa; neque nunc, si Tridentum capiatur, conspiraturos; fassuros potius atque affirmaturos iure id meritoque Sigismundo accidisse, qui amicae civitati bellum temere intulerit. Nam quod ad viarum angustias attinet, quantulum esset iter Tridentum usque? Id tamen ipsum patefieri ante oportere, quaeque sint castella Germanorum ipsa in via, ea esse capienda, ne quid hostile post tergum relinquatur.

20   Extremum autem quod fuerit in collegae rationibus, defessam civitatem belli oneribus malle quiescere, ad id respicere ipsos non oportere; Tridento enim capto non eam modo pecuniam, quam hanc in belli partem paucorumque dierum moram erogari oportuerit, sed illam etiam quae toto in bello per tot menses esset insumpta cumulate sarcitum iri, vel magno potius cum faenore magnisque utilitatibus repensum et restitutum; vindicatum praeterea iniurias ab iniquo acceptas hoste; auctum imperii fines; auctum etiam gloriam nomenque reipublicae clarius factum. Quae quidem omnia nisi tanti esse, quanti aestimanda iure sunt, maiores nostri duxissent, numquam ipsos tot labores atque tantos perlaturos, numquam ullum bellum suscepturos fuisse, ut suam et reipublicae gloriam una cum imperii finibus protenderent.

21   Postremo occasionis esse rem, ut Tridentum capiatur, vel militibus sua celeritate atque virtute in oppidum non praemunitum irrumpentibus, vel quod repentino nostri exercitus adventu oppidani perterriti, ne deripiantur, deditionem faciant. Itaque ad eos casus eventusque temptandos, in iis quas haberent ipsi copiis satis virium atque praesidii fore. Id si recte cesserit, ipsum illum suum collegam imprimis imperatorem summis laudibus laturum, qui eius rei consilium inierit. Sin se oppidum tuebitur, vastatis finibus,

concert to expel the Venetians from those towns and territories, nor would they do so now if Trento were taken. They would more likely admit, indeed positively assert, that it was quite right that that had happened to Sigismund for having recklessly attacked a friendly state. And as for the narrowness of the roads, what a trifling matter it was to get to Trento! That was the route that ought to be opened up first, and any German fortresses on the way would have to be taken, in case the Venetians left any enemy force to their rear.

Coming to the final point in his colleague's argument, that a citizenry worn out by the burdensome costs of war is inclined to remain at peace, he said they should pay no attention to it. If Trento were taken, not only would the money necessarily spent on that phase of the conflict, involving the passage of a few days, be handsomely restored, but also all the money that had been been expended over so many months on the war as a whole — or rather it would be repaid and made good with great interest and to great advantage. Added to that, the ill-handling they had received from a treacherous enemy would be avenged, the borders of their domain extended, the glory of the Republic increased, and its reputation enhanced. Had our ancestors not reckoned all those matters to be as important as they undoubtedly are, they themselves would never have endured so many great hardships, they would never have undertaken any war to enhance their own and the Republic's glory hand in hand with the advance of the boundaries of empire.

Finally (he said), there was an opportunity to take Trento: the speed and courage of our soldiers could break into the unfortified town, or the townsfolk might take fright at the sudden arrival of our army and surrender to avoid being destroyed. They had sufficient strength and security in their present forces to try for such an outcome. If the matter should turn out well, it would be his colleague Pisani himself who would be the first to praise the general to the skies for having formed the plan. But if the town de-

incensis eius regionis castellis vicisque, incusso magno terrore hostibus, exercitum ultorem reduci oportere. Id autem procliviore omnium hominum venia posse tum fieri, quam si iam nunc inulti domum redeant. Porro non horis omnibus rei bene gerendae
facultatem exercitibus dari. Quare cum datur, ab iis qui praesunt
ea esse magnopere utendum, ne lapsae temere atque praeteritae recordatione paenitentiaque diu atque incassum torqueantur.

22   Hac habita oratione a Marcello, Pisanus in collegae sententiam
se traduci facile passus est. Itaque ambo imperatori permiserunt
uti de eo, quemadmodum sibi agendum videretur, ita statueret.
Ille, dimissis legatis, ad rem explicandam maturandamque se dedit. Sed quod erat, in ipsa laeva fluminis ripa qua Tridentum
quaque Roveretum est, inter utrumque oppidum ter mille ab Rovereto passus castellum Petra, loco alto atque edito viae imminens
sic ut Petrensibus invitis ea commeari tuto non posset, Petram in
potestatem suam redigere, et itineris et commeatus causa, et quod
ita Marcellus censuerat, ne quid inimicum post se relinquerent,
primum omnium decrevit.

23   Iis constitutis rebus, propterea quod a Rovereto venientibus, ob
praecipitem montis et crepidinum declivitatem, aditus ad Petram
omnino nullus erat, ab altera eius montis parte, qua adiri facile poterat, castellum oppugnare instituit. Transmisso itaque Athesim,
per eum pontem quem initio fecerat, exercitu, atque adverso flumine sesquihorae itinere confecto, ad Callianum vicum, quod ultra
Petram est passus circiter mille, ponte altero navibus imposito iterum Athesim exercitum traducit; atque in planitie sexcentorum

fended itself, they would have to lay waste to the territory, burn
the forts and settlements of the area, and strike terror into the enemy before withdrawing an army which had taken its vengeance.
Everyone would be more inclined to make allowances for this
course of action than if they went back home just as things stood,
without taking their vengeance. It was not every day, furthermore,
that an army was given the chance of carrying out a successful action. When the chance did arise, therefore, it was up to those in
charge to make the most of it, or they would be long haunted by
the memory and prey to vain regret for carelessly letting the opportunity slip and pass them by.

After this speech by Marcello, Pisani readily allowed himself to   22
be won over to his colleague's views. Both of them accordingly left
the decision as to how to proceed to the captain-general. The
proveditors were discharged, and the general devoted himself to
organizing the matter and moving it forward. But on the same left
bank of the Adige on which Trento and Rovereto lie, there was a
fort called Castel Pietra, between the two towns and some three
miles from Rovereto. From its lofty position it overlooked the road
in such a way that it was impossible to come and go in safety if the
people of Pietra were against it. So he decided to take control of
the fort before anything else, both to secure their route and supplies and in view of Marcello's warning not to leave any enemy
force to their rear.

In this situation, as there was absolutely no way of approaching   23
Pietra from Rovereto on account of the sheer steepness of the
mountain and its spurs, he set about attacking the fort from the
other side of the mountain, where there was an easy approach.
And so he had his army cross the Adige on a bridge he had constructed at the outset, and marched upriver for an hour and a half.
He then led his troops across the Adige again on a second pontoon bridge to the village of Calliano, about a mile beyond Pietra,
and took up position on level ground extending about 600 yards

ferme passuum, quae a montis radicibus ad flumen pertinet, consedit, praemissis equitibus levis armaturae, qui praecurrerent atque an manus aliqua hostium cogeretur cognoscerent sibique renuntiarent. Equites spretis imperiis praedae spe vagari et populationem facere coeperunt.

24   Interim cum Tridentini pontem esse factum cognovissent, non Petrensibus modo sed sibi etiam suisque rebus veriti, soluto exercitu, oppido non communito, imparati ab rebus omnibus, a Georgio Petraeplanae principe, quod est castellum ultra Tridentum, impetrant uti cum iis qui eo se receperant militibus, coacta celeriter agrestium et montanorum hominum manu, ire obviam properet hostemque, si potest, moretur, dum a Sigismundo auxilia conveniant. Ille, collectis quos ei casus obtulit militibus, et tum suorum, tum eorum qui Besinum vicum in summis Alpium Calliano imminentium culminibus incolebant rapto agmine, ad mille hominum numero, magno cum timpanorum et cornuum strepitu, eo de monte se demittere incipit; atque, ut se iugum implicabat agmenque partim se ostendebat, partim latebat, magnae ad speciem esse copiae iis equitibus qui praedatum ierant videbantur, magnae succedere et priores consequi existimabantur. Itaque cum propius maioreque cum strepitu descenderet, illi in fugam vertuntur atque, in alios incurrentes, eos in fugam vertunt. Iamque permixti passim equites peditesque tumultuose revertebantur. Id cum fieret adessentque Germani, fuga magis hostium quam sua virtute incitati, manus Venetae, quas ea planitiei pars exceperat, retrocedere ac fugere contendunt atque in aciem imperatoris, qui, acceptis de suorum fuga nuntiis, eo properabat, implicantur.

between the foot of the mountain and the river. He sent forward light cavalry who were to run ahead and find out if there was any concentration of enemy forces and report back to him. But ignoring their orders, the cavalry took to roaming about in hope of booty and to plundering the countryside.

The people of Trento, meanwhile, discovered that a bridge had been made, and began to fear not only for the people of Pietra but for themselves and their property as well, since their army was disbanded, their town unfortified, and they themselves were unprepared in all respects. They secured the agreement of Giorgio, the lord of Pietrapiana, a castle beyond Trento, that he would quickly collect a band of men from the mountains and countryside and, with the soldiers who had taken refuge there, would hasten to confront the enemy and delay them, if possible, until reinforcements from Sigismund arrived. Gathering together the soldiers that chance presented to him, and at the head of a column 1,000 strong, some of them his own men, some the men who lived in Beseno, a village at the very top of the Alps that overlook Calliano, Giorgio began to march down the mountain amid a great din of drums and horns. As there was a fold in the ridge, the column was partly visible and partly hidden, so that to the cavalrymen who had gone out for plunder there seemed at first sight to be a great number of troops; great forces were thought to be coming up and following on the earlier ones. And so when the column came down closer and ever noisier, the cavalry turned and fled, and as they met others, caused them to flee too. Now randomly muddled together, cavalry and infantry alike retreated in confusion. While this was going on and the Germans, spurred on more by the enemy rout than by their own courage, were coming upon them, the Venetian forces who were stationed on that part of the plain hastened to turn and flee. In doing so they became mixed up with the column of the captain-general, who was hurrying there on the news of his men's flight.

25   Tum imperator, quantum temporis exiguitas patiebatur, suos
perterritos foedeque fugientes increpitare atque convertere, hostem
sustinere ac reprimere adnixus fortiterque diu pugnans, ingenti
caede utrimque facta, urgentibus Germanis, cum suorum globo in
flumen deicitur, ibique periit. Reliqua multitudo magis magisque
perterrita pontem fuga petere contendit. Id conspicatus Andreas
Burgius, praefectus militum, sperans, si pons rescindatur, fore ut
milites equitesque, ablata fluminis transeundi facultate, contine-
rentur seque in hostes necessario converterent, accurrens solutis
retinaculis pontem propulit; quae res in contrarium atque ipse
existimaverat vertit, propterea quod timor consilium plerumque
non recipit. Qui enim semel fugae se mandaverant, ea spe ut, si
flumen transire possent, in tuto sese crederent futuros, ubi pontem
sublatum viderunt, plerique omnes se in flumen praecipitaverunt
et armis equisque depressi atque impliciti perierunt. Pauci ripam
tenere potuerunt, quod flumine maximo, rapido et vorticuloso impediebantur; ut essent omnes, qui ab hostibus pugnantes interfecti
sunt quique vi fluminis rapiente interierunt, circiter mille.

26   Unus Guidus Maria Rubeus, cum sua equitum turma pugnae
initio per medios hostium cuneos viam sibi armis et virtute cum
fecisset atque in campum evasisset, Germanos exultantes in se
convertit; quibuscum dimicans, quid in bello animus constan-
tiaque possent palam fecit. Eorum enim partem cecidit; reliquos
disiecit, fugavit; atque ita clariorem sibi victoriam ex hostibus victoribus, quod raro fieri assolet, comparavit. Reliqui centuriones
equitumque praefecti, ceterique qui fuga se abstinuerant, per montium invia, superatis iugis, nonnulli naviculis excepti ad Rovere-

In the short time at his disposal, the general then strove to ca- 25
jole his terrified men into turning back as they fled ignominiously,
to check the enemy, to drive them back. But after a long and val-
iant struggle, with massive slaughter on both sides, he was beset
by the Germans, pushed into the river with a band of his men,
and there perished. More and more terrified, the large number of
men that were left fled and tried to head for the bridge. Catching
sight of this, Andrea dal Borgo, the captain of infantry, hoped that
if the bridge were cut loose, the soldiers and cavalry would hold
fast and of necessity turn against the enemy, since there was now
no way of crossing the river. He ran up, cut the cables and pushed
the bridge away. But it turned out quite contrary to what he had
expected, since fear does not generally encourage rational judge-
ment. Of those who had once taken to flight in the belief that if
they could cross the river, they would be safe, when they saw the
bridge gone, nearly all leapt into the river and perished, burdened
and tangled up in weapons and horses as they were. Few of them
were able to hang onto the bank, thwarted by the great size and
speed of the river and its eddies. The result was that about 1,000
in all were killed by the enemy in combat, or died from the brute
force of the river.

At the outset of the battle, one Guido Maria de' Rossi made his 26
way with his cavalry company straight through the enemy lines by
force of arms and military valor, and coming out onto the open
ground, drew the exultant Germans upon himself. As he fought
them, he made it plain how much courage and perseverance could
achieve in warfare. Part of them he cut down, the rest he scattered
and put to flight. And thus he won from the victorious enemy an
even more famous victory, something that very rarely happens.
The remaining infantry officers and captains of horse, and others
who had declined to flee, crossed the ridges through the trackless
mountains, a number of them picked up by boats, and made their

tum redierunt; ex quibus fuit Rubeus, qui se atque suos magno labore noctu flumen traiecit.

27   Interfecti ex Germanis permulti non incruentam suis eam Venetorum cladem fecerunt. Veneti complures dies redintegrandis copiis consumpserunt. Neque interea Germani iis in locis quidquam moverunt, quando, clade non multo leviore accepta quam illata, exercitu et ipsis reparando opus fuit. In Vicentinis tamen et Feltrinis Alpium iugis, atque in Benaci lacus regione, ea manu quam conficere per occasiones poterant utrique saepe congressi, caede facta castellisque aliquot vel captis vel incensis, sese invicem inferendis cladibus intentos paratosque tenuerunt.

28   Arcum autem municipium, quod quidem abest tria milia passuum a Benaci litore, magnis et obsessum antea et expugnatum viribus, cum propterea quod ei bello causam dederat, inita de finibus altercatione cum vicinis sibi in ora lacus populis, Sigismundoque ad arma capienda incitato, tum quod eius oppidi principes Veneti hostes nominis existimabantur, senatus incendendum et diruendum censuit. Burgius interea proditionis apud decemviros accusatus, quod pontem ad Callianum, ut exercitum in fraudem coniceret, dolo malo propulisset, atque in vincula coniectus, Marci Beatiani, senatus scribae, qui ei bello cum legatis interfuerat, testimonio absolutus est ordinibusque redditus.

29   Miserat ante eos dies ad Sigismundum Innocentius Roma Paridem, episcopum Auximi, qui eum hortaretur uti bello finem imponeret: non esse tempus, imminente regno Italiae et Romanis rebus Turca, ut duo potentissimi ad illum repellendum populi levissimis de causis armis inter se decertarent odiisque mutuis contererentur; ipso arbitro suarum cum senatu Veneto discordi-

way back to Rovereto. One of their number was de' Rossi, who
with great effort got himself and his men across the river at night.

Very many Germans were killed, making the defeat of the Ve-   27
netians far from bloodless for them. It took the Venetians a good
many days for their forces to recover. Not that the Germans in the
meantime made any hostile move in those parts, since they too
needed to have their army recuperate, having suffered a disaster
not much less serious than the one they inflicted. In the Alpine
ranges around Vicenza and Feltre, however, and in the area of
Lake Garda, they often came into conflict, putting forces together
as occasion offered. With the consequent slaughter and the capture or burning down of a number of fortresses, they kept themselves ready and willing to visit destruction on one another.

The Senate decided that the town of Arco, three miles from the   28
shore of Lake Garda, which had already been besieged and taken
by a great force, should be burnt down and laid waste, and this not
only because it had given the occasion for the war by starting a
border conflict with the neighboring peoples on the lake shore,
and so provoking Sigismund to take up arms, but also because
the leading citizens of the town were thought to be hostile to Venetian power. Andrea dal Borgo, meanwhile, was accused of
treachery before the Council of Ten for having maliciously cut
loose the bridge at Calliano so as to drive the army into a trap, and
was thrown into jail. But he was acquitted by the testimony of
Marco Beazzano, secretary to the Senate, who had been with the
proveditors in the war, and was restored to his command.

Pope Innocent had earlier sent Paride [Ghirardelli], Bishop of   29
Osimo, from Rome to Sigismund, to urge him to put an end to
the war: this was not the time, he said, with the Turks threatening
the realm of Italy and the affairs of Rome, for the two nations best
fitted to drive them back to engage one another in armed conflict
for the most trivial of reasons, and to wear themselves down in
mutual hatred. Sigismund might, if he wished, use the pontiff

33

arum, si vellet, uteretur; se ei pro rerum aequitate non defuturum. Is apud illum legatus dies aliquot tractandis pacis condicionibus fuit. Venetias deinde cum mandatis est profectus; quibus a senatu non probatis, re infecta Romam rediit de mense Septembri, cum ante Idus Sextiles Severinas imperator interiisset. Egerat illud idem etiam cum senatu Veneto pontifex per suum apud ipsos internuntium Nicolaum Francum, episcopum Taurisanorum, qui civitatem et hortari et monere non destiterat; sed nihilo minus irritus omnis eius conatus fuit, quoad, fessus belli dispendio, Sigismundus (alere enim exercitum non poterat), missis saepe inter eos legatis, foedus cum Venetis percussit Idibus Novembris. Foederis condiciones fuerunt uti bello ablata, quae antiquitus eorum qui amisissent fuerint, restituerentur, et negotiatoribus Venetis damna illata sarcirentur; quae superessent inter eos res, quibus de rebus non convenerat, de iis Innocentii iudicium esset. Is finis bello Raetico fuit.

30   Milites deinde in hiberna sunt deducti, dimissusque ob rem publicam segniter gestam Iulius Camers. Roberti vero duo liberi, Gaspar atque Antonius, in reipublicae militiam conscripti, sexcentis equitibus praeficiuntur; centurionesque aliquot qui egregiam operam navaverant donis militaribus aucti, quorum uni etiam dos filiae numerata, auri ternae librae. Erantque iam Sebastianus Baduarius, Bernardus Bembus, pater meus, legati ad Innocentium profecti, cum aliis de causis, tum ut apud illum de castellis Nomio et Ivano captis a Veneto exercitu, de quibus erat lis, disceptarent.

31   His ita constitutis rebus, quod exhilarata pacis nomine civitas iam etiam ante hoc bellum in omnem luxum domesticum sese

himself as arbiter in his dispute with the Venetian Senate. He would not fail him in impartial adjudication of the matter. The legate stayed with Sigismund for several days to negotiate peace terms. He then set out for Venice with his instructions, but when they did not meet with the Senate's approval, he returned to Rome in September without accomplishing his mission, the captain-general Sanseverino having died a short while before 13 August. The pontiff had also entered negotiations on the same matter with the Venetian Senate through his nuncio to Venice, Niccolò Franco, Bishop of Treviso. He continued to give the state both encouragement and warning, but his efforts were nevertheless all in vain until Sigismund became weary of the expense of war, being unable to support his army, and struck a treaty with the Venetians on 13 November after frequent exchanges of ambassadors. The terms of the treaty were as follows: goods lost in the war were to be restored to their former owners; losses inflicted on Venetian merchants were to be compensated; and the remaining matters of dispute between them for which no provision had been made were to be decided by the pope. So ended the war in the Tyrol.

The soldiers were then led off to winter quarters, and Giulio   30
Cesare Varano, lord of Camerino, was discharged for want of vigor in his conduct of the state's business. But the two sons of Roberto da Sanseverino, Gaspare and Antonio, were taken into the service of the Republic and put in charge of 600 cavalry, and some officers who had served with distinction were honored with military decorations, one of them even being awarded a dowry of three gold pounds for his daughter.[12] Sebastiano Badoer and my father Bernardo Bembo had already set out as ambassadors to Innocent, in order (among other reasons) to discuss with him the forts of Nomio and Ivano, which had been captured by the Venetian army and about which there was a dispute.

With these matters settled, the sumptuary laws were revived at   31
the beginning of the following year, since the spirits of the citizens   1488

effuderat, insequentis anni initio leges sumptuariae revocantur. Itaque cenis pavones, phasianae aves lautioresque epulae, cubiculis stragulae vestes ex auro, argento, purpura interdicuntur; omnis ornatus muliebris decem auri libras excedere non permittitur; ampla delatoribus praemia, servis insuper libertas decreta. Quamquam caverant etiam patres, in Raetici fervore belli, ne alea neve ullo alio praeter ludum latrunculorum cum in urbe, tum per viginti quinque milia passuum extra urbis fines in pecunia luderetur, exceptis nuptiarum celebritatibus et cauponis, et ea fori parte quae ad columnas est, atque ipsa fori porticu; editumque ne iis in locis lusio auri unciae partem quintam excederet. Viarum etiam urbanarum angustiis prospectum est, sublatis tabernarum pluteis qui in vias prominebant; pontesque lignei, quibus universae prope urbis insulae, aquis interfluentibus discretae, coniungebantur, ex lateribus et lapide Istrico publice tota urbe fieri coepti.

32   Atque inter haec Ioannes Bentivolus Bononiensis, eius oppidi princeps, visendae urbis et salutandorum patrum causa Venetias venit; atque a senatu liberaliter acceptus, cum plures dies ea in re atque studio consumpsisset, donatus civitate ac iure comitiorum domum rediit. Quo quidem tempore infans biceps Patavii natus est vixitque horas aliquot. Eum nos pueri ad urbem vidimus, cum pro miraculo circumferretur. Eorum duorum capitum utrumque suo cum collo atque cervicibus a summo ita pectore suspendebatur, ut toti corpori esse par atque proprium posset; utrique ori eadem species inerat. Post eos dies regina Daciae, Roma domum rediens, Venetias et ipsa se contulit; acceptaque regio apparatu, urbe inspecta suburbiisque perlustratis, viae se reddidit.

had been lifted by the peace and they had abandoned themselves to domestic luxury of all sorts, even before the war started. Peacocks, pheasants, and the more sumptuous dishes were forbidden at dinner, and in bedrooms coverings of gold, silver, and purple cloth; the whole of a woman's jewellery was not permitted to exceed ten gold pounds in value; large rewards, and for slaves their freedom too, were laid down for informers. To be sure, in the heat of the Tyrolean war the senators[13] had also stipulated that neither dice nor any game but chess should be played for money, not just in the city but for 25 miles around, except at weddings and in inns, in the part of St. Mark's Square by the columns,[14] and in the portico of the Square itself; and in those places the stakes were not to exceed a fifth of an ounce of gold. They also did something about the city's narrow streets, by removing the shop-counters projecting into them; and the wooden bridges, by which almost all the islands of the city were joined across the canals flowing between them, began to be constructed in brick and Istrian stone at public expense throughout the city.

While this was going on, Giovanni Bentivoglio of Bologna, the 32 lord of that town, came to Venice to see the city and pay his respects to the senators. He was given a warm reception by the Senate, and spent several days in those pursuits before being granted citizenship and noble status and returning home. It was at this time that a two-headed child was born at Padua and survived for some hours. We saw it ourselves as boys in Venice when it was being paraded as a wonder. Each of the two heads had its own neck and shoulders, and rose from the top of the chest in such a way as to seem a natural part of the body as a whole; both faces had the same appearance. After that, the queen of Denmark made her way to Venice on her return home from Rome.[15] She was received with royal pomp, and after touring the city and traveling around the outlying islands, resumed her journey.

33   Eo tempore Hieronymus Rhearius, qui Sixti pontificis maximi beneficio duorum in Flaminia oppidorum, Fori Livii et Fori Cornelii, regnum obtinebat, suo in cubiculo a suis civibus trucidatus atque in forum de fenestra proiectus, foedum spectaculum populo praebuit implicuitque intestinis exterisque bellis atque incendiis civitatem; quae quidem incendia vix aegreque nobilitatis interitus et multorum hominum consecutae caedes restinxerunt. Neque multo post Galeotus Manfredus, Faventiam item obtinens, admissis noctu ab uxore sicariis, suo et ipse in lectulo confossus, oppidum tumultu et seditionibus implevit.

34   Haec senatui nuntiata eum a rei maritimae cura non averterunt. Erat iam antea sane rumor classem ingentem, a Baiasete Turcarum rege comparatam, in mare Aegaeum vela facturam. Itaque Francisco Priolo classis praefecto designato mandarunt patres, maturaret proficisci; et quoniam existimabant Baiasetem eo quidem maxime tempore mentem atque animum ad Cyprum insulam adiecisse, eo, quo celerius posset, contendere iusserunt. Is, mense Aprili conscendens, Corcyram, deinde una cum Cosma Pascalico legato Methonem adnavigavit. Quem subsecutus Nicolaus Capellus, item legatus, auxit earum quae Methone erant longarum navium numerum. Quibuscum navibus praefectus (erant autem triremes viginti quinque, minora navigia longa plus minus decem) die quinto Cyprum attigit. Ea intellecta re, Turcarum classis omnis generis longarum navium, cum a Cypro non longe abesset, mare Issicum praetervecta, sine ullo usu in Hellespontum rediit.

35   Auxerat Cypriam patribus curam, quod intellegebant Ferdinandum regem Neapolis, in Federici filii sui nuptias regina pellecta, occupandae insulae occasionem quaerere. Ea erat Caterina, Venet-

At this time Girolamo Riario, who by the munificence of Sixtus   33
IV had become lord of two towns in Romagna, Forlì and Imola,
was slaughtered in his bedchamber by his own townsfolk, and
thrown from a window into the square: a horrible spectacle for the
people, and one that brought upon the citizens war and fiery conflicts at home and abroad; and those flames were scarcely extin-
guished even by the destruction of the nobility and the mass
slaughter that followed. Not long afterwards Galeotto Manfredi,
who had similarly become lord of Faenza, was himself stabbed in
his bed after his wife let in assassins by night, and the town was
filled with uproar and civil unrest.

These matters were laid before the Senate, but did not distract   34
them from their concern for their maritime interests. There had
indeed already been a report that a huge fleet assembled by the
Turkish sultan Bayazid was about to set sail for the Aegean. The
Signoria accordingly instructed Francesco Priuli, appointed captain of the fleet, to set out with all haste, and in the belief that
Bayazid had at that particular time set his heart on Cyprus, they
told him to make for the island as quickly as he could. He embarked in April and sailed to Corfu, and from there to Methoni, in
the company of the proveditor Cosma Pasqualigo. He was followed by another proveditor, Niccolò Capello, who added his galleys to those already at Methoni. With those ships (numbering 25
galleys and about 10 smaller vessels), the captain of the fleet
reached Cyprus in five days. The Turkish fleet was made up of
warships of every kind, but when they realized what had happened, though their ships were not far from Cyprus, they returned
to the Hellespont by way of the Gulf of Alexandretta without seeing any action.

The senators' concern over Cyprus was increased by their learn-   35
ing that Ferrante, King of Naples, had inveigled the queen of Cyprus into marrying his son Federico,[16] and was looking for an opportunity to occupy the island. The queen was Caterina, who was

iis oriunda e gente Corneliorum clara atque illustri, quam Marcus
Cornelius pater Iacobo Lusiniano regi Cyprio in matrimonium
collocaverat, numerata regi pecunia dotis nomine auri ad libras
mille. Eam rex, brevi tempore profluvio ventris sublatus, prae-
gnantem reliquit, scriptis tabulis quibus illam regni heredem nas-
citura cum subole instituerat sub Veneti senatus tutela; quo a senatu Corneliam, tamquam reipublicae filiam, publica interposita
fide acceptam, uxorem duxerat. Itaque post mortem patris natus
filius, anno vertente natali suo, diem cum obiisset, novasque res
nonnnulli eo in regno principes molirentur, classe ad insulam celeriter missa cum legatis et Cornelio patre, qui reginae assiderent,
eos senatus facile tumultus compressit.

36   Tranquillitate insulae restituta, mulier vidua auctoritate reipublicae quindecim iam annos post viri mortem pacate regnum obtinuerat, cum per internuntios Ritium Marinum Neapolitanum, qui
regi Cyprio perfamiliaris fuerat, et Tristanum Cibeletum Cy-
prium, cui erat soror e reginae famulis, Ferdinandus rex clam eas
quas dixi nuptias procurabat. Ii cum a rege missi in insulam des-
cendissent, a praefecto classis capti atque in vincula coniecti sunt
Venetiasque transmissi. Tametsi Tristanus, qui, propterea quod
post regis Cyprii mortem tumultu excitato Andream Cornelium
reginae patruum interfecerat exulque factus fuerat, sui poenas sce-
leris se persoluturum sciebat, adamante quem in anulo gestabat
per os in stomachum recepto, aqua insuper quae metalla dividit
epota, dum portaretur interiit.

37   Iis permoti rebus decemviri, quamquam quidem non Ferdinandi modo artes, sed Turcarum quoque insidias inceptaque timuerant, neque nihil etiam ab rege Syriae propter vicinitatem me-
tuebant, Georgio Cornelio, reginae fratri, dant negotium, uti se ad

born at Venice into the prominent and distinguished Cornaro family. Her father Marco Cornaro had given her in marriage to Jacques Lusignan, King of Cyprus, paying him by way of dowry about 1,000 gold pounds. The king was carried off by a stomach ailment shortly thereafter, leaving her pregnant. By his will he made her heir to the kingdom, along with the child about to be born, under the protection of the Venetian Senate. It was from the Senate that he had taken Cornaro to wife, taken on, as it were, as a daughter of the Republic guaranteed by the state. The son who was born after the death of his father met his end on his birthday a year later, and some of the leading nobles of the kingdom began to plot a coup, but the Senate quickly sent a fleet to the island, with ambassadors and her father Marco Cornaro to support the queen, and so easily suppressed the uprising.

With tranquillity restored to the island, under the aegis of Ven- 36
ice the widow had governed Cyprus in peace for some fifteen years after the death of her husband, when through the go-betweens Rizzo di Marino of Naples, who had been very close to the king of Cyprus, and the Cypriot Tristano Cibelletto, who had a sister among the queen's attendants, King Ferrante began in secret to arrange the marriage I mentioned. When the men sent by the king reached the island, they were seized by the captain of the fleet, thrown into irons, and sent to Venice. Tristano, however, realized that he would pay the penalty for his crime, for in the unrest that followed the death of the king of Cyprus, he had killed the queen's uncle Andrea Cornaro and been sent into exile: he swallowed a diamond that he wore on a ring, and with a further draught of the liquid that separates metals,[17] died in the course of the journey.

Disturbed by these events (they already had fears not only 37
about Ferrante's schemes but also the treacherous plans of the Turks, and were somewhat concerned about the sultan of Syria too, being so close by), the Council of Ten gave the queen's brother Giorgio Cornaro the task of going to his sister and per-

sororem conferat eique persuadeat ut, relicta regni procuratione reipublicae, ad urbem revertatur atque in patria malit interque suos quod reliquum est vitae secure atque tranquille degere, quam in remota suspectaque insula alienigenis hominibus sese vitamque suam credere. Cornelius, parvulo navigio, ut celerius iter faceret, parte itineris confecta, brumalibus diebus in Cyprum transmisit et sorori quam ob causam venisset exposuit. Novitate rei permota, recusare illa neque sibi persuaderi velle uti regnum opulentum relinqueret, mulier regio victu, regiis honoribus assueta, quaeque sciret quam nullo praecipuo iure quamque parce in republica viveretur; satis esse dicere, si, se mortua, ea insula in reipublicae potestatem redigatur.

38   Contra Cornelius niti rogareque ne pluris terram Cypriam quam natale solum quamque rempublicam faceret; casus humanarum rerum esse incertos; fieri momento horae posse ut regno expellatur, tam potentibus regibus quasi obsessa atque praecincta eius insulae dominationem affectantibus, quamplurimis etiam Cypriis principibus a femina sese regi non obscure indignantibus. His eam casibus et periculis una modo re atque consilio pulcherrime ire obviam posse, suum si regnum, quoniam liberis careat, reipublicae fidei iam nunc vivens florensque commiserit. Dum insidiarum et suspicionum tempora non plenissima fuerunt, eam regno suo frui non permisisse solum rempublicam, sed etiam uti frueretur adiuvisse; idque ipsi iucundissimum accidisse. Nunc autem, cum nihil a quoquam tuti sit, cum omnibus a vicinis regibus, atque etiam a longinquis et magno seiunctis atque separatis mari, omnes artes adhibeantur et tamquam retia ei insulae tendantur, quibus capi et teneri possit, senatum ad id descendisse quod unum

suading her to leave the governance of her realm to the Republic and to return to Venice. She was to be urged to live out what remained of her life in her own country and among her own people, in security and tranquillity, rather than trust herself and her life to foreigners on a remote island of uncertain loyalty. Making part of the journey in a small boat for speed, Cornaro crossed to Cyprus in midwinter, and explained to his sister his reasons for coming. Taken aback by this turn of events, she protested and would not be prevailed upon to abandon her wealthy kingdom, accustomed as she was to a royal way of life and the honors paid to royalty. She well knew that she would have no special prerogatives, and greatly reduced circumstances, if she lived at Venice; it was enough, she said, if the island were to come back under the control of the Republic at her death.

In his reply Cornaro urged her with all the emphasis at his 38 command not to prize the land of Cyprus more highly than her native soil and the Republic. The outcome of human affairs was uncertain: she might be thrown out of her kingdom in the space of an hour, being as good as besieged and encircled by such powerful kings aspiring to mastery of the island, as well as having a great many Cypriot nobles who made no secret of their resentment at being ruled by a woman. There was only one plan and course of action that could successfully meet these perils and risks, and that was (since she had no children) to entrust her kingdom to the protection of the Republic now, while she was alive and well. When the times were not so full of plotting and mistrust, Venice had not only allowed her to enjoy her kingdom but had even helped her to do so, and it had been a cause of great satisfaction to the Republic to have it so. But now nothing was safe from anyone; every art was being employed by all the neighboring rulers, and even by distant ones separated from Cyprus by a great expanse of sea. Snares, so to speak, were being laid for the island, by which it could be seized and occupied. In the circumstances, the Senate had been driven to

sibi visum esset omnium impendentium malorum et periculorum remedium; quorum si reliqua ipsa nihil timeret, num illud non perhorresceret, quod, nisi praesidio celerrime comparato insulam senatus firmavisset, aestate illam proxima Turcarum classis occupavisset atque ipsam vel fugae sese dare coegisset vel captam Byzantium duxisset? Quod eam casus aut offensio aliqua compellere turpiter uti faciat potest, praestare id incredibili reipublicae gratia suique facti summa cum gloria celebritateque antevertisse.

39   Occasionem esse variam, multiplicem, subitam; non singula hostium consilia provideri semper posse; non semper homines in tempore adesse. Inter intimum Adriatici maris sinum Cypriaque litora multum terrarum, multa maria interesse. Haec illi cogitanda, haec imprimis pensitanda esse. Quod si nulla necessitas urgeat, quid esset tandem aptius atque commodius ad eius famam nominis sempiternam, quam suae illam patriae regnum nobilissimum tradere, ut in annalibus referatur Venetam rempublicam a sua cive Cypri insulae opulentissimae imperio auctam atque condecoratam fuisse? Omni eam in regione nomen regium obtenturam. Si optio ipsius sit, cum tot annos apud Cyprios vixerit, debere eam cupere suis etiam ab civibus aliquando suaque in patria se salutari atque conspici, splendorem suum fratri, sororibus, propinquis, familiae, demum ei urbi in qua nata alitaque sit communicare. Nullius umquam feminae, neque etiam viri, tam gratum adventum reipublicae fuisse quam ipsius futurum. Quod si Venetiae abiectum aliquod oppidulum esset, locoque aspero atque ignobili situm, esse tamen eius pietatis atque humani plane animi, qua in terra nascens caelum hauserit, revisere eam velle seseque suis omnibus tanto post tempore ostendere. At cum ea omnino

the view that this was the only remedy for all the trouble and peril that hung over her. If she had no fear of the rest, did she not shudder at the thought that, had it not been for the quick action of the Senate in supplying a garrison and securing the island, the Turkish fleet would have attacked it the previous summer and would have forced her to flee or taken her to Constantinople as a prisoner? It was better to forestall what some misfortune or mishap might compel her to do to her shame, and earn thereby the extraordinary gratitude of the Republic, and for her actions the highest glory and renown.

The right moment, he said, was different in each case, change- 39 able, suddenly presented. One could not always anticipate every last intention of the enemy. Men were not always there to help in time. Between the innermost gulf of the Adriatic and the shores of Cyprus there was much land and many seas. These were the things she had to think about, this above all was what she had to weigh up. Even if there were no pressing need, what in the end would be more apt and conducive to the eternal glory of her name than for her to make over that splendid realm to her fatherland, so that history might say that the Republic of Venice was increased and enhanced with the rule of the wealthy island of Cyprus thanks to its own citizen? She would obtain a royal renown in every land. If the choice was hers, even though she had lived so many years among the Cypriots, she should desire to be greeted and seen by her own citizens as well, and in her own country; she should want to share her glory with her brother, sisters, relations, and household, in a word, with the city in which she was born and raised. Never was a woman's arrival, nor even a man's, so gratifying to the Republic as hers would be. If Venice were some miserable little town in a rough and undistinguished location, to wish to see again the land in which she first drew breath at birth, and present herself to all her people after so long a time, would still show a proper patriotism and humanity. But since the city was celebrated

urbs omnes alias urbes quas sol aspicit prope excellere omnium hominum consensu praedicetur, atque ipsa in Italia omnium sit eius terrae urbium opportunissima, quidnam esse causae posse quamobrem, a senatu atque a republica tanto post tempore invitata, non se eo libentissime conferat? Quod regina sit, quod multos annos secure atque feliciter regnarit, gratiam esse senatui, a quo id acceperit, referendam; eam gratiam pessime relatum iri, si senatum se vocantem omnibusque honoribus prosequi cupientem despexerit.

40   Postremo cum ipse ei frater sit, atque is frater cui multum illa semper tribuerit, si hoc non impetret, non tam eam adduci non potuisse ut reipublicae satisfaceret, quam se noluisse, omnes homines existimaturos; eoque se nomine magnam totius civitatis invidiam subiturum liberisque relicturum. Itaque flecti se sineret et cum sibi ipsa in praesentia consuleret, tum in posterum respiceret ad suos. Nihil esse laudabilius quam secunda fortuna moderate uti neque in summo semper gradu velle consistere. Deos etiam immortales consuevisse, quibus se diu benevolos praestiterunt, eos aliqua non iucunda re interdum probare an se homines esse natos reminiscantur. Nullas eam preces posse illis gratiores adhibere, nullam potiorem victimam caedere quam eorum voluntati atque numini sese praesto esse profiteri. Deorum autem voluntatem eam esse existimare nos oportere, quae patriae sit optimeque constitutae reipublicae.

41   Haec Cornelius cum dixisset, homo apprime eloquens, non doctrina ille quidem aut sapientiae studiis, sed naturae quadam vi liberali atque munere, regina obortis iam lacrimis, ubi primum fari potuit: "Si tibi hoc ita frater videtur, et mihi," inquit, "videtur; aut ut videatur meo animo imperabo; sed magis a te patria regnum

by the all but universal opinion of mankind as surpassing all other cities under the face of the sun, and since in Italy itself it was the best situated of any city in the land, what possible reason could there be for her not to seize the chance to go there at the invitation of the Senate and the Republic after such a long time? She had the Senate to thank for the fact that she was a queen, and had reigned in security and prosperity for many years. And the favor that she had received from them would be ill repaid if she were to hold in contempt the Senate's invitation and their desire to attend her with every mark of respect.

Finally, he said, as her brother, and one whom she had always 40 highly regarded, if his plea were unsuccessful, everyone would think not so much that she could not be brought to meet the Republic's wishes, as that he had not wanted her to do so. He would incur the great resentment of the entire city on that score, and leave it as a legacy to his children. She should therefore let herself be won over and consult her own best interests here and now, as well as having regard to her family's position in the future. Nothing was more praiseworthy than to use good fortune in moderation, and to forbear to remain forever at the very summit of things. Even God was on occasion accustomed to test with some unwelcome situation those to whom He had long shown favor, to see whether they remembered they were of mortal birth. She could offer no more acceptable prayer to Him, she could slaughter no more welcome victim, than to profess that she was at the disposal of His will and power. And God's will we should regard as identical to the will of our country, the best regulated Republic.

Cornaro was a man eloquent in the highest degree, not indeed 41 because of his learning or philosophical studies, but because he was endowed by nature with a certain gift and a noble forcefulness. When he had finished his speech, the queen, already in tears, said, as soon as she could speak: "If this is your view, my brother, it is mine too, or rather I shall tell my heart it is so; but our father-

meum acceperit, quam a me." His dictis, constitutoque quid facto
opus esset, anno insequente iam inito, classis praefectus legatique,
re divina facta, in Famagustae oppidi foro, regina inspectante
atque iubente, reipublicae vexilla erexerunt, Cypriumque regnum
in provinciam est redactum. Regina posthaec, supellectili regia im-
posita, Cornelio cum fratre naves longas conscendit atque ad portus Veneti angustias aestate media appulit; exceptaque ab Augustino Barbadico, civitatis principe, et patribus, qui ei obviam ierant
ad Nicolai fanum, quod est in portus litore, magna omnium ordi-
num, atque adeo omnium hominum, in cymbis impositorum pro-
sequentiumque laetitia, ipsa vecta Bucentauro navi, media inter
patres matronasque nobilissimas civitatis, urbem est ingressa,
quod ante id tempus Venetarum feminarum contigerat nulli; lae-
tissimusque is profecto dies civitati fuit. Asulum subinde, oppidum in Taurisanis collibus, ei a decemviris dono datum, atque auri
quinquaginta librae in annos singulos constitutae pensionis nomine, tum muneris in praesentia decem librae.

42   Superiore anno autem (ut ad eas res, quibus de rebus ante dicendum fuerat, revertamur), ne civitatem onerariarum navium numerus proventusque deficeret, senatus consultum factum est: quae
in navibus exterarum nationum mercaturae causa imponerentur,
ea fisco deberi, vino Cretico excepto; pro quo tamen portorii nomine Venetis magistratibus pares amphorarum numero auri se-
muncias mercatores solverent. Tum quicumque navem magnam
onerariam fabricandam institueret, uti ei quaestores de triginta
auri libris commodarent, eodem senatus consulto continebatur.
Posthaec cum Tremezeni rex, quod est oppidum Africae, non longissime a freti angustiis contra Hispaniam situm, a senatu per legatos petiisset uti civem Venetum eo mitteret, qui suis in oppidis
tribus ius reipublicae hominibus diceret, senatus censuit, quo

land will receive my kingdom more from you than from me." On these words, arrangements were made for what had to be done. The new year had already begun when, after celebration of mass, the captain and ambassadors raised the flag of the Republic in the town square of Famagusta, the queen looking on and giving directions. And so the kingdom of Cyprus was reduced to a province. After this the queen's royal trappings and accoutrements were loaded, and she and her brother embarked on the warships, putting in at the basin of the port of Venice in the middle of summer. She was greeted by the Doge Agostino Barbarigo and the senators, who had gone to meet her at the church of San Niccolò dei Mendicoli on the harbor shore, to the great joy of Venetian society and of the people as a whole, who followed her on board little boats. Amid the senators and the noblest ladies of the city, Caterina herself made her entry into Venice borne on the Bucintoro,[18] something which had never before happened to any Venetian lady: indeed a day of great rejoicing for the citizenry. Presently Asolo, a town in the hills of Treviso, was given her by the Council of Ten. Her annual pension was fixed at 50 gold pounds, along with an immediate gift of 10 pounds.

But to return to those events of which mention should have been made earlier, in the previous year the Senate took measures to ensure adequate numbers and development of the city's merchant fleet by decreeing that cargo loaded onto foreign ships by way of trade was owed to the state treasury. An exception was made for Cretan wine, for which, however, the merchants were to pay the Venetian authorities duty of half an ounce of gold on every cask. The same decree of the Senate made provision for the proveditors to lend up to 30 gold pounds to anyone undertaking to build a large merchant vessel. Following that, ambassadors of the king of Tlemcen (an African town facing Spain, not far from the Straits of Gibraltar) petitioned the Senate to send a Venetian citizen to administer justice in his three towns for men of the Repub-

regiae postulationi satisfieret, uti magistratus crearetur eoque mit-
teretur, ad quem centesima mercium omnium, quae merces eis in
oppidis venderentur, perveniret; estque ad ea oppida omnium pri-
mus Aloisius Pizamanus missus.

43   Eodem tempore senatus iussu in Idri lacus ripa, loco alto atque
edito, quo in loco Anfo, Brixiani agri vicus, est, magni arx operis
crebraeque munitiones institutae, ac tertio confectae anno, omnem
illam oram tutiorem ac celebratiorem reddiderunt. Eodem quoque
anno decemviri legem tulerunt, ne aperte suffragia inirentur; qui
secus fecisset, suffragiorum iure magistratibusque annos duos ca-
reret. De Graecis item equitibus qui reipublicae militiam facie-
bant, lex est lata: qui eorum coloniae nomine ad insulam Zacynthum ire vellent, uti iis agri publice darentur, imprimisque
Theodoro Palaeologo, si eo mittere aliquem suorum vellet, propter
eius summum in rempublicam studium, summam fidem singula-
remque constantiam. Regis etiam Roxolanorum legatio cum pre-
tiosarum pellium muneribus ad senatum venit petiitque ut ad ipsorum litora reipublicae onerariae naves longae ad mercaturam
exercendam mitterentur. Ea de re propter longinquitatem itineris
navigationisque taedium atque pericula, quod Maeotis erat palus
emetienda, nihil est impetratum. Legati, qui duo erant fratres, ho-
norifice accepti, veste uterque aurea, et auri libra publice donati,
Romam profecti sunt.

44   Insequente vero anno, de quo paulo ante dicere incepimus,
Franciscus Gonzaga, qui Mantuae regnum a maioribus traditum
obtinebat, in reipublicae militiam conscriptus est, eique senatus
consultum est missum; quo ex senatus consulto equitibus cataphractis trecentis, sagittariis qui equo uterentur quadringentis, militibus ducentis et quinquaginta praeesset. Cum autem Mathias,

lic. The Senate decided to satisfy the royal request by despatching a newly-created magistrate, to whom would accrue one percent of the value of all merchandise sold in the towns; the first to be sent out there was Alvise Pizzamano.

At the same time the Senate ordered the construction of a massive fortress with numerous towers at the Brescian village of Anfo, high up on the shores of Lake Idro. It was finished in two years and made the whole shoreline more secure and populous. Also in the same year, the Council of Ten passed a law forbidding open balloting; any contravention was to be punished by the loss of voting rights and eligibility for magistracies for two years. Another law was passed concerning the stradiots[19] serving in the Republic's army, that those who wished to go to form a colony on the island of Zante should be given land at public expense. This was especially aimed at Theodore Palaeologus, in case he should want to send some of his men there, in the light of his great attachment to the Republic and the high degree of loyalty and steadfastness he had shown it. An embassy of the king of the Rossolani[20] also came to the Senate with gifts of precious skins to ask that Venetian merchant galleys should be sent to their shores to carry on trade. But on this matter, owing to the length of the journey and the wearisome and dangerous sailing (the Sea of Azov would have to be traversed), their request met with a peremptory refusal. The two brothers who formed the embassy were honorably received at Venice, and each was given a golden robe and a gold pound at public expense before they set off for Rome.

In the following year, about which I started to write a little earlier, Francesco Gonzaga, who had inherited the marquisate of Mantua, was taken into the Republic's service by decree of the Senate. Under the terms of the decree, he was to be in command of 300 heavy cavalry, 400 mounted archers, and 250 infantry. King Matthias of Hungary, a man famous for his knowledge and success in military matters, had attacked the Emperor Frederick by

43

44
1489

Pannoniae rex, homo rei militaris scientia atque gloria clarus, bellum Federico imperatori duobus exercitibus intulisset, uno in Carnos, altero in Liburnorum fines immisso, senatus vicinitate belli adductus per Antonium Bolduum, Dominicum Bolanum legatos, illum ad Federicum, hunc ad Mathiam missos, eorum regum animos iam exulceratos leniit. Itaque indutiae inter eos dictae.

45   Earum indutiarum tempore, solutus belli occupationibus, Federicus Tridentum venit, omnem illum Italiae tractum qui a lacu Benaco ad Aquileiam secundum Alpes est, si per Venetos liceat, animi causa perlustraturus. Ea intellecta re, senatus Hieronymum Barbarum, Dominicum Grimanum (qui postea cardinalis fuit), Paulum Trivisanum, Hieronymum Leonem legatos ad eum misit; qui ei venienti obviam Roveretum profecti sunt reique publicae nomine illum salutatum exceperunt. Eaque postea legatio, quoad is in Italia fuit, ei praesto omnibus in reipublicae locis fuit, atque uti pro copia locorum quam maximi ei honores haberentur, studium et diligentiam adhibuit. Federicus, Benacum primum invisens omniaque litora biremi circumvectus, eius praesertim orae quae ad meridiem vergit aspectu atque fragrantia, quod est pomi medici plena, mirifice exhilaratus, tum aquae perlucidissimae amoenitate oblectatus piscationibusque delectatus est. Capitur eo in lacu prope medio, quaque altissima est aqua, piscis clarus carpio ab incolis dictus, pedis plerumque longitudine; qui omnino piscis alibi non capitur. Eum piscem capere atque cognoscere Federico voluptati fuit. Veronam deinde, tum Vicetiam,[3] Bassianum, Taurisum, Cornelianum, Forum Iulii, Aquileiam, Portumque Naonis, qui locus in ipsius dictione est, lento itinere pervenit. E Naonis vero Portu tres legatos ad senatum misit actum gratias, quod per eius loca tam liberaliter tantisque honoribus susceptus fuisset

sending two armies against him, one in Friuli and the other in Croatia. Concerned at the proximity of the hostilities, the Senate sent ambassadors to the kings, Antonio Boldù to Frederick and Domenico Bollani to Matthias, who managed to soothe the rancor that had arisen between them, and a truce was accordingly declared.

Free of his military preoccupations while this truce was in force, 45 Frederick went to Trento with the intention of taking a pleasure trip through the whole stretch of Italy from Lake Garda to Aquileia along the Alps, provided the Venetians were agreeable. When they learned of this, the Senate sent an embassy to him made up of Girolamo Barbaro, Domenico Grimani (the later cardinal), Paolo Trevisan, and Girolamo Leone. They went to Rovereto to meet him on his progress and welcomed him in the name of the Republic. As long as he was in Italy, this legation was subsequently at his service throughout the Republic's territory, and so far as the resources of the places allowed, they took great pains to have him paid the greatest possible honors. Frederick first visited Garda and had himself conveyed all around the shore in a small galley.[21] He was very taken by the views and scents of the southern side specially, being full of citron trees, and also took great pleasure in the clear, beautiful water, and the fishing that went on there. Around the middle of the lake where the water is deepest, a well-known fish is taken which the natives call a carp, generally about a foot in length and not caught elsewhere. Frederick enjoyed catching the fish and learning about it. He then made his way by slow degrees to Verona, followed by Vicenza, Bassano, Treviso, Conegliano, Cividale, Aquileia, and Pordenone, the last a place in his own territory. It was from Pordenone that he sent three ambassadors to the Senate to thank them for having welcomed him so generously and with such marks of honor throughout their domain, and for the great goodwill that he had learned

53

tamque benivolam in sese civitatis voluntatem cognovisset. Ab
Aquileiae finibus suum in regnum concessit.

46   Eodem tempore, ut infantibus vulgo quaesitis, qui publice ale-
bantur quorumque magnopere numerus excreverat, largius ube-
riusque esset, in senatu lex est perlata, ut navalium urbanorum
magistratus in annos singulos tritici molita sestaria, quae appellant, ducenta, vini amphoras duodecim eorum curatoribus darent;
iisque rebus ex reipublicae horreis silvae caesae ad ignem domesticum carros ducentos eorum praefecti adderent. Terruit non multo
post civitatem, quod ad diem tertium Iduum Sextilis duae turres,
omnium quae in urbe essent maximae atque altissimae, noctu de
caelo tactae conflagraverunt, culminibus incendio late spectabili as-
sumptis; una, quae in foro est, cuius erat culmen inauratum; altera, quae est media in urbe ad Francisci. Senatus posthaec legibus
aliquot promulgandis operam dedit, quae leges ad portoria urbis
conservanda pertinerent. Etiam in Mariae clarum miraculis, unde
ei nomen est, fanum exaedificatum iam eo luculentiore opere, quo
ipsum angustius est, ut eius artificii elegantia et sumptus aliorum
templorum magnitudinem exaequarent, extremo anni die virgines
inductae sunt.

47   Anno insequente, quod in urbe saevire pestilentia coeperat,
triumviros sananda civitate[4] senatus creavit; isque postea magistratus numquam est creari desitus. Eo anno, cum increbuisset rumor
Baiasetis regis classem non multarum navium in Aegaeum pro-
vehi, ut Nicolaum Sumaripam e Paro insula, quam obtinebat, expelleret eaque potiretur, Nicolaus Capellus legatus cum triremibus
quattuor Zacynthum contendit, ei praesidio, si opus esset, futu-
rus. Sumaripa ubi adesse legatum cognovit, insigne Venetum sustulit seseque reipublicae addixit. Neque multo post Ioannes Cerno-

the Republic bore toward him. From the borders of Aquileia he retired into his own realm.

At that time too, the Senate passed a law to give more generous 46 treatment to the illegitimate children who were raised at public expense and whose numbers had greatly increased, by having the officers of the Arsenal make their keepers an annual grant of 200 bushels (as they call them)[22] of wheat and twelve casks of wine, and by having their superintendents add on top of that 200 cartloads of timber for firewood from the Republic's stores. Not long afterwards, the city was thrown into panic when on 11 August the two greatest and tallest towers in the city, one in St. Mark's Square whose roof was gilded and the other in the middle of the city at the church of the Friars Minor,[23] were struck by lightning at night and caught fire, the blaze that consumed their roofs visible far and wide. Following that the Senate gave its attention to promulgating various laws directed at maintaining the city's revenue from tariffs. Also, on the last day of the year, nuns were brought into the church of Santa Maria, famous for the miracles from which it takes its name:[24] the building was now finished with workmanship all the more splendid for its being so small, so that the beauty and richness of its materials equalled the grandeur of other churches.

In the next year, plague began to rage in Venice and the Senate 47 appointed a Board of Three to see to restoring the city to health, a *1490* magistracy that became a permanent body from that time on. In that year a rumor spread that a fleet of Sultan Bayazid was sailing with no great number of ships into the Aegean to expel Niccolò Sommaripa and take control of the island of Paros, of which he was lord. The proveditor Niccolò Cappello made haste to Zante with four galleys, so as to be in a position to give assistance if the need arose. When Sommaripa learned that the proveditor was there, he raised the Venetian flag and declared himself a subject of the Republic. Not long afterwards Ivan Cernovich, a man of great

ichius, cuius erat magnum in Illyrico nomen, magna auctoritas, legatos ad senatum misit: cupere sese ut Georgius, filius suus, Antonii Erici senatoris filiam in matrimonium duceret; petere ut sibi id facere senatus voluntate liceret. Ea de re consultus, senatus censuit uti nuptiae fierent. Erat eo tempore Antonius reipublicae nomine Ferrariae magistratus qui prodominus appellabatur. Itaque facta potestate ad urbem venit, Georgio filiam spondet. Ea dum per legatos in Illyricum traducitur, pater moriens filio regnum tradit; ita nuptiae, inter lacrimas et gratulationem concelebratae, clariorem exitum habuerunt. Guidus Maria Rubeus paulo post Venetiis moritur, magno totius civitatis dolore; funus ei publice atque magnifice factum laudatusque a Sabellico est. Eius stipendium equitumque numerus duobus eius liberis aequis partibus distributus.

48　　Eodem anno tametsi pacata neque ullo bello implicata esset civitas, rei militaris tamen studium non neglexit. Invaluerat iam in bellis consuetudo, invento Germanorum nobis tradita, ut milites fistulis ferreis uterentur; quibus fistulis glandes plumbeas magna vi ignis impetu mitterent atque hostem e longinquo vulnerarent. Eae erant fistulae ad formam atque imaginem eorum tormentorum quibus muri oppidorum deiciuntur, nisi quod illa ex aere fusili fiunt maximique saepe sunt ponderis, ut carris solidissimis ferratisque ac magno iumentorum numero egeant, quibus sustineri atque regi possint. Fistulae e ferro sunt gestanturque singulis ab militibus singulae ligneis alligatae armamentis, per quae capiuntur; et pulvere ad ignem celeriter comprehendendum idoneo infarciuntur; et glande immissa humeris sublatae in hostem convertuntur. Eo telo qui uti scirent ut reipublicae suppeterent, peritissimos eius rei homines undique conquisitos accersitosque decemviri suas ad

renown and standing in Illyria, sent ambassadors to the Senate to say that he wanted to marry his son Zorzi to the daughter of the senator Antonio Erizzo and to ask for the Senate's approval to do so. After consultation on the matter, the Senate agreed to the marriage taking place. Antonio was at that time acting as a magistrate (called a *visdomino*) on behalf of the Republic at Ferrara, and when the permission was granted he came to Venice and betrothed his daughter to Zorzi Cernovich. While she was being conducted to Illyria by ambassadors, the father Ivan bequeathed the realm to his son on his deathbed, and so the marriage, taking place amid tears and rejoicing, took on an enhanced significance.[25] Guido Maria de' Rossi died at Venice a little while later, much mourned by the whole city: his splendid funeral was held at public expense, with a eulogy by Sabellico. His pay and the number of lances assigned to him were distributed equally between his two sons.

Though the city was at peace that year and not involved in any war, it did not neglect military matters. The German innovation of soldiers using guns[26] had been taken over by the Italians and was by now well established in our warfare. With these they would shoot lead bullets, driven by fire with great force, and wound the enemy from a distance. These guns were in shape and appearance like the cannons used to knock down town walls, except that those are made of cast bronze and often extremely heavy, so that they need very substantial iron-clad carriages and a good many beasts of burden to carry and operate them. Guns are made of iron and are carried by a single soldier, with a wooden casing to hold them by. They are crammed with an explosive powder, and with the bullet loaded, they are lifted onto the shoulder and turned on the enemy. To ensure that those who knew how to use the weapon would answer to the needs of the Republic, the Council of Ten scoured the land for the greatest experts in its use, gathered them together and sent them to the subject towns to train the

48

urbes miserunt, qui iuventutem instituerent. Atque ut agrestes maxime homines id armorum genus docerentur, singulis in vicis pagisque uti duo puberes ei artificio assuefierent edixerunt; atque iis omnium onerum immunitatem concesserunt, quo studiosiores et diligentiores unum ad id munus obeundum reliquis liberati oneribus ac tributis fierent; eosque puberes die dicta ad suum quosque oppidum quotannis signo glande feriendo convenire voluerunt; qui vicisset, eius toti pago aut castello vacationem esse munerum annuam, eo excepto munere quo ad Medoaci fluminis derivationem tenebantur, imperaverunt.

49   Inter haec, cum antea fures domestici, lege antiquitus instituta, poena multo leviore plecterentur quam ii qui eandem domum non incolerent, qua ex re fiebat uti, aucta servorum et inquilinorum audacia, omnibus paene in domibus furta exercerentur, maioribus in comitiis mense Sextili lex est perlata, qua lege eadem esset in servos reliquosque fures contubernales poena constituta, idem ius, qua poena quoque iure in alienos exterosque fures animadvertere civitatis magistratus consueverant.

50   At ea quae subsecuta est hieme tantus tamque perpetuus nivium rigor fuit, ut omnia urbis aestuaria congelaverint, neque pedibus modo, sed in equis etiam homines ex agris ad extremum urbis marginem commeatibus importandis sine periculo ventitarint; magistratusque Mestrinus ad Secundi fanum, quod est in mediis ad urbem vadis, curru pervenerit. Quibus quidem diebus etiam in media latissimaque urbis via, per quam unam naves onerariae magnae permeant, constricto glacie mari niveque superaddita, admissis per ludi speciem equis, Graeci hastati equites concurrerunt. Vini, ficus, oleae anni aliquot, intra Alpes Athesimque atque

young men. And so that countrymen in particular might learn
how to handle weapons of the sort, they ordered that in every village and hamlet two young males should be made familiar with
the device. They granted them immunity from all financial burdens, so that they might meet that one obligation all the more
keenly and attentively for being free of taxes and tribute, and they
required those young men to meet on a fixed day each year in their
several towns to hit a target with a bullet. They ordered that the
entire village or castle of the winner should enjoy a year's exemption from taxes, with the exception of the tax which they were required to pay for the diversion of the Brenta river.

In the meantime, by a law of long standing, thieves who belonged to a household had previously received a much lighter punishment than those who did not live in the same house. The result
was that the boldness of slaves and lodgers increased, and thefts
were happening in nearly every home. So in the Great Council of
August [1490] a law was passed which laid down that the same
penalty and the same judicial process should apply to slaves and
other thieves occupying the same dwelling as those which the state
magistrates had customarily applied to foreigners and people outside the household who committed thefts.

In the winter that followed, the snows came so continuously
and with such severity that all the estuaries of the city froze over.
People could travel back and forth bringing supplies in from the
countryside in perfect safety, not only on foot but even on horseback, right up to the edge of the city. The magistrate of Mestre
drove in a chariot to the church of San Secondo, which is in the
middle of the lagoon near the city. And indeed in that period,
with the sea icebound and snow covering it, horses were sent for
sport onto the central and widest canal of the city, the only one
through which large merchant ships can pass, and stradiots
jousted with lances there. For some years there was a reduced har-

49

50
1490–91

Padum flumina, exustis super terram arboribus, proventum angustiorem habuerunt.

51   Vere insequente Innocentius pontifex maximus per suos internuntios eiusmodi sententiam Tridenti pronuntiavit: quod Veneti, a Sigismundo lacessiti, bello Rhetico se defendissent impensasque magnas eo in bello fecissent, Nomium et Ivanum castella iure ab iis capta atque retenta sibi videri. A senatu tamen petiit, vellet ea ipsa Sigismundo ultro reddere, id se propterea cupere ostendens, ne pax inter ipsos inita ea de causa violaretur. Cuius auctoritate moti, patres praesidiis abductis Nomium et Ivanum Sigismundo restituerunt.

52   Obiit per eos dies mortem Romae Marcus Barbus, Pauli secundi pontificis maximi fratris filius, e cardinalium collegio, vir et doctrina et probitate et sanctitate vitae et Romanorum civium gratia egregie insignis; quique, comitiis pontificalibus Sixti morte habitis, parum abfuit quin a collegio summum locum adipisceretur. Eo mortuo Innocentius patriarchatum (sic enim appellant) Aquileiensium, quem is multos annos obtinuerat, Hermolao Barbaro, legato apud se Veneto, attribuit. Quod ubi civitas intellexit, tametsi Hermolaus ad senatum scripserat coactum se a pontifice vestem senatoriam mutavisse, quoniam tamen sacerdotiis cooptari cives Veneti qui legati Romae essent lege prohibebantur, graviter tulit ausum illum contra leges patrias facere. Auxit eius rei magnopere invidia, quod antea ex Hermolai litteris, quas ad senatum de Barbi morte dederat, more institutoque maiorum comitiis senatoriis praeiudicium patres fecerant, cuius ipsi civis nomen ad id adipiscendum sacerdotium Innocentio commendarent. Itaque deceptos in eo sese ac prope delusos querebantur.

vest of wine, figs, and olives in the land between the Alps and the Adige and the Po, the trees having withered above ground.

At the beginning of spring, Pope Innocent delivered his adjudication through intermediaries at Trento, as follows: because the Venetians had been provoked by Sigismund in the war of the Tyrol, and had defended themselves at great expense in that war, the castles of Nomio and Ivano had in his view been lawfully captured and retained by them. He nevertheless asked the Senate to agree to return them to Sigismund voluntarily, intimating that his reason for doing so was to avoid the peace between them being broken on their account. The pope's authority induced the senators to withdraw their garrisons and to restore Nomio and Ivano to Sigismund. 51

During this period Marco Barbo of the college of cardinals died at Rome, the nephew of Pope Paul II and a man of great distinction for his learning and the probity and holiness of his life, as well as his influence with the people of Rome. In the papal conclave held on the death of Sixtus, he came very close to winning first place in the vote of the college. At his death Innocent conferred the Patriarchate (as it is called) of Aquileia, which Barbo had held for many years, on Ermolao Barbaro, the Venetian envoy to the pope. When this became known at Venice, although Ermolao had written to the Senate that he had been obliged by the pontiff to put off his senatorial robes, the Venetians were offended that he had ventured to breach the ancestral laws, since citizens who were ambassadors at Rome were prohibited by statute from holding priestly office. Anger at this turn of events was greatly increased by the fact that, following the letter which Ermolao had sent the Senate on the death of Barbo, the senators had earlier made a pre-election of the citizen whose name would be recommended to Innocent for appointment to the post, in accordance with ancestral custom and precedent. And so they complained that they had been misled and practically duped in the matter. 52

1484

53   Erat omnino Hermolai, propter eius summam in litterarum
atque optimarum artium studiis praestantiam, magnum apud ex-
teras nationes nomen, apud suos quidem certe maximum; nam ad
doctrinae singularem opinionem etiam vitae perpetuam innocen-
tiam adiunxerat. Simul is multum patris opibus et gratia, qui
summo proximum in civitate magistratum gerebat, multum clientelis, necessitudinibus propinquitatibusque pollebat. Quibus tamen in rebus omnibus satis sibi praesidii non habuit, cum pluris a
patribus una legum caritas maiestasque, quam ullorum civium
omnibus aucta nominibus dignitas atque claritas, fieret. Decemviri
enim litteras ad eum severe scriptas dederunt: mora omni excusa-
tioneque sublata, sacerdotium repudiaret; id si non faceret, patrem
magistratu remoturos et bona eius publicaturos prae se tulerunt.
At pater, perspecta civitatis voluntate, omnibus temptatis rebus,
cum iam eam flecti et leniri posse diffideret, aegritudine animi est
mortuus. Filius non multo post Romae, editis Plinianis castigatio-
nibus, immensi prope laboris opere, privatus plebeio morbo periit.
Eum vitae finem Hermolaus habuit, omnium ex sua civitate qui
ante illum nati essent Latinorum et Graecorum litteris plane doc-
tissimus.

54   Eo tempore ab Hieronymo Marcello litterae Byzantio venerunt;
erat is Venetus eo in oppido vetere consuetudine magistratus; quibus litteris Marcellus senatum certiorem faciebat sibi ab rege imperatum statim Byzantio discederet; eius rei causam fuisse, quod
rex diceret Marcellum suis de rebus et consiliis ad senatum scripsisse; velle se atque decrevisse posthac suo in oppido ei magistratui
locum non esse; foedere tamen quod cum Venetis haberet, uti antea tenebatur, sese teneri. His de causis senatus ad regem Dominicum Trivisanum legavit, qui prima ad navigandum idonea tempestate proficisceretur. Neque multo post, anno insequente vix inito,

To be sure, Ermolao had attained considerable fame for his   53
great gifts in the study of literature and the liberal arts, both with
foreign nations and above all among his own people: to his unique
reputation for learning he had joined a life of unbroken innocence.
At the same time he had great power, owing to the wealth and influence of his father (who held the next to highest magistracy)[27]
and to patronage and the ties of friendship and family. But all that
was not enough to protect him against every eventuality, since es-
teem for the law and its majesty in itself counted for more with
the senators than the repute and renown of any of its citizens,
whatever famous names they boasted. The Council of Ten sent
him a severely worded letter to say that he should without delay or
excuse decline the prelacy, failing which they threatened to remove
his father from office and confiscate his property. His father tried
everything but saw that the mind of the citizens was made up, and
believing that it could be neither altered nor mitigated, died of a
broken spirit. Not long afterwards, his son, having published his   1492
textual observations on Pliny the Elder, a work of almost infinite
labor, died of plague at Rome a private citizen.[28] And so ended the
life of Ermolao Barbaro, undoubtedly the greatest scholar of Latin
and Greek literature the city had produced to that point.

About this time a letter came from Girolamo Marcello at Con-   54
stantinople, where he had long been the Venetian magistrate, in-   1491
forming the Senate that he had been told to leave the city at once
by the sultan. The reason for this, Marcello wrote, was that according to the sultan Marcello had written to the Senate about his
activities and plans. The sultan had therefore resolved and decreed
that there should be no place for the magistrate in his city hence-
forth, while still regarding himself as bound by the treaty that he
had with the Venetians, just as he had been before. On this account the Senate sent Domenico Trevisan as ambassador to the
sultan, who was to set out when the first opportunity of sailing
arose. Shortly afterwards, with the new year scarcely begun, the

regis legatus ad senatum venit exposuitque patribus quas ob causas Baiasetes magistratum eorum Byzantio removisset; erant autem fere illae ipsae de quibus ad senatum Marcellus perscripserat; adiunxitque illud idem etiam omnibus aliarum nationum magistratibus fuisse denuntiatum quod rex Marcello imperavisset.

55   Iisdem diebus, antequam mensis Ianuarius desineret, ornandi eos cives causa qui pro patria mortem oppetiissent, senatus decrevit uti Damiani Mauri, eius classis praefecti quae prior bello Ferrariensi Padum flumen est ingressa, hostium castellis aliquot in ripa fluminis vi captis, bellicis ex laboribus mortui, duabus filiis dotis nomine quadraginta auri librae ex publica pecunia darentur; sacerdotii autem nomine, si ei vitae se dederent, senae librae.

56   Post dies paucos, cum esset nuntiatum Baiasetem regem classem et exercitum parare, senatus consultum est factum, uti sedecim triremes naves, alteraque navis oneraria magna reipublicae, quae ad ancoras erat deligata, confestim ornarentur; altera, quae aquam non tetigerat, deduceretur atque instrueretur. Sed eo tamen anno eis navibus respublica non est usa, classis exercitusque comparatione a Baiasete penitus intermissa.

57   Neque multo post, maiorum comitiorum lege, quam Lucas Pisanus consiliarius tulit, quadragintavirale iudicium tertium duobus prioribus est additum. Nam sunt in urbe magistratus duo, quos appellare in civilibus actionibus licet: unum ab iudicibus urbanis, alterum ab iis qui publice in oppida atque provincias ad ius dicendum mittuntur. Ii tamen ipsi per se magistratus nihil statuunt, nisi de minimis quibusdam rebus. Sed ante eum diem ad alterum tantummodo eorum duorum iudiciorum quadragintaviralium, quae antiquitus sunt instituta, res ab aliis iudicatas deducebant; illi

sultan's ambassador came before the Senate and explained to the senators the reasons for Bayazid's dismissal of their magistrate from Constantinople, very much the same reasons, in fact, which Marcello had expounded to the Senate. He added that the order which the sultan had given to Marcello had been likewise communicated to all the magistrates of other nations too.

At the same time, before the end of January, as a way of honoring citizens who had died for their country, the Senate resolved that the two daughters of Damiano Moro (the captain of the fleet that was the first to enter the Po in the war of Ferrara, who had died of his labors in the war after storming a number of enemy fortresses on the banks of the river) should be given 40 gold pounds from the public treasury by way of a dowry, or if they gave themselves over to the religious life, 6 pounds for their vocation. 55

A few days later it was reported that Sultan Bayazid was getting ready a fleet and an army, and a senatorial decree was consequently enacted to have sixteen galleys fitted out immediately, along with one of the two large merchant vessels of the Republic, which was tied up at anchor. The other, which had not yet touched the water, was to be launched and fitted out. But in the event the Republic did not draw upon the ships that year after Bayazid abandoned the preparations for his army and navy altogether. 56

Not long afterwards, a third court of appeal was added to the two existing ones by a law of the Great Council proposed by the councillor Luca Pisani.[29] There are two magistracies in the city to whom one may appeal in civil actions: one for appeals of cases heard by the urban judges, the other of cases heard by those who administer justice on behalf of the Republic in the towns and provinces. These magistrates, however, do not decide anything on their own, except in certain very minor matters. But up to that point the Venetians had only two courts of appeal, both long established, and they would lay before one or other of them matters 57

sententias ferebant, quibus aut probarent quae deducebantur, aut
rescinderent; eas ratas haberi oportebat. Alterum iudicium vitae
necisque habet potestatem, aliusque ad eos iudices magistratus
causas defert. Illud igitur iudicium quadragintavirum, ex duobus
apud quos ex provocationibus quae ad duos illos magistratus fiebant disceptabatur, cum actionum et causarum multitudini non
sufficeret, tertium simile ita est institutum, ut veteri illi alteri ab
urbanis iudicibus, huic recenti et novo ab exteris interpositae iudicibus appellationes proponerentur. Ea re provocantium querelis
aditus et iuris persecutio duplo facilior et explicatior est facta.

58   Aliam etiam magnopere utilem civitati legem maioribus comitiis Antonius Tronus consiliarius paucis post mensibus tulit; qua
lege ferendorum suffragiorum nimiam creandis magistratibus li-
centiam, quae ferri iam non poterat, facile sustulit. Porro ante id
tempus suffragiorum ferendorum ratio erat eiusmodi. Loculi lignei
tornatiles, pedis altitudine bini, civibus per subsellia consedenti-
bus, alter prasinus, albus alter, afferebantur. Eorum loculorum superiore parte detecta patulaque, uti manus inferri posset, media in
angustum atque artum pars contrahebatur, eo usque ut uni modo
suffragio viam interius daret, extrinsecus ad circumferendum captu
multo esset etiam habilior. Infima erat pars plurimorum suffragiorum capax, eaque detrahi atque reponi poterat. Detrahebatur autem numerandorum suffragiorum causa. In eorum loculorum
utrum quisque vellet suffragium inferebat. Id erat glandula, parvi
pomi cerasi magnitudine, ex tela facta, non quidem solide com-
pacta atque firmiter, sed consuta leviter, quod in quem cecidisset
loculum glans sentiri posse nolebant. Itaque pugno etiam clauso
manum lege in utrumque loculum demittebant, ut ea quoque re
cognosci non posset quo in loculo suffragium esset relictum. Nam
quae album in loculum glandulae cecidissent, eae candidato fave-

adjudicated by others. That court would hand down judgments either approving or rejecting what was brought before them, and those judgments had to be taken as binding. The second court has the power of life and death, and a different magistrate brings cases before those judges.[30] Since the first of the two courts before which judgment of appeals to those two magistracies was made was insufficient for the sheer number of actions and cases, a third of the same sort was instituted: appeals emanating from the urban judges were to go before the old civil court, while those from the judges of the *terraferma* were to go before the new one. By this expedient access to the courts for the complaints of appellants and prosecution of the legal process was made twice as easy and straightforward.

A few months later another law which greatly benefited the city   58
was brought before the Great Council by the councillor Antonio Tron. His law on casting votes soon put an end to abuses in the election of magistrates, which had become by now intolerable. The system of voting in place up to that time was as follows: with the citizens seated on benches, two boxes of turned wood, each a foot high, were brought in, one green, the other white. The upper part of the boxes was open and they spread out so that a hand could be put in, while in the middle they contracted to a narrow passage so that only a single ballot could get further inside, while also making it much handier to pick up and carry around. The bottom could hold a great many votes, and could be removed and replaced, as it was when the votes were counted. Each voter would cast his ballot into his preferred urn. The ballot itself was a little ball the size of a small cherry and made of cloth, not hard and solid, but loosely sewn together so as to make it impossible to hear into which urn the ball had fallen. By law the voters would put their hands into both urns with fist clenched, again to make it impossible to know in which urn the ballot had been left. The balls

67

bant; quae in prasinum essent coniectae, iis glandulis candidati re-
pellebantur.

59   Haec cum ita essent antiquitus constituta, ambitio, cui plane
locus omnibus in rebuspublicis semper fuit, eo licentiae creverat,
ut qui suorum aliquem creari magistratum volebat et ipse summis
prehensam digitis glandulam album in loculum palam proiceret, et
qui ei proximi erant idem uti facerent postularet. Illi, candidato-
rum veriti invidiam, non suo plerumque iudicio, sed ad gratiam
suffragium aperte ferebant. Ea re fiebat ut indigni saepe homines,
propterea quod plus aut opibus aut propinquitatibus aut omnino
clientelis valuissent, bene de republica meritis optimisque civibus
anteferrentur magistratusque adipiscerentur; boni reiecti ac repulsi
iacerent.

60   Eam ad perniciem atque malum cum plures latae leges nihil
profuissent, uti e civitate tolleretur, una omnino Antonii legis latio
saluti atque decori civibus fuit. Nam qui bini ad eam diem loculi
patuli atque aperti binos erant per ministros publice circumferri
soliti, eos et a superiore tectos parte, et una coniunctos inter seque
continentes fieri statuit oportere; iisque ambobus sic connexis et
conglutinatis unum tantummodo in superiori parte laterorsum os
dedit eique ori tubum prominentem circumduxit semipalmae spatio, ad interiores loculorum aditus obtegendos; quem per tubum
recta utrumque ad loculum manus inferri apte posset. Rursus eorum loculorum prior tuboque proximus is collocabatur cuius loculi
glandulae candidatos reiciebant. Id ea causa excogitaverat Antonius, ut si quis aliter atque ipsi liberet suffragio ferendo cuipiam
favere cogeretur, is, dum manum per tubi os ad posteriorem loculum protenderet, quod is esset loculus cuius suffragia magistratum
crearent, apertis clam digitis in anteriore sineret loculo glandulam

that were cast into the white urn represented votes for the candidate, those in the green one votes against.

Although this system had been set up long before, electoral 59 fraud (to which every republic in history has obviously been exposed) had become so outrageous that someone who favored the election of one of his followers would take the ball in his fingers and openly cast it into the white urn, and demand that those around him should do the same. They in turn would fear the resentment of the candidates, and would cast their vote in full view, not usually following their own judgment but in order to curry favor. And so it came about that men who were not worthy of it were often preferred to citizens who had served the Republic well, simply because they had greater influence thanks to their wealth or family or patronage in general. They won the magistracies while good men were spurned and rejected.

Numerous laws in the past had done nothing to counter this 60 pernicious evil and eradicate it from civic life. It was only with the passing of Antonio Tron's legislation that integrity and honor were restored to the citizens. His plan was that the two urns, which it had hitherto been customary to have carried around open and uncovered by two civil servants, should be covered in their upper part and joined together side by side. He made a single opening in the urns thus connected and welded together, towards the side of the top covering, and around it he put a projecting cuff the width of half a palm, so obscuring the openings to the insides of the boxes. Through this tube a hand could be inserted and easily turned towards either of the boxes. Another feature was that the first of the two urns, the one placed next to the cuff, was the one whose balls rejected candidates. By this device Tron intended that if a man was compelled to vote for someone against his will, he could secretly open his fingers and drop the ballot in the near compartment as he extended his hand through the mouth of the tube towards the far one, the one whose votes elected a magistrate. In this

decidere. Ita cives unum simulando, alterum dissimulando, illud re quod cuique esset prius audacter efficerent, neque deprehendi aut cognosci posset quid fecissent. Ea lege post id tempus civitas maioribus in comitiis atque in senatu et decemvirum collegio creandis magistratibus semper est usa; liberumque illi iudicium ab gratia atque invidia semper fuit. Tametsi capitalibus ceterisque omnibus in iudiciis, uti, si cui non liqueret, is eo deferri posset, tertium etiam loculum adhibuerunt; eumque seiunctum a duobus atque separatum esse voluerunt.

61   Neque vero minus decemviri ante anni exitum alia ex parte surgentem malorum civium ambitum severo iudicio represserunt. Erat in quadragintaviris rerum capitalium iudicibus, qui omnes in senatu adhibentur, Gabriel Bonus, eorumque magistrum gerebat. Creantur autem semel a collegio magistri numero omnes duodecim. Eorum magistrorum tres bimestre tempus apud principem omnibus rebus praesunt habentque cum in senatu, tum vero etiam maioribus in comitiis ferendi leges potestatem. Post eos tres item alii ex eodem numero tres eodem loci tantundem temporis praeficiuntur usque eo, quoad octo menses abeunt, quod est eius collegii temporis universum spatium. Eo cum esset in magistratu Gabriel, Francisco Falerio auctore, principi et reliquis ex eius collegio patribus legem a se scriptam proposuit; qua lege civibus omnibus qui re familiari angusta uterentur, quadraginta annos natis, auri libra singulatim ex publica pecunia quotannis daretur, qua se stipe honestius liberosque suos alerent; qui intra eos annos nati essent, annum autem vigesimum quintum excederent, ii semilibram eodem nomine acciperent. Eam ipse legem ferre ad senatum maioraque comitia statuerat. Itaque ut consultis patribus ferretur (id enim fieri aliter non poterat), eis tradiderat legendam.

way the citizens could pretend to do one thing and not the other and so actually bring about what each of them wanted, nor could what they had done be detected or discovered. Thenceforth the citizenry always used this procedure in the Great Council and in appointing magistrates in the Senate and the Council of Ten, its decisions free of favor or spite. In capital cases and all other judicial proceedings, however, they brought in an additional third urn, so that if someone was undecided, he might place his vote there. They resolved to keep this urn separate and unconnected to the other two.[31]

Nevertheless, before the year was out the Council of Ten took 61 harsh measures to stem corruption in bad citizens that arose from a different quarter. Gabriel Bon was one of the *Quarantia* for capital crimes, all of whom sit with the Senate, and he was acting as their Head. The Heads number twelve altogether and are elected all at one time by the college.[32] Three of these Heads are in charge of all matters before the doge for a period of two months, and they have the power of proposing legislation not only in the Senate but in the Great Council too. After these three, another three from the same body of twelve are in charge for the same length of time, until eight months have passed and the period of office of the college expires. When Bon occupied that position, at the instance of Francesco Falier he laid before the doge and the other senators of his *Collegio*[33] a law drawn up by himself. This provided for an annual gift of a gold pound from the public purse to all citizens in straitened personal circumstances who were at least forty years of age, so that with this support they might make decent provision for themselves and their children. Those under forty but over the age of twenty-five were to receive half a pound on the same account. He had himself decided to propose that law to the Senate and the Great Council, and so that it might be carried after consultation with the *Collegio* (for it could not be done otherwise), he handed it over for their perusal.

62   Patres ubi legem inspexerunt, quae morem improbi exempli in
rempublicam induceret, ut unus temere civis tantum pecuniae publicae ceteris civibus elargiretur; idque nulla alia de causa eum et
Falerium esse aggressos animadverterent,[5] nisi uti civium gratiam
ad magistratus adipiscendos aucuparentur, principi negotium dederunt, ut utroque ad se vocato eos moneret ne quod amplius ea
de lege verbum facerent. Illi cum dies aliquot siluissent, multorum
autem civium, quorum vitae lex erat opportunissima, vocibus in-
creparentur suam ipsorum dignitatem ab eis negligi — si legem fer-
rent, sese quos vellent magistratus adepturos principesque civitatis
e vestigio futuros — ut si quid eius facere possent experirentur, curam et studium adhibuerunt. Ea re ad collegium delata, decemviri
Gabrielem Bonum et Franciscum Falerium statim comprehensos
atque in vincula coniectos in Cyprum insulam deportandos cura-
verunt, poena capitis adiecta, ab oppido Nicosiensium ullo tempore si emigravissent. Binos autem scribas fisci reipublicae, quibus
illi usi fuerant eius legis consultoribus et tamquam administris, in
Cretam insulam exulatum miserunt, eadem eis poena proposita ab
Rhythymna Cretae oppido diffugientibus. Atque hoc omnino decemviri gravioris animadversionis esse iudicium voluerunt, non
tam quidem ut de iis supplicium sumerent qui legem, tametsi per-
niciosam, neque dum tamen ad senatum tulerant poterantque per
se ab ea re desistere, quam ut reliqui etiam cives ab eiusmodi quic-
quam in posterum cogitandi consilio similis timore poenae, duorum civium exemplo, absterrerentur.

63   Eiusdem anni vere Laurentius Medices Florentinus, excellenti
vir ingenio, qui principatum in sua civitate obtinebat, vita functus
est; aestate media Innocentius. Ille tres reliquit liberos, qui omnes
brevi tempore, et principatu et civitate eiecti, exulatum abierunt.
Huius locum Alexander Borgia Valentinus, opibus et largitione

The senators gave the law their consideration, and concluded 62 that it would set a bad precedent to introduce the custom into the Republic of a single citizen lavishing public funds so prodigally on the rest of the citizen body. They observed that he and Falier had embarked on this course for the sole reason of finding favor with the citizens so as to get their hands on magistracies. The senators gave the doge the task of summoning the pair before him and warning them not to say another word about the law. They remained silent for some days, but were verbally attacked by many citizens (for whom the measure was greatly to their advantage) for neglecting their own political standing: if they carried the law, they would get whatever magistracies they wished, and would at once become the leading men in the city. And so they made efforts to see if they could put some part of the law into effect. When this was reported to the *Collegio*, the Council of Ten immediately had Bon and Falier arrested and thrown into prison, then saw to their deportation to the island of Cyprus, imposing the death penalty if they should ever leave the town of Nicosia. Two secretaries of the state treasury that they had used as consultants, almost as assistants, in the legislation, were also sent into exile on Crete, with the same penalty laid down if they fled from the Cretan town of Rethymno. No doubt the Council of Ten decided on this severe sentence not so much to punish men who had not at that point actually proposed the law, no matter how pernicious, and who might desist from their undertaking on their own, as to deter other citizens by the example of these two from thinking up any such plan in the future, for fear of a similar penalty.

In the spring of the same year, Lorenzo de' Medici, a man of 63 extraordinary talent who was the leading citizen of Florence, met 1492 his end, and Pope Innocent too died in midsummer. Lorenzo left three children, who were all soon stripped of their position and thrown out of city, going into exile. Innocent's place was taken by Alejandro Borgia of Valencia, who could rely on wealth and lar-

nixus, tenuit. Atque hoc plane tempore civitas prope quievit. Insequente autem iam in ver progresso anno, ut, firmatis inter se trium
maximarum Italiae civitatum rebus, tempora etiam pacatiora fierent, ab Alexandro pontifice maximo et Venetis et Ioanne Galeatio
adolescente, regnum in Mediolanensibus obtinente, auctore Ludovico patruo, qui civitati eius nomine praeerat, foedus in viginti
quinque annos percussum, atque uno eodemque die ab singulis
concelebratum est; quo quisque foedere ad reliquorum sociorum
diciones defendendas hostesque propulsandos teneretur. Et quod
erat ea tempestate Romae Giemes Sultanus, Baiasetis regis frater,
homo magni inter suos nominis, qui ab eo armis regno pulsus
Rhodum confugerat, Rhodii, ne bellum in se converterent, eum ad
regem Galliae, rex ad Innocentium rogatu eius miserat, itaque is
ab Alexandro adhibitis custodibus asservabatur, cum ne fratri re-
novare bellum posset, cuius rei causa quadringentae ab eo auri
librae quotannis pontifici dependebantur Romamque mittebantur,
tum ut eo nomine Baiasetem a bello Christianis inferendo abster-
reret, est in foedere additum ut, si Veneti armis a Baiasete lacesse-
rentur, Alexander eis Giemem traderet, cuius auctoritate atque
gratia contra illum uti possent. Ei foederi Hercules Atestinus, dux
princepsque Ferrariensium, Ludovico suadente paucis post diebus
se adiunxit.

64   His confectis rebus, cum prope omnia spectare ad quietem vi-
derentur, Leonora, Ferdinandi regis Neapolitani filia, Herculis
Atestini uxor, cum duabus filiis, altera Ludovici, altera Francisci
Gonzagae uxore, atque Alfonso cum filio, et eius uxore Anna,
Ioannis Galeatii sorore, conscensis ad Padi ripam navibus, secundo

gesse. At this time the city was more or less completely at peace.
But as the following year moved into spring, Pope Alexander, the   *1493*
Venetians and Giangaleazzo Sforza of Milan concluded a 25-year
peace to put the affairs of the three greatest states of Italy on a
firmer footing and bring about even more peaceful times. Sforza
was a young man who held the duchy of Milan thanks to the
backing of his uncle Ludovico [il Moro], who ruled the state in his
name. The parties to the peace all celebrated it severally on one
and the same day. Under the terms of the treaty each of the signatories was obliged to defend the territory of the other allies and
drive off their enemies. The Sultan Djem was at Rome at the
time, the brother of Sultan Bayazid and a man of high standing
among his own people, who had fled to Rhodes when he was
driven by force of arms from the Ottoman realm by Bayazid.
Fearing that they might get involved in their war, the people of
Rhodes had sent him to the king of France, and the king had sent
him to Innocent at the pope's request. Djem was in consequence
now being kept under guard by Alexander, not only so that he
could not renew war with his brother (for which service Bayazid
sent to Rome 400 gold pounds every year for payment to the
pontiff), but also to deter Bayazid from making war on the Chris-
tians on that account. In view of all this, an addition was made to
the treaty to the effect that if the Venetians were attacked by
Bayazid, Alexander would surrender Djem to them, and they
could use his prestige and influence against Bayazid. A few days
later Ercole d'Este, Duke and lord of Ferrara, joined the parties to
the treaty at the urging of Ludovico il Moro.

When these matters were settled and almost everything seemed   64
set fair for peace, a party consisting of Eleonora, the daughter of
King Ferrante of Naples and wife of Ercole d'Este, her two daugh-
ters, one the wife of Ludovico il Moro, the other of Francesco
Gonzaga, and Alfonso d'Este with his wife Anna (the sister of
Giangaleazzo Sforza) and his son, boarded ships on the Po and

flumine in aestuaria Venetiasque se contulit, ut urbem laeto illo tempore inviserent. Quibus quidem feminis uti quam amplissimi honores haberentur, senatus decrevit. Itaque et obviam eis publice itum in Bucentauro navi, qua in navi a magna senatus parte atque a matronis centum triginta, tota paene civitate circumfusa atque adnavigante, sunt exceptae; et per eos dies quos in urbe confecerunt nullum eis genus publicae voluptatis aut liberalitatis defuit. Nam et choreae electissimarum feminarum a principum liberis in comitio celebratae sunt; et bellaria magni et operosi sumptus data; et ludi tota urbe certaminaque multifariam edita. Quibus ex omnibus unum novum civitati fuit, ut complures cumbae, quibus in singulis quattuor feminae remigarent, cursu propositis praemiis contenderent. Quo in certamine prope mira res accidit, quae a civitate animadversa diei spectaculique laetitiam et hilaritatem conduplicavit, ut, quem ad modum Leonora duabus cum filiis et nuru aderat, quarum causa ea fiebant, ita cumba, qua in cumba mater cum duabus filiis ac nuru remos impellebat, vicerit.

made their way downstream into the lagoon of Venice to visit the city at that happy time. The Senate resolved to pay these women the most extraordinary compliments: not only did they go out to give them a public welcome in the Bucintoro, where they were received by a substantial number of the Senators and 130 ladies, amid the accompanying boats of practically the whole city; but in the course of the days they spent in the city, they also wanted for nothing in the way of entertainment or munificence that the state could lay on. Dances by the élite of the female aristocracy were attended by the children of the leading citizens[34] in the Hall of the Great Council, elaborate refreshments were provided at great expense, and games and contests of every sort were put on throughout the city. Of all these diversions, one was quite new to the city: a number of boats, each rowed by four women, taking part in a race for which prizes were offered. In this contest a marvellous thing occurred, which when the citizenry observed it redoubled the happiness and fun of the day, and of the spectacle itself: just as Eleonora was present with her two daughters and daughter-in-law — it was because of them that these events were taking place at all — so the race was won by the boat in which a mother was plying the oars with *her* two daughters and daughter-in-law.

LIBER SECUNDUS

1   Vix eae mulieres domum redierant, cum ab Carolo rege Galliae, eius nominis octavo, certus homo ad senatum venit; cuius oratio eiusmodi fuit: quoniam Carolus in Italiam cum exercitu sit venturus ad regnum Neapolitanum, quod ad se iure hereditario spectaret, in suam potestatem redigendum, scire eum cupere, quo in se animo civitas esset futura; velletne, qua in amicitia et necessitudine adhuc quidem egregia et constanti secum fuisset, in ea etiam in posterum manere. Civitas, nova intellecta re, quaeque magnam rebus Italis commutationem esse allatura videretur, consulto senatu, ne regis in se invidiam prima omnium excitaret, praesertim cum fieri posset, uti is vel per sese, ut sunt plerumque hominum mobiles ad omnem ferme impetum animi, ab incepto desisteret, vel difficultate atque magnitudine belli gerendi, adolescens neque rei militaris gnarus, absterreretur, vel aliqua interposita mora atque a ceteris regibus impedimento, explicare se non posset, respondit se quidem omni tempore pacem bello praetulisse, optareque ut et ipse quiesceret et reges principesque Italos quiescere permitteret; sed si veniat, ea de causa nihil moturam, neque ab eius amicitia recessuram. Pero (id enim erat ei nomen), accepta civitatis voluntate, Romam abiit. Eumque alii postea regis interpretes duo paucorum mensium spatio cum eisdem fere mandatis separatim sunt subsecuti; quibus interpretibus idem est responsum datum quod Pero ante acceperat.

2   Sed omnino ad eam belli ab rege capessendi causam quae ab illis praedicabatur, quod ei regnum Neapolitanum hereditatis nomine deberetur, etiam aliae causae accedebant; ex quibus una haec

78

BOOK II

These ladies had scarcely returned home when a certain man came
to the Senate from King Charles VIII of France. The burden of
his message was that since Charles was about to come into Italy
with an army to take control of the Kingdom of Naples (which
belonged to him by hereditary right), he wanted to know what the
attitude of the Venetians would be toward him. Did they wish in
future to remain on the extremely amicable and close terms they
had had with him in the past? When they had grasped the novelty
of the situation, which seemed likely to bring about great changes
in the affairs of Italy, after debate in the Senate the city responded
that though she had always preferred peace to war, and hoped that
Charles would himself take no action and suffer the kings and rulers of Italy to do the same, yet if he should come, Venice would
make no move on that account, nor would she withdraw from her
alliance with him. This was so that Venice would not be the very
first to arouse the king's ill-feeling, especially since it was possible
that Charles would abandon the undertaking of his own accord, as
the generality of men change their minds almost at whim[1]; or,
young and ignorant of the military arts as he was, he might be put
off by the difficulty and scale of the war to be waged; or again, if
some delay arose or other rulers put difficulties in his path, he
might be unable to extricate himself. Perron [de Basche] (for that
was the envoy's name) heard the city's decision and left for Rome.
Two further emissaries of the king followed on his heels in the
space of a few months with much the same instructions, and received the same response as Perron had been given earlier.

In addition to the reason they gave in public for the king's willingness to go to war, that the Kingdom of Naples was owed to
him by hereditary right, there were doubtless other causes as well.

1

1493

2

79

fuit. Galeatio Sfortia, qui Mediolani regnum obtinebat, complures
ante annos per insidias interfecto, Ludovicus frater, uxore Galeatii
e regni procuratione, quam illa, ut Ioanni Galeatio, filio suo admo-
dum parvulo, in fide atque officio civitatem contineret, post viri
mortem susceperat, reliquisque administris paulatim deiectis, ipse
se ei rei praeposuerat annosque tredecim praefuerat. Fratris autem
filium, cui se regnum procurare prae se ferebat, ita porro aluerat
iisque moribus instituerat, ut omnem curam videretur adhibuisse,
ne puer ullam ad frugem perveniret. Non rei militaris, non litterarum studia, non denique artem ullam et disciplinam regiam edo-
ceri illum voluerat, adhibitis etiam ad puerile ingenium depravan-
dum corruptoribus, quorum ille convictu in omnem luxum atque
inertiam assuefieret.

3   Ei nondum plane puberi Alfonsus, Ferdinandi regis filius, Isa-
bellam filiam in matrimonium collocaverat, ex eaque is etiam liberos procreaverat. Ad regni tamen sui gubernaculum a patruo nullam in partem admittebatur. Id cum graviter ferret non Alfonsus
modo socer, assiduis prope filiae litteris lacrimisque permotus, sed
multo etiam magis avus Isabellae Ferdinandus, primo petere a Ludovico coeperunt, vellet pro sua fide atque iustitia fratris sui filio
non adulto modo atque firmo, sed etiam plane iam viro atque adeo
duorum filiorum patri, aliquando tandem regnum tradere suique
illum imperii, suarum rerum compotem facere. Ea postulatio cum
saepius interposita nihil profuisset, gravioribus apud illum expos-
tulationibus et querelis non semel egerunt; postremo eo rem de-
duxerunt, ut dicerent sese illum bello persecuturos, ni Ioanni Galeatio, quicum affinitatem, uti cum rege, contraxissent, regiam

One of them was the following: Galeazzo Sforza, the former duke of Milan, had been killed in a plot some years earlier, and his brother Ludovico il Moro had gradually removed Galeazzo's wife and his other ministers from the governance of the duchy, something she had taken on after her husband's death so that she might hold the state in trust for her son Giangaleazzo, still at that time very young. Ludovico had assumed control of the state himself and had been in power for 13 years. He professed to be acting as regent for his brother's son, but he had at the same time raised him and moulded his character in such a way that he appeared to have made every effort to see that the boy would never come to anything. He had declined to have him taught the arts of war and literature, or any skill or discipline befitting a ruler. He even employed people to corrupt and deprave his childish nature, so that in their company Giangaleazzo might become habituated to every sort of indulgence and idleness.

Alfonso, the son of King Ferrante of Naples, had given his 3 daughter Isabella in marriage to this boy before he even reached puberty, and he had actually had children by her. Notwithstanding, his uncle still utterly refused to admit him to the government of his own realm. This caused great offense not only to his father-in-law Alfonso, filled with dismay as he was at his daughter's almost constant tearful letters, but even more so to Isabella's grandfather Ferrante. And so they began to ask Ludovico for an undertaking to show his integrity and fairness by at length handing over the duchy to his brother's son and making him master of his own realm and his own affairs, for Giangaleazzo was by now not just grown up and in robust health, but really quite a man, to the extent of having two children. Further repeated requests being made to no effect, they more than once put sterner protests and remonstrations to Ludovico, and finally got to the point of threatening him with war if he did not restore ducal power to Giangaleazzo, since they had contracted the marriage with him on the under-

potestatem remitteret. Horum ille regum minas atque potentiam veritus, ne tam amplae civitatis principatum atque imperium ulli tradere cogeretur, quod suum unius efficere in animo magnopere habebat filiisque suis relinquere, cum intelligeret Galliae regibus in regnum Neapolitanum ius esse, celatis ea de re Alexandro Venetisque, quibuscum paulo ante foedus percusserat, ad speciem salutandi regis legationem maxime celebrem ad Carolum misit, hortatum ut id bellum susciperet; suasque illi opes copiasque pollicetur: facillimum factu esse, modo Alpes traiceret atque in Italiam se ostenderet, eo regno potiri. Ea tanti hominis hortatio apud Carolum momenti plurimum habuit.

4   Altera fuit eius rei causa in Antonio, qui Salernum a maioribus suis traditum obtinuerat. Is cum ob Ferdinandi regis inimicum in sese animum sedibus patriis excessisset seque in Galliam ad Carolum contulisset, prope cottidianis eum sermonibus admonebat, ut tam propriam regni opulentissimi capiendi oblatam sibi a diis immortalibus facultatem ne praetermitteret. Ferdinandum hominem esse avarum, crudelem, nulla fide, nulla iustitia; omnes eius regni principes, omnes populos illum odisse; nullius esse negotii rem eum regno expellere, praesertim Galliae regibus, quorum nomen atque auctoritas illis in regionibus maxime omnium tum vigeret fueritque semper plurimi. Alexander etiam pontifex maximus, moleste ferens Virginium Ursinum, eius familiae principem, ausum esse a Francisco Cibo, Innocentii pontificis ante se maximi filio, oppidum Anguillariam in Sabatini lacus ripa, quod erat in pontificum maximorum dicione abestque ab Urbe sedecim milia passuum, nulla facta sibi ab ipso eius rei potestate, coemisse, quoniam Virginius a Ferdinando fovebatur, ne quid facere invitus cogeretur, Carolum et ipse ad id suscipiendum bellum hortabatur, vindicandi

standing that he was the duke. Ludovico grew afraid at the threats of these powerful monarchs, in case he was forced to hand over to someone else the leadership and control of so rich a state as Milan, which he had very much in mind to keep for himself alone and to leave to his sons. He learned that the kings of France had a claim on the Kingdom of Naples, and so keeping Pope Alexander and the Venetians in the dark (though he had a little earlier struck a treaty with them), he sent a very grand embassy to Charles, ostensibly to greet the king but really to urge him to undertake the war, promising him his resources and troops. It would be very easy, he said, once Charles had crossed the Alps and shown himself in Italy, to take control of the Kingdom. The encouragement of such an important personage carried a great deal of weight with Charles.

Another cause of the war lay in Antonello da Sanseverino, who 4 had inherited from his ancestors the lordship of Salerno. He had left his ancestral seat in view of King Ferrante's hostility towards him and had made his way to Charles in France. There in almost daily conversations he advised him not to pass up the real chance that heaven had offered him of taking over such a wealthy kingdom. Ferrante, he said, was a greedy man, cruel, untrustworthy and unjust. All the princes and all the people of the Kingdom hated him. It would be no trouble to drive him from the Kingdom, especially for the kings of France, whose renown and authority in those parts had always been very great, never more so than now. Pope Alexander was further aggrieved that Virginio Orsini, the head of the family, had ventured to purchase from Francesco Cibo (the son of his predecessor Innocent VIII) the town of Anguillara Sabazia on the shores of Lake Bracciano, which is under papal jurisdiction and 16 miles from Rome, without Alexander's granting him permission to do so. Since Orsini was being encouraged by Ferrante not to do anything against his will, the pontiff too urged Charles to embark on war, so that he might take

sese de adverso suis rebus suaeque dignitati rege causa. Quas ad
res omnes etiam illud adiungebatur, quod ex Gallis principibus iis
qui apud Carolum auctoritate gratiaque pollebant, nonnulli rerum
Italicarum Romanique pontificis, qua erat iter faciendum, occasione amplissimis sacerdotii dignitatibus sese iri auctum et hones-
tatum confidebant; alios exercituum et regendorum populorum
quos essent subiecturi spes et cupiditas incendebat. Multi etiam
sua levitate et novarum rerum studiis movebantur, ut regem ad
profectionem impellerent.

5   Interim autumni mensibus tota fere citeriore Gallia eiusmodi
tempestates tamque continentes pluviae fuerunt, ut in Bergomatium finibus aqua denos quinos pedes praeter consuetudinem ex-
creverit, aedificiisque quamplurimis dirutis ac pontibus lapideis
abreptis, magnum puerorum et mulierum, magnum etiam viro-
rum numerum repentino impetu oppresserit. Neque in Brixianorum finibus flumina non ingentem stragem ediderunt. Athesis quidem cum Veronae urbis magnam partem pervasisset et complures
domorum parietes subruisset, etiam pontem firmissimum medio
in oppido deiecit. Medoacus, et ipse ripas non uno loco transgres-
sus, optimam Patavini agri partem illuvie vastitateque foedavit. Pa-
dus omnino utriusque ripae vicinitates ita est depopulatus, ut omnia luctu et maeroribus impleverit. Atque hanc quidem esse quasi
deorum immortalium significationem quae Gallorum in Italiam
adventum portenderet, omnes paene homines interpretabantur et
prodigii loco ducebant; erantque permulti, qui maxime ad Venetos, quod eorum regionibus et oppidis aquae magnum detrimentum intulissent, eam rem atque id prodigium existimabant perti-
nere.

6   Ordo rerum me admonet ut duo civitatis iudicia, hoc ipso facta
tempore, silentio ne obruam. Erat in civium nobilitate Ioannes
Georgius, homo ferox nullaque pietate, qui ab Antonio Bernardo

vengeance on a king hostile to his interests and prestige. Added to all these reasons was the fact that some of the French princes who carried most weight and influence with Charles were confident that they could profit from their involvement with Italian and papal affairs (where their journey would take them) to get preferment and honors in the highest positions of the church. Others were spurred on by the hope and longing to lord it over the armies and peoples they meant to conquer. Many again were motivated by mere frivolousness and passion for novelty to urge the expedition on the king.

Meanwhile, in the autumn months almost the whole of Lombardy suffered such storms and such continuous rain that in the area around Bergamo the waters rose 15 feet above normal. A great many buildings were destroyed and stone bridges carried off, drowning women and children in great numbers in its sudden flood, and even a good many men. Nor was the territory of Brescia spared massive destruction from the rivers. The Adige penetrated a large part of the city of Verona and demolished the walls of many homes, even destroying the strong bridge in the center of town. The Brenta too overflowed its banks in more than one place, and fouled the best part of the Paduan countryside with mud and waste. The Po as a whole wrought such destruction on the areas around both its banks that the entire land was filled with grief and sorrow. Nearly everyone interpreted this as some sort of sign from heaven portending the arrival of the French in Italy, taking it for an omen. There were a great many who felt that the event and the omen were specially aimed at the Venetians, because it was their towns and lands that bore the brunt of the flood damage. 5

The sequence of events reminds me not to pass over in silence two court cases held in Venice at just this time. Among the city nobility was a violent and impious man, Giovanni Zorzi. Antonio Bernardo, the governor of Treviso, had exiled him from that town 6

Taurisanorum praetore, ob maledicta in deos aliaque scelera, exul
eius oppidi factus fuerat damnatusque ut, si eo rediret, lingua ei
amputaretur manusque altera praecideretur. Is Taurisum alio praetore cum revertisset virginemque vi adhibita violavisset, decemviri,
missis illo suis rerum capitalium ministris atque vindicibus, Georgium comprehendi deque eo Antonianum supplicium medio in
foro sumi iusserunt; eo sumpto Venetias adductum in Cretam deportari mandaverunt. Neque multo post Antonius Bolduus,
triumvir ex advocatis reipublicae, Dominicum Bolanum, Candiani
filium, collegam suum, accusatum acceptae eo in magistratu ab
reis et litigatoribus pecuniae, ad senatum detulit. Cum senatus
eum comprehendi atque ex vinculis causam dicere iussisset, ille autem fuga se iudicio eripuisset; absens damnatus est ut intra mensem se carceri dederet Caniam, Cretae oppidum, exulatum depor-
tandum; quod si non faceret, comprehenso cervices abscinderentur
bonaque publicarentur, magnis propositis praemiis iis qui eum aut
vivum magistratibus tradidissent aut ipsi occidissent.

7   Post haec de adventu Gallorum fama percrebrescente, ac Ferdinando rege exercitum et classem ad hostes repellendos comparante
atque omnibus Alexandrum pontificem maximum pollicitationibus, ut suarum partium esset, sollicitante, Ludovicus, veritus ne, si
inter eos convenisset, Ferdinandus, praemissis in Galliam suis et
Alexandri celeriter copiis, e regni eum procuratione atque fastigio
ante Caroli adventum expelleret ereptamque filii sui genero dignitatem atque imperium restitueret, a senatu petiit ut quos haberet
milites equitesque ad Ollii fluminis ripam, quod est in Brixianorum finibus, iuberet proficisci, uti regem ab eo ineundo consilio
abduceret aut, si id non posset, ipsi flumen transirent seseque tuerentur. Ea re a senatu non impetrata, quod diceret sibi id necesse
eius tam firmis rebus non videri, iterum ad Carolum legatos misit

for blasphemy and other crimes, and had condemned him to have his tongue cut out and a hand cut off if he should return. When he did return to Treviso under another governor and violently raped a girl, the Ten despatched there the court officials for capital offences, and those charged with carrying out punishments for them, having given orders that Zorzi should be arrested and Bernardo's sentence carried out on him in the middle of the town square. This done, they ordered him to be taken to Venice and deported to Crete. Not long afterward Antonio Boldù, one of the three state attorneys,[2] denounced his colleague Domenico di Candiano Bollani to the Senate, accusing him of taking money while in office from defendants and litigants. The Senate ordered that he should be arrested and plead his case from prison, but he escaped the trial by taking to flight. In his absence he was sentenced to deliver himself to prison within a month, and then to be exiled to Canea,[3] a town on Crete. Failing which, he would be arrested and decapitated and his goods confiscated, with large rewards offered to those who handed him over to the officials alive, or killed him themselves.

Rumors of the advent of the French subsequently grew apace 7 and King Ferrante got ready his army and fleet to repel the enemy, offering the pope all manner of promises to induce him to take his side. Ludovico il Moro feared that if they came to an agreement, Ferrante would quickly send his troops and Alexander's into Lombardy and drive him from his position as regent of the duchy before Charles could arrive, and so restore Giangaleazzo (the son-in-law of Ferrante's own son)[4] to the position of power that he had usurped. He accordingly asked the Senate to have all the infantry and cavalry at their disposal sent to the banks of the river Oglio in the territory of Brescia to deter Ferrante from any such plan, or, failing that, to cross the river themselves to defend him. The Senate turned down this request, on the grounds that it was in their view unnecessary when his position was quite secure, so Ludovico

rogatum, ut maturaret Alpes transmittere; sese ei de pecunia com-
modaturum suasque copias cum illo coniuncturum, ubi primum
terram Italiae attigisset.

8   Carolus, qui plures iam menses in ea modo praedicatione
consumpsisset, velle se Neapolim armis suam facere, atque iis qui
apud illum plurimum poterant partim bellum suadentibus, partim
dissuadentibus, nihil etiam nunc constituisset quod pro firmo
atque certo haberetur, acceptis Ludovici tum hortationibus dili-
gentioribus, tum pollicitis, foedus cum Ferdinando et Elisabeta,
Hispaniae regibus, percussit, non nullis eis oppidis in Pyrenaeo
saltu gratis restitutis; quae pridem oppida Aloisius rex, eius pater,
a Ferdinandi patre pignoris nomine acceperat. Deinde ad diem no-
num Kalendarum Ianuarii, adhibitis totius Galliae principibus,
statuit, omnibus aliis omissis rebus, proficisci. De eo cum esset
amicorum litteris celeriter Ferdinandus certior factus, primis anni
diebus e venatu lectulum petens, acri urgente pituita, intra bi-
duum est mortuus; cuius Alfonsum maiorem natu filium Federicus natu minor reliquique Neapolitani principes regem salutave-
runt.

9   Alfonsus, regno patris inito, per legatum Venetum, qui paulo
ante ad Ferdinandum venerat insolitisque ab eo et obviam itioni-
bus et aliis honorum generibus exceptus fuerat, a senatu petiit ut
cum Ludovico ageret, ne is Carolum ad profectionem incitaret
praedemque se apud illum constitueret; nihil ipsum ullo tempore
moturum, quominus is regni Mediolanensis procuratione, quoad
vellet, uteretur. Senatus ea de re cum apud Ludovicum Alfonsi
verbis egisset eumque esset magnopere hortatus, ne Gallis in Italiam veniendi auctor adiutorque esset, ille autem nihil eiusmodi
respondisset, quo se ab eo consilio remoturus videretur, ne frustra
operam insumeret, destitit neque amplius eam cogitationem est
aggressus.

again sent ambassadors to Charles to ask him to hurry across the Alps. He would make him loans of money and unite his troops with those of Charles as soon as he reached Italian soil.

Charles had already spent several months simply proclaiming 8 his intention to bring Naples under his sway by force of arms. He had even now come to no firm and definite decision, his most influential advisors being partly for the war and partly against. But in the light of Ludovico's attentive encouragement, and his promises too, he struck a treaty with the Spanish sovereigns Ferdinand and Isabella and returned to them without recompense a number of towns in a stretch of the Pyrenees that his father, King Louis, had earlier had from Ferdinand's father as security for a loan. Then on 24 December, in the presence of all the chief nobles of France, he announced his decision to put everything else to one side and set out for Italy. Letters of friends soon made Ferrante aware of this, but after returning from a hunt at the beginning of the new year, he took to his bed with a severe chest infection and *1494* died within two days. His elder son Alfonso was acclaimed king by the younger son Federico and the other Neapolitan princes.

Taking on his father's realm, Alfonso asked the Senate through 9 the Venetian ambassador to negotiate with Ludovico (the ambassador had come to Ferrante shortly before and had been welcomed by him with rare personal audiences and other honors) to stop him encouraging Charles to undertake the expedition and setting himself up as his guarantor. For his part, he would never take any action to prevent Ludovico enjoying the regency of Milan for as long as he liked. The Senate put the matter to Ludovico in Alfonso's terms, and strongly urged him against provoking the French to come to Italy, or helping them to do so. In his reply, however, Ludovico gave no indication that he would back down from his plan, and to avoid wasting their labor, the Senate gave up and pursued their designs no further.

10   Miserat ante eos dies ad senatum Carolus Philippum Argentonium legatum: si se respublica in belli Neapolitani societatem cum ipso coniungeret, quam vellet eius regni partem sibi deposceret, nihil illum recusaturum; id si non vellet, quod pollicita esset se ab eius amicitia non discessuram, in eo perseveraret; iussum se esse apud patres moram trahere omniaque regis consilia cum ipsis communicare. Ad haec civitas ita respondit: tantas esse Caroli regis ad id gerendum bellum facultates, tam praesentem omnium rerum copiam, ut sui auxilii nihil indigeat; itaque se more exemploque maiorum, qui bella nisi lacessiti non fecissent, quieturam; nec partem sibi eius regni postulaturam cuius nullum ipsa ius habeat; ceterum, quod aliis regis nuntiis dixisset pollicitaque esset, ab eo non recedere; regisque benivolentiam sese plurimi semper facturam; ipsum quidem eo nomine et nunc libenter vidisse et, si maneat, eo libentius visuram, quo erit etiam urbana mora et cottidianis collocutionibus familiarior; quaeque regis intererunt, pro sua vetere in patrem eius atque ipsum necessitudine, ea in dies, ut ipsi nota sint, curaturam.

11   Iisdem prope diebus senatus Bartholomaeo Collioni Bergomati, imperatori suo, quod multa bella singulari virtute, fide incomparabili gessisset, remque militarem, superiorum imperatorum negligentia collapsam, restituisset, quodque, de republica optime meritus, auri libras decies centies ei moriens testamento legavisset, statuam equestrem aeream inauratam in Ioannis et Pauli area ponendam censuit. Ea tempestate vita functus est apud Naxios Ioannes Crispus, qui eam ex Cycladibus insulam tresque alias obtinebat, Rhenem Scyrum Melum, duobus liberis parvulis ex paelice

Prior to this, Charles had sent Philippe de Commines as am-   10
bassador to the Senate: if the Republic allied herself with him in
the Neapolitan war, she could claim any part of the Kingdom she
wished and he would refuse her nothing. If Venice was unwilling
to do so, she should stand by her promise not to withdraw from
her friendship with him. The ambassador said that his instructions were to extend his stay with the Signoria and to share with
them all the king's plans. To this the city replied that Charles' resources for waging the war were so great, he had such a ready supply of everything needful, that he had no need of their assistance.
In consequence they would follow the custom and example of
their ancestors, who had not made war unless attacked, and remain neutral. Nor would they ask for a part of the Kingdom, on
which they had no claim. But they would not renege on the state-
ments and promises they had made to other emissaries of the
king, and would always place the highest value on his friendship.
They said they had been glad to see Commines on that account
and, if he remained, would see him all the more gladly as he became closer to them through his stay in the city and his daily in-
tercourse with them. As for matters that concerned the king, they
would make every effort to keep Commines informed of them on
a day-to-day basis, in view of the long-standing bond they had
with his father and with the king himself.

At much the same time, the Senate decreed that a gilt bronze   11
equestrian statue should be erected in the square of SS. Giovanni   1494
and Paolo to their general Bartolomeo Colleoni of Bergamo.
Colleoni had fought many wars with remarkable bravery and in-
comparable loyalty, he had revived the art of war after it had been
brought low by the slovenliness of his predecessors, and after this
distinguished service to the Republic, he had left her at death
1,000 gold pounds in his will. At that time Giovanni Crispo died
among the people of Naxos, the island he ruled along with three
others in the Cyclades, Rinia, Scyros and Melos, leaving behind

relictis. Is propterea quod avare atque crudeliter regnaverat, civitas
concilio coacto statuit reges ulterius non perpeti. Erat tum forte
fortuna in insulae oppidique portu Nicolaus Capellus legatus, eo
cum sex longis navibus ad piratas insequendos profectus. Itaque
nacti occasionem cives plebsque omnis, ipsis cum natu maioribus
matribusque familias infantes in ulnis gestantibus, cumque virginibus et pueris, legatum adierunt, orantesque uti se reciperet — mori
enim malle omnes, quam amplius sub tyrannis esse — miro se studio reipublicae dediderunt. Nicolaus, principibus eorum liberaliter
appellatis, reliquam turbam solatus, civitatem in reipublicae fidem
recepit; civemque Venetum, qui praeesset iusque diceret, attribuit.
Naxii paucis post diebus legationem ad senatum miserunt, quae
apud patres sacramentum diceret, se in eius fide perpetuo futuros.
Ea legatione adhibita, senatus consultum factum est, uti Naxii,
qui sponte in deditionem venerant, reciperentur; recepti autem
non essent, nisi prius Crispi liberis et eorum matri alimenta prae-
berentur. Itaque omnis insularum earum proventus illis, quoad viverent, dono datus est eo nomine.

12   Interea cum inter Alexandrum, quem quidem multis de causis
magnopere paenituerat Carolum regem ad id bellum incitavisse,
atque inter [sic] Alfonsum, qui ambo ad Vari vicum venerant, ut
ipsi inter se colloquerentur, iis condicionibus esset foedus amici-
tiaque inita, ut pontifex regem in Romanae reipublicae fidem reciperet omnique illum ab hoste, qua posset, tueretur; ille autem
pontifici ob tributi veteris reliqua auri libras mille se repraesenta-
turum, in annos vero singulos quadringentas persoluturum polliceretur; desponsa etiam filia Giufredo Alexandri filio, ut societas

two small children by his concubine. His rule had been avaricious and cruel, and the citizenry consequently held a meeting in which they resolved that they would no longer tolerate a lord over them. By a lucky chance the proveditor Niccolò Capello happened to be in the port of the island, the main town, having gone there with six galleys in pursuit of pirates. And so the citizens and the populace as a whole — including the old folk, matrons bearing infants in their arms, girls and boys — seized their opportunity and accosted the proveditor, begging him to take them under his protection: they would all rather die, they said, than live any longer under tyranny, and with this remarkable display of devotion they surrendered themselves to the Republic of Venice. Obligingly summoning the leading men, and giving words of comfort to the rest of the crowd, Niccolò took the city under the protection of the Republic, and assigned a Venetian citizen to govern it and administer justice. A few days later, the Naxians sent an embassy to the Senate to swear an oath before the senators that they would remain loyal to the Republic in perpetuity. Having heard the ambassadors, the Senate passed a decree that the Naxians, who had come to surrender of their own accord, should be taken under their protection; not, however, unless they first provided support for Crispo's children and their mother. And so on that account all the profit made from the islands was given them for as long as they lived.

Meanwhile Alexander had for a number of reasons come to 12 greatly regret that he had encouraged Charles to go to war. He and Alfonso went to Vicovaro to discuss matters between themselves, and entered into an alliance on the following terms: the pope would extend the protection of Rome[5] to the king, and would defend him against any enemy as far as he was able. For his part, in view of the sums of tribute money outstanding from the past, Alfonso undertook to make the pontiff an immediate cash payment of 1,000 gold pounds, and to pay 400 pounds each year in future. Alfonso's daughter was also promised in marriage to Al-

eo pignore firmaretur, utrique se ad bellum communire modis omnibus explicareque coeperunt. Fuerat ea in re Alexander, ut sunt
hominum mutabilia saepe ingenia et voluntates, Virginio ipso usus
interprete, qui etiam illum et Alfonsum lautissime splendidissi-
meque sua in domo tunc suscepit. Erat enim Virginii oppidum
Vari, de quo diximus, vicus. Iamque Alfonsus, classe longarum navium amplius triginta, onerariarum maximarum duodeviginti, ad
Ligustici maris oram infestandam navesque hostium quae Genuae
instruebantur impediendas comparata, equitatu peditatuque co-
gendo eque Brutiis educendo atque in Galliam mittendo distinebatur, cum ob Baiasetis regis novos motus, qui et classem et exercitum comparabat, respublica et ipsa parare classem instituit.
Itaque primis comitiis, Antonio Grimano classis praefecto decla-
rato, naves longas quas confectas habebat deduci atque instrui iubet; quibuscum navibus Antonius mense Quintili solvens in Illyricum traiecit.

13   Eo tempore Florentinorum legatio ad senatum venit, petens,
propterea quod Carolus rex a civitate postulaverat ut per eorum
fines exercitum ducere sibi liceret, uti senatus consuleret quid ipsis
esset ad regis postulata respondendum; tum hac tota in causa
atque adventu regio quid cavere, quid praestare ipsos opus esset,
pro sua fide atque consilio existimaret; magnopere enim se eius
prudentiae tribuere confidereque optimum factu id futurum quod
senatus censuisset. Senatus unum modo existimans fore ut quidquid Florentinis consuluisset neque Carolum neque Alfonsum la-
teret, legatis respondit nescire omnino se, tam ardua in re tamque
casibus et eventui proposita, quid praestaret; quod si se plures in
unam sententiam coniecturae quam in alia omnia traherent, non
tamen id audere ipsis dicere, propterea quod fortuna plerumque in

exander's son Jofré, a token to cement their alliance. Then the pair
of them began to gird themselves for war and to take every measure to prepare for action. Men often change their minds and their
desires, and so it was with Alexander when he used Virginio
Orsini himself as his intermediary in the matter: Orsini actually
gave Alexander and Alfonso a most sumptuous and splendid welcome in his own home, Vicovaro, which I mentioned above, being
a town of his. Alfonso had already put together a fleet of more
than 30 galleys and 18 large merchant ships[6] to harass the Ligurian
coast and block the enemy ships that were being fitted out at
Genoa. He was now occupied with collecting cavalry and infantry,
marching them out of Calabria and sending them to Lombardy,
when new moves on the part of Sultan Bayazid, who was raising a
fleet and army, caused the Republic to set about putting together
its own fleet. So at the next meeting of the Great Council Antonio
Grimani was appointed captain-general of the fleet and the galleys
which were ready were ordered to be fitted out and put to sea.
Grimani set sail with these ships in July and crossed over to
Dalmatia.

A Florentine embassy came to the Senate at that time to ask its   13
advice on how to respond to Charles' demand that he should be allowed to march his army through their territory. And on the
whole question of the king and his descent into Italy, they sought
its confidential and considered opinion on what they should do
and what avoid doing, for they greatly respected the Senate's wis-
dom and were sure that the best course of action would be what
they recommended. The Senate saw only one outcome, that whatever it recommended to the Florentines would come to the attention of Charles and Alfonso. It responded to the ambassadors that
it was quite at a loss to know what was best in such a thorny situation, where so much was at the mercy of chance and events. Even
if a number of considerations were to lead them to one single view
above any other, they would still not dare tell them what it was,

bellis dominatur, temereque facta saepe melius quam ratione atque consilio suscepta ceciderunt; itaque auxilium a diis immortalibus implorandum; eos unos scire quid quaque in re quemque aut sequi aut fugere oporteat.

14   Antonius Venetiis profectus cum esset in Illyrico, legati ad eum ab Scardona atque ab Clissa venerunt, qui dicerent cupere sua municipia sub reipublicae imperio esse; orare, ut ab eo reciperentur. Antonius, legatos cohortatus ut reipublicae voluntatem exspectarent, litteras ea de re ad senatum dedit Corcyramque contendit. At Alfonsi classis, cui Federicum fratrem praeposuerat, mare Ligusticum invecta, Obiecto Flisco Genuensi, non minimae inter suos auctoritatis, militibusque ad Veneris Portum expositis atque ab hostibus repulsis, infecta re Triturritam rediit. Confecerat autem per eos dies Genuae Carolus itemque Ludovicus classem satis idoneam ad hostem repellendum. Itaque et adverso proelio suorum et classis hostium timore perterritus Federicus, neque amplius temptandam iis in locis fortunam belli ratus, sese recepit.

15   Ea spe lapsus, Alfonsus suas cum Alexandri copiis coniunctas copias in Flaminiam propere misit, quod intelligebat Caroli exercitus praemissam iam partem Padum flumen traiecisse. Eae cum Ariminensium finibus copiae appropinquarent, Pandulfi eorum principis rogatu, qui erat in reipublicae militia, suisque rebus veritus tam suspecto atque ambiguo tempore, opem a senatu postularaverat, Georgius Emus est eo missus, qui auctoritate reipublicae oppidum finesque tueretur. Per quos dum ii pacate iter facerent, Alexander, Ioannis Galeatii frater nothus, qui erat in Ludovici partibus, Parma fugiens ad eos se contulit, ut contra patruum esset. Erant in eorum exercitu Ferdinandus Alfonsi filius, magnae spei

since Fortune is generally the master in war and actions taken at random often turned out better than rationally planned ones. They should accordingly beg Almighty God for help, for He alone knew what each man should pursue or avoid in each situation.

Having left Venice and arrived in Dalmatia, Antonio Grimani 14 had ambassadors come to him from Scardona and Clissa[7] to say that their towns wished to be taken under Venetian rule, and they begged to be admitted as subjects by him. Antonio urged the ambassadors to await the Republic's decision and sent a letter on the subject to the Senate, and then made for Corfu. Alfonso's fleet meanwhile, which he had put under the command of his brother Federico, sailed into the Gulf of Liguria. They put Obietto Fieschi of Genoa, a man of considerable importance with his people, on land at Portovenere along with his soldiers, but they were repulsed by the enemy and the fleet returned to Livorno having accomplished nothing. On the other hand, during that time Charles and Ludovico had put together at Genoa a joint fleet quite capable of driving the enemy off. And so, thoroughly alarmed at the defeat of his forces and in fear of the enemy fleet, Alfonso withdrew, thinking not to try the fortunes of war further in those places.

Frustrated of his hopes there, Alfonso straightaway sent his 15 forces, now united with those of Alexander, into Romagna, because he had heard that part of Charles' army had been sent ahead and had already crossed the Po. As their forces neared the territory of Rimini, Pandolfo Malatesta, the lord of Rimini who was in the Republic's service, began to fear for his realm at such a critical and uncertain time, and asked the Senate for aid. At his request, Giorgio Emo was sent there to protect the town and its territory by dint of the Republic's prestige. And while the troops were marching through the district undisturbed, the illegitimate brother of Giangaleazzo, Alessandro Sforza,[8] who had been on the side of Ludovico, fled from Parma and made his way to them to fight against his uncle. Their army included Alfonso's son

adolescens; Nicolaus Ursinus, qui Petilianum oppidum in Etruria
obtinebat, belli rebus atque artibus clarus; Virginius item Ursinus,
de quo superius diximus, Romanae factionis princeps; Ioannes Iacobus Triultius Mediolanensis, homo magna inter suos gratia.
Hos est paulo post Guidus Ubaldus, Urbinas dux princepsque
Metaurensium, ad Cesenam consecutus. Atque ii omnes equitum
cataphractorum duum milium quingentorum, militum octo milium numerum habebant. Ad eos cum praemissae Caroli atque
Ludovici copiae appropinquavissent, universi congredi non sunt
ausi; itaque, aut oppidi plane firmi aut fluminis interiectu munitis
castris, complures se dies continuerunt. Per occasiones tamen parvulis minutisque proeliis quid utrique possent aliquoties periculum fecerunt.

16   At Carolus, qui Aloisium propinquum suum, principatum in
Genabensibus obtinentem, et Iulianum cardinalem, Sixti pontificis
maximi fratris filium, et Antonium Salernitanum, de quo supra
dictum est, Genuam cum pedestri exercitu miserat, ut naves iam
paratas conscenderent, suique itineris ratione habita, se subsequi
iusserat, ut ingressum in regnum Neapolitanum suum mari etiam
aperiret, cum reliquo exercitu bene magno planeque paratissimo
primis Septembris diebus Alpes traiecit atque Astam venit. Ibi illum Ludovicus cum muliebri uxoris Beatricis comitatu, et Ioannes
Galeatius fratris filius Herculesque Atestinus socer, obviam progressi, venientem exceperunt; quicum de rebus utriusque Ludovicus collocutus cum eisdem illis quos adduxerat Ticinum rediit. Ea
itio atque reditio itinerum omnium postrema Ioanni Galeatio fuit.
Profluvio enim ventris, ut videbatur, lectulo impositus — ut vero
creditum est, veneni a patruo dati haustu — insequente mense

Ferrandino, a youth of great promise, Niccolò Orsini, who was lord of Pitigliano in Tuscany and distinguished in the art and practice of war, Virginio Orsini likewise, whom I mentioned above, the leader of the Roman party, and Giangiacomo Trivulzio of Milan, a person of great authority among his people. A little later they were joined near Cesena by Guidobaldo, the Duke of Urbino and lord of the people of the Metauro. These leaders together had troops numbering 2,500 heavy cavalry and 8,000 infantry. When the advance forces of Charles and Ludovico approached them, none of the parties dared to join battle, and so with their camps secured by the protection of some strong town or a river, they stayed where they were for a good many days. Notwithstanding, they several times engaged in tiny and trivial skirmishes as occasion offered, to see what each side was capable of.

But Charles had sent to Genoa his relative Louis, the Duke of   16 Orleans, and Cardinal Giuliano della Rovere (nephew of Pope Sixtus), and Antonello da Sanseverino, Prince of Salerno, whom I mentioned before, along with an infantry army, to board the ships now made ready. He explained his plans for the journey and ordered them to follow close behind him, so he might clear a way for his entry into the Kingdom of Naples by sea too. With the rest of the army, in very large numbers and certainly at the height of readiness, he crossed the Alps at the beginning of September and reached Asti. Accompanied by his wife Beatrice d'Este and her female retinue, Ludovico il Moro, Giangaleazzo his nephew, and his father-in-law Ercole d'Este went to meet Charles there, welcoming him on his arrival. After discussions with him on their respective situations, Ludovico returned to Pavia with the same people he had brought with him. This traveling there and back was the last journey Giangaleazzo ever made. Having taken to his bed with an apparent case of diarrhea — though really, it was believed, through drinking poison given him by his uncle — he died the following

periit. Tantum in animis mentibusque hominum mala regnandi cupiditas atque ambitio potest.

17 Carolus inter haec Astae cum esset, Aloisium Genua, mutato consilio, accersivit ibique iussit esse. Erat autem Aloisii oppidum Asta, quod quidem eius avia dotis nomine a patre, Mediolani rege, acceperat. Ipse pustulis correptus est, eoque in oppido commoratus dum convalesceret, itineri deinde se dedit; atque ad diem duodecimum Kalendarum Novembris Placentiam pervenit. Processerat eo una cum illo Ludovicus; qui postridie eius diei, de fratris filii morte nuntio accepto, Mediolanum rediit, urbemque in veste regia perambulans, salutari regem se non modo passus est sed maxime omnium voluit; neque ei minus id deliberatum propterea fuit, quod Ioannes Galeatius moriens duos liberos, Franciscum et Mariam, superstites reliquisset.

18 Carolus, qui antequam e Gallia proficisceretur, tametsi Florentinis ostendisset se per eorum fines iter Neapolim esse facturum, per Flaminiam tamen ire constituerat, ob eamque rem exercitus sui partem eo miserat, cum Laurentini Medicis, Florentini civis, suasu, qui cum Petro Medice, propinquo suo, cuius erat in potestate civitas, magnas atque acerbas simultates exercebat, tum Ludovici, qui eundem Petrum, quod is, uxore ex Ursina gente ducta, in eorum atque Alfonsi partes se traduxerat, ingenti odio prosequebatur, ire Florentiam decrevit. Ea res Florentiam perlata civitatem ad novum atque subitum capiendum consilium perpulit. Rex post haec Placentia profectus, dextra se per Tari fluminis vallem flectens, ad Apuanos, in Apennini radicibus municipium, legatos Florentinorum obvios habuit, quos ad regem civitas, ut cum eo agerent, ne inimico ad sese animo accederet, misit. Eius legationis Petrus Medices princeps fuit. Is cum regem a se alienatum Laurentini et Ludovici maledictis calumniisque comperisset, omnibus

month. Such is the hold that ambition and the corrupt desire to
rule have on the hearts and minds of men.

In the meantime, while Charles was at Asti, he changed his　17
plans and summoning Louis from Genoa, ordered him to stay
there. The town of Asti in fact belonged to Louis in virtue of his
grandmother's having received it by way of dowry from her father,
the duke of Milan. The king himself suffered an attack of the pox
and stayed in the town until he recovered. He then took to the
road and arrived at Piacenza on 21 October. Ludovico had accompanied him there, but returned to Milan the next day on hearing
of his nephew's death. As he walked through the city dressed in
ducal clothes, he permitted himself to be hailed as duke, though in
reality he craved it more than anything else — nor was this action
any the less deliberate for the fact that Giangaleazzo had left behind at his death two children, Francesco and Maria.

Although he had indicated to the Florentines that he was going　18
to make his way to Naples through their territory, Charles had
nevertheless resolved to go through Romagna even before he set
out from France, and had for that reason sent part of his army
there. He now decided to go to Florence at the urging of Lorenzo
[di Pierfrancesco] de' Medici, a Florentine citizen who was engaged in a long and bitter struggle with his relative Piero de'
Medici, the ruler of the city, and at Ludovico il Moro's urging as
well: Ludovico had formed a fierce hatred of Piero for having
taken a wife of the Orsini family, and crossing over to their party
and Alfonso's. When this news reached Florence it forced the city
to improvise a new policy. The king then left Piacenza, turning
right along the valley of the river Taro, and at Pontremoli, a town
at the foot of the Apennines, he met a Florentine embassy sent by
the city to make sure the king was not going to approach Florence
with hostile intent. The head of the embassy was Piero de' Medici.
When he learned that the king had been turned against him by
the abuse and slander of Lorenzo and Ludovico, he attempted to

illum condicionibus lenire benivolumque sibi reddere est aggressus. Itaque tria civitatis oppida in Apennini iugis, quae Genuensium antea fuerant, tum Pisas et Triturritam in praesentia regi tradere, certasque quotannis, quoad is in Italia esset, pecunias tributi
nomine atque equitatum pollicitus, cum illo in amicitiam rediit.
Quibus intellectis rebus, civitas incitata illum et Ioannem et Iulianum, eius fratres, urbe finibusque suis expulit, domo eorum opu-
lentissima direpta bonisque fisco addictis. Quorum duo se Venetias contulerunt. Ioannes, Petro natu minor, Bononiae primum,
deinde in Tifernatibus apud propinquos suos complures se menses
continuit; erat tamen e cardinalium collegio.

19   Rex, Apennini superato iugo, Lucam, inde Pisas venit idque
oppidum a Florentiae imperio dicioneque removit, et sui iuris liberumque iussit esse, quod quidem civitas plebsque omnis cupidissime arripuit. Florentiam paucis post diebus est profectus; li-
brisque auri duodecies centies imperatis, in reipublicae formam
civitatem redegit. Pisis libertati restitutis, senatores reliquique cives concilio coacto magistratus qui Florentia venerant ex oppido
suisque vicis et castellis expulerunt; ex sese quos visum est magistratus creaverunt. Leones marmoreos depictosque, quod est insigne Florentinorum, e foro locisque omnibus sustulerunt. In exi-
lium qui essent a Florentinis magistratibus missi, ii ut in oppidum
atque in suos quisque lares remigrarent edixerunt. Iisdem diebus
ea Gallici pars exercitus quae in Flaminiam praecesserat, tribus in
agro Forocorneliensium et Foroliviensium tum vi, tum deditione
captis castellis, Faventiaque in suas partes traducta, a Bretinoro
vico, qui eos recipere noluerat et indignantes oppugnareque aggressos sustinuerat, Apenninum traicere atque, ut cum rege se

placate him and gain his friendship with all sorts of proposals. And so Piero resumed friendly relations with the king after promising to hand over to him at once three Florentine towns in the Apennines which had previously belonged to Genoa, then Pisa and Livorno, a certain annual sum of money by way of tribute for as long as he remained in Italy, and some cavalry. When the Florentines learned of this they were enraged, and expelled Piero and his brothers Giovanni and Giuliano from the city and its territory, plundering their palatial home and confiscating their property. Two of them went to Venice. Giovanni, the next eldest after Piero, stayed with relations for several months, first in Bologna, then in Città di Castello, though he was a member of the college of cardinals.[9]

The king crossed the Apennines and came first to Lucca and 19 then Pisa. This latter town he rid of Florentine domination and rule, bidding it be free and independent, something that the citizenry and the common people seized on with enthusiasm. Charles set out for Florence a few days later, and levying a sum of 1,200 gold pounds, imposed a republican form of government on the city again. When their freedom was restored, the senators and the rest of the citizens of Pisa held a meeting and expelled the magistrates imposed by Florence from their city, its villages and castles. They elected from among themselves such magistrates as they saw fit, and removed the marble and painted lions, the insignia of Florence, from the town square and elsewhere. They issued an edict that those who had been exiled by the Florentine magistrates could all return to Pisa and to their own homes. At the same time the part of the French army which had been sent on ahead into Romagna captured three castles in the territory of Imola and Forlì, either by force of arms or surrender, and Faenza too came over to them; they then began to cross the Apennines and set out on their journey to join up with the king, starting from the village of Bertinoro, which had refused to admit them and had managed to

coniungeret, iter facere coepit. Ferdinandus cum omnino Gallos
intercludere morarique non posset, suis cum ducibus, quo itinere
venerat, Romam rediit.

20   At Veneti, ubi Carolum magna cum manu Padum flumen traiecisse nuntiatum est, legatos ad eum mittere decreverunt, qui ei honoris gratia praesto essent, seque ad omnes casus praemunire
constituerunt. Missi legati Dominicus Trivisanus, Antonius Lauredanus regem Florentiae convenerunt eumque postea sunt subsecuti. Illis ipsis diebus Ioannes, Senogalliam obtinens, Iuliani cardinalis frater, Baiasetis regis legatum, qui Anconae navi expositus
Romam proficiscebatur, Alexandro pensionem annuam librarum
auri quadrigentarum, Giemis nomine dependi solitam, afferens,
intercepit ablataque pecunia dimisit. Carolo Senas urbem trans-
gresso, Alexander Virginium et Nicolaum, Alfonsi exercitus duces,
et Ferdinandum, regis filium, qui Romae appropinquaverant, intra
moenia recepit, ut et loca tuta hostibus praeripere, et adversarios
cohibere atque reprimere, et urbem ad Gallos repellendos velle
communire magnopere videretur. Verum tamen paucis post diebus, Carolo Romam recta veniente, Ferdinandum reliquosque duces est hortatus uti Roma proficiscerentur; neque Gallos, quibus
quidem iam nihil esset impeditum, exspectarent. Illi, quos omnia
plane deficerent, pontifici paruerunt Tiburque cum ea quam habebant manu se contulerunt. Alexander, qui quidem Gallos veritus
de capienda fuga non semel cogitaverat, demum in Hadriani mo-
lem, commeatu et tormentis communitam, se recepit.

21   Carolus omni cum exercitu pridie Kalendarum Ianuarii Romam venit. Pauloque post, cum inter ipsum atque Alexandrum
Ascanio interprete de pace sermones haberentur, Ascanius autem

hold out against them when they took offense and went on the attack. Since Ferrandino was quite unable to head off the French and slow them down, he and his captains returned to Rome by the way they had come.

When the Venetians learned that Charles had crossed the Po 20 with a large force, they resolved to send an embassy to wait upon him as a mark of honor, determined that they should safeguard themselves against every eventuality. Domenico Trevisan and Antonio Loredan were sent out as the ambassadors and met the king at Florence, afterwards following in his train. It was at that time that an emissary of Sultan Bayazid landed at Ancona and set out for Rome with the customary pension of 400 gold pounds paid each year to Alexander on account of Djem, when he was intercepted by Giovanni della Rovere, the lord of Senigallia and brother of Cardinal Giuliano, who relieved him of the money and let him go. Once Charles had got beyond Siena, Alexander admitted within the walls of Rome Virginio and Niccolò Orsini, the captains of Alfonso's army, and the king's son Ferrandino, who were close by the city. In this it seemed his chief desire was to forestall the enemy by seizing strongholds first, and so control and check his adversaries' advance, and also to strengthen the city for repelling the French. But when Charles was making straight for Rome a few days later, Alexander urged Ferrandino and the other captains to leave the city and not wait for the French, who now had no obstacle in their path. Those men, now plainly bereft of all resource, followed the pontiff's suggestion and went to Tivoli with the men they had. Alexander, who had thought more than once of taking to flight for fear of the French, in the end withdrew into Castel Sant'Angelo, which was well supplied with provisions and artillery.

Charles entered Rome with his entire army on 31 December. A 21 little later peace talks were held between him and Alexander with *1495* Cardinal Ascanio Sforza acting as intermediary. When Ascanio

duras nimium et severas condiciones Alexandro imponeret, Alexander, eam hominis audaciam compescendam ratus, cardinalium concilio ad speciem quaerendarum ab eis sententiarum coacto, illum, qui ad concilium venerat, retinuit nec nisi pace cum rege facta dimisit. Romae Carolus complures dies commoratus, Alexandrum, quicum foedus certis condicionibus percusserat, separatim primo, deinde publico in concilio salutavit, eius ad pedes advolutus, sollemnibusque sacris ministrante illo interfuit. Post haec pontifex episcopum Macloviensium, cuius unius magnopere consiliis rex omnibus in rebus nitebatur, petente rege cardinalem creavit. Navesque onerariae viginti commeatum e Gallia provincia regis exercitui supportantes ad Centumcellarum portum appelluntur.

22   Iisdem prope diebus ex tribus Venetorum longis navibus, quae publice in Britanniam ad mercaturam exercendam mittebantur, duae in oceano tempestatis vi absorptae sunt fluctibus; quibus in navibus complures ex ipsa nobilitate cives, reliqui amplius quingenti perierunt, mercium ad quater mille auri libras summa deperdita. Quod quidem antea numquam acciderat, ut eiusmodi naves, terra non tacta, mari atque undis absumerentur. Tametsi anno ab urbe condita millesimo decimo sexto duae item naves longae onustae mercibus, eo ipso in mari ventorum contumelia impactae litoribus, sunt amissae.

23   Dum ea Romae apud Carolum geruntur, Alfonsus, suis rebus plane diffidens, Ferdinando filio Neapolim accersito regnum tradit, Federico fratre adhibito; eumque uti deos immortales vereatur monet. Ea oratione apud filium habita, in arcem, quae est in oppidi litore et mari undique adluitur, quae castellum Ovi appellatur, noctu se contulit, ut naves longas conscenderet. Quod tum facere austro magno coorto vento prohibitus, paucis post diebus, nactus idoneam tempestatem, in Siciliam transmisit; eoque anno in Pan-

began imposing excessively harsh and severe conditions on Alexander, the pope thought the man's effrontery had to be checked and summoned a consistory of the cardinals, ostensibly to ask their opinions. He had Ascanio, who had come to the consistory, put under arrest and did not let him go until peace was concluded with the king. Charles remained at Rome for some days, and having agreed a treaty with a number of conditions with Alexander, paid his respects to him first privately and then in public consistory, when he prostrated himself at his feet and took part in a mass celebrated by him. After this, at the king's request, the pontiff raised to the cardinalate the bishop of Saint-Malo, on whose advice the king specially relied in all his affairs.[10] Twenty merchant vessels carrying provisions for the king's army from Provence put in at the port of Civitavecchia.

At about the same time, two of three Venetian galleys which the Republic had sent to Britain[11] to engage in trade were engulfed by the waves of the ocean during a violent storm. A number of citizens of the nobility itself perished in the ships, and more than 500 others, the merchandise lost amounting to some 4,000 gold pounds. It had never before happened that ships of this type were swallowed up by the sea and the waves without running aground, although in the 1016th year of the city's foundation [1437], another two galleys loaded with merchandise had been lost when they were driven ashore by the violence of the winds in the same sea.

While all this was going on at Rome with Charles, Alfonso, despairing of his situation, summoned his son Ferrandino to Naples and handed the kingdom over to him, in the presence of his brother Federico, adjuring him to respect Almighty God. Having delivered this speech in his son's presence, he made his way by night to the fortress called Castel dell'Ovo, which is on the shore of the town and washed by the sea on all sides, in order to board his galleys. This he was prevented from doing at the time by a strong south wind, but a few days later, having met with suitable

ormitano agro privatus moritur. Ferdinandus, profecto patre, regni principibus quattuor, qui erant in custodia, primum omnium dimissis, oppidum in veste regia una cum Federico patruo perequitavit; salutatusque rex, cum se ad carceris parietem contulisset, reclusis patefactisque foribus, rebelles aliquot[1] damnatosque complures et libertati et municipio restituit, privatas publicasque iniurias omnes remisit, pollicitusque est se proscriptos quosque revocaturum. Militibus deinde appellatis, eos stipendio donavit, atque oppida novis praesidiis firmavit.

24   Carolo ad diem quintum Kalendarum Februarii Roma profecto Velitrasque progresso, Caesar Borgia cardinalis, Alexandri filius, quem quidem pater legati nomine Carolo dederat, ut obsidis loco apud illum esset, noctu aufugit; neve patris voluntate videretur id fecisse, non Romam sed Spoletum se contulit. Eodem tempore missi a rege milites, qui ex foedere Ostiensem et Centumcellarum Anxurisque arces, quoad is in Italia esset, custodirent, repulsi sunt ab Alexandri custodibus. Arcem enim Ostiensem, quam Iulianus cardinalis exaedificaverat praesidiisque firmaverat, cum is Alexandri pontificatus initio, nihil illi fidens, speculatoria biremi se ex ea sustulisset, conscendensque Fabricio Columnae, amico sibi homini et magni ac erecti animi viro, illam commendavisset, Genuamque ac deinde in Galliam esset profectus, Alexander, Nicolao Ursino, Petilianorum principe, cum exercitu eo misso, acri obsidione cinctam expugnaverat suique iuris fecerat.

25   Rex, Velitris profectus, Fortini montis oppidum munitissimum, quod quidem capi posse nisi longa obsidione non videbatur, paucarum horarum spatio cepit, itemque Ferentinum; quae utraque in Ferdinandi erant partibus. Ea re confecta suum hominem ad pont-

weather, he crossed to Sicily, and in that year he died a private citizen in the countryside of Palermo. Once his father had left, Ferrandino in the first place released four princes of the realm who were in custody, and accompanied by his uncle Federico, rode on horseback through the town in his royal robes. Acclaimed as king, he made his way to the walls of the prison, unlocked the gates and threw them open, and returned freedom and civic rights to a number of rebels and a number of condemned men. He pardoned all private and public crimes, and promised to recall all those who had been exiled. He then summoned his soldiers and gave them a gift of money, and strengthened his towns with new garrisons.

Charles left Rome on 28 January and proceeded to Velletri. The 24 cardinal Cesare Borgia, Alexander's son, had been assigned to the king by his father, nominally as a legate but really to serve as a hostage. Cesare fled from him under cover of night, and to avoid the appearance of having done so at his father's wish, he made his way not to Rome but to Spoleto. At the same time soldiers sent by the king under the terms of the treaty to take custody of the fortresses of Ostia, Civitavecchia and Terracina for as long as he was in Italy were driven off by Alexander's guards. The fortress at Ostia had been built by Cardinal Giuliano della Rovere and furnished by him with a garrison. At the outset of the pontificate of Alexander, whom he thoroughly distrusted, Giuliano had taken himself off from there in a brig, entrusting it as he boarded ship to Fabrizio Colonna, a friend of his and a man of great and noble spirit, and had left for Genoa and from there to France. Alexander sent Niccolò Orsini, Count of Pitigliano, there at the head of an army, stormed it after a bitter siege and made it his own.

The king set out from Velletri and in the space of a few hours 25 captured the strongly fortified town of Montefortino, which it seemed impossible to take without a long siege, and Ferentino as well, both of which were on Ferrandino's side. This accomplished, he sent his agent to the pope: unless Alexander stood by the agree-

ificem misit: ni pactis quae sunt in ipsorum foedere steterit, sese primum omnium sua in illum arma conversurum; quo accepto nuntio, pontifex regis militibus arces tradidit. Ferociore regis milites impetu primum in Alfonsi dicione castellum in Cassinate saltu, et militibus et commeatu communitum, vi captum diripuerunt, propugnatoribus incolisque omnibus ad unum interfectis, quod praemissi ad oppidanos de deditione nuntii ab iis male accepti fuerant. Id castellum sancti Ioannis mons ab incolis appellatur, tenebaturque ab Aterni regulo, quo uno nemo erat Ferdinando regi carior. Itaque hoc successu rerum suarum Carolus, cum exercitu equitum militumque numero triginta milium in regnum Neapolitanum ingressus, ad Cassinum venit. Quo in oppido Ferdinandus cum esset (haberet autem milites numero ad quattuor mille, equites alteros totidem), oppidanos cohortatus ne se diripi sinerent sed fortunae cederent seque in aliud tempus reservarent, oppido profectus Capuam suis cum copiis contendit. Cassinates eo profecto sese Carolo dediderunt. Ad quem, non intermissis itineribus Capuae appropinquantem, Caietae civitas legatos misit: ei se oppidum traditurum imperataque facturam. Caieta in deditionem recepta, Capuani et ipsi regi oppidum tradiderunt. Capuam ubi rex venit, Giemes, quem Roma secum abduxerat, in morbum incidit, cuius sustinere vim non potuit.

26   At Ferdinandus cum Neapolim petiisset, eius exercitu intra moenia non admisso, ipse cum suo comitatu equitibusque paucis est receptus. Qui, voluntate civitatis intellecta, quae Gallos exspectare, ne diriperetur, nolebat, combustis duabus navibus magnis, ex tribus quas in portu habebat, ne in manus hostium pervenirent, tertia Obiecto Flisco tradita, equos prope trecentos egregiae sobolis suis civibus amicisque distribuit. Deinde Neapolitana arce

ments in the treaty, the first thing he would do would be to turn his arms against him. On receipt of this message, the pope handed over the fortresses to the king's soldiers. A more ferocious attack led to the king's forces taking and looting the first castle in Alfonso's lands, in the neighborhood of Montecassino, well supplied with soldiers and provisions though it was, and this after killing every last one of its defenders and inhabitants because messengers sent ahead to discuss surrender with the townspeople had been maltreated by them. The fortress is called by its inhabitants Monte San Giovanni and was held by the Marquis of Pescara,[12] the favorite of King Ferrandino. And so with this success Charles entered the Kingdom of Naples with an army numbering 30,000 cavalry and foot soldiers, and arrived at Montecassino. Although Ferrandino was in the town (and had some 4,000 foot soldiers and the same number of cavalry), he urged the townspeople not to let themselves be pillaged, but to yield to Fortune and save themselves for another time. On which he left the town and made for Capua, the people of Montecassino surrendering to Charles once he had gone. Without breaking his march, Charles was approaching Capua when the people of Gaeta sent envoys to say that they would surrender the town to him and do his bidding. Once Gaeta had surrendered to the king, the people of Capua too handed over their town to him. When the king reached Capua, Djem, whom he had carried off from Rome, succumbed to the violent attack of an illness he had contracted there.

When Ferrandino sought to enter Naples, his army was refused 26 admittance within the walls, though he himself was received with his retinue and a few cavalrymen. Sensing the temper of the city, which did not want to await the French and the likelihood of being sacked, he burned two of the three large ships that he had in the harbor, in case they should fall into enemy hands. The third he made over to Obietto Fieschi, while he distributed nearly 300 thoroughbred horses to his fellow citizens and friends. Ferrandino

quam appellant Novam militibus reliquisque rebus ad obsidionem sustinendam idoneis apprime communita, cum Federico patruo et uxore Ferdinandi avi sui atque filia in insulam Megarem sese contulit. Ex ea insula, quae est non longe ab oppidi litore, Neapolitani reges arcem munitissimam effecerunt. Carolo recta Neapolim cum exercitu properante, Virginius Nicolausque, Ferdinandi duces, quod intellexerant civitatem legatos de deditione ad Carolum misisse, Nolam se cum ea quam habebant manu receperunt. Quos praemissi Caroli equites cum insequerentur, Nolani Gallis portas aperuerunt, retentis interceptisque Nicolao atque Virginio; qui ambo in Gallorum potestatem venerunt, tametsi iam ante a Carolo petiissent ut in suam fidem sese reciperet, idque eis Carolus esset pollicitus. Itaque in eo fides est regia desiderata. Carolus, intellecta Ferdinandi fuga, Neapolim venit, praemissis suis ducibus, ne militum et equitum introitu oppidum egregium atque opulentum diriperetur. Eo potitus, per legatos Venetos perque litteras senatui gratias egit, quod otium sibi atque benevolentiam quam pollicitus fuerat praestitisset.

27   Ferdinandus, suis cum mulieribus et supellectili bene magna, navibus longis duodecim ad Aenariam traiecit, insulam et situ et opere munitissimam; abest a Neapoli duodeviginti milia passuum. Interim fama de adventu deque successu rerum Caroli ad Turcas perlata, propterea quod rex palam dictitaverat, Neapolitano regno capto, se in Turcas profecturum eisque bellum terra marique illaturum, tanta fuit eius rei opinio tantusque omnes eas gentes terror invasit, ut in Illyrico Epiro Acarnania Macedonia qui maritimas earum regionum oras atque portus incolebant se introrsus reciperent atque in longinquas a litoribus et remotas latebras abderent.

then greatly strengthened the Neapolitan citadel called Castelnuovo with soldiers and the other things needed for withstanding a siege, and took himself off to the island of Megaride with his uncle Federico and the wife and daughter of his grandfather Ferrante. The kings of Naples had made a very strong fortress of the island, which is close to the shore of the city.[13] As Charles hastened straight to Naples with his army, Ferrandino's captains Virginio and Niccolò Orsini, realizing that the citizens had sent spokesmen to Charles to discuss surrender, retreated to Nola with what forces they had. When they were pursued by the cavalry sent on ahead by Charles, the people of Nola opened their gates to the French, holding Niccolò and Virginio back and cutting off their escape. And so they both fell into the hands of the French, although they had earlier asked Charles to take them under his protection, and Charles had promised to do so. Thus it was that the trustworthiness required of a king was found wanting in him. When Charles learned that Ferrandino had fled, he went to Naples, sending his captains on ahead in case that fine and wealthy city should be pillaged when the foot soldiers and cavalry entered the city. Once he had taken charge of it, he sent thanks to the Senate, through the Venetian ambassadors and by letter, for giving him the peace and goodwill which they had promised.

With his womenfolk and a good deal of baggage loaded on 12 galleys, Ferrandino crossed to Ischia, an island about 18 miles from Naples, very secure both in its location and its defenses. Meanwhile news of Charles' arrival and his successes reached the Turks. The king had openly declared that once the Kingdom of Naples was taken, he would proceed against the Turks and wage war on them by land and sea. Such was their expectation that this would happen, and such the terror that gripped them, that all the people who dwelt on the shores and in the ports of Croatia, Albania, Acarnania, and Macedonia retreated inland and hid themselves away in remote fastnesses far from the coast. A letter also came to

27

Litterae etiam ab Antonio Grimano ad senatum venerunt: cum ad
Naupactum Aetoliae litora navibus longis praeterveheretur, Turcas, eam esse classem Gallicam verentes, omnes aufugisse vacuaque
litora custodiis reliquisse; ut quilibet existimare potuerit, si se
modo Carolus illis in locis ostendisset, parvo eum negotio omnes
eas regiones in suam potestatem redigere potuisse. Baiasetes quidem rex iam inde, cum primum Florentiam Carolum esse ingressum cognovit, veteres triremes reficere, novas instituere coepit, militibusque suis et equitibus edixit se compararent, ut cum vellet
sibi praesto esse possent.

28   Eodem quoque tempore et naves sexaginta, quibus in navibus
erant militum sena milia, equites sexcenti, ab Hispaniae missae regibus, ut Siciliae praesidio essent, Triturritam appulerunt; et Laurentius Suares, quem iidem reges legatum ad senatum miserant,
Venetias venit. Causa mittendi fuit quod timuerant ne Carolus,
Neapolitano regno capto, in animum induceret etiam Siciliam insulam, quae aliquando Galliae regibus paruisset, eodem quo Neapolim iure velle suam facere. Ii cum suis rebus timerent, Gallorum
audaciam atque potentiam veriti, existimabant Venetos, vicinitate
periculi adductos, quod magnum regem in Italia pollentem viderent, eodem in timore versari, propterea quod res omnes publicae,
validae praesertim atque firmae, suspectae ac formidolosae sunt regibus. Itaque Suari mandaverant ut, salutato principe et patribus,
eos certiores faceret sese, quo ipsi animo in Carolum essent, eodem esse Venetos existimavisse. Quod si cavere sibi ab illo cupe-
rent, se paratos esse una cum ipsis omnem fortunam experiri.
Scire se, qua prudentia, qua fide senatus Venetus esset; nemine
cum rege libentius quam cum ipso foedus percussuros. Venturum
in societatem periculi Alexandrum pontificem maximum, qui nihil

the Senate from Antonio Grimani: when he was sailing in his galleys past the shores of Aetolia on his way to Lepanto, all the Turks took to flight, fearing that it was the French fleet, and left the coast completely without protection, from which one might conclude that if Charles were just to put in an appearance in those places, he would have little trouble in gaining control of them. Sultan Bayazid had in fact already begun to refit old galleys and construct new ones as soon as he found out that Charles had entered Florence, and he ordered his infantry and cavalry to get themselves ready for war so that they would be at his disposal when he wanted them.

Also at this time, the 60 ships carrying 6,000 infantry and 600   28 cavalry which had been sent by the Spanish sovereigns to protect Sicily put in at Livorno, and Lorenzo Suarez, whom they had sent to the Senate as their envoy, arrived at Venice. The reason for sending Suarez was that they were worried that once the Kingdom of Naples was taken, Charles would take it into his head to seize control of Sicily as well, on the same basis as he had Naples, since the island had once been subject to the kings of France. Anxious about their own situation and fearful of the boldness and power of the French, they supposed that the Venetians would be moved by the proximity of the danger when they saw a great king wielding power in Italy and would be prey to the same fears, since all republics, strong and stable ones especially, were objects of suspicion and dread to kings. The sovereigns accordingly instructed Suarez, once he had paid his respects to the doge and senators, to inform them that they believed the Venetians to be of the same mind toward Charles as themselves. If the Venetians wanted to safeguard themselves from Charles, the sovereigns were perfectly willing to try their luck at their side. They were aware of the Venetian Senate's sagacity and steadfastness, and would rather make a pact with them than with any king. Pope Alexander would come forward to share in the danger, since he would like nothing better than to

aeque cupiat atque hoc, ut ipsos et Venetos sibi coniunctos habeat, quorum armis, si quid durius accidat, se munire ac tueri possit. Eo socio non minimum roboris atque virium, plurimum quidem certe auctoritatis in commune accessurum; ut magnopere sperandum sit, si consenserint, omnia prospere atque feliciter casura.

29   Ea legati oratio gratissima fuit patribus; quos iam Caroli rerum successus circumspicere sesemet et vereri multa cogebat, quae ambiguo adhuc eventu belli non aestimabantur. Huc accedebat quod Ludovicus ipse diffidere Carolo coeperat, cum ob eius litteras imperiosiores ad se missas, quibus eum litteris rex Neapolim evocabat, tum propterea quod Ioannem Iacobum Triultium, quem quidem ipse Mediolano expulerat exulemque fecerat, hominem sibi multis de causis inimicum, Carolus suam in fidem apud Neapolim receperat; postremo quod Aloisium propinquum suum, quem Astae relictum supra demonstratum est, inde postea discedere Carolus noluerat. Eae res, quod nonnullam ostendebant in Caroli animo inesse de Ludovici fide suspicionem, Ludovicum item suspensum animi fecerant, quantum regi esset credendum. De eo ipse apud legatum Venetum questus, ei ostendit libenter se ab Gallis discessurum foedusque cum republica renovaturum.

30   Erant praeterea in urbe Maximiliani regis legati, cuius pater Federicus imperator eo anno mortem obierat, qui senatum in Gallos incitare non desistebant. Eorum oratio, propterea quod Maximilianus Ludovici fratris filiam in matrimonium duxerat eratque cum eo plane coniunctissimus, ex ipsius ore Ludovici mitti propemodum videbatur. Tametsi Maximiliano quidem ipsi omnis erat ad Gallorum opes atque potentiam invisa molestaque accessio; quem quidem etiam recens accepta insignis iniuria contra Carolum stimulabat, Margarita filia sua, cum dote plures ante annos ei tradita,

have themselves and the Venetians as allies, by whose arms he could protect and defend himself if anything untoward should happen. With him as their ally, their common enterprise would gain not a little strength and force, and certainly a great access of prestige, and so there was good reason to hope that if they agreed, everything would turn out for the best.

The ambassador's speech was very welcome to the senators. 29 They had already been forced by Charles' success to consider their position and to fear many possibilities which, while the outcome of the war was still uncertain, had not been contemplated. To this was added the fact that Ludovico il Moro himself had begun to distrust Charles, not only on account of a rather imperious letter he had received in which the king summoned him to Naples, but also because Charles had taken under his protection at Naples Giangiacomo Trivulzio, a man with many reasons to hate him and whom he had expelled and exiled from Milan; and lastly, because Charles had not wanted his relative Louis, the Duke of Orleans (left behind at Asti, as I mentioned) to leave that town. These indications that there was some doubt in Charles' mind about Ludovico's loyalty had made Ludovico himself doubtful as to how much trust he could put in the king. His complaint on this score in the presence of the Venetian ambassador showed that he would be glad to abandon the French and renew his pact with Venice.

Apart from that, there were also in Venice ambassadors from 30 King Maximilian, whose father the Emperor Frederick had died that year [1495], and they were constantly stirring up the Senate against the French. Their words might as well have come from the mouth of Ludovico himself, for Maximilian had married the daughter of Ludovico's brother and was clearly very close to him. Nonetheless Maximilian himself hated every advance in French wealth and power and found them hard to bear, having indeed recently suffered a notable injury that turned him against Charles. His daughter Margaret had been betrothed to Charles with a

cui tamen Carolus propter aetatem puellae nondum se adiunxerat, repudiata, Annaque Armoricarum gentium regina, quam Franciscus pater Maximiliano spoponderat, sibi a Carolo praerepta et uxore ducta.

31   Interim, Neapolitanis arcibus duabus partim vi, partim pretio expugnatis, magna Calabrorum populorum, magna Brutii, magna etiam Apuliae parte in deditionem recepta, Carolo non iam ea qua consueverat facie facilitateque legatos Venetos admittente, nonnihil etiam interdum iactante brevi fore ut, qui se noluerant in Italiam traicere Neapolimque capere, eos suae malevolentiae paeniteret, de foedere inter eos sanciendo diligentius est agi coeptum per eorum omnium legatos apud senatum; ad quem quidem Ludovicus eam ob rem novam etiam legationem miserat. Suares quidem ipse iam ab initio suarum hortationum patribus dixerat iussum se ab regibus, quamcumque foederis legem senatus iuberet, in eius verba iurare; satis sibi fore, si unum modo scirent, senatum ita statuendum iudicavisse. Nam omnino Alexander, qui iam Gallos esset expertus dixissetque palam, si redeant, se Venetias, ne eos iterum videat, profecturum, cupidissime avidissimeque illum ipsum exspectabat diem, quo se cum republica reliquisque coniungeret.

32   Itaque pridie Kalendas Aprilis foedus initum ab iis sancitumque est in annos viginti quinque, maiestatem Romani pontificis, dignitatem, libertatem, iura eorum dicionesque omnium tuendi et muniendi causa. Quo ex foedere equitum triginta quattuor milia, peditum viginti confecta parataque habere universi tenerentur, suo cuique singillatim attributo numero. Is erat equitum quidem Alexandro quattuor milium, Maximiliano sex, Hispaniae

dowry many years before, but owing to the girl's age, he had not yet married her when he repudiated the match. Anne of Brittany was then snatched away by Charles and married to him, although her father Francis had betrothed her to Maximilian.

The two castles of Naples had meanwhile been conquered, 31 partly by force of arms, partly for a price, and large parts of the peoples of Calabria, of the Abruzzi, even of Apulia had surrendered to Charles. He no longer received the Venetian ambassadors with the countenance and affability he had used with them before, and even bragged a bit now and then that those who had not wanted him to descend into Italy and take Naples would soon come to regret their ill-will toward him. In these circumstances, serious discussions began about concluding a treaty between them through the ambassadors of each party to the Venetian Senate,[14] to which Ludovico too had sent a new embassy for the purpose. Suarez himself at the very outset of his address to the senators said that he had been told by the sovereigns to give his oath to whatever form of treaty the Senate might require. It would be enough for them simply to know that the Senate had judged that it should be settled in that way. Pope Alexander (Suarez concluded) had already had experience of the French and had openly said that if they returned, he would leave for Venice rather than see them again: he was waiting for the day when he could join the Republic and the other allies with the keenest anticipation and enthusiasm.

On the last day of March, accordingly, they signed and ratified 32 a twenty-five-year treaty to defend and protect the majesty of the pope of Rome, and the dignity, liberty, rights and dominions of all the parties. By the terms of the treaty, they were jointly responsible for providing a standing force of 34,000 cavalry and 20,000 infantry, each of them being assigned their individual contribution. These were 4,000 cavalry for Alexander, 6,000 for Maximilian, 8,000 for the sovereigns of Spain and the same number for the

regibus octo, reipublicae totidem, Ludovico item octo; peditum
vero singulis quattuor milium. Quem si quis equitum peditumque
numerum, propter longinquitatem itineris ac rei bene gerendae celeritatem, mittere in tempore non possit, ei sit in socios eorum stipendium conferendum auri sexcentenae librae; ii exercitum pro
illo conficiant. Quod si classis bellum indigeat, quibus adest pa-
randarum navium facultas, ii tantam, quanta opus erit, parent; ab
reliquis pro sua cuiusque parte stipendium attribuatur.

33   Ea lex eius foederis fuit. Quo omnino in conficiendo cum tot
adessent legati, tot civibus tractandae rei adhibitis, toto demum
vocato saepius et consulto senatu, tanta tamen fuit iussu decemvirum in patribus reliquisque omnibus continendae vocis cura, ut
Philippus, Caroli regis legatus, cum in curiam cottidie ventitaret
atque ab legatis reliquis appellaretur, nihil eius tamen cognoscere
potuerit. Itaque cum postridie eius diei, quo die scripta lex est, in
curiam vocatus a principe, foedus esse percussum intellexisset et
nomina foederatorum cognovisset, mens paene hominem reliquit.
Tametsi princeps ei dixerat ea quae fecissent non propterea esse
facta, uti bellum cuiquam inferrent, sed ut, si inferretur, propulsa-
rent. Demum is, revocato ad se paulisper animo, "Quid," inquit,
"meus rex in Galliam reverti non poterit?" Tum princeps, "Ille
vero," inquit, "poterit, si redire amicus volet; nosque illum rebus
omnibus iuvabimus." Quo responso accepto discessit; atque ubi,
curia egressus, remensis quas ascenderat scalis, in aream descendit,
ad scribam senatus, qui eum comitabatur, conversus, "Rogo te,"
inquit, "sodes, mihi eum sermonem recenseas, quem princeps me-
cum habuit; nihil enim iam eius memini."

Republic of Venice, and 8,000 again for Ludovico il Moro, but each was to provide 4,000 infantry. If any of the signatories was unable to send his allotted number of cavalry and infantry in time, due to the distance to be traveled or the haste needed for success, he would have to give to the allies the soldiers' pay of 600 gold pounds, and they would provide the army on his behalf. If on the other hand a fleet was required for a war, those who had the ability to build ships were to build a fleet as large as was needed, and the costs would be borne by the others paying in proportion.

Such were the provisions of the treaty. And though so many 33 envoys took part in drawing it up and so many citizens were involved in discussing it, with the whole Senate in the end often meeting for consultations, nevertheless at the bidding of the Council of Ten, the senators and everyone else took such care to keep talk about it to a minimum that Philippe de Commines, King Charles' ambassador, was unable to learn anything about it at all, even though he came to the Doge's Palace every day and received calls from the other ambassadors. And so when he was summoned to the Doge's Palace the day after the text was drawn up and learned from the doge that a treaty had been signed, and found out the names of the allies, he was dumbstruck. The doge, however, told him that they had done what they did not to wage war on anyone, but to defend themselves against any war that might be waged on them. Recovering his spirits a little, Commines at last said, "What, will my king not be able to return to France?" Then the doge said, "Certainly he will, if he is willing to return there as our friend, and we shall in that case render him every assistance." On receiving this reply, Commines left, and when he came out of the palace down the stairs by which he had entered and into the courtyard, he turned to the chancellor of the Senate who had accompanied him and said, "Please remind me what the doge just said to me: I cannot now recall a word of it."

34   Petierat a senatu Alexander, antequam de foedere esset confectum, vellent patres, pro ea qua semper civitas fuerat in Romanos
pontifices pietate, equites levis armaturae quingentos, milites bis
totidem praesidii ad se causa mittere. Ea enim factione quae regi
se adiunxerat Romanorum principum omnia eius consilia magnopere impediebantur. Itaque percusso statim foedere, patres iusserunt ex illis qui Ravennae hiemaverant equitibus, quique ibi adhuc
quidem morabantur, is ut Romam numerus celeriter contenderet,
tum ut Hieronymo Georgio, qui apud Alexandrum legati munere
fungebatur, pecuniam quaestores e vestigio curarent, qua is pecunia mille in Urbe milites conscriberet. Litteras ad Ludovicum
praeterea dederunt: ipse quoque idem faceret mitteretque alteros
totidem Romam milites equitesque; quo fultus auxilio pontifex dignitatem posset suam facilius atque honestius tueri. Legati post
haec qui ad Carolum a senatu missi fuerant domum sunt redire
iussi.

35   Ipse vero interea Carolus, cognito de quo dictum est foedere,
veritus ne, si moram Neapoli traheret, dum ii novas copias coge-
rent exercitusque coniungerent, ab eis intercluderetur, ne in Galliam reverti posset, statuit optimum esse quamprimum discedere,
sperans, si modo antequam ii omnibus ad bellum rebus instructi
paratique essent proficisceretur, Italiae itinera sibi ipsum, illis
etiam nolentibus, patefacturum. Nam mari tantum exercitum traiciendi navium ei facultas non erat. Quam enim Genuae paraverat
classem, ea, maxima coorta tempestate afflicta atque in litus ad Populoniam eiecta, nullum ei usum praebuerat; cuius quidem praefectus et princeps Salernitanorum Antonius pedibus se ad eum
contulerunt. Interim a Ludovico maxime omnium se deceptum
dictitans, avertere ab illius imperio Genuensium civitatem summo
studio concupivit. Itaque Petro Fregosio cardinale, qui dux eorum

Before the treaty was concluded, Alexander had asked the Sen- 34
ate, in view of the dutifulness that Venice had always shown to the
Roman pontiffs, to agree to send him for his protection 500 light
cavalry and twice as many infantry, for all his plans were being
greatly obstructed by the group of Roman nobles which had
joined King Charles. As soon as the treaty was struck, the senators therefore ordered 500 of the cavalrymen that had been in winter quarters at Ravenna and still remained there, to make for
Rome with all haste. They further told the treasurers to make an
immediate payment to Girolamo Zorzi, who was serving as their
ambassador to the pope, to enable him to recruit 1,000 soldiers in
Rome. The Senate also sent a letter to Ludovico saying that he
should do the same and send a similar force of infantry and cavalry to Rome, so that with their support the pontiff would be able
to defend his position with greater ease and seemliness. After that,
the ambassadors that the Senate had sent to Charles were ordered
to return home.

Meanwhile Charles himself learned of the treaty described 35
above, and grew fearful that if he tarried at Naples until they gathered new forces and united their armies, he would be cut off by
them and consequently unable to return to France. He decided
that the best thing to do would be to leave as soon as possible, in
the hope that if he could only set out before they had finished all
their preparations for war, he would be able to force a passage
through Italy whether they liked it or not. He did not have ships
in sufficient numbers to convey so large an army by sea, for the
fleet which he had got ready at Genoa had been damaged in a
great storm. It had been driven onto the shore at Piombino and
was now useless to him, its captain and Antonello, the Prince of
Salerno, making his way to him overland. In the meantime he
kept repeating that he had been deceived by Ludovico il Moro
above all, and he conceived a burning desire to detach the city of
Genoa from his dominions. He accordingly secured the adherence

fuerat, suas in partes traducto, eum et Obiectum Fliscum et praefectum ex suis, Segusianorum principem, cum navibus longis un-
decim quas habebat ex sua classe reliquas, eo misit. Ipse, equitum
et militum octo milibus regni praesidio relictis, ad diem tertium-
decimum Kalendarum Iunii cum reliquo exercitu Neapoli profectus viae se dedit.

36   Alexander, ad quem quidem Veneti, de Carolo id quod accidit
opinione existimantes, futurum ut, nuntio de foedere accepto, in
Galliam redire contenderet, pontificis timentes rebus, iam ante eos
dies alteros equites levis armaturae quingentos, ex iis quos ab
Epiro Laconiaque accersitos celeritate praestantissimos habebant,
miserant, quibus ad omnes casus uti posset, regem Romae appropinquantem, cardinalibus Romanisque principibus adhibitis, non
exspectare decrevit; saeptusque equitum numero duum milium,
peditum trium milium quingentorum discessit atque Urbem veterem biduo venit. Illis diebus Carolus certum hominem ad senatum
misit, qui ei diceret suum regem nulli umquam homini supplica-
visse; scire tantum velle, utrum civitas amico in se an hostili animo
esset. Ad ea princeps ita respondit: prudentium esse hominum
planeque sapientium aliorum interdum voluntati se permittere,
aliorum opem poscere, precari; illud in ipso esse, amicus ne an ini-
micus reipublicae velit esse. Is postea nuntius et Philippus, regis
legatus, una Venetiis discesserunt.

37   Florentini autem cum intellexissent Venetos cum pontifice ac
Ludovico reliquisque regibus consensisse, Carolumque Neapoli, ut
in Galliam rediret, discessisse, novas militum copias celeriter con-
scribere seseque praesidio communire coeperunt ut, si Carolus ea
vellet iter facere oppidumque ingredi, repellere illum possent. Statuerat enim civitas nullis iterum condicionibus esse regem moenibus recipiendum. Pontifice profecto Carolus Romam venit atque

of Cardinal Pietro Fregoso,[15] who had been the doge of Genoa, and sent to the city Fregoso, Obietto Fieschi and one of his captains, the count of Bresse [Philippe de Savoie], with 11 galleys remaining from his fleet. Leaving behind 8,000 cavalry and infantry to defend the Kingdom, he himself set out from Naples on 20 May with the rest of his army and began his journey.

The Venetians had supposed that things would fall out with 36 Charles as they in fact did—that when he heard about the treaty he would make haste to return to France—and so growing anxious about the pope's situation, they had already shortly before sent him another 500 light cavalry, the speediest they had, fetched from Albania and the Morea, for Alexander to make use of against every eventuality. As the king approached Rome, Alexander gathered the cardinals and Roman nobles and decided not to wait for him. Accompanied by 2,000 horse and 3,500 infantry, he left the city and in two days reached Orvieto. Charles sent one of his men to the Senate at this time to tell them that his king had never made supplication of any man, but that he merely wished to know whether the city regarded him as a friend or an enemy. To this the doge replied as follows: it was the custom of wise and prudent persons to entrust themselves on occasion to the will of others, and to ask or entreat their aid. It was up to him whether he wished to be a friend or an enemy of the Republic. This messenger and the king's ambassador Philippe de Commines afterwards left Venice together.

When the Florentines learned that the Venetians had joined 37 forces with the pope and Ludovico and the other rulers, and that Charles had departed from Naples to return to France, they quickly began to raise fresh troops and to strengthen their defenses, so that if Charles intended to make his way there and attack the town, they would be able to repel him. The city had decided that on no account would the king be received within the walls again. After the pope had left, Charles reached Rome and

ad Alexandrum legatos misit: velle se eum alloqui; plurimum
utriusque interesse sibi eius rei fieri potestatem. Colloquio non im-
petrato, Tuscanellam, in via Cassia oppidum, quod quidem magna
opposita ruricolarum manu Gallos intromittere noluerat, eius milites, itemque Fisconis fontem, vi ceperunt. Quod ubi senatus
cognovit, reipublicae socium, et quidem omnium dignitate principem, a Gallis violatum, bellique factum a Carolo initium in foederatos, eosque homines, cum intra fines imperii vel reipublicae
vel Ludovici venissent, a maleficio non temperaturos existimaret,[2]
praeter id quod in Gallia terrestrium copiarum comparabatur, decrevit uti Antonius, ea cum classe quam civitas illis ipsis auxerat
diebus, ad Sasonem insulam accederet, ut in Apuliam traiciendi,
cum iuberetur, mora ei nulla fieret. Optimum enim esse statuerat,
si Galli furere inciperent, ea etiam a parte illos lacessere. Carolus
relicta Florentia, quae se praesidiis firmaverat, Pisas, deinde Lucam venit. Pontifex, qui Perusiam erat profectus, equitibus quos a
Venetis et Ludovico acceperat reverti iussis, Romam rediit.

38   Haec dum agerentur, Aloisius, princeps Genabensium, Astae a
Carolo relictus, Salassis adiuvantibus, tum e Gallia transalpina
atque ab Helvetiis milite celeriter accersito, vastatis Ludovici finibus, transmisso furtim Pado flumine, Novariam per proditionem
cepit. Erat eo in oppido civis, cuius fratris fundos, valde quidem
fructuosos, Ludovicus post eius mortem dolo malo suorum cuipiam addixerat, ipso ad sepulcrum in iudicium sisti iusso. Is, fra-
ternos ulciscendi manes studio, milites Aloisianos, reclusis bene
mane portis, intra moenia recepit. Ita Galli apertius eodem tem-

sent ambassadors to Alexander to say that he wished to speak to him, and that it was very much in both their interests that he should have a chance to do so. When the meeting was declined, his soldiers took Toscanella by force of arms, a town on the Via Cassia where a great horde of peasants had opposed the entry of the French, and Montefiascone too was taken. The Senate got to hear of this attack by the French on their ally (indeed the chief of all their allies in terms of the position he occupied) and realized that Charles had begun hostilities against the League. They judged that the French would not hold themselves back from further injury once they had entered their own dominions or Ludovico's, and so in addition to the land forces being assembled in Lombardy, they ordered Antonio Grimani to go to the island of Saseno[16] with the fleet, lately augmented by the Republic, with the idea that he would face no delays in crossing into Apulia when the order came: they had decided that if the French rage was unleashed on them, it would be best to attack them from that direction as well. Florence having strengthened its defenses, Charles left it aside, and made for Pisa and then Lucca. The pope, who had set out for Perugia, told the cavalry which he had been given by the Venetians and Ludovico to turn back, and he returned to Rome.

Meanwhile Louis, Duke of Orleans, whom Charles had left behind at Asti, laid waste to Ludovico's territory with the aid of the people of Saluzzo and with soldiers fetched quickly from France and Switzerland. Crossing the Po by stealth, he captured Novara by means of a traitor within. There was in that town a citizen whose brother's extremely fertile farms Ludovico had fraudulently made over to one of his own men following the brother's death, the citizen himself being ordered to stand trial at the burial. Keen to avenge his brother's shade, he opened the gates very early in the morning and let Louis' soldiers inside the walls. In this way the

38

pore alterius regnum socii reipublicae invadere ac priores bellum gerere coeperunt.

39   Illis ipsis diebus patres consulto senatu decreverunt uti quina milia Italorum equitum nova conscriberentur; bina milia ex Epiro Graeciaque, praeter illos qui imperati iam erant, accerserentur. Francisco autem, Mantuanorum principi, senatus consultum prius in annos quattuor renovatum est, stipendiaque uberiora consti- tuta. Tum scriptus una Rodulfus eius patruus. Scriptus etiam ante eos quidem menses Guidus Ubaldus Feltrius, qui regnum in Me- taurensibus obtinebat, cum equitibus quadringentis septuaginta; illis autem diebus Hannibal Bentivolus, Ioannis filius, cum qua- dringentis, et Paulus Manfronius Vicetinus, qui Neapolitano in regno tunc erat, cum ducentis; equitesque ab Epiro Acarnaniaque ad litus Venetum advecti circiter mille. Exercitu deinde lustrato, milites equitesque in fines Brixianorum iussi procedere; creatique legati Malchio Trivisanus, Lucas Pisanus ad exercitum profecti sunt. Senatus etiam scriba Bononiam missus, qui Ioannem Benti- volum in officio contineret. Itaque cum rex paulo post ad eum mi- sisset, petens ut itineris per eius fines oppidumque faciendi facul- tas sibi fieret, impetrare nihil potuit. Auri praeterea quingentae librae Ludovico petenti mutuo a senatu datae, deinde etiam tre- centae.

40   Post haec senatus consultum factum est uti militum in Gallia et Venetia quina milia imperarentur, ex Helvetiorum pagis bina milia accerserentur; qui autem iam tum pedites equitesque convenissent, ii omnes in Parmensem agrum mitterentur. Neque multo post alio senatus consulto Franciscus imperator dictus est, eique res milita- ris permissa. Praefectus etiam Graecis equitibus Bernardus Conta-

French began simultaneously to invade the realm of another Venetian ally and to take the initiative in making war.

In the same period the Signoria resolved by decree of the Senate that 5,000 cavalry should be newly recruited among the Italians, and that 2,000 should be fetched from Albania and Greece, beyond those that had already been ordered. The Senate's existing agreement[17] with Francesco Gonzaga, the Marquis of Mantua, was renewed for four years, and at a higher rate of pay. His uncle Rodolfo was recruited with him at the time. Also recruited, actually somewhat earlier, was Guidobaldo da Montefeltro, who held the duchy of Urbino, with his 470 cavalry, and Annibale Bentivoglio, son of Giovanni, and Paolo Manfrone of Vicenza, who was then in the Kingdom of Naples, were also taken into service at this time, with 400 and 200 horse respectively. About 1,000 cavalry were brought to the Lido of Venice from Albania and Acarnania. Once the troops had been passed in review, the foot soldiers and cavalry were ordered to proceed to the territory of Brescia, and Melchiorre Trevisan and Luca Pisani, appointed proveditors, set out to join the army. A secretary of the Senate was also sent to Bologna to ensure that Giovanni Bentivoglio observed his obligations. In consequence, when a little later the king sent word to him to ask for permission to march through his territory and town, he was unable to prevail upon him. Besides that, the Senate made a loan of 500 gold pounds to Ludovico il Moro at his request, and later another 300.

A decree of the Senate was made that 5,000 of the foot soldiers in Lombardy and the Veneto should be mobilized, and 2,000 more levied from the Swiss cantons. The infantry and cavalry already assembled were to be sent into the countryside of Parma. Soon afterwards Francesco Gonzaga was named captain-general by another senatorial decree and the conduct of the war entrusted to him, while Bernardo Contarini was appointed captain of the stradiots. The Republic's standard was then officially sent to

renus datus; tum vexillum imperatorium publice Francisco missum. Qui, facto ad Ollium flumen ponte, exercitum traduxit; et firmato munitionibus ponte ab ea ripa quae in Cremonensi agro est, alterum pontem in Pado flumine navibus imposuit, atque ex utraque ripa fossa et vallo aggereque praealto muniit. Tum exercitus in Parmensem est agrum traductus. Eius rei litteris acceptis, imperator a senatu iussus est: si Galli, dum redeunt, ei molestiam exhibeant, ipse autem sine reipublicae incommodo posse id fieri videat, in eos impetum faciat; sin res in angusto sit, proelio abstineat suoque se loco atque milites contineat; quod si pacati iter faciant, nihil eis noceat, sed sinat intactos discedere.

41   Eo accepto nuntio, imperator, ad Tari fluminis pontem ducto exercitu, qui pons abest a Parma oppido passuum milia quattuor, castra posuit. Cumque eo Ludovici equites bis mille, milites totidem Ioanne Francisco Severinate duce convenissent, exercitum traduxit; atque ad Oppianicum vicum, qua Gallis erat iter faciendum, in ipsa Tari fluminis ripa, quod pedibus transmitti poterat (neque enim ripas praealtas habebat), consedit, non omnino pleno exercitu, quod non omnes qui exspectabantur erantque iam in itinere equites peditesque convenerant. Reliquae Ludovici copiae apud Novariam distinebantur. Ad quem quidem, a senatu petentem ut Graecos equites ei mitteret, quibus eo bello uti posset, senatus Bernardo Contareno praefecto sexcentos misit.

42   Rex Luca profectus per Apennini iuga ad Apuanos, Ludovici municipium, venit. Oppidani, Ioannis Iacobi Triultii suasu, sese regi dediderunt; quos tamen paulo post eius milites pace fracta diripuerunt oppidumque incenderunt. Ex eo loco rex Triultium cum prima acie praemisit, qui, montano confecto itinere, se exspectaret

Francesco, who constructed a bridge over the Oglio and led his army across the river. Having secured the bridge with defense works on the Cremonese side of the river, he made a second bridge of pontoons over the Po, and fortified it on both banks with ditch and palisade and a very high rampart. Then the army was led across into the territory of Parma. Having informed the Senate of this by letter, the general was given instructions that if the French on their return caused him any difficulty, and he saw it could be done without harm to the Republic, he should attack them, but if the situation was dangerous, he should hold off from battle and keep himself and his soldiers where they were. If again the French were proceeding peaceably, he should not attack them but allow them to leave unharmed.

On receipt of this message the captain-general led his army to   41
the bridge over the river Taro, which is four miles from Parma, and pitched camp. When Ludovico's 2,000 cavalry and an equal number of foot soldiers had assembled there under the leadership of Gianfrancesco da Sanseverino, he led the army across. The village of Oppiano, where the route of the French lay, actually lies on the Taro. As the river did not have very steep banks, it could be crossed on foot, and there Gonzaga halted with his army, still a little under strength because not all the cavalry and foot soldiers which were expected and which were already on the march had yet come together. The rest of Ludovico's troops were kept back near Novara. When Ludovico asked the Senate to send him stradiots to use in the war, the Senate sent him 600 under the command of Bernardo Contarini.

The king set out from Lucca across the Apennine hills and   42
came to Pontremoli, a town belonging to Ludovico.[18] At the urging of Giangiacomo Trivulzio, the townspeople surrendered to the king, though a little later his soldiers broke the truce, plundered them and set fire to the town. From that place the king sent Trivulzio on ahead with the first column, to wait for him when the

exploratoresque mitteret, ut quid hostes molirentur scire posset. Interim imperator, praemissis equitibus atque militibus quot visum est ad Gerulam vicum, qui a Foro Novii abest passuum milia tria, uti regis itinera cognoscerent locumque castris caperent, postridie eius diei mane cum reliquis copiis omnibus eo venit. Erat autem universus exercitus equitum ad duodecim milia, militum prope altera totidem. Ibi cum esset imperator, a speculatoribus certior factus est Triultium, cum equitum cataphractorum et militum Helvetiorum manu praemissum, e iugis in planitiem ad Forum Novii descendere. Ille autem, ut postea cognitum est, vicum illum magnopere opportunum, in quo se regiae copiae confirmarent atque ab Apennini itinere reficerent, capere volebat eoque partem suorum praeire iusserat; ipse cum reliquis se, ut sequeretur, comparabat.

43   Ea intellecta re, imperator Graecos equites sexcentos praemisit, qui eos impedirent; ipse cum equitum firmiorum agmine illis praesidio est subsecutus. Graeci, velocitate sua usi, ubi primos venientes conspexerunt, in eos impetu facto proelioque commisso, universos reppulerunt; repulsos usque ad castrorum munitiones consecuti, complures eorum occiderunt, complures captivos fecerunt, uno suorum tantummodo amisso, quem parvi tormenti pila e vallo missa traiecerat. Eo mortuo captivos prope omnes interfecerunt, capitaque abscissa in castra revertentes attulerunt circiter quadraginta. Triultius, sibi suisque veritus, extremum in iugum sese recepit, regemque ibi triduum exspectans est commoratus. Quo si tempore Venetus illum adortus esset, ea se manu defendere non potuisset; quo capto reliquum exercitum expugnare haud maximi negotii fuisset.

44   Ea re ab imperatore atque ab legatis et principibus iactata, quod existimabant, si primam aciem proelio vicissent, Carolum reli-

march through the mountains was accomplished, and to send out scouts to find out what the enemy was up to. Meanwhile the captain-general sent forward as many cavalry and foot soldiers as he thought necessary to the village of Giarola, three miles from Fornovo, to discover what route the king was taking and to pick a site for the camp, and there he arrived with all the rest of his troops on the morning of the following day. His whole army amounted to about 12,000 cavalry and almost as many foot soldiers. When the captain-general got there, he heard from the scouts that Trivulzio had been sent on ahead with a troop of heavy cavalry and Swiss infantry and was descending from the heights to the plain near Fornovo. But it was later learned that Trivulzio wanted to take the village as a place ideally suited for the king's troops to gather their strength and recover from the Apennine march. He had ordered part of his men to go there as an advance party while he prepared to follow with the rest.

When he learned this, Gonzaga sent on ahead 600 stradiots 43 to obstruct their passage, and he himself followed with a column of his stronger cavalry to protect them. Using their speed, the stradiots charged when they saw the first ones coming, engaged them in battle and drove them all back. Pursuing them in their flight all the way to the camp's defenses, they slew a good number of them and took a good number captive, losing only one of their own, struck by the ball of a light cannon fired from the rampart. When he died, they killed almost all the captives, and returned to camp with about 40 of their severed heads. Trivulzio, fearing for himself and his men, retreated onto the far ridge, and he stayed there for three days awaiting the arrival of the king. Had Gonzaga attacked him then, he would not have been able to defend himself with the force he had, and with Trivulzio taken, there would have been no great difficulty in defeating the rest of the army.

The situation was discussed by the captain-general with the 44 proveditors and captains in the field. Reckoning that if they de-

quasque copias Lucam reversuras seque in tutum recepturas, ne
qua eos manus elabi effugereque posset, ab illo aggrediendo desti-
terunt. Quamquam postea fuere qui crederent Severinatem, qui
eius consilii princeps fuerat, non eam ob causam de qua dixi, sed
propterea quod ex Ludovici praescripto regi magnum fieri detrimentum nolebat, ne civitatis ex eo Venetae nomen existimatioque
augeretur, summopere in concilio, id ne fieret, obstitisse. Civitas
interea, cum intellexisset regem magno animo in Venetos impetum
facturum, quos imparatos adhuc plurimis ab rebus esse audierat,
permota largitiones in sacrarum virginum collegia precesque ad
omnia templa fieri iussit, votaque pro salute patriae publice suscepta sunt.

45   Rex triduum illud, tormentis bellicis ex aere magni ponderis
impeditissimis itineribus per invia atque abrupta montium convehendis moratus, non iis modo quae priore itione secum habuit,
sed illis etiam quae cum reliquo exercitu in Flaminiam praemise-
rat, cum omnibus copiis Forum Novii ante meridiem se contulit.
Eo die remissi Graeci equites usque ad regis castra compluribus
cum Gallorum capitibus ad imperatorem redierunt. E Foro autem
Novii missus tubicen a Philippo Argentonio, qui regis nomine itineris propter castra faciendi facultatem ab legatis peteret, ea non
impetrata, quod legati dicerent, nisi rex capta ab se atque suis sociorum reipublicae oppida restitueret, se id non concessuros, ad regem reversus spem pacis omnem sustulit.

46   Ea intellecta res magnum attulit Gallis timorem, qui e collibus
castra Veneta prospexerant in amplissimum tabernaculis porrecta
campi spatium; visumque eis est, tantis oppositis hostium copiis,

feated Charles' forward lines in battle, he would turn back to Lucca with the rest of his troops and retire to safety, they stopped attacking him, so as to prevent any units from slipping through their fingers and escaping. Though afterwards there were those who believed that Gianfrancesco da Sanseverino, who took a leading part in the discussion, strongly opposed the action in council,[19] not for the reason I mentioned, but because on Ludovico's instructions he did not want any great harm to come to the king, in case the renown and repute of Venice should be enhanced on that account. Meanwhile, when the city learned that the king was going to make a spirited onslaught on the Venetians, whom they had heard to be still unprepared in many respects, they were greatly disturbed and ordered alms to be given to the female convents and prayers said in every church, and public vows were undertaken for the salvation of the homeland.

Though the king had been delayed for those three days by having to convey his heavy bronze artillery by the most difficult of routes through the sheer and trackless mountains[20] (not only the artillery pieces which he had with him on his earlier passage, but also those which he had sent on ahead into Romagna with the rest of the army), before noon he made his way to Fornovo with his entire force. On that day the stradiots were sent back to the king's camp and returned to Gonzaga with a great number of French heads. Philippe de Commines sent an army trumpeter out from Fornovo to ask the proveditors in the king's name for permission to march past their camp. The request was declined, the proveditors saying that they would not grant it unless the king restored the towns of the Republic's allies which he and his men had taken, and so the trumpeter returned to the king, and all hope of peace was gone. 45

A great fear seized the French when they learned of this, for they looked out from the hills over a Venetian camp whose tents covered a great stretch of the plain below, and it seemed to them that 46

rem ipsorum in angusto esse. Itaque vulgo qui sapientiores erant tribuni ducesque magis magisque regi sibique verebantur, gravissimumque omnibus impendere casum atque periculum arbitrabantur. Qui quidem timor ea quae secuta est nocte auctus conduplicatusque est. Magnae enim pluviae ingentiaque tonitrua et crebrae atque terrificae coruscationes fuerunt, ut caelum prope discedere videretur, ultimamque plurimi sibi noctem illam fore, ea deorum immortalium quasi denuntiatione moniti, crederent. Solet autem fere semper accidere ut, cum semel vehemens aliquis mentes hominum incessit timor, etiam iis quae timenda non sunt animi eorum magnopere perturbentur. Quam ob rem cum parum in somno, multum in consiliis inter se fuissent, orta vix luce, qui fuit dies pridie Nonas[3] Iulias, Caroli praefecti aciem instruxerunt atque iter facere coeperunt.

47 Interim, consultis legatis principibusque reliquis quidnam esset potissimum agendum, legatis proelium dissuadentibus, cum propter senatus consultum, de quo supra dictum est, tum vero etiam quod complures equitum turmae militumque centuriae neque dum venerant (nam et Pandulfus Ariminensium et Ioannes Pisaurensium principes, et Paulus Manfronius, cum sua quisque cataphractorum equitum copia, innumerique milites exspectabantur), tandem Gallos aggredi, qui reipublicae sociorum oppida cepissent atque incendissent, proeliumque committere placuit.

48 Erant Gallorum copiae tres in acies instructae; quarum in priore magnam spem duces habebant, quod eam et numero equitum ac militum et robore munierant eique addiderant quatercentos ex cohorte regia eorum qui sagittis in equo utebantur; quos quattuor milibus Helvetiorum militibus, quibus maxime confidebant, immiscuerunt. In media erat acie rex, eaque prope omnis Galliae nobilitas continebatur. Ab postremae laevo latere impedi-

their situation was critical when they had such a huge enemy force
to contend with. And so the more prudent of their officers and
captains began generally to fear for themselves and the king,
thinking that grievous disaster and peril threatened them all.
Their fear was increased and redoubled by the night that followed:
there were heavy rains, prodigious thunder and frequent terrible
lightning, so that it almost seemed the sky was splitting open.
Many believed that it was effectively a warning from Almighty
God and that this would be their last night. It almost always happens that once some powerful fear has invaded the minds of men,
their spirits are thrown into turmoil even by things not in themselves fearful. And so it came about that after little sleep and much
discussion among themselves, Charles' commanders drew up their
formation and set out on their march at the crack of dawn on 6
July.[21]

Meanwhile in consultations among the proveditors and the   47
other officers as to the best course of action, the proveditors coun-
selled against a battle, not only because of the Senate decree I
mentioned above, but also because a good number of the cavalry
squadrons and infantry companies had not yet arrived — they were
waiting for Pandolfo Malatesta, lord of Rimini, Giovanni Sforza,
lord of Pesaro, and Paolo Manfrone, each with his own force of
heavy cavalry, besides countless foot soldiers — but it was finally
decided to attack the French for having taken and burned towns of
the allies, and to engage them in battle.

The French forces were drawn up in three columns. In the first   48
of them the captains had great hopes, because they had reinforced
it with the pick of their cavalry and infantry units, and had added
from the royal guard 400 mounted crossbowmen and interspersed
among them 4,000 Swiss soldiers, in whom they had great confidence. In the middle column was the king with almost the entire
nobility of France. On the left of the last column followed the bag-
gage-train. Artillery was positioned in front of all the columns.

menta sequebantur; tormenta omnibus aciebus erant praeposita; eaeque acies, non ita magno inter se relicto spatio constipatae, celeriter, uti si possent Venetos effugerent, vadebant. Interea nuntii ad Venetorum castra, qui pacem ab legatis peterent, fallendi gratia mittebantur. Ubi id imperatori nuntiatum est, militibus ut arma caperent imperavit. Ipse deinde, armato exercitu et insessis equis, copias omnes ita disposuit, ut ex iis novem acies efficeret; quarum quinque equitum cataphractorum essent, tres militum, equitum levis armaturae una; quae res impetum exercitus imminuit; nulla enim earum satis virium ad hostem propellendum habebat.

49   Erat inter utrumque exercitum Tarus, de quo dictum est, flumen, quod ea nocte creverat; eius autem vallis planities, impedita non ripis modo fluminis, sed glarea etiam grandibusque saxis, tum et virgultis et, quod magnae pluviae fuerant, lubrico et lacunoso caeno, ut inaequabilem et difficilem transitum daret. Gallorum prima acies cum ante castra Veneta pervenisset, armari milites conspicata, magnum in eos pilarum ferrearum numerum tormentis immisit; quas tamen prope omnes supra militum capita vis ignis impetusque abstulit, ne magnopere nocerent; percommodeque ea in re accidit, quod tum caelum erat pluvium, ut sua Galli tormenta, quorum magnum numerum habebant, amplius exercere non potuerint. Tum vero imperator, moras omnes posthabendas ratus, magno ipse animo et rei bene gerendae fiduciae pleno, quem etiam provehebat adolescentia, instructo exercitu constitutoque quid fieri oporteret, ac permissa patruo reliquas acies submittendi potestate, signo pugnae dato, et transmisso pedibus flumine, regis exercitum, qui quidem mille passuum iter eoque amplius iam

Packed close together with no great space between them, these columns proceeded at quick march so as to escape the Venetians, if
that were possible. In the meantime, in an attempt to deceive
them, messengers were sent to the Venetian camp to sue for peace
with the proveditors. When the captain-general learned of it, he
ordered his soldiers to arm themselves. With the men armed and
the horses mounted, Gonzaga then disposed his entire force in
such a way as to make nine battle-formations, five of them of
heavy cavalry, three of infantry, and one of light cavalry. This arrangement weakened the fighting power of the army, since none of
them by itself had sufficient strength to fend off the enemy.

Between the two armies was the river Taro mentioned above, 49
which had become swollen overnight. The plain of the Taro valley
was not easily traversed, owing not only to the banks of the river
but to pebbles and large rocks too, also to the scrub that covered it
and the slippery mud full of puddles that followed the heavy rains,
so that progress was patchy and difficult. When the first column
of the French arrived in front of the Venetian camp and saw the
soldiers arming themselves, they fired a large number of iron cannonballs at them, almost all of which, however, were carried away
over the heads of the soldiers by the strength of the discharge, and
no great injury resulted. It turned out very happily for the Venetians that the weather was wet at the time, and the French were
unable to make further use of the great quantity of artillery they
had with them. But then the captain-general, a man of great courage and completely confident in the success of his action, something which his youth also encouraged, reckoned that they should
delay no further. With his army all ready and the decision made as
to how to proceed, he gave his uncle [Rodolfo Gonzaga] authority
to send the other formations as reinforcement, and gave the signal
for battle. Crossing the river on foot, he began to pursue at full
speed the king's army, which had already gone ahead a mile or
more. When he had come roughly to the middle of the army, he

praecesserat, citato gradu insequi coepit; eumque prope medium
assecutus, in regis aciem, quae se converterat, impetum fecit.

50   Proelio acriter commisso cum fortissime ab utrisque pugnare-
tur, Rodulfus, acie una maxima atque plenissima, cui Antonius
Feltrius, Guidi Ubaldi frater nothus, praeerat, iussa consistere, altera castris praesidio esse, neque se loco ambas movere, donec ipse
eas vocet, imperatorem subsecutus, cum secunda acie in Gallorum
globum sese iniecit, acerrimeque pugnans eum disiecit; neque imperatori modo auxilium peropportune attulit, cum illius acie se
coniungens, sed magnum etiam addidit suo adventu eius militibus
animum. Itaque ambae acies parvo temporis spatio magnum Gallorum numerum occiderunt, magnum ex suis amiserunt; rex cum
paucis relictus, admonitus a suis, pugnantibus se subripuit. Eodem fere tempore acies tertia, cui Severinas praeerat, primam Gallorum aciem consecuta, pedem statim rettulit, non ausa vel potius
non iussa progredi. Omnibus autem equitum aciebus quae ad regis
exercitum contenderunt idem fere perincommode accidit, ut et flumine transeundo et ripis superandis et saxis pervadendis et virgultis ac caenosa via conficienda, multa etiam pluvia, non solum ordi-
nes servari non potuerint, sed complures prolaberentur, complures
se medio itinere continerent, multi aliorsum flecterent; ut parva
eorum pars proelio interfuerit. Nam milites plerique omnes, exceptis ducentis, Genua Veneto duce, paucisque ex imperatoris comitatu, qui equitibus interiecti eius latus muniebant, pugnam de-
trectaverunt.

51   At vero Itali equites levis armaturae, quos una cum Graecis imperator iusserat ab hostium tergo laevum latus montium capere

launched an attack on the king's column, which had turned about to face him.

Battle was raging fiercely, with extremely hard fighting on both 50 sides, when Rodolfo Gonzaga ordered one of the units to stay where it was (the largest formation, and one at full strength, under the command of Antonio da Montefeltro, illegitimate brother of Guidobaldo), and a second to keep watch over the camp. Neither was to move from its position until he gave the word. Accompanied by the second unit, he followed the captain-general, threw himself upon the massed French troops, and after fierce fighting put them to flight. Rodolfo not only brought very opportune assistance to the captain-general by joining up with his battle-unit, but his arrival also greatly heartened the general's soldiers. In a short space of time the two units slew a great number of the French, but lost a great number of their own. The king, who remained behind with a few retainers, was warned by his men and stole away from the fighting. At about the same time, the third formation, under the command of Gianfrancesco da Sanseverino, caught up with the leading French column, but immediately retreated, as they did not dare, or rather, had not been ordered, to proceed. All the cavalry units which were making for the king's army, on the other hand, suffered pretty much the same major reverse, that when they were crossing the river or climbing the banks, or passing through rocky terrain or scrubland, or traveling along the muddy roads, and in heavy rain too, they were not only unable to keep formation but some of them took a tumble, some stopped in mid-course, while many made off elsewhere, so that few of them actually took part in the battle. For almost all the soldiers shirked combat, except for 200 under the command of Genova Veneziano, and a few of the captain-general's company who were interspersed with the cavalry and protecting his flank.

The Italian light cavalry had been ordered by the captain- 51 general to seize, in concert with the stradiots, the left flank of the

atque ab latere adverso in eos impetum facere, ubi impedimenta
conspexerunt, in ea spretis imperiis prope omnes convolaverunt,
custodibusque aliquot occisis, ea rapere atque abducere contenderunt; quos Graeci equites imitati idem fecerunt, exceptis eorum
ducibus, qui cum paucis ad hostes lacessendos contenderunt. Ea
res magna ex parte reipublicae victoriam interpellavit. Nam si in
hostium acies ab latere, ut debebant eratque eis imperatum, ii omnes impetum fecissent, Galli se pugnae subducere sine certa clade
non potuissent. Tametsi alia etiam ex parte casus adiumento atque
praesidio Gallis fuit. Duae enim equitum acies, quem ad modum
Rodulfus imperaverat ne se loco moverent, proelio non interfue-
runt, exspectantes quam is in partem eas vocaret. Ille autem a Gallis interfectus fuerat. Ita qui repulsi atque fracti fugae se mandare
cogitabant, restituto ab reliquis aciebus quae regi auxilio venerant
proelio, se continuerunt. Pugnatum igitur est acriter, ut ante dictum est, ab utrisque, caedesque ingens facta; eoque res horae spatio deducta, ut, neutris plane victoribus, defessis potius pugnando
quam permittentibus Venetis, Galli se celeriter subriperent; ac magna impedimentorum parte direpta, cumque iis regio tentorio et
cubiculo et supellectili sacra qua rex in templo utebatur, signisque
militaribus aliquot amissis, tantum itineris, quantum lassitudine
atque vulneribus confecti poterant, contenderent; noctemque illam
magno cum timore sub dio sine tabernaculis, sine castris exigerent.

52 Imperator sua in castra rediit. Desiderati sunt ex Venetis circiter mille quingenti; quorum non minimam quidem partem, vel
iniquitate loci detentam et vagam, vel acceptis vulneribus aut suff-
ossis equis prolapsam et morantem, calones lixaeque Galli,

mountain at the enemy's rear, and to launch an attack on them
from the opposite side. But when they caught sight of the bag-
gage-train, almost all of them disregarded their orders and flocked
to it: they killed some of the guards, and pressed forward to lay
their hands on the baggage and carry it off. The stradiots followed
their lead and did likewise, except for their officers, who with a
few men exerted themselves to harass the enemy. This circumstance was chiefly responsible for preventing the Republic's victory,
for if they had all made a flank attack on the enemy columns, as
they should have and as they had been ordered, the French would
not have been able to withdraw from the fight without certain defeat. Nonetheless, a further chance came to the aid and succor of
the French. Since Rodolfo had commanded them not to move
from their positions, two of the cavalry formations took no part in
the battle as they waited to see where he would summon them.
But Rodolfo had been killed by the French. So it happened that
those Frenchmen who had been beaten back and broken and were
thinking of taking to flight, held their ground when the fortunes
of the battle were retrieved by the remaining units which had
come to the aid of the king. Fierce fighting therefore ensued on
both sides, as I mentioned above, and massive slaughter. In the
space of an hour things had come to a point where, with no clear
victor, the French were able to quickly withdraw, the Venetians not
so much allowing them to do so as simply worn out with fighting.
With much of the baggage plundered (including the king's tent,
his bedchamber and the liturgical articles he used in church),[22]
and with a number of their standards lost, the French marched as
far as their exhaustion from fatigue and wounds allowed, and
spent the night in great fear under an open sky, with no tents and
no camp.

The captain-general made his way back to his camp. The Vene- 52
tians had suffered about 1,500 casualties. A substantial number
had been found wandering by the French servants and camp-

quorum permagnus erat numerus, qui ab equitatu leviore disiecti se ad acies referebant, desertos a reliquis militibus plures singulos adorti, securibus interfecerant. Ex iis qui fortiter pugnantes interierunt fuere, praeter Rodulfum, imperatoris praefectus militum Ranutius Farnesius Romanus, claro loco natus, vir magna virtute, Alexandri Farnesii, illius qui postea, pontifex maximus creatus, Paulus tertius dictus est, patruelis frater; et familiaris imperatoris comitatus parte plus media; tum praefecti equitum viri fortissimi duodecim, centuriones quattuor. Bernardinus autem Montonius, multis vulneribus acceptis, equo deiectus, inter caesorum corpora repertus, per suorum umeros relatus in castra servatusque est.

53   In ipso vero proelio Nicolaus Ursinus, quem Nolae captum a Gallis dixeramus, et rex custodiri iusserat, pugnantibus omnibus elapsus, ad legatos Venetos contendit; suamque operam reipublicae pollicitus, Gallos prope fractos esse, eos, si quaevis una ipsorum acies insequatur, terga daturos confirmans, contestansque deos id ut legati mandarent, magnopere suadebat; qui, perculso temere exercitu, militibusque aut dispersis aut pedem referentibus, eam rem aggredi non sunt ausi. Ex Gallis interfecti sunt ad mille, atque ex iis dux vigilum regis, itemque sagittariorum, et magistratus is quem ipsi Magnum Maressalem appellant, aliique praefecti militum decem; tum nothus Boius, primae fere apud regem auctoritatis et magni inter Gallos nominis, vulnere accepto, duoque magnorum principum liberi, et sacerdos regius aliique captivi facti,

followers after getting stuck in the rough terrain, or collapsed and immobilised by their wounds or their horses disemboweled, and were killed by them with axes. These camp-followers had been scattered by the light cavalry and were returning to their units in great numbers, attacking en masse individuals deserted by the other soldiers. Besides Rodolfo, among those who died fighting bravely were Ranuccio Farnese of Rome, Francesco Gonzaga's captain of infantry, high born and a man of great courage, a cousin of the Alessandro Farnese who was later elected Pope Paul III, and more than half of the captain-general's personal company, twelve brave cavalry officers, and four of infantry. Bernardino [Fortebraccio] da Montone, on the other hand, who had been thrown from his horse after taking many wounds and found among the bodies of the slain, was carried back into camp on the shoulders of his men and saved from death.

It was in this very battle that Niccolò Orsini, whom I mentioned as having been captured by the French at Nola, and whom the king had ordered kept under guard, slipped away while everyone else was fighting. He hastened to the Venetian proveditors and promised his assistance to the Republic, asserting and calling God to witness that the French had almost been broken, and that if any single unit of theirs gave chase, the French would turn and run. He strongly urged the proveditors to give the orders to do so, but since the army was demoralised and the soldiers were either dispersed or returning to base, they did not dare embark on such an action. About 1,000 of the French were killed, and among them the captain of the king's bodyguard, and the captain of the crossbowmen too, and the officer they call the Grand Maréchal, and ten other infantry officers. Among the prisoners were the Bastard of Bourbon, taken following a wound (perhaps the man of greatest influence with the king, and famous among the French), two sons of great princes, the royal chaplain, and others, while not

53

cum eo proelio ex Venetorum exercitu nemo vivus in hostium potestatem venisset.

54   Postero die rex ante lucem, igne plurimo facto, ut eius copiae ibi
esse viderentur, sine ullo strepitu abiit; celeritateque usus, quam
longissime potuit antecessit. Veneti mane consequi regem cum vellent, Taro flumine, quod ea nocte creverat, impediti restiterunt.
Tum Severinas, qui proelio cum suis abstinuerat, imperatori legatisque sese obtulit: si sibi equitatum leviorem traderent, se regem
remoraturum, dum ipsi cum reliquo exercitu veniant. Re impetrata, cum equitibus mille quingentis Italis profectus, longiore itinere per occasionem suscepto, quod flumen crevisset, consequendi
regem eo die volens tempus omisit. Quem postea cum esset consecutus, ei dux ministerque itineris potius quam morator fuit Astam
prope usque; ut id quod petierat ab imperatore legatisque propterea videretur petiisse, ut illum in tuto sisteret. Id ab eo de Ludovici
sententia esse susceptum ea res indicio fuit, quod Bernardo Contareno, ab Ludovico petenti uti se cum suo equitatu extremum regis agmen aggredi sineret, Ludovicus non permisit.

55   Eo biduo magnus equitum conscriptorum, multo maior militum numerus ad exercitum Venetorum venit. Imperator, subsi-
dente flumine cum exercitu profectus, cum rex bidui eum itinere
praecederet, consequendi regem facultate amissa, Graecos equites
levissimos sexcentos misit, qui eius agmen carperent, quaque possent, exercitui nocerent. Ii dum iter facerent, multa in via cadavera
Gallorum passim iacentia conspexerunt; ut plus etiam quam cre-
debatur exercitui regio esse illatum caedis appareret. Atque ii qui-

one man of the Venetian army came into the enemy's hands alive
in that battle.

Before dawn on the following day, the king had a great number   54
of fires lit so as to have it appear that his troops were still there
while he departed noiselessly, and putting on a turn of speed,
moved as far away from them as he could. In the morning, although the Venetians wanted to pursue the king, they were prevented by the river Taro, which had risen in the night, and so remained where they were. Then Gianfrancesco da Sanseverino,
whose men had taken no part in the battle, offered his services to
the captain-general and the proveditors: if they gave him the light
cavalry, he would delay the king until they arrived with the rest of
the army. His request granted, he set out with 1,500 Italian cavalry, and taking a rather lengthy route on the grounds that the
river was in spate, deliberately passed up the opportunity of catching up with the king that day. And when he did catch up with him
later on, he proved to be no hindrance but rather a guide and
helper on the king's journey, almost as far as Asti, so that it appeared that he had made his request of Gonzaga and the
proveditors simply in order to get the king to safety. That he did
this at Ludovico's bidding was indicated by the fact that when
Bernardo Contarini asked his permission to attack the king's rearguard with his cavalry, Ludovico refused to give it.

Over those two days a great number of conscript cavalry and an   55
even larger number of infantry reached the Venetian army. The
captain-general had set out with his army as the river subsided,
but since the king was two days' march ahead and there was no
chance of catching up with him, Gonzaga despatched 600 very
lightly armed stradiots to harry his lines and damage the army
wherever they could. While they were on their way, they noticed
many corpses of the French lying scattered about the road, so that
it appeared that even more casualties had been inflicted on the
king's army than had been previously thought. The cavalry moved

dem equites, postremum regis agmen celeritate consecuti, compluribus interfectis, praeda etiam facta ad imperatorem redierunt. Eo de proelio a senatu supplicatio decreta est; gratiaeque diis immortalibus actae, quod civitatem, magnopere suspensam tantarum rerum exspectatione, fuga hostium liberavissent; Nicolaoque Ursino auri librae decem dono datae.

56   Sed rege Carolo Neapoli profecto (ut paulisper ad superiora revertamur), Veneti, de classe regia in Liguriam missa, ut supra demonstratum est, certiores facti, suum hominem cum pecunia Genuam, ad naves onerarias, quibus ad mercaturam uti civitas privatim consuevit habetque in portu fere semper multas, militibus rebusque omnibus ad bellum propulsandum idoneis celeriter armandas, contendere iusserunt, cum Ludovicus item instrui naves longas aliquot ibidem iussisset. Pollicitae praeterea sunt, procurantibus patribus, foederatorum legationes Genuensium magistratui, ut libentius contra Gallos arma caperent, se curaturas effecturasque ut eis Florentinorum civitas Serezanam Serezanulamque ac Petram Sanctam in Apennino oppida restitueret; eiusque rei petentibus ipsis senatus praedem se dedit. Fuerant ea oppida complures ante annos Genuensium magistratus, qui publicae privataeque pecuniae quae in aerario vulgo deponitur praeest, ob eamque pecuniam dominis ternas centesimas quotannis solvit. Sed ab iis qui civitati tum praeerant pignoris nomine ad rempublicam Florentinorum pervenerunt, tercentum auri libris mutuo ab illa eis datis. Ea sibi reddi oppida civitas magnopere studebat; erantque illa ipsa quae Carolo tradere Petrus Medices pactus fuerat. Regis igitur classis, ad litora Genuensium appulsa, cui quidem etiam ex Apennini iugis rex equites aliquot peditesque Gallos quingentos auxilio miserat, totam illam oram quae ad orientem solem spectat

swiftly and caught up with the rearguard of the king's army. Having killed a fair number of them, and taken some booty as well, they made their way back to the general. The Senate decreed a public procession to mark the battle, and thanks were paid to Almighty God for liberating the city by putting the enemy to flight, after the great suspense which it had felt at the prospect of such momentous events, and Niccolò Orsini was given an award of 10 gold pounds.

But to go back in time for a moment, when the king left Naples, the Venetians learned (as I mentioned above) that he had sent a fleet to Liguria. They told their agent to hasten to Genoa with money to have merchant vessels quickly armed with soldiers and all the other things needed to prosecute a war, Ludovico too having ordered a number of galleys to be fitted out there. These merchant ships were generally used at Genoa for the purposes of private trade and the city nearly always had large numbers of them in port. At the instance of the Senate, the ambassadors of the League also made this promise to the Genoese authorities to encourage them to take up arms against the French: they would see to it that the state of Florence restored the Apennine towns of Sarzana, Sarzanella and Pietrasanta to them, and at their request the Senate offered itself as guarantor. Many years before, these towns had been in the possession of the magistracy of Genoa which supervises the public and private monies regularly deposited in the treasury,[23] paying out three per cent per annum to the depositors. But they passed to the Florentine Republic from those who ruled the city at the time, as security for a loan of 300 gold pounds. Genoa was very keen to have the towns returned — the very same towns, in fact, which Piero de' Medici had agreed to hand over to Charles. The king's fleet, then, put in at the Genoese shore, the king having sent in support from the Appenine heights some cavalry and 500 French infantry, and brought the whole shore to the east of Genoa [the Riviera di Levante] under his con-

56

in eius potestatem redegit, Portu Veneris excepto. Ita belli ab Carolo initium ea etiam ab regni parte in Venetorum socios est factum. Postremo cum Galli, Paulo et Obiecto ducibus, successu rerum elati, pedibus Genuam aggrederentur, civitas armata illos fudit fugavitque, eo ipso die quo rex ad flumen Tarum adverso cum Venetis proelio dimicavit.

57   Tum pridie Idus naves onerariae longaeque, maiori ex parte reipublicae instructae opibus, obsessam in portu Rapalo classem Gallicam Rapalique arcem expugnaverunt, navibus omnibus cum earum praefecto captis; quibus in navibus mulieres erant captivae permultae, virginesque sacrae aliquot suis e Caietae fanis abreptae atque violatae, aurumque item sacrum et argentum; ac fores aëneae portarum, affabre illae quidem factae magnoque comparatae pretio, quas arci Neapolitanae Galli detraxerant. Pauloque post Carretii principes, qui Finarium oppidum a Genuensibus acceptum obtinebant, Intemelium[4] oppidum, quod ad occidentem solem est, et Galli occupaverant, recuperaverunt; omnisque utrumque ora brevi ad Genuenses rediit. Atque haec quidem in Liguribus gesta sunt. Cumque ad Ludovicum signa Caroli regis quattuor, e Gallorum capta navibus, Genuensis civitas dono misisset, Ludovicus, magno reipublicae merito id se facere pronuntians, duo eorum legato apud se Veneto dedit. Eodem quoque Genuenses tempore legationem Venetias miserunt, quae senatui gratias ageret, quod ea, quae feliciter contra Gallos gesserant, eius liberalitate atque ductu, primo et initium et incrementum, postremo etiam exitum habuissent.

58   Imperator autem Clastidii cum esset, regem subsequens, Ludovico postulante, equites militesque ad bis mille Dertonam Alexandriamque senatus iussu praesidio misit. Eodem etiam petente ut respublica legatos ex principibus civitatis ad se duos mitteret, qui

trol, with the exception of Portovenere. So it was that Charles embarked on war against the League from that corner of his dominions too. When the French, buoyed up by their success, at length attacked Genoa by land under the leadership of Paolo Fregoso and Obietto Fieschi, the citizens took up arms and routed them, putting them to flight on the very day that the king fought the unsuccessful battle against the Venetians at the river Taro.

Then on 14 July the merchant vessels and galleys, which had been for the most part fitted out at the Republic's expense, overcame the French fleet, which was blockaded in the port of Rapallo, and took the fortress there as well. All the French ships were captured along with their commander, and in them were found a great many female prisoners and a number of nuns who had been carried off from their convents at Gaeta and raped, also ecclesiastical gold and silver, and bronze doorpanels, masterfully made and very expensive, which the French had removed from the castle at Naples. A little later the del Carretto princes, lords of the town of Finale Ligure which they had had from the Genoese, recovered Ventimiglia, which lies toward the west, and had been occupied by the French. In a short while the whole coast on either side of Genoa returned to the Genoese. When the city of Genoa sent Ludovico a present of four of King Charles' standards which had been seized from the French ships, Ludovico gave two of them to the Venetian ambassador at his court, declaring that he was doing so in recognition of the Republic's signal services in the war. At the same time, the Genoese also sent an embassy to Venice to thank the Senate, because their successful campaign against the French had begun and grown and in the end reached its happy outcome thanks to the Senate's liberality and leadership. 57

When Francesco Gonzaga, the captain-general, was at Casteggio in pursuit of the king, at the request of Ludovico and on the Senate's orders he sent to Tortona and Alessandria nearly 2,000 cavalry and infantry as garrisons. And when Ludovico fur- 58

secum rebus omnibus tam ambiguo tempore praeessent, uti sui cives omnesque homines cognoscerent ei se curae regnumque suum
esse, Lucam Zenum, Andream Venerium, legatos senatus creavit.
Ab iis legatione propter aetatem renuntiata, Marcus Georgius, Benedictus Sanutus ad id muneris eorum loco Mediolanum sunt ire
iussi. Inter haec senatus decrevit ut eorum qui fortiter atque
amanter ad flumen Tarum contra Gallos rempublicam gesserant
vel viventium vel mortuorum ratio haberetur. Itaque imperator
Rodulfi patrui equitatu stipendioque auctus est, nomenque ei clarius datum, ut latissime imperator appellaretur; praeterea dono
quotannis auri triginta librae constitutae, centumque in stipendium in praesentia missae. Auctus et Bernardino Montonio equitum numerus ad mille, sexque auri librae dono datae in annos singulos; quae quidem etiam nunc ad inutiles servato annos
ultimumque senium, et vitam modo producenti, pecunia penditur.
Nicolao item Nonio tum equitum Graecorum auctus numerus,
tum vero etiam stipis summa, qua in annos singulos a republica
donatus antea fuerat, amplior facta.

59   Rodulfi vero liberi in reipublicae fidem recepti, pensioque librarum auri decem victus annui nomine eis[5] data, decretumque uti
maribus singulis equitum turmae singulae praefectique earum at-
tribuantur, quoad ipsi exercere se per aetatem possint; feminis,
cum erunt nubiles, dos e pecunia publica pro earum gentisque nobilitate numeretur. Farnesii duobus liberis maribus equites quad-
ringenti, quos primo a republica stipendio pater eorum habuerat,
cum praefecto dati; dosque ampla feminis publice pollicita. Vin-
centii Corsii liberis patris equitatus datus; filiae quam unam reliquit dos auri librarum quadraginta[6] constituta; intereaque, dum fit

ther asked the Republic to send him two of their leading citizens as proveditors to take overall charge of things alongside him at such an uncertain time, Luca Zen and Andrea Venier were appointed to the posts by the Senate. They refused the commission on account of their age, however, and Marco Zorzi and Benedetto Sanudo were ordered to go to Milan and take up their duties instead. In the meantime the Senate decreed that those who had served the Republic with courage and devotion against the French at the Taro, whether living or dead, should receive recognition. And so the captain-general was additionally given the cavalry and pay of his uncle Rodolfo, and a more distinguished title with enhanced authority as captain-general.[24] On top of that, he was to be made an annual gift of 30 gold pounds,[25] and 100 were sent at once for his pay. As for Bernardino da Montone, the number of his cavalry was increased to 1,000, and 6 gold pounds were to be given him every year. The money is still paid to him to this day, though in extreme old age and of no use to the Republic, as he merely hangs on to life.[26] Again, Niccolò da Nona had not only the number of his stradiots increased, but the annual pension which the Republic granted him was raised too.

Rodolfo Gonzaga's children were taken under the protection of the Republic, and an annual pension of 10 gold pounds was given them to live on.[27] By decree of the Senate, each of the males was to be assigned a company of cavalry and a captain of horse, for as long as they were of an age to take part in the activity. The females of marriageable age were to be given a dowry from the public purse according to their rank and that of their family. To the two male children of Ranuccio Farnese were given the 400 cavalry which their father had had at his original engagement with the Republic, along with a captain of horse, and an ample dowry was promised for the daughters from the public purse. Their father's cavalry was given to the sons of Vincenzo Corso, and a dowry of 40 gold pounds was settled on his only daughter.[28] In the mean-

nubilis, in virginum sacrarum collegio uti victus publice subministretur, senatus consulto additum. Alexandri Beraldii Patavini equitatus Francisco fratri, qui cum illo ea in pugna fuerat vulneri-
busque acceptis superfuerat, et pensio annua, quae ei a
quaestoribus curabatur, attributa. Idem in Roberti Strotii item Patavini fratre superstite servatum. Litterae praeterea publice ad legatos datae: curarent ne quis qui bene de republica meritus esset ab
ipsis praeteriretur; quin de eo ad senatum scriberent; ex eorumque
litteris in complures compluriumque liberos fratresque senatus
pietas liberalitasque exstitit.

60   At vero interea rex, septimo post proelium die Astam ingressus,
fugae finem fecit, confecto cum timore ac labore viae, tum commeatus non omnino magna inopia exercitu. Nam ut sunt ad
conserendas manus proeliaque committenda Galli omnium prope
hominum paratissimi atque fortissimi, ita ad perferendos paulo
diutius labores inediamque tolerandam supra ceteros animus eorum mollis infirmusque est; omnisque illa ardens ac vehemens
brevi tempore virtus elanguescit atque restinguitur. Paucis post
diebus, edicto magistratuum Gallorum, Veneti Mediolanenses Li-
guresque omni e Gallia quae in imperio Caroli erat exules facti
sunt, poena iis qui recepissent constituta. Itaque Petrus Pascalicus
Venetus, qui Lutetiae Parisiorum philosophiae studiis sacrisque
litteris operam dabat, servili veste sese occultans, in Morinos aufugit.

61   Deinceps autem cum Ludovicus legatique Novariam omnes
copias adduxissent, hostesque crebris ex oppido excursionibus eos
lacesserent, secundiora cum iis fere semper Veneti proelia fecerunt;
quibus in omnibus Bernardi Contareni virtus egregia extitit. Postea vero quam communi consilio oppidum obsidione cingi placuit,

time, the decree added, until she was of marriageable age her life
in the convent was to be supported at public expense. The cavalry
of Alessandro Beraldo of Padua was assigned to his brother
Francesco, who had been with him in the battle and had survived
despite receiving wounds, along with the annual pension which
the treasurers had been paying to Alessandro. The same thing
happened with the surviving brother of Roberto Strozzi, also of
Padua. In addition a public letter was sent to the proveditors to
say that they should take pains not to overlook anyone who had
served the Republic well, and should write to the Senate about all
such cases. As a result of their letters, the Senate manifested its
liberality and sense of duty toward a good many men, and toward
the children and brothers of many others.[29]

Meanwhile the king entered Asti a week after the battle and   60
there called a halt to his retreat, his army worn out not only from
fear and the effort of the march but also from a certain want of
supplies. For while the French are of almost all mankind the readi-
est and bravest at engaging in close combat and joining battle, yet
their spirit is surpassingly weak and yielding when it comes to en-
during more protracted labors and tolerating hunger, and in a
short while all that fierce and ardent courage grows faint and cool.
A few days later a proclamation of the French authorities expelled
Venetians, Milanese and Genoese from France and all of Lombardy that was in Charles' hands, with penalties for those who
took them in. It was on this account that the Venetian Piero
Pasqualigo, who was studying philosophy and theology at Paris,
fled to Thérouanne disguised as a servant.

When, later on, Ludovico and the proveditors had taken their   61
entire force to Novara, and were being harassed by the enemy's
frequent sallies from the town, the Venetians almost always got
the better of them in the skirmishes, in all of which Bernardo
Contarini displayed his exceptional valor. But after the allies fixed
on a concerted plan to lay siege to the town, the king's kinsman

et Aloisius, regis propinquus, quique cum eo erant in oppido equites militesve numero ad milia octo, inopia frumenti laborare com-
meatusque coeperunt, quod ante hostium adventum eius rei nullam curam habuerant, missi ad eos furtim cum iumentis
frumentariis, equites regii ab eodem Contareno saepe intercepti,
saepe una cum illis ii qui ex oppido regiis equitibus subsidio venerant caesi fugatique sunt. Neque rex interim novas copias, ut Aloisium obsidione liberaret, e Galli cotidie postulare, accersere, scriptis ad suos magistratus atque ad uxorem litteris, intermittebat;
quas ad litteras illa se iam viros qui velint Alpes traicere omnino
nullos habere regi respondit, feminas viduas se permultas habere,
quarum viri in Italia periissent. Ab Helvetiis etiam per legatos
atque interpretes idem petebat; sed stipendiorum inopia, ne rem
conficeret, impediebatur. Quin etiam ea de causa ex Helvetiis quos
habebat milites centum, ex Germanis alteri totidem ad Venetos
transierunt. Tum vero ab iis suburbana aedificia incensa tormentaque muralia oppido propius admota; et obsessi modis omnibus
acrius premi coepit; quibus in rebus administrandis Nicolaus Ursinus, fistulae glande plumbea supra renes percussus, pro mortuo
sublatus atque in castra relatus est; neque postea ei bello interfuit.

62   Gallos igitur, qui obsidebantur, magis magisque in dies rerum
omnium egestas atque inopia premebat, ut equis in escam uti co-
gerentur, compluresque corruptis farinis aut pane furfuraceo ves-
centes, tum aquae potu, quo Galli Germanique minime omnium
uti assolent, interirent. Percusserat autem paulo antea nummum
aereum Aloisius, cum pecunia eum defecisset, qui pro argenteo
polleret. Haec cum crebris occulte nuntiis litterisque regi ab Aloisio significarentur, quorum plerique ab hostibus intercipiebantur,

Louis, Duke of Orleans, and the 8,000 or so cavalry and foot soldiers that were with him in the town, began to suffer from a
dearth of grain and supplies, which they had not given thought to
before the enemy's arrival. The king's cavalrymen were secretly
sent to them with pack-animals carrying grain, but were often intercepted by Contarini, and those that had come from the town to
help the cavalry were frequently killed and routed along with
them. Every day, meanwhile, the king continued to demand and
solicit fresh troops from France to free Louis from the siege, in letters written to his officials and his wife. In reply, however, she told
him that she now had no men at all who were willing to cross the
Alps, but she did have plenty of widows whose husbands had perished in Italy. Through envoys and intermediaries he was making
the same demands of the Swiss as well, but lack of funds meant he
could not achieve his object. It was in fact for this very reason that
a hundred of the Swiss soldiers that he had with him, and another
hundred Germans, went over to the Venetians. The Venetians
then burnt down the outlying buildings and moved their siege artillery closer to the town, so that the defenders began to be put
under greater pressure in every way. As he organized these actions,
Niccolò Orsini was struck in the kidneys by a lead bullet shot
from a gun; he was taken for dead, picked up and taken back to
camp, and took no further part in the war.

As each day passed, then, the besieged Frenchmen were in-   62
creasingly hard pressed by their total lack of resources, to the extent that they were compelled to eat their own horses. Many of
them died through eating flour or bran bread that had been
spoiled, and by drinking water, which the French and Germans
are quite unaccustomed to. Since his money had run out, Louis
had a little earlier struck a bronze coin, intended to have the value
of silver coinage. Louis often communicated this state of affairs to
the king by secret messengers and letters, most of them intercepted by the enemy, but some got through to the king by travel-

nonnulli, noctu magnisque imbribus profecti, diversis atque occul-
tis itineribus ad regem perveniebant, seque ille perpaucos posse ulterius dies obsidionem sustinere diceret, deceptum autem et desti-
tutum quereretur, rex ab hostibus pacem petere constituit. Itaque
per Argentonium temptare imperatorem ea de re coepit. Ab eo ad
legatos, ab iis ad Ludovicum, cuius causa bellum gerebatur, re delata, saepius deinceps eo libentissimo iactata, qui iam quiescere
quam alendis exercitibus conteri et bello periclitari malebat, indutiae primum factae; deinde Aloisio cum paucis abire Novaria
permissum.

63   Demum pax ab rege atque ab Ludovico circiter Nonas Octo-
bres concelebrata, iis condicionibus: ut Novaria Ludovico reddere-
tur; tum ex libris auri vicies centies, quas ab Ludovico rex in Neapolitanum bellum mutuo acceperat, mille ei et quingentae
rependerentur, quingentae regi cederent; Ludovicus autem naves
Gallicas, in Rapali captas portu, nuntiis regiis reddendas curaret;
et Triultium, cuius bona publicaverat exsulemque ipsum fecerat,
ab exilio revocaret, in integrumque restitueret, neve auxilia Ferdinando regi mitteret; et Carolus quantam vellet classem in Liguribus comparare posset; easque ob res Genuae arx Herculi Ferrariensium principi vice obsidum traderetur, quam ille regis nomine
biennium obtineret. Quam quidem ad pacem celerius sanciendam
ea etiam causa regem impulit, quod Helvetiorum multo maior
quam ipse petierat manus domo tandem egressa, ut regi auxilio
eo in bello esset, partim Vercellas ad regem venerat, partim appro-
pinquare nuntiabatur, omnes numero ad viginti milia. Quibus
quidem iam stipendium, quod rex pollicitus fuerat, arroganter ac
seditiose postulantibus, rex persolvere non poterat, emuncta creb-

ing at night and in heavy rain by a variety of secret routes. When Louis told him that he could withstand the siege for no more than a few days, and complained of being misled and abandoned, the king decided to sue the enemy for peace, and so he began to sound out the captain-general through Philippe de Commines. Gonzaga relayed this to the proveditors, and they to Ludovico il Moro, on whose account the war was being fought. There was thereafter much discussion of the offer, which was very much to Ludovico's liking, since he now preferred to remain at peace to shouldering the burden of supporting an army and facing the dangers of war. After an initial truce, Louis was allowed to leave Novara with a few of his men.

Peace was finally concluded between the king and Ludovico 63 about 7 October [1495] on the following conditions: Novara would be returned to Ludovico; 1,500 gold pounds of the 2,000 which the king had received as a loan from Ludovico for the Naples war would be repaid to him, while 500 would fall to the king; Ludovico would see to it that the French ships taken in the port of Rapallo were returned to the king's representatives; and Trivulzio, whom Ludovico had exiled and whose property he had confiscated, would be recalled from exile and restored to his original position; Ludovico would send no further assistance to King Ferrandino; and Charles could build a fleet in Liguria of any size he liked; and on that account, in lieu of hostages, the fortress of Genoa would be handed over to Ercole d'Este, Duke of Ferrara, who would hold it for two years in the king's name. The king was induced to ratify this peace treaty all the more quickly for the further reason that a Swiss force, much greater than he himself had sought, had finally left home to assist him in the war. Some of them had come to the king at Vercelli, others were said to be approaching, altogether numbering about 20,000. They were already demanding in an insolent and mutinous fashion the wages that the king had promised them, which the king was unable to pay:

errimis ingentibusque in bellum thesauris regi subministrandis transalpina Gallia, vicinisque regibus fere omnibus, accepta superioribus mensibus mutuo ab eis pecunia, prorsus exhaustis. Itaque cum intellexisset eos unos, qui venerant, nocturna concilia de se capiendo habuisse, veritus ne, si reliqui Helvetii propius accessissent, vim eorum subterfugere non posset, pace statim facta, eos sero venisse ad speciem questus atque in Taurinos propere abiens, domum, qua condicione potuit, remisit.

64   Ea de pace cum rege ineunda Veneti ab eius interpretibus, tum a Ludovico saepe invitati, consulto senatu responderunt sese omnino, nisi de sociorum voluntate atque consilio, quibuscum foedus percussissent, nihil acturos. Nam quoniam ex iis quae eo in bello gesserat Ludovicus quantum ei esset credendum non ambigue cognoverant, novo se foedere implicari cum tam infido homine plane nolebant. Id aegerrime cum ferret Ludovicus, existimans Venetos alieno ab sese animo esse, questusque apud legatos senatum omnia alia praeterquam de sua salute cogitare, suis militum praefectis clam imperavit uti flumine, qua esset exercitui reipublicae transeundum, si domum redire vellet, communirent navesque abigerent, ne traicere se invito posset. Ea per amicos reipublicae delata res ad legatos magnopere eos commovit, quod tantis obiectis fluminibus iter se impeditissimum habituros intelligebant, Ludovici exercitu munitissimis in locis se opponente. Pontium autem efficiendorum facultatem sibi datum iri non videbant, praereptis navibus quibus imponi possent. Tum illud etiam timebant, ne, si vis adhiberetur, perfidia Ludovicus sua Gallos sibi adiungeret, ut rerum dominus et pacis ac belli arbiter videri posset.

France itself had been cleaned out in furnishing the frequent and massive imposts for the king's war, and pretty well all the neighboring rulers were quite drained of funds, having already loaned the king money in the preceding months. When he learned that the Swiss who had arrived at Vercelli had held meetings at night about taking him prisoner, he feared that if the rest of them came any closer, he would not be able to avoid falling into their power, and so made peace at once, making a show of complaining that they were late in turning up. Departing in haste for Turin, he sent them back home on any terms he could.

The Venetians were often approached about taking part in this 64 peace treaty with the king, both by his messengers and by Ludovico, but after discussion in the Senate they replied that they would do absolutely nothing without the consent and counsel of the parties with whom they were allied. From what Ludovico had done in the war, they were perfectly aware how far he was to be trusted, and they were by no means willing to involve themselves in a new treaty with such a treacherous man. Ludovico took this very ill, judging that the Venetians took a hostile view of him, and complained in the presence of the proveditors that the Senate was thinking of everything but its own security. He secretly ordered his infantry officers to strengthen the defenses on the rivers where the Venetian army would have to cross if it wanted to return home, and to remove boats so that it would not be able to cross against his will. Friends of the Republic reported this to the proveditors, who were greatly disturbed since they realized that they would have a very difficult journey with such rivers in the way and Ludovico's army opposing them in well-defended strongholds. Nor could they see that they would get a chance to build bridges without the boats on which they might be laid. There was also the fear that if force were used, Ludovico would turn traitor and ally himself with the French, so that he might appear master of the situation and the arbiter of peace and war.

65   Haec versantibus legatis, Contareno adhibito, neque satis tutum eius rei exitum reperientibus, ubi omnes paulisper conticue-
runt, "Ego," inquit Contarenus, "iter vobis domum, si annuitis, pa-
tens atque tutum comparabo." Ad ea, cum legati quonam id
tandem modo quove consilio esset effecturus ab eo quaesivissent,
"Hodie," inquit, "ut consuevistis, vos et Ludovicus una eritis, com-
munibus de rebus consulturi; aderunt cum illo sui duces, vester
vobiscum imperator praefectique; fores claudentur, disceptabitur.
Tum ego illum, tamquam allocuturus, hoc vobis gladio confossum
atque confectum dabo. Ea re patrata, neminem ex eius ducibus
ferrum educturum certo scio. Quis est enim eorum omni non femina timidior? aut quis illum non pessime odit, uno aut altero excepto? qui tamen ipsi, ad Carolum legati de pace profecti, adesse
non poterunt. Ludovici etiam exercitus ipso mortuo ad vos signa
transferet, si se receptum iri intelliget, praesertim spe largitionis
aliqua oblata. Quod si fit, eius quoque regnum vestris in manibus
versabitur. Ita ille, ut meritus est, suorum scelerum poenas pendet;
vos, reipublicae iniurias nullo dispendio ulti, vestram dignitatem
pulcherrime retinebitis."

66   Erat Contareno procerum sane corpus et vividum solidumque,
vires immanes vastaeque ac prope inexsuperabiles, animus cum
prudens, tum omnium magnarum rerum capax, ut, quod is polliceretur, etiam praestari posse confideres. Itaque ea legati cum intellexissent, maximis illum laudibus certatim efferentes, quod tantam rem aggredi pro communi salute non dubitaret, constituerunt,
hoc ad extremum reservato consilio, experiri num Ludovicus ad
sanitatem bonis artibus converti posset. Ea tamen de re quam

As the proveditors mulled over these matters in consultation 65
with Contarini, without finding a viable solution to the problem,
everyone had fallen silent for a moment when Contarini spoke up:
"I will find you a way back home, if you agree, that is accessible
and safe." At this, the proveditors demanded to know how on
earth he meant to do such a thing, and he replied, "Today, as
usual, you will be holding discussions with Ludovico about matters of common concern. His captains will be with him, and you
will have your captain-general and officers with you. The doors
will be shut, and debate will ensue. I shall make as if to address
him, but will then run him through with this dagger and kill him.
That done, I know for sure that none of his captains will draw his
sword—which of them is not more timid than any woman?
Which of them, one or two excepted, does not regard him with
the utmost loathing? And those one or two will have gone to
Charles as peace envoys and will not be present. Ludovico's army
will also surrender their standards to you once he is dead, if they
realize that you will accept them, especially if some prospect of
largesse is held out to them. And if that happens, his duchy too
will be in your hands. In this way he will pay the penalty for his
crimes as he deserves, while you will have taken vengeance for the
wrongs done to the Republic without cost, and so keep your reputation untarnished."

Contarini had a very tall, vigorous and strongly built physique. 66
His brute strength was immense and almost unparalleled, his
mind not only intelligent but capable of any great enterprise, so
that you could be confident that he would deliver what he promised. Though the proveditors grasped this, and competed with
each other to praise him to the skies for not hesitating to take on
such an important task for the common good, they decided to
keep the plan as a last resort and to see whether Ludovico could
be brought to his senses by honorable means. They did, however,
make haste to send a coded letter to the Heads of the Council of

Contarenus proposuerat notis scriptas litteras ad decemvirum magistros confestim dederunt, postulantes uti rescriberent, vellentne atque permitterent, si necessitas urgeat, eo consilio ipsos uti. Qui de collegii sententia rescripserunt ex reipublicae dignitate sibi eam rem non videri. Ludovicus interea cum legatorum dissimulatione atque prudentia, qui ea se nescire quae ab illo parabantur ostendebant, tum sua sponte, quod nihil omnino tuti irritandis legatis in tam nova suspectaque dominatione se habiturum videbat, ab eo per se consilio destitit. Iis confectis rebus, milites obsessi oppido Novaria emittuntur; oppidum Ludovico restituitur. Legati Veneti post haec omni cum exercitu Cremam cum venissent, militesque quos oportuit dato stipendio missos fecissent, reliquosque milites equitesque in hiberna deducandos curavissent, cum imperatore Mantuam profecti, ludis ab eo dies aliquot habitis, ad urbem reverterunt. Carolus, cupidissimis suis omnibus, multo cupidius ipse traiectis Alpibus suum in regnum concessit.

Ten regarding Contarini's proposal, asking them to write back whether they were agreeable to their adopting the plan should it become necessary. The Heads responded that in the Council's opinion the procedure was not consonant with the dignity of the Republic. Meanwhile Ludovico, prompted not only by the disingenuous cleverness of the proveditors in pretending not to know what he was up to, but also of his own accord, since he saw that he would find no security at all in irritating the proveditors when his rule was so new and distrusted, spontaneously abandoned his plan. The affair concluded, the French soldiers under siege at Novara were let go, and the town was restored to Ludovico. The Venetian proveditors subsequently went to Crema with the whole army and dismissed such soldiers as they needed to after paying them off, arranging for the rest of the foot soldiers and cavalry to be conducted to their winter quarters. They left for Mantua with the captain-general, who held games there for a number of days, and then returned to Venice. With all his men earnestly desiring it, none more so than Charles himself, the king crossed the Alps and withdrew into his own realm.

LIBER TERTIUS

1   Ferdinandus ubi Carolum Neapoli profectum cognovit, acceptis Messanae militibus ad mille (ibi enim tunc erat), quos quidem civitas in vicini atque amici regis gratiam, depenso trium mensium stipendio, ei praesto esse iussit, navibus longis duodecim in Calabros traiecit et Rhegium Crotonemque recepit; ac secundo cum Gallis pedestri facto proelio, interfectis captisque compluribus, reliquos cum eorum duce in proximum oppidum compulit. Ad quos cum auxilia undique convenissent, victus ab iis ingenti clade, cum paucis Rhegium fugiens, uni saluti consuluit suae. Idem autem, paulatim sese confirmans, cum iam Gallorum imperii plerosque eorum qui eos libenti animo exceperant magnopere paeniteret (nihil enim fere cuiusquam neque sanctum neque tutum ab illis erat), cum Hispanae classis navibus quadraginta, quam superiore libro missam in Siciliam dixeramus, et suis cum triremibus duodecim Aenariam ad insulam, quae ab eo non defecerat, venit.

2   Atque illis ipsis quidem diebus res eiusmodi acciderat, quae magnam invidiam in Gallos conflaverit. Nam cum ii qui Caietae praeerant navem longam remigibus instruere vellent municipesque imponere, illi se cogi passi non sunt, palamque praedicaverunt nolle se contra Ferdinandum regem duci, atque ad arma capienda prosilierunt. Galli eos veriti se in arcem oppidi receperunt atque ad auxilia proximis ex oppidis evocanda miserunt; quibus adductis magnam civium caedem fecerunt, magnam in oppidanos stragem ediderunt, matribus familias et virginibus vulgo in servitutem

BOOK III

The town of Messina, where Ferrandino had been staying, had arranged to have about 1,000 soldiers put at his disposal and their wages paid for three months, to oblige a neighboring king with whom they were on friendly terms. When Ferrandino learned that Charles had left Naples, he took the soldiers and crossed over to Calabria with 12 galleys, taking back Reggio and Crotone. After a successful land battle with the French in which a good number of them were killed or captured, he forced the rest into a nearby town along with their commander. When reinforcements came to their aid from all sides, however, he suffered a calamitous defeat at their hands, and fled with a few of his men to Reggio, taking thought only for his own safety. But he also little by little recovered his strength, since most of those who had welcomed them with open arms had now come greatly to regret French rule—hardly anything at all was sacrosanct or safe from them, no matter who owned it. And so Ferrandino reached the island of Ischia, which had remained true to him, with 40 ships of the Spanish fleet (which I mentioned in the preceding book as having been sent to Sicily)[1] and his own 12 galleys.

At this same time there occurred an event that aroused great resentment against the French. The authorities at Gaeta wanted to find rowers for a galley and man it with local people, but they refused to be coerced. They openly declared that they would not be led against King Ferrandino, and they rushed to take up arms. The French retreated into the town fortress for fear of them, and sent for reinforcements to be fetched from the nearby towns. When they arrived, they carried out a massacre of the citizens, inflicting great slaughter on the townspeople and abducting matrons and maidens en masse as slaves or objects of their lust. When they

atque libidinem abductis. Quae intellecta res Neapolitanorum animos, iam ante infensos et labantes, ab Gallis magnopere averterat.

3 Ea cum sic cecidissent, ipse autem Ferdinandus Neapolim non
obscuris multorum vocibus sermonibusque accerseretur, quem
etiam adventare intelligebant, spei atque fiduciae plenus ab Aena-
ria naves solvit; atque ad litus Neapolitanum classe appulsa, non
longe ab oppido exponere milites cum vellet, impeditus a Gallis
atque reiectus, de tota re desperans, quod ab oppidanis nihil sibi
auxilii emitti, nihil tumulti fieri animadverterat, ad Aenariam re-
vertebatur. At civitas, aegre id passa, armis captis Gallos partim
eiecit, partim in arces quae ab illis tenebantur coniecit. Id, a pisca-
toria navicula Ferdinando nuntiatum, spem ei pristinam facile restituit. Quamobrem sua cum navi incitatis remigibus statim Neapolim rediens, magno populi consensu in oppidum receptus est.
Ita parvo temporis spatio saepius modo bonam, modo adversam
expertus fortunam, ac variis rerum suarum eventis tamquam fluctibus iactatus, cum id minime fieri posse confideret, ab eadem
quasi tempestate atque ventis in portum coniectus est.

4 Pauloque post Galli qui ei arci praeerant quae Capuana appellatur sese atque arcem Ferdinando dediderunt. Tum naves Gallicae
sexdecim, quae in portu Neapolitano erant, veritae ne interciperentur, egressae ad insulam Megarem iactis ancoris se continuerunt. Ferdinandi classis ad Baias substitit. Iis nuntiatis rebus, Nolani Atellani Capuani aliaque vicina municipia propenso ad illum
studio celeriter redierunt; videbanturque reliquae eius regni civitates idem facturae, si modo rex firma cum manu eodem accederet.
Ille autem, per se omnibus ab rebus quae ad bellum sunt usui
praesertimque a pecunia plane imparatissimus, magistratum Venet-

learned of these events, the Neapolitans, already hostile and wavering before this, became greatly alienated from the French.

In these circumstances, with many men openly calling on 3 Ferrandino to return to Naples, in the belief that he was actually on his way, he set sail from Ischia full of hope and confidence. His fleet making land on the Neapolitan coast, he wanted to put his soldiers ashore not far from the city, but the French stopped him and forced him back. Ferrandino saw no sign of help arriving from the townspeople, nor any sign of an uprising, so he despaired of the whole enterprise and turned back towards Ischia. But the citizenry took this ill and seizing their arms drove out some of the French and forced others into the castles they held. Ferrandino heard about this from a fishing boat and his original hopes were soon rekindled. He therefore returned to Naples at once with his boat, himself urging the oarsmen on, and was welcomed into the town on a tide of popular support. So in a short space of time Ferrandino several times experienced good fortune and bad by turns. Battered as if by waves by the varying success of his fortunes, and just when he was sure that it was the least likely outcome, the same storm winds, as it were, brought him back into harbor.

A little later on, the French who controlled the castle called 4 Capuano surrendered it and themselves to Ferrandino. Then 16 French ships that were in the port of Naples departed for fear that they might be captured. They dropped anchor at the island of Megaride and stayed there, while Ferrandino's fleet stayed at Baiae. When these events became public knowledge, the people of Nola, Aversa, Capua, and other nearby communities, who were already inclined to favor Ferrandino, quickly returned to him, and the remaining towns of his kingdom seemed ready to do the same if only the king would appear in those parts with a strong military force. But Ferrandino, who was conspicuously lacking in everything needed for war, in money above all, made this kindly address

um, qui vetusta consuetudine ea in urbe reipublicae hominibus iuri dicendo praeerat, perhumaniter est allocutus: sese, quod Neapolim recuperavisset, reipublicae acceptum referre, quae foedus cum Alexandro reliquisque regibus iniisset; quod autem superesset (quod quidem certe magnum atque perplexum sciret esse, tot municipiis toto in regno, tot munitis oppidis Gallorum imperium secutis) eius se fidei liberalitatique permittere. Eo sermone apud illum habito, Federicum patruum cum navibus longis tribus ad Antonium, quem in Apuliam cum classe venisse intellexerat, conveniendum seque illi commendandum propere misit.

5   Antonius, paulo ante ad Sasonem insulam senatus consulto accepto, tantum ut in Apuliam traiceret, Brundusium, quod municipium ad Gallos non transierat, venit. Oppidani Antonium amice atque benevole exceperunt eique se dedere voluerunt, atque ut insigne reipublicae in oppidi foro sustolleret ab eo magnopere petiverunt. Antonius, Brundusinis collaudatis, atque ut in regis sui fide permanerent cohortatus, ibi dies aliquot, dum quid imperarent patres scire posset, est commoratus. Illi autem, nisi de foederatorum sententia, Hispaniaeque imprimis regum consociata voluntate, qui classem paratam habebant, nihil omnino agere constituerant. Itaque a legato regio missi in Siciliam nuntii eius rei eventum tardiorem reddiderunt.

6   Accepto tandem altero senatus consulto, quo bellum Gallis inferre iubebatur Antonius, biduo scalis reliquisque rebus ad oppugnationem oppidorum comparandis consumpto, cum triremibus viginti naveque una oneraria bellica, et altera in qua erat equitum Graecorum non magnus numerus, ad oppidum Monopolitanorum, quod est in maris litore a Gallisque obtinebatur, accessit; praefectumque Gallorum uti se dederet per internuntios cohorta-

to the Venetian magistrate who by ancient custom was responsible for administering justice in that city for the men of Venice: he owed his recovery of Naples to the Republic, which had entered into an alliance with Pope Alexander and the other rulers. What remained to be done (and that to be sure was a large and complex undertaking, given that so many communities and fortified towns throughout the entire kingdom had gone over to French rule), he entrusted to the Republic's steadfastness and liberality. After delivering himself of this speech before the Venetian consul, Ferrandino made haste to send his uncle Federico with three galleys to welcome Antonio Grimani and pass on his greetings to him, having learned that Antonio had arrived in Apulia with a fleet.

A little earlier Antonio had received the Senate decree at the island of Saseno that he should cross only as far as Apulia, and he went to Brindisi, a town that had not gone over to the French. The people gave him a friendly reception and were happy to surrender to him, earnestly entreating him to raise the flag of the Republic in the town square. Antonio praised the people of Brindisi but exhorted them to remain loyal to their king. He remained there a few days, waiting to learn what the senators would tell him to do. But the Senate had decided to do nothing at all except by agreement with the allies, and in particular not without the assent of the sovereigns of Spain, who had a fleet ready. For that reason the despatch of messengers to Sicily by the king's ambassador delayed the resolution of the situation.

Receiving at length a second decree of the Senate which ordered him to take the war to the French, Antonio spent two days in putting together siege-ladders and other gear for storming towns, and then made for Monopoli, a town on the [Adriatic] coast held by the French, with 20 galleys, an armed merchant ship, and another in which there was a small force of stradiots. Through intermediaries he urged the French commander to surrender, but

tus, ubi illum ad propugnationem paratum vidit, expositis equitibus, qui discurrerent populationemque facerent, et aliquid in agris
aut vitis aut oleae succiderent tectorumque incenderent, si ea re cives ad deditionem compelli possent, ubi neque id quidem quidquam proficere animadvertit, tormentis e nave oneraria murum
oppidi deicere aggreditur. Id cum propter longinquitatem parum
ex usu administraretur, Hieronymo Contareno legato praefectisque triremium uti naves tegerent ad ictus cum tormentorum,
tum vero lapidum atque telorum quae de muro adigerentur imperavit; postridieque eius diei mane, iis qui primi murum ascendis-
sent propositis praemiis, navibusque omnibus sub conspectum
hostium dispositis, oppugnare oppidum multo acrius est adortus;
qua in oppugnatione Petrus Bembus, navis longae praefectus, vir
egregia virtute, cohortans suos pila ferrea traicitur.

7   Antonius cum horas aliquot, Gallis atque oppidanis acerrime
propugnantibus, suos vulnerari, hostes non defatigari, minus denique rem procedere animadvertisset, oppidum militibus diripien-
dum proposuit. Tum vero praedae spe milites remigesque incitati
cohortatique inter se ad murum convolaverunt; scalisque positis
cum amplius horis duabus continenter atque fortissime pugnavissent, deiectis interfectisque propugnatoribus, in oppidum se iniecerunt diripereque contenderunt; Aloisiumque Tintum Venetum,
qui eo in oppido mercaturam exercebat, imprudentes occiderunt
domumque eius diripuerunt. Antonius, reclusis portis in oppidum
ingressus, mulieres, quae, natu maiorum usae consilio, ad aras
deorum immortalium cum infantibus confugerant, a militum iniuria defendit oppidoque est potitus; sectionemque earum rerum
quae distractae nondum essent, multo minoris quam vendi aliis

when he saw that he was prepared to defend the town, he put his cavalry ashore to fan out and lay waste to the land, cutting down a number of vines and olive trees in the fields, and setting fire to houses, to see if this would force the townsfolk to surrender. Seeing that even with all that they were making no progress, he set himself to wrecking the town walls with the artillery on the merchant ship. When this tactic proved of little use because the ships were too far away, he told the proveditor Girolamo Contarini and his captains to take measures to protect the ships against the enemy artillery and the impact of the stones and missiles that were being shot from the walls. The next morning, he offered rewards to the first to climb the walls, and drawing up his entire fleet in full view of the enemy, he launched a much fiercer attack on the town. In the course of the attack the captain Pietro Bembo, a man of extraordinary courage, was shot by an iron ball as he urged his men on.

After several hours Antonio saw that in the face of the vigorous 7 resistance of the French and the townsfolk, his men were being wounded, the enemy were not tiring, and the operation was not going well, so he held out to his soldiers the prospect of plundering the town. Spurred on then by hope of booty, the soldiers and rowers hurled themselves against the walls, urging each other forward. They set up the ladders there and fought with great bravery for more than two hours continuously. After throwing the defenders to the ground and killing them, they thrust themselves into the town and set about plundering it. In doing so they unwittingly killed a Venetian, Alvise Tinto, who had business in the town, and pillaged his house. Once the gates were opened, Antonio entered Monopoli, protecting the women there from injury by the soldiers (on the advice of their elders they had fled with their infants to the churches), and took possession of the town. He sold the remnant of the property which had not yet been carried off to the townspeople themselves, for much less than it could have been sold to

potuissent, die laxissima oppidanis ipsis vendidit. Quibus etiam,
quo minore damno amissis rebus suis afficerentur, annos decem
omnium munerum et tributorum levationem concessit.

8   Eo oppido capto, nonnulla eius regionis municipia se Antonio
dediderunt. Atque haec quidem adhuc ipsa Ferdinando Neapolim
recipienti nota non erant. Antonius, Nicolao Cornelio, qui Mono-
politanis praeesset, relicto, missoque Pulinianum, quod oppidum
abest a litore eique se dederat, Alexandro Pisauro eodem nomine,
Sipontum est profectus, quod iam per sese ob Gallorum insolen-
tiam atque libidinem in Ferdinandi partes oppidum redierat, eiec-
tis Gallis, qui se in arcem contulerunt. Ad quos cum Antonius misisset, uti arcem Ferdinando restituerent, id ni facerent, eos se
hostium loco habiturum, responderunt nihil sibi cum Ferdinando
rei esse; ipse si velit eos recipere, eius se fidei libenter permissuros.
Itaque acceptis in fidem Gallis, Antonius Federico, qui iam ad se
Ferdinandi missu venerat, arcem reddendam curavit. Eodem tempore qui Tranensium arcem tenebant, missis ad illum interpretibus, velle se eius imperata facere Antonio significaverunt. Ille, ut
Ferdinando sese dederent hortatus, eos non tam libentes quam
auctoritate sua compulsos tamquam de manu Federico tradidit.
Eidemque Graecorum equitum dimidiam partem, quorum iam
erat numerus ad quadringentos quinquaginta, petenti dedit.

9   Patres cum intellexissent Ferdinandum Neapolim recuperavisse,
decreverunt ne quid Antonius oppidorum, neve omnino locorum
amplius reipublicae nomine in regno Neapolitano caperet. Tum
Petri Bembi uxori liberisque victus annuus a senatu dono datus;

others and giving them plenty of time to pay. He also granted them relief from all duties and tribute for ten years, so that they might feel less keenly the loss of their property.

After the taking of Monopoli, a number of towns in the region 8 surrendered to Antonio, developments which were as yet unknown to Ferrandino while he was engaged in the reconquest of Naples. Antonio left Niccolò Corner as governor of Monopoli, and sent Alessandro da Pesaro for the same purpose to Polignano, a town a long way from the coast which had surrendered to him. He himself left for Manfredonia, which owing to the high-handedness and depravity of the French had already come back to Ferrandino of its own accord — the citizens had expelled the French, who had withdrawn into the fortress. Antonio sent word to them that they should return the fortress to Ferrandino, and that if they did not, he would treat them as an enemy. They replied that they had no business with Ferrandino but that if Antonio wished to take them under his protection, they would gladly surrender themselves to him. And so with the French under his protection, Antonio saw to it that the fortress was returned to Federico, who had been sent by Ferrandino and had already arrived. At the same time, those [Frenchmen] who held the castle of Trani sent messengers to Antonio to let him know that they were willing to do his bidding. He encouraged them to surrender to Ferrandino. Though they they were not happy about it, they were forced to comply by his personal authority, and so Antonio practically delivered them to Federico with his own hands. At Federico's request, he also gave him half of his stradiots, who now numbered about 450.

When the senators learned that Ferrandino had recovered Na- 9 ples, they ordered that Antonio should take no further town or any place at all in the Kingdom of Naples in the name of the Republic. The Senate then granted the wife and children of Pietro Bembo an annual living allowance, and also 40 gold pounds to

duabus quoque filiis dotis nomine librae auri quadraginta; duabus alteris, in sacrarum virginum collegia iam destinatis, quod ad id satis esset constitutum. Antonio autem Tinti fratri, ab adolescente me in amici hominis afflictis rebus causa bis apud patres perorata, proventus est annuus senatus decreto et liberalitate attributus; quo se nunc quoque familiamque suam senex oculisque captus sustinet. Post haec, Alexandro a senatu postulante ut illam ipsam classem Neapolim ad Ferdinandum auxilio levandum tam opportuno tempore mitteret, tametsi permagnis Gallici exercitus impensis civitas distinebatur, concedendum tamen censuit. Itaque Antonius, Graecis equitibus centum et navibus duabus Monopolitanorum praesidio relictis, Tarentum adnavigavit; quod quidem oppidum, appulso eo cum septem navibus longis, quas ad eius tres Antonius addiderat, Federico, ad Ferdinandum tamen non redierat. Ibi ventris profluvio arreptus Antonius, navibus viginti, quibus Contarenum legatum praefecit, Neapolim ad Ferdinandum iussis contendere, ipse cum reliquis navibus (aliae enim nonnullae ad illum interea naves convenerant) Corcyram est profectus.

10   Eodem anno cellis farinariis urbanis, quae publicae ad Rivum altum antiquitus sunt institutae, longinquae plebis et inquilinorum parti usum incommodiorem praebentibus, alterae apud forum reipublicaeque horrea exaedificatae, Kalendis Sextilibus exerceri coeptae sunt, magistratibus adhibitis.

11   Iisdem fere diebus, Florentinis Pisas bello repetentibus, cum per se oppidani contra tantas opes municipium diutius se tueri posse diffiderent, suum ad senatum interpretem secreto miserunt: velle se sub reipublicae imperio esse; petere, rogare ut reciperentur.

two of his daughters by way of dowry; another pair of daughters who were already destined for the convent were apportioned an amount sufficient for that purpose. As for Antonio, Tinto's brother (I had twice pled his case before the Senate in my youth, moved as I was by my friend's sorry plight), he was awarded a yearly subvention by generous decree of the Senate, by means of which he even now, in old age and blindness, supports himself and his family. Following that, Pope Alexander asked the Senate to send the same fleet to Naples to assist Ferrandino, since circumstances were so favorable. Although the city was distracted by the vast expense of keeping the army in Lombardy, they nevertheless agreed to grant the request. Antonio accordingly sailed for Taranto, leaving behind a hundred stradiots and two ships to guard Monopoli. Though Federico had landed there with seven galleys (which Antonio had increased from Federico's original three), Taranto had nevertheless not returned to Ferrandino. There Antonio came down with a gastric disorder, but he ordered 20 ships to make for Ferrandino at Naples, putting the proveditor Contarini in command of them, and himself set out for Corfu with the remaining ships, some other ships having reached him in the meantime.

In the same year, the urban grain stores long established for 10 public use at the Rialto having proved inconvenient for some of the commoners and inhabitants living at a distance, another set of storerooms was built next to St. Mark's Square and the state granary. They came into use on 1 August under the supervision of their own magistrates.

At more or less the same time, the Florentines were seeking to 11 regain Pisa by force of arms. The Pisans were not confident that they could defend their town against the might of Florence, and so they secretly sent a messenger to the Senate to say that they wanted to be taken under the sway of the Republic, and begged and prayed to be admitted to their protection. The situation at

Res primum nova patribus, quae neque statim reicienda neque temere suscipienda esse videretur; deinde magis magisque in eorum animos irrepere, pulchrum existimantium augeri imperii fines atque ad mare Ligusticum protendi: magnum porro esse Venetum nomen, cui sponte tam longinqua civitas tamque nobilis sese dederet; sed factum prope similibus rerum eventis; quos si maiores nostri despexissent, nulli nunc populi eius imperium appeterent; itaque recipiendas esse Pisas, quas dii immortales reipublicae addicerent. Ea cum sententia maiori patrum numero probaretur, res in decemvirum collegio agitari coepta est, quo lex occultius ferri posset.

12   Tum Marcus Bolanus, sexvir ex iis qui principi assident, tacentibus reliquis ac legis lationi prope assentientibus, suggestum ascendens, debere eos dixit, qui de rebus dubiis agunt, non tam quid velint ipsi aut cupiant, quam quid sit utile reipublicae constituere; necesse enim esse, si suam modo libidinem sequantur, ut sui eos consilii tum paeniteat, cum ea quae provisa ipsis non sunt magna interdum et formidolosa rerum momenta atque pericula exsistunt. "An me quoque," inquit, "patres, idem quod vos et optare maximopere, et optato frui cupere non existimatis? Non Pisas modo, de quibus nunc consulimur, sed reliquas etiam Italiae civitates, oppida, populos iuris nostri esse, mareque superum atque inferum in reipublicae imperio contineri? Ego vero ista percupio; meaque morte cum fortuna paciscar ut tam prospera reipublicae sit. Sed cum hoc opto, tum illud timeo, ne, si Pisas receperimus, magno cum nostro dedecore reique publicae incommodo eas ipsas brevi

first seemed entirely unprecedented to the senators, and not something they should either reject out of hand or take on without much thought. It then began to grow upon them more and more, as they came to think that it would be a good idea to enlarge their dominion and extend its boundaries to the Ligurian sea: the prestige of Venice must be great indeed if a state as far away and as well known as Pisa was prepared to hand itself over to her of its own accord. But that prestige had come about through events of much the same sort, and if their ancestors[2] had disdained to capitalize on those opportunities, no communities would now be looking to be ruled by Venice. Let them therefore admit Pisa to their dominion, as a gift awarded the Republic by Almighty God. This view having prevailed among a majority of the senators, the matter went to be discussed in the Council of Ten so that the law could be brought forward in greater secrecy.

Then while the rest remained silent and as good as agreed to 12 the law's passage, one of the six ducal councillors, Marco Bollani, mounted the platform and said that it was incumbent on those who debated such delicate matters to propose not so much what they themselves might wish or desire as whatever was in the Republic's interest. It was inevitable that if they simply followed their heart's desire, they would come to regret their decision, when from time to time serious and formidable crises and dangers arose which they had not foreseen. "Or do you senators not think," he said, "that I desire just the same as you, and just as much, and that I too want to avail myself of the object of my desires just like you? Do you not think that I not only want Pisa under our sway, the present subject of debate, but all the other states and towns and peoples of Italy as well, and for the Venetian empire to embrace the Adriatic and the Tyrrhenian? I want those things very much indeed, and I would stake my life with Fortune if she would look with such favor on the Republic. But much as I desire this, I fear something else: that if we admit Pisa to our dominion we shall in

tempore amittamus. Nam quemadmodum quidem sitae posi-
taeque sunt Pisae, ad eas defendendas auxilia mittere per alienos
fines multorum dierum itinere nos oportebit. Quorum populi nostris conatibus si adversabuntur, aut erunt ipsi bello prius atque armis subigendi, ut quidquid inter nostros ac Pisarum fines iacet pa-
catum iter atque tutum nostris exercitibus praebeat, aut nobis
turpiter ab incepto desistendum. Nam mari tanto circuitu, tam
suspectis litoribus, tantum exercitum transmittere, quanto erit
opus, ut cum unis Florentinis bellum geramus, qui poterimus?
Nullus vicinorum Pisis regum, nulla natio est, quae non Florentinos malit quam nos suae dicioni finitimos habere, propterea quod
nostram potentiam nostrasque opes magis quam illorum verentur,
magis nos quam illos sibi esse metuendos intelligunt.

13   "Est autem a natura omnibus animantibus comparatum atque
insitum, ut quae eis plurimum obesse possunt fugiant, ad ea se ap-
plicent quibus ad nocendum minus est virium et facultatis attributum. Itaque passerculi gallinas anseresque non vitant; cum colum-
bis vero etiam nidificant; ab accipitre autem, et ab iis quae raptu
vivunt avibus, maxime quidem semper volatu latebrisque sese au-
ferunt. Quamobrem cogitare debemus etiam Ligures — quae una
quondam natio quam infesta reipublicae fuerit, annales nostri testes sunt; quantas a nobis clades acceperit, omnis eius posteritas
memoria retinebit — si suae spontis sint, nos Pisarum dominos
fieri nullis condicionibus concessuros, sed sua cum Florentinis
arma, suas classes atque opes communicaturos, ut nos potiri Pisis
ne permittant. Quamquam, ut horum temporum mores sunt, ut
fides in plerisque fluxa, vereor ne ii etiam qui foedera nobiscum
pepigerunt, qui nobis sua regna se debere profitentur, ubi nos eo
usque velle fines proferre nostros intelligent, nos celeriter deserant;
neque deserant modo, sed arma etiam contra nos capiant, cumque

short order lose it, to our disgrace and the Republic's loss. Given Pisa's location and situation, we shall have to send troops to defend it on a march of many days through alien territory. If the people of those lands oppose our efforts, they will either have to be themselves first subjugated by war and force of arms, so that everything lying between our territory and that of Pisa will offer peace and security for our armies on the march, or we shall have to desist from the enterprise to our discredit. Consider how vast will be the resources we shall need to transport an army on such a sea journey and to such dangerous shores, just to wage war on the Florentines. How on earth shall we be able to do it? There is not one of the rulers around Pisa, there is no nearby people, that does not prefer to have the Florentines as neighbors of their domains rather than us. Being in greater awe of our power and strength than of theirs, they realize that they should be more afraid of us than of them.

"All living things naturally and instinctively shun what most 13 harms them and cleave to what has less power and ability to injure them. Sparrows do not flee from hens and geese, indeed they even nest with doves. But from hawks and other birds of prey, they always fly away or conceal themselves as far as they can. We ought to think, then, that the Genoese likewise, if it were up to them, would under no circumstances permit us to become masters of Pisa: our histories bear witness to how hostile that people was to Venice in the past and all posterity at Genoa will remember what great defeats it suffered at our hands. They would share their armies, fleets and wealth with the Florentines to prevent us gaining control of Pisa. Though such is the temper of the times and so uncertain most people's loyalty that I fear that even our allies, even those who profess that they owe their realms to us, will soon desert us when they learn that we mean to enlarge our borders as far as that; and not only desert us, but actually take up arms against us and make common cause with our enemies, in the belief

hostibus nostris coniuncti, communi nos bello atque consilio esse avertendos et repellendos putent.[1]

14   "Maiores nostri Vicetinos, cum a rege Patavino premerentur, sese illis dedere, missis ad eos legatis, cupientes atque orantes in fidem receperunt. Quid in illa huic simile deditioni fuit? oppidum vicinitate propinquum ac prope coniunctum, ut iter impediri atque accessio non potuerit; ipsum liberum, quodque Patavini reges antea non obtinuissent. Itaque remissis cum auxilio legatis, facile defensum atque retentum est. Hostis autem eam ob rem novus nullus factus; sed cum eo qui semper hostis reipublicae fuerat bellum acrius renovatum maiores iidem nostri prospere atque feliciter gesserunt.

15   "Quod si tam facilem rerum statum paresque condiciones in Pisis recipiendis esse vobis propositas hoc tempore videtis; si non amico populo et reipublicae, a qua lacessiti nulla re sumus, ut id quod volumus assequamur, insignis est iniuria atque calamitas inferenda; si non, quae in animis hominum iam pridem insedit opinio, nos regnandi cupiditate supra ceteros efferri, eam hoc exemplo sic confirmaturi sumus, ut non sit posthac infitiandi locus; si non etiam Ferdinandi regnum adhuc quidem multo maxima ex parte, Ludovici haud ex minima Gallorum, quos hostes nostros fecimus, praesidiis et exercitibus tenentur, neque quem finem eae res habiturae sint satis consequi coniectura possumus, ut non tam de novo bello capessendo, quam de institutis conficiendis, flammaque illa quae optimas atque pulcherrimas Italiae regiones incendio corripuit exstinguenda, cogitare nos oporteat, legem, patres, quam rogamini, decernite; ego ipse meum suffragium ad eam sanciendam volens ac libens affero. Sin vero longe aliter omnibus a partibus se

that we can be routed and repelled by their collective military action and strategy.

"When the people of Vicenza were being hard pressed by the 14 ruler of Padua, and sent our ancestors emissaries to express their desire and willingness to hand themselves over to them, Venice took them under her protection. In what way did that surrender resemble this one? Vicenza was in close proximity and practically bordering our lands, so that the way there and access to the town could not be blocked. It was itself a free city, and not one previously subject to the rulers of Padua. When therefore the ambassadors returned with Venetian forces to support them, it was easily defended and held. Nor did Venice make any new enemies on account of Vicenza, but those same forebears of ours started war again on a fiercer footing with the Republic's traditional enemy, and brought it to a successful conclusion.

"If you now see things as being just as straightforward, how- 15 ever, and the terms held out to you for taking on Pisa as just the same; if you do not see that to gain our ends we shall have to inflict a grave injury and misfortune on a friendly people and a republic which has never provoked us in any manner; if you do not see that we will confirm by this precedent, and in a way we could not afterwards deny, the view long settled in the minds of men that we above all others are preoccupied with a passion for dominance; if it is not the case, too, that much the greatest part of Ferrandino's realm, and no small part of Ludovico's, is still occupied by the garrisons and armies of the French, whom we have made our enemy — nor can we guess with any accuracy where all this will end, so we should really be considering not so much the start of a new war as concluding those already started and quenching the flames that have set the finest and most beautiful parts of Italy alight; then, senators, pass the law that is proposed for your consideration, and I myself will be only too glad to cast my vote for its approval. If on the other hand things are quite different in

res habet, antequam Pisas esse recipiendas statuatis, ea quae ad bellum cum positis inter nos atque Pisas nationibus cumque finitimis ei civitati populis agitandum erunt usui comparate." Hac a Bolano dicta sententia, magna est commutatio facta voluntatum; neque quisquam omnium fuit, cui non Bolanus prudens ac sapiens videretur. Itaque lex in praesentia reiecta.

16   Atque eo quidem tempore Alexander, certior factus Carolum regem ad Novariam obsidione liberandam multa cottidie aggredi, multa moliri, neque adhuc Neapolitani regni cogitationem abiecisse illum intelligens, quod quidem et firmis etiam nunc veteribus praesidiis, et novis comparandis, tuebatur (naves enim Genuae atque Massiliae complures ad bellum instrui ornarique mandaverat), gravioribus eum litteris monuit ut intra mensem ex omnibus Italiae locis omnem belli apparatum abduceret; id ni faciat, sese illi eiusque populis aqua et igni interdicturum. Novaria deinde Ludovico restituta paceque facta, dedit etiam litteras ad Genuensium civitatem: eodem se in eos interdicto usurum, si quid in classem opis Carolo contulissent. Atque id ab eo Ludovicum petiisse nemini dubium fuit, ut ea se re, si uni foederis capiti non steterit, Carolo purgaret, quod pluris apud eam civitatem Alexandri auctoritas fuerit, divino praesertim iure adhibito, quo plerumque homines magnopere continentur, quam omnino sua.

17   Miserat ad senatum, prosperis reipublicae rebus cognitis, Turcarum rex certum hominem gratulatum, quod Carolum Galliae regem Italia suis armis expulisset. Is equum egregia forma dono patribus attulit; patres Bernardo Contareno miserunt.

every respect, then before you decide that Pisa is to be taken on, you must build up your stocks of materiel for the coming war against the people who lie between us and Pisa, and against its immediate neighbors." This expression of Bollani's views brought about a great change in opinion: the senators to a man now regarded him as prudent and wise, and the law was consequently deferred for the time being.

At the same time, the Pope learned that King Charles was 16 making constant and strenuous efforts to relieve the siege of Novara, and he realized that Charles had still not abandoned hope of the Kingdom of Naples, which indeed he was protecting with the old but still strong garrisons, as well as getting new ones ready. To that end he had ordered a good number of ships to be fitted out and readied for war, at Genoa and at Marseilles. Alexander sent him a letter to warn him in no uncertain terms to take all his military forces out of every part of Italy within a month, failing which he would excommunicate him and his subjects. Once Novara was restored to Ludovico il Moro and the peace concluded,[3] he sent a letter to the citizens of Genoa as well, to say that he would employ excommunication against them too if they gave Charles any assistance with his fleet. No one doubted that Ludovico had asked this favor of Alexander so that he could thereby excuse himself to Charles if he failed to meet just one clause of the treaty, for the pope's authority certainly carried more weight with Genoa than his own, especially when bolstered by religious sanction, which is a great restraint for the generality of mankind.

When he heard of the Venetian success, the sultan of Turkey 17 sent one of his men to the Senate to congratulate them on having expelled King Charles of France from Italy by force of arms. The messenger brought an extraordinarily fine horse as a gift for the senators; the senators sent it to Bernardo Contarini.

18   Interea, Ferdinando rebus modo prospere cedentibus, qui etiam
Luceriam in Dauniis vi cepit, modo autem relabentibus, cum eum
Galli aliquando intra oppidum ad Neapolim compulissent, diversisque in locis ei fortuna laeta interdum, saepius tristi se osten-
dente, ac spe regni sui recuperandi apud illius animum plane la-
bante, Alexander, eius precibus atque periculo permotus, a senatu
magno studio petiit uti exercitus partem aliquam, eius qui Novaria
redierat, ad Gallos expellendos Ferdinandumque sublevandum
mitteret; se curaturum uti aliquot eius regni oppida, quae mare at-
tingant, pignoris nomine, quoad quidquid ea in re senatus sumpti
fecisset Ferdinandus reponeret, reipublicae tenenda traderentur.
Senatus, nondum decreta exercitus profectione, inclinatis tamen
ad eam rem civium animis, Bernardum Contarenum cum Graecis
equitibus sexcentis Ravennam praemisit, quo minus ei, cum decerneretur, itineris illo perveniendi superesset. Quod posteaquam est
Romam renuntiatum, Ascanii suasu, qui diceret Venetos sua
sponte bellum suscepturos, non oportere quidquam eis oppidorum
sumpti nomine a Ferdinando tradi, res dilata legatique regii, qui
iam Venetias ad paciscendum cum senatu venerant, rogare tantum
de exercitu; nihil ultra polliceri. Id ubi senatus cognovit, et Ludovicum invidiae suae in rempublicam stimulis impelli agique animadvertit (nihil enim fere iis de rebus umquam Ascanius, nisi a
fratre monitus iussusque loquebatur), legatos ab se reiecit, nihil
esse confirmans, quod ea de causa in urbe horae spatium morarentur.

19   Interim cum Faventini, qui aestate proxima petierant a senatu
ut, quoniam certorum exulum insidias magnopere timerent, ipse
pro sua pietate oppidique vicinitate eius regendi curam susciperet,
Hestoremque plane puerum, Galeoti eius de quo priore libro sermonem habuimus filium, cuius erat in potestate civitas, auctoritate

Meanwhile matters were at times turning out well for 18 Ferrandino, as when he stormed Lucera in Apulia, at times badly, as when the French from time to time forced him back inside the walls of Naples. His luck in different places proved sometimes good but more often bad, and his hope of regaining the Kingdom was clearly faltering. Much moved by his entreaties and his dangerous plight, the pope urgently requested the Senate to send some of the troops that had returned from Novara to expel the French and relieve Ferrandino. He said he would arrange for a number of coastal towns of the Kingdom to be handed over to Venice to be held as security until Ferrandino repaid whatever expenses the Senate incurred in the matter. As yet undecided on the despatch of the army, though the citizens were minded to do so, the Senate sent Bernardo Contarini ahead to Ravenna with 600 stradiots to make the journey shorter when the order came. When this became known at Rome, Cardinal Ascanio Sforza[4] said that the Venetians would go to war anyway and that there was no need for Ferrandino to hand over any towns to them for their expenses. At his instance the matter was put off, and the king's ambassadors, who were already at Venice to seek an agreement with the Senate, asked only about the army without making any further promises. When the Senate came to learn of it, they realised that Ludovico was motivated and driven by his hatred of the Republic (for Ascanio hardly ever said anything on such matters unless he was advised or bidden by his brother), and dismissed the ambassadors with the observation that there was no reason for them to linger another hour in the city on that account.

Meanwhile, much alarmed at plots laid by a number of their 19 exiles, the people of Faenza had in the previous summer asked the Senate to take on the burden of ruling them, out of a sense of fellow feeling and in view of their proximity, and to defend by its authority Astorre Manfredi, the very young son of the Galeotto Manfredi I mentioned in an earlier book,[5] who was the lord of the

sua tueretur, postea rogandi et obtestandi patres ea de re tempus
nullum intermisissent, mense Decembri senatus decrevit uti Faventinorum civitas puerque princeps in reipublicae fidem reciperentur, mitterentque patres eo civem Venetum, qui pueri nomine
ius diceret; ipse autem puer equites cataphractos centum haberet,
stipendiumque in eos libras auri annuas octoginta. Neque non tamen, antequam decerneretur, iisdem exulibus, Florentinorum
adiutis ope, in eorum fines irrumpentibus, Bernardus Contarenus,
qui Ravennam venerat, cum Graecis equitibus militumque manu
auxilio a senatu missus, eos fudit fugavitque; ac regnum illud
puero, quod iam prope amiserat, plane constituit. Pauloque post
patrum suffragiis Dominicus Trivisanus, vir gravis atque prudens
habitus, qui puerum senatus nomine tueretur, oppidanisque ius
diceret, legatus est Faventiam profectus. Atque ante eos quidem
dies, uti horologium in foro ex reipublicae dignitate fieret, cui aedis Marciae procuratores aream darent, senatus censuit.

20   At Ferdinandi legati cum multos dies patribus placandis
consumpsissent, pollicitique essent Ferdinandum tria oppida nobi-
lissima cum eorum agris atque finibus, Tranum, Brundusium,
Hydruntum,[2] eo quo dictum est nomine, reipublicae traditurum,
anni insequentis initio, foederatorum omnium non approbantibus
modo, sed etiam adnitentibus legatis, pacta inita foedusque percussum est; quo civitas foedere traditis oppidis equites cataphractos septingentos, milites ter mille ad Ferdinandum mittere celeriter
teneretur; qui una cum ea classe quam Neapolim Contarenus legatus adduxerat tam diu eius imperata facerent, quoad bellum esset
confectum. Capitaque foederi sunt addita: uti a quaestoribus urbanis librae auri centum quinquaginta mutuae Ferdinandi legatis e

town. They had since then never stopped sending a constant stream of supplications and petitions to the senators on the matter, and in December the Senate decreed that they would take the city of Faenza and its young lord under their protection, and that they would send a Venetian citizen there to govern in the child's name. The boy himself was to have 100 heavy cavalry, and 80 gold pounds a year for their pay. Before the decree was passed, however, the exiles invaded the territory of Faenza with the aid of the Florentines, but were routed and put to flight by Bernardo Contarini, now arrived at Ravenna. Having been sent by the Senate to assist with light horse and a troop of infantry, Bernardo strengthened the boy's hold on the state that he had nearly lost. A little later, Domenico Trevisan, who was accounted a solid and prudent man, left for Faenza as a proveditor elected by the senators to watch over the boy in their name and to administer justice for the people. A short while before, the Senate resolved that a clock befitting the dignity of the Republic should be constructed in St. Mark's Square, and that the Procurators of St. Mark's should make space available for its erection.

Ferrandino's ambassadors spent many days placating the sena- 20 tors, and promised them that Ferrandino would give the Republic three fine towns with their lands and territories — Trani, Brindisi, and Otranto — on the terms previously agreed. At the beginning of the following year, with the representatives of all the allies 1496 not just approving but actively pressing the issue, agreement was reached and the treaty was concluded. Under the terms of the treaty, once the towns were handed over, Venice would be responsible for the quick despatch to Ferrandino of 700 heavy cavalry and 3,000 infantry. Together with the fleet that the proveditor Contarini had taken to Naples, they were to be under his command for as long as the war lasted. Certain clauses were subsequently added to the treaty: the city treasurers were to make an immediate loan of 150 gold pounds to Ferrandino's ambassadors. If

vestigio curarentur; uti si parte aliqua Ferdinandus Graecis equitibus quam cataphractis uti mallet, pro eo cataphractorum numero
quem de summa detraxisset Graecos sesquialteros haberet; uti ex
publicis oppidorum proventibus, si quid in magistratuum et prae-
sidiorum stipendia factis impensis superesset, id in accepti a Ferdinando tabulis ferretur; uti quemquam eo in regno virum principem civitas in fidem, nisi Ferdinandi permissu, ne reciperet; uti
frumentum, oleum reliquumve commeatum eis ex oppidis et finibus asportari sine solitis portoriis ne liceret; uti Gargani montis
saltum, qui a Gallis tenebatur, cum illum Ferdinandus recuperavisset, reipublicae traderet; quod tamen caput scriptum non est, voce
tantum atque verbis fidem fore quod convenerat facientibus agita-
tum. Atque id omnino foedus Alexander, suis ad senatum scriptis
litteris, ratum sanctumque iussit esse. Nam quoniam antiquitus in
regnum Neapolitanum pontifices maximi ius habent, caverant cum
primis patres, ea ut res Alexandri auctoritate perscripta firmaretur.

21   Foedere confecto, qui oppida reipublicae nomine a Ferdinando
reciperent missi; imperatorque Franciscus, cum ea de qua dictum
est manu, iussus in regnum sine mora proficisci. Iis cognitis rebus,
quas porro celerius more atque instituto civitatis fama vulgaverat,
quam plurima eius regni municipia brevi tempore ad Ferdinandum
redierunt. Arces autem Neapolitanae munitissimae duae, longa
obsidione certisque condicionibus separatim Ferdinando sunt hos
intra menses pauloque post redditae, cum Galli, qui eas obtinebant, Alfonsum Avalum, Aterni principem, virum magna excellen-
tique virtute, ad colloquium vocatum occidissent; quae quidem
plane mors Ferdinando, qui eum impense amabat (aliti enim edu-
catique una fuerant), incredibilem maerorem aegritudinemque at-

Ferrandino preferred to use light rather than heavy cavalry, whatever number of heavy cavalry he forwent, he could have half as many again of light horse. If there was anything left over from the public revenues once the wages of the magistrates and garrisons had been paid, it would be put down to Ferrandino's credit in the accounts. The city would not take any lord in the Kingdom under its protection except with Ferrandino's permission, nor would it be permitted to carry off grain, oil, or other provisions from the towns without paying the customary tariffs. The wooded promontory of Monte Gargano, presently under French control, would be transferred to Venice by Ferrandino when he recovered it. This last provision, however, was not written down, and there was only verbal assurance that the agreement would be put into effect. In a letter sent to the Senate, Pope Alexander asked for the treaty to be approved and ratified. The popes having had jurisdiction over the Kingdom of Naples from ancient times, the senators had been extremely careful to see that the business was confirmed by Alexander's written authority.

With the signing of the treaty, men were sent to receive the towns from Ferrandino in the name of the Republic, and the captain-general Francesco Gonzaga was ordered to set out for the Kingdom at once with the force I mentioned above. When this state of affairs became known — and rumor spread the news much more quickly than was usual in the city [Naples] — a great many communities of the Kingdom returned to Ferrandino within a short time. And in the space of those months and a little later, both of the two very strong castles at Naples were separately returned to Ferrandino. This followed a long siege and was subject to certain conditions, the French, who held the castles, having killed Alfonso d'Avalos (the Marquis of Pescara and a man of quite exceptional courage) after summoning him to a parley. His death brought extraordinary grief and pain to Ferrandino, who loved him dearly, for they had been raised and educated together. 21

tulit. Qua tandem excussa, Ioannam, Ferdinandi avi sui filiam, Alfonsi patris alia matre sororem, in matrimonium duxit; easque nuptias Alexander, quando legibus fieri non poterant, sua indulgentia comprobavit. Atque haec tunc quidem in Ferdinandi partibus agitabantur.

22   At Carolus, in Galliam rediens, nondum traiectis Alpibus, Philippum Argentonium ad senatum misit: existimare se eodem in foedere quod cum Ludovico fecisset rempublicam esse comprehensam, propterea quod imperator Venetus legatique ei foederi, cum scriberetur, adfuissent; quod si aliter se res habeat, scire se cupere, an vellet civitas tum demum comprehendi; petere autem ut Monopolitanorum oppidum, quod ab suis vi atque armis classis reipublicae praefectus cepisset, senatus restitueret, atque a Ferdinando auxiliis iuvando abstineret. Quarum is rerum neutra impetrata discessit. Carolo in Galliam profecto, filius, quem unicum habebat, tres natus annos moritur. Qua quidem morte accidit ut, cum postea Carolus iterum exercitum coegisset, quem ad Ferdinandum repellendum, Aloisio propinquo suo duce, mari Caietam mitteret, Aloisius, cui regnum Galliae, Carolo sine liberis maribus moriente, lege Gallorum obveniebat, profectionem respuerit. Itaque Carolus, cum alio duce nollet exercitum mittere, rem iam prope confectam distulit; pauloque post, dilapsis cunctando militibus, ea omnino missio, magnis impensis instituta, certissimaque iis quos Neapoli reliquerat ducibus cum verbis, tum litteris ac nuntiis promissa totiens auxilia interpositaque regia fides ad nihilum reciderunt.

23   Ludovicus autem, Gallici belli metu deposito, cum id quod Pisarum civitas a senatu petierat amicorum litteris cognovisset, Pisani vero, patefacta ipsorum postulatione, legatos etiam palam

At length he shook off his grief and took in marriage Giovanna, the daughter of his grandfather Ferrante and sister of his father Alfonso by another mother. Alexander gave his approval to the marriage by papal dispensation, since it could not take place lawfully. Such were the events touching Ferrandino's affairs at that time.

King Charles, meanwhile, had not yet crossed the Alps on his 22 return to France. He sent Philippe de Commines to the Senate to say that he believed that the Republic was included in the treaty he had made with Ludovico il Moro, because the Venetian general and proveditors had been present at the signing. But if things were otherwise, he wanted to know if the city was prepared to be included in it now. He asked the Senate to give him back the town of Monopoli, which the captain of the Venetian fleet had seized from his men by force, and to refrain from assisting Ferrandino with reinforcements. Commines departed without achieving either of these aims. After Charles left for France, his only son died at the age of three. Charles subsequently assembled another army under the leadership of his relative Louis to send overseas to Gaeta and drive Ferrandino back, but on account of the death of Charles' son, Louis refused to set out, as under French law the kingship of France devolved upon him if Charles were to die without issue. And so, since Charles was unwilling to despatch the army under another leader, he put off a matter that was practically concluded, and shortly afterwards, when the soldiers had melted away due to the delay, the expedition which had been undertaken at great expense and the troops promised as a certainty to the captains left behind at Naples, verbally and in writing and by messenger, all came to nothing, and with it the pledge the king had given.

But once the fear of a war with France was removed and 23 Ludovico learned from letters of friends what Pisa had asked of the Senate (indeed, the Pisans themselves had made their request plain by openly sending ambassadors to Venice on the matter), he

Venetias eadem de re misissent, ne id quod verebatur accideret, uti ea civitas sub unius reipublicae imperium redigeretur, sese senatui obtulit, si Pisas esse defendendas existimaret, eius rei socium et adiutorem futurum; videri autem sibi aequissimum esse eas defendi, propterea quod Florentini foedus cum Carolo percussissent; cuius ipse foederis legatum, occulte ad Carolum proficiscentem, suis in finibus interceperit. Re saepius a patribus agitata, Ludovico magis magisque cottidie adnitente, lex tandem in senatu lata est, foederatorum omnium legatis approbantibus, uti Alexandri et reipublicae ac Ludovici armis atque opibus Pisae defenderentur; additumque legi, ut in Liguribus milites bis mille reipublicae pecunia conscriberentur Pisasque mitterentur. Id autem uti Ligures permitterent, Ludovicus antea se receperat effecturum.

24   Iis intellectis rebus, Florentini, antequam auxilia contra se convenirent, omni cura diligentiaque adhibita, sex militum milibus celeriter coactis, non sine spe potiundi oppidi Pisas contenderunt atque ad portas cum tormentis accesserunt. Hostes patefactis portis impetum in illos fecerunt, fortiterque pugnantes propulerunt eorumque tormentis sunt potiti. Neque multo post Paulus Vitellius, ex Ursina Romanorum factione ac gente, vir fortis, quem Pisani suis copiis praefecerant, eorum stipendio emerito, ad Florentinos sese contulit; ac praefectura quam ei contulerant inita, cum exercitum decem milium hominum confecisset, Pisas acerrime adortus, in oppidi suburbium se iniecit; ex quo tamen ab oppidanis, qui quam magnam potuerant manum et ipsi coegerant, reiectus expulsusque est. Sed illud idem suburbium Florentini postea cum cepissent retinerentque, Petrum Medicem veriti, qui, Ursinos

offered his services to the Senate, in case his fears were realised and the city fell into the power of Venice alone. If they were minded to defend Pisa, he said, he would be their ally and helper in the enterprise. He said that he thought it quite right that Pisa should be protected, since the Florentines had formed an alliance with Charles — he himself had intercepted in his own territory the legate who negotiated the treaty as he returned in secret to the king. After lengthy discussions among the senators, and with Ludovico pressing them harder each day, a law was finally passed in the Senate with the approval of the ambassadors of all the allies that Pisa should be defended with the combined arms and resources of the pope, Venice and Ludovico. Appended to the law was a provision that 2,000 soldiers should be raised in Liguria at the Republic's expense and sent to Pisa. Ludovico had earlier undertaken to see to it that the Genoese would permit this to happen.

When they learned of this, the Florentines quickly assembled 24 6,000 foot soldiers before the troops could unite against them, and with might and main hastened to Pisa in the hope of taking the town, arriving before the gates with their artillery. Opening the gates, the enemy charged them, and fighting manfully drove them off and seized their artillery. Shortly afterwards Paolo Vitelli, one of the Roman Orsini party and faction, and a brave man whom the Pisans had put in command of their forces, went over to the Florentines when he had fulfilled his contract with Pisa. Taking on the captaincy which the Florentines conferred on him, he put together an army of 10,000 infantry and made a fierce attack on Pisa. Vitelli rushed into the outskirts of the town, but was driven back and forced out by the Pisans, who had themselves gathered as many troops as they could. The Florentines later retook and held on to those outskirts, but they then abandoned Pisa and turned to defending themselves for fear of Piero de' Medici, who

affines suos secum ducens, in ipsorum fines iam iamque irrupturus dicebatur, Pisis relictis ad sua se tuenda converterunt.

25   Interim, conscriptis per internuntios reipublicae quingentis Genuae militibus Pisasque missis, Ludovicus Gasparem Severinatem cum militibus, ut pollicitus est, alteris totidem, ut re evenit, paucissimis illo misit, qui utrisque praeesset. Quo quidem tempore, Florentinis ab Carolo contendentibus, ut Pisarum arcem, quae ab eius militibus tenebatur, pretio redimere sibi liceret, Pisani, maiore etiam quam illi pollicebantur pecunia partim pollicita, partim iam tradita, arcem receperunt, receptamque diruerunt. Eius pecuniae partem decemviri Genuae curatam persolverunt, libras auri ad quadraginta.

26   Vere autem iam adventante, quod Dominicus Calbus maioribus in comitiis Bernardino Minoto, Petri filio, pugnum in os impegerat, decemvirum magistri Calbum e comitiis in carcerem duci iusserunt; deinde collegii decreto in insulam Cyprum exulatum deportari mandaverunt. Tum, ut urbanorum navalium res multiplices atque variae, quaeque magna et perpetua indigent cura, diligentius administrarentur, ad reliquos navalium magistratus qui antiquitus maioribus comitiis creantur, triumviri ex principibus civitatis ex senatorum suffragio adlecti sunt additique illis tamquam magistri. Iique postea triumviri numquam sunt creari desiti. Aestate vero proxima, ne possessores bonae fidei omni tempore turbarentur (nonnumquam enim accidebat delatorum improbitate atque audacia uti de suis rebus periclitari aliquem contingeret, etiam si per multos annos possedisset), legem decemviri iusserunt: quarum rerum quis triginta annos in possessione fuisset, earum rerum peti ab eo nihil licere; neque deferri quemquam licere, nisi si decemvirum magistri permisissent.

was reportedly on the point of bursting into their territory at the head of his Orsini relatives.[6]

In the meantime 500 foot soldiers were recruited at Genoa by 25 Venetian agents and despatched to Pisa. Ludovico then sent Gaspare da Sanseverino there, as it turned out with very few soldiers and not the further 500 that he had promised, to take command of both contingents. It was at this time, when the Florentines were pressing Charles to sell them the fortress at Pisa which his soldiers held, that the Pisans retook the fortress and at once destroyed it, having handed over or promised to hand over even more money than the Florentines were offering. The Council of Ten discharged part of this debt, arranging for the payment of about 40 gold pounds at Genoa.

As spring arrived, the Heads of the Ten ordered Domenico 26 Calbo to be taken from the council chamber to prison because he had punched Bernardino di Pietro Minotto in the face in the Great Council. By a subsequent decree of the Council of Ten they ordered his deportation and exile to Cyprus. Then to improve the complicated and disparate administration of the Arsenal shipyards, which needed constant and concentrated attention, to the other magistrates of the Arsenal, who had long been elected by the Great Council, a board of three chosen from the leading citizens by senatorial vote was added to act as their Heads. This board of three has continued to be elected uninterruptedly from that time onwards. In the previous summer, the Council of Ten enacted a law to put a stop to the constant harassment suffered by bona fide property owners, for it sometimes happened that owing to the shameless effrontery of informers a man might find his property at risk, even if he had owned it for many years. By the terms of the law, no property that had been in someone's possession for 30 years could be claimed from him, nor could anyone lodge an accusation without permission of the Heads of the Ten.

27   Ludovicus cum eiusdem veris tempore a Maximiliano magnis
largitionibus impetrasset ut eum regem Mediolani appellaret, ea
de re gratulatum Hieronymum Leonem, quem antea ad Ludovicum senatus legaverat, ire patres iusserunt. Atque illis etiam diebus a praefecto classis reipublicae certum hominem Naupliam cum
pecunia missum, ut equites quot posset illis in locis conscriberet
navigiisque imponeret ad urbem deportandos, adversa tempestate
complures Maleae dies cum detineretur iterque pedibus facere vellet, accersitis Nauplia equitibus ducentis, qui ei praesidio essent,
saeptum in itinere Turcarum equitatus magno impetu est aggressus, numero amplius sexcenti; quibuscum Nauplii equites fortissime pugnantes maiorem eorum partem interfecerunt, reliquos
fugae mandarunt, paucis ex suis desideratis, vulneratis paulo pluribus.

28   Contarenus autem, cum Graecis equitibus quingentis petente
Ferdinando in eius regnum a senatu praemissus, ubi Suessam venit seque cum Federico, regis patruo, qui Suessae erat, coniunxit,
oppida quattuor quae a Gallis tenebantur se uti dederent compulit. Idem cum ad Gallutianos temptandos cum tercentis equitibus
se contulisset, Galli autem, ut eos tuerentur, pluribus ex locis
manu coacta, impetum in illum fecissent, fortiter pugnans eos sustinuit, proelioque non intermisso, interfectis compluribus in fugam
vertit oppidumque cepit. Idem etiam paulo post, eodem equitum
numero[3] in insidiis se occultans, praemissis Frangetium, quo in
oppidulo erant Galli, paucis ex suis, qui discurrerent, Gallos, pau-
citatem illorum suam praedam opinantes insecutosque, ubi ad insidias pervenerunt, evolans, incitatis in eos equis, cum multo illi
plures essent, tamen fudit, non parvo eorum interfecto numero
atque capto.

In that spring too, Ludovico prevailed upon Maximilian to   27
name him duke of Milan by means of substantial bribes, and the
senators told Girolamo Leone, whom they had previously sent to
Ludovico as their envoy, to go to offer him their congratulations. It
was also in those days that the Venetian captain of the fleet sent a
man to Nauplia with money expressly to recruit as many cavalry as
he could in those parts and put them on ships to be taken to Venice. Detained at Cape Malea for some days by bad weather, he decided to make the journey on foot, but accompanied by 200 horse
brought from Nauplia for his protection he was attacked en route
by a great onslaught of more than 600 Turkish cavalry. The
Nauplian cavalry fought with great valor and killed the larger part
of them, putting the rest to flight with the loss of a few of their
own men and rather more wounded.

At Ferrandino's request the Senate had sent Bernardo   28
Contarini on ahead into the Kingdom with 500 stradiots.
Reaching Sessa Aurunca and joining forces with the king's uncle
Federico, who was at Sessa, he forced the surrender of four towns
held by the French. With 300 cavalry he turned to an assault on
the people of Galluccio, but the French had assembled forces from
a number of places to defend them and launched an attack on
him. Fighting bravely, he managed to hold them off, and after killing many of them as the battle raged without respite, he put them
to flight and took the town. A little later, the same Contarini lay
in ambush with another 300 horse, after sending up a few of
his men to wander around Fragneto Monforte, a small town where
the French were. When the French saw how few they were, they
thought them easy prey and gave chase. As they reached the ambush, Contarini sprang forth, driving the horses on against them,
and although the French were much more numerous, he nevertheless put them to flight, killing and capturing a considerable
number.

29   Interim, imperatore cum reliquo exercitu adventante, Philippum Rubeum, Guidi filium, per silvam Casinatem sua cum equitum turma temere vadentem, Ioannes, Iuliani cardinalis frater, magna equitum, multo maiore militum manu, clamore sublato, excepit; quibuscum Rubeus diu pugnans, paucis ex suis interfectis atque captis, sarcinariis iumentis aliquot amissis, ad imperatorem se recepit. Quod tamen detrimentum Contarenus facile sarciit; nam cum Ferdinandi missu excursionem in Severinatum fines usque ad ipsorum oppidi muros atque portas fecisset, quo in oppido esse Virginium Ursinum atque Vitellios ab exploratoribus cognoverat, neque quisquam egredi ausus ei se obviam ostendisset, rediens Troianum Sabellum, cum equitibus cataphractis quinquaginta se ad illos conferentem, in itinere deprehensum fudit, parte plus equitum media tum interfecta, tum capta.

30   Paulo autem post, cum Gallorum exercitus timore, qui erat equitum cataphractorum ad octingentos, levis armaturae ad quingentos, militum Helvetiorum ad quattuor milia, rex in oppidum Foliam se cum suo exercitu contulisset, praesertim quod illis diebus Galli septingentos milites Germanos, qui in Raetis conscripti ad illum se conferebant, interceptos male habuerant, seque oppidi muro Gallis obsidentibus tueretur, Contarenus, qui cum illo erat, apud eum questus non esse aequum Graecos equites moenibus inclusos contineri, petiit uti se emitteret. Qua impetrata re, Gallos saepe lacessendo, saepe imparatos aggrediendo, saepe in vigiliis noctem totam continendo, nonnumquam male multando, obsidionem relinquere ac longius recedere seseque in tutum recipere coegit. Neque multo post imperator, Gallis alio conversis, Valacam oppidum cingens, murorum parte tormentis diruta scalisque positis, vi captum diripuit, interfectis qui in oppido erant omnibus,

As the captain-general Gonzaga arrived with the rest of the   29
army, meanwhile, Filippo di Guido de' Rossi and his troop of cavalry were passing in loose formation through the forest of Cassino
when with a great shout he was attacked by Giovanni della
Rovere, Cardinal Giuliano's brother, with a great many horse and
even more infantry. After a lengthy fight in which a few of his men
were killed or captured and some pack animals lost, de' Rossi
withdrew to join the general. But Bernardo Contarini easily made
up for this loss. Ordered by Ferrandino to make an incursion into
the territory of San Severo, he had gone right up to the walls and
gates of the town (where Virginio Orsini and the Vitelli were, according to his spies) without anyone daring to come out and face
him. On his way back he caught Troiano Savelli and 50 heavy cavalry heading towards the enemy at San Severo, and routed them,
more than half of them being killed or captured.

But a little later, in fear of the French army, which consisted of   30
about 800 heavy cavalry, 500 stradiots, and 4,000 Swiss soldiers,
Ferrandino had taken himself and his army into the town of
Foglia.[7] He was particularly prompted to do so by the recent inter-
ception and maltreatment by the French of 700 German infantry
who had been recruited in the Tyrol and were making their way to
him. So Ferrandino defended himself behind the town walls from
the besieging French. Contarini, who was with him there, protested that it was not right to keep the stradiots shut up inside the
walls and asked to be sent out. His request granted, by frequent
harassment of the French, and frequent attacks on them when
they were unprepared, by repeatedly keeping them awake throughout the night, and on occasion dealing out harsh punishment,
Contarini forced them to abandon the siege and withdraw to a safe
position at a distance. Not long afterwards, when the French had
turned elsewhere, the general surrounded the town of Vallata, and
after breaching part of the walls with his artillery and putting
siege-ladders in position, he took it by force and sacked it. Every-

cum milites nec mulieribus nec infantibus pepercissent, propterea quod ea in oppugnatione centum ex imperatoris exercitu fortes viros hostes oppidanique interfecerant. Eodem impetu imperator multa eius regionis oppida brevi ad deditionem compulit. Galli, Canusium aggressi, cum ab oppidanis quinquaginta auri libras accepissent, ne oppidum diriperent neve ingrederentur, tamen, Helvetiis militibus irrumpentibus, caedes ingens facta oppidumque direptum est.

31 In ea vero regione quam Basilicatam appellant, trium oppidorum populi per sese Gallos a quibus regebantur occiderunt seque regi dediderunt. Contarenus, et ipse multa cum praeda per Severinatum fines ad exercitum se referens, magnam hostium manum oppido egressam secumque congressam disiecit, militibus equitibusque septuaginta interfectis, captis nonaginta. Tum Consalvus, Hispanae classis praefectus, vir magni animi egregiaeque virtutis, in Calabris egressus, Crotonem, quod fugato pridem rege ad Gallos oppidum redierat, vi cepit, Gallosque, quique eorum erant partium, iusto proelio fudit, interfectis centurionibus praefectisque equitum septem, militibus et equitibus ducentis, captis egregii nominis plus viginti, equis militaribus sarcinariisque quadringentis.

32 Iis diebus naves longae sex, ex classe reipublicae quae in portu Neapolitano erat, Genuam sunt ire iussae (rumor enim invaluerat Carolo regi classem in Galliae Provinciae portubus comparari), ut quae a Gallis administrarentur inspicerent et, si possent, impedirent navesque incenderent. Haec dum sic agitarentur, diversisque in locis, dispari etiam eventu belli, meliore tamen quam antea fortuna, Ferdinandi regnum caedibus et rapinis arderet, Galli, ex eventu rerum timidiores aliquanto facti, Telam, quod a Venusia oppidum duodecim milia passus abest, non magna spe eius pot-

one in the town was killed: the soldiers spared neither women nor children, because in the course of the attack the enemy and the townsfolk had killed 100 brave men of the general's army. In the same campaign the general forced many towns in the area to surrender in short order. When the French launched an attack on Canosa di Puglia, despite the fact that they had taken 50 gold pounds from the inhabitants not to plunder the town or even enter it, their Swiss soldiers nevertheless broke in, resulting in massive slaughter and the sack of the town.

In the region called Basilicata, on the other hand, the people 31 of three towns killed their French rulers of their own accord and surrendered themselves to Ferrandino. As he returned to his army through the lands of San Severo with a good deal of booty, Contarini himself put to flight a large enemy force that had left the town and engaged him in combat, killing 70 foot soldiers and cavalry and capturing 90. Then Gonzalo de Córdoba, the admiral of the Spanish fleet, a man of great spirit and remarkable courage, disembarked in Calabria and took Crotone by force of arms, the town having returned to the French after the king had fled long before. Gonzalo broke the French and their supporters in a pitched battle. Seven infantry officers and captains of horse were killed, as were 200 infantry and cavalry, and more than 20 nobles were taken prisoner, plus 400 warhorses and packhorses.

Around that time six galleys of the Venetian fleet in Naples 32 harbor were ordered to Genoa to find out what the French were up to and, if possible, to block and burn their ships, for there was a persistent rumor that a fleet was being assembled for King Charles in the ports of Provence. While all this was going on, and Ferrandino's kingdom was ablaze with slaughter and pillage in various places and with varying fortunes of war, though attended with better success than before, the French and their general, somewhat more timid now in view of what had happened, attacked Tela, a town twelve miles from Venosa, though with no

iundi cum eorum duce aggressi, oppidanos, certis condicionibus se
dedentes, fide fracta ingressi diripuerunt. Id intelligens Ferdinandus Contarenum eo praemisit, qui Gallorum partem, prope oppidum repertam, in fugam atque intra muros compulit, equitibus cataphractis plus triginta captis. Eum subsecutus rex mille ad
oppidum passus loco tuto castra posuit. Eodem Consalvus e Calabris cum ea quam habebat manu, Guidus Ubaldus Metaurensium
dux, quem senatus foederatique auxilio regi submiserant, e Brutiis
venerunt.

33   Aucto exercitu apud Telam rex cum esset, ad molas frumentarias corrumpendas, quibus oppidani utebantur, itineraque duo in-
tercludenda, Consalvi milites qui tragulis utebantur misit, cum
paulo ante Contarenum Venusiam misisset, veritus ne inde hostibus, quorum erat in potestate oppidum, auxilia mitterentur com-
meatusque subministraretur. Relinquebatur hostibus iter unum
montanum, quo itinere commeatus in iumentis subvehi poterat;
idque magnis adhibitis praesidiis cum fieret, Contarenus congressus praesidium dissipavit commeatumque cum iumentis omnibus
interceptum abduxit. Posteroque die centum ex suis uti Venusiam
adcurrerent imperavit; ii praeda facta sub oppidi muris cum essent, oppidani autem milites ter centum, cum paucis equitibus
egressi, recuperandae praedae spe proelium commisissent, ex illis
octoginta occiderunt captivosque complures fecerunt; ex quibus
erat Fundos obtinens.

34   Eo tempore, Antonio primum anno superiore propter valetudi-
nem a classe reipublicae quae Neapolim mittebatur remoto, deinde
domum revocato, Malchio Trivisanus ei suffectus cum navibus
longis aliquot Corcyra in Apuliam traiecit atque, in Calabros
contendens, cum reliqua classe, quam ad se vocaverat, coniunctus,
complura in litore aut vicina mari oppida regis imperium recipere

great hope of gaining it. While the townspeople were arranging the terms of their surrender, the French broke their word, entered the town and plundered the inhabitants. When he learned of this, Ferrandino sent Contarini on ahead to Tela. Coming upon some of the French near the town, Contarini forced them to flee inside the walls, taking captive more than 30 of the heavy cavalry. The king followed him and pitched his camp in a secure spot a mile from the town. Gonzalo de Córdoba, too, came there from Calabria with whatever troops he had, and Guidobaldo, Duke of Urbino, from the Abruzzi, sent by the Senate and the League to help the king.

Settled at Tela with his army thus enlarged, the king des- 33 patched Gonzalo's soldiers to use their spears to wreck the grain mills used by the townspeople and block two of the roads, having a little earlier sent Contarini to Venosa for fear that reinforcements and supplies might be sent from there to the enemy, who controlled the town. The enemy was left with a single route through the mountains by which supplies could be carried on pack animals. This was being done under heavy guard when Contarini engaged them, put the guard to flight, and seized the supplies, carrying them off with all the animals. The next day he told 100 of his men to hurry to Venosa. They were by the town walls with the booty they had taken when 300 soldiers of the town emerged with a few horsemen and joined battle in the hope of recovering the booty, of whom they slew 80 and took many captive, among them the lord of Fondi.[8]

The previous year, on account of his ill health, Antonio 34 Grimani had first been relieved of his command of the Venetian fleet being sent to Naples and then called back home. Now his replacement Melchiorre Trevisan crossed from Corfu to Apulia with some galleys and hastened to Calabria. Having summoned the rest of the fleet, he joined up with them there and forced a number of towns on the coast or nearby to accept the king's authority. When

coegit. Demum Paulam veniens, cum oppidani, missis ad eos qui
oppidum regi peterent, deditionem renuissent, ille autem ad oppugnationem se comparavisset velletque muro succedere, mulieres,
passis crinibus porta cum infantibus egressae, ad illius se navem
plorantes ac pacem petentes profuderunt. Quibus commotus milites continuit oppidumque Paulam in regis fidem omnibus incolu-
mibus oppidanis recepit. Ferdinandus, quo ad Telam Gallos diligentius obsideret omnemque iis commeatus facultatem eriperet,
castra propius oppidum admoveri mandaverat. Ea re Gallis enun-
tiata, magnum calonum et lixarum numerum equitesque cataphractos, qui eis praesidio essent, centum quinquaginta, levis armaturae, qui sagittis utebantur, alteros totidem celeriter portis
emiserunt, uti ex vicinis oppido villis vicisque quidquid possent
pabuli colligerent atque in oppidum comportarent, reliquum omne
succenderent, ne hostes eo uti possent.

35   Imperator, ea de re certior factus, cum Philippo Rubeo equitibusque Italis levis armaturae quos circum se habere consueverat
celeriter insecutus, proelio cum Gallis acriter commisso caedeque
facta, refugere illos in oppidum compulit. Quibus pulsis castrisque
regis prope oppidum positis, cum Galli commeatu laborarent
diesque complures sine spe levandae inopiae se continuissent,
equitibus praeterea et militibus stipendium deberetur neque pecunia suppeteret, missis ultro citroque internuntiis ipsoque duce
cum rege ad colloquium admisso, tertiodecimo Kalendas Sextiles
pacti sunt uti, si auxilia intra mensem ab rege Carolo ad sese non
mitterentur, quibus auxiliis exire oppido atque in aperto consistere
audeant, regno Neapolitano cederent, exceptis oppidis Venusia,
Caieta, Tarento; ipsis interim ab rege commeatus copia fieret; cedentibus autem rex suum praesidium adiungeret, quo Puteolos ac-

he came at length to Paola, the inhabitants refused to surrender to
envoys asking for the town in the king's name. Trevisan prepared
to attack and was ready to approach the walls when the women of
the town, their hair undone and with infants in their arms, came
out of the gate and streamed toward his ship, weeping and begging
for peace. Moved at their plight, he held off his soldiers and took
Paola's submission to the king, with no harm coming to the
townspeople. In order to place the French at Tela under more
effective siege and ensure that they had no access to provisions,
Ferrandino ordered the camp to be moved closer to the town.
When this was revealed to them, the French quickly sent out of
the gates a great number of servants and camp-followers, and 150
heavy cavalry to protect them and the same number of mounted
crossbowmen, so that they might gather and bring back to town
whatever food they could from the neighboring farms and villages,
burning the rest so the enemy could not use it.

When the general Gonzaga learned of this, he at once set off in   35
pursuit, accompanied by Filippo de' Rossi and the Italian light cavalry that he generally kept about him. After a fierce engagement
with the French, with casualties on their side, he forced them to
retreat into the town. When they had been driven back and the
king's camp pitched close to the town, the French faced great difficulties in getting supplies, staying put for many days without hope
of relief. In addition pay was owed to the cavalry and foot soldiers,
but there were no funds to give them. In this situation they sent
out envoys far and wide, and their commander was actually
granted an audience with the king. On 20 July they came to an
agreement that if within a month King Charles had not sent them
reinforcements with which they might venture to leave the town
and take a stand in the open, they would quit the Kingdom of Naples, except for the towns of Venosa, Gaeta, and Taranto. In the
interim, they would be given provisions by the king, and as they
departed, the king would give them a guard to enable them to

cedere navesque in Galliam traiecturi conscendere tuto possent. Eiusque rei cum ipsi obsides regi dedissent, legatum Venetum, quem cum Ferdinando esse intellexerant, ab rege adhiberi voluerunt, qui eis ita fore uti convenerat reipublicae nomine sponsor esset.

36   Iis scriptis firmatisque condicionibus, Gallorum dux regi est pollicitus, si sibi centum auri libras mutuo det, quibus stipendia quae debet exercitui persolvat, sese triduo cessurum oppidumque traditurum. Accepta rex condicione quinquaginta ei libras numerari statim iussit; reliquas alteras quinquaginta Helvetiis militibus, quibus debebantur quosque sacramentum apud se dicere cupiebat, quaestorem suum numeraturum recepit. Illi a Gallis missi regi libentes paruerunt, ad illumque transierunt. Gallis oppido tradito abeuntibus, rex imperatorem Venetum adiunxit, qui cum Graecis equitibus reliquisque Italis levis armaturae curaret ne quid eis in itinere noceretur. Contarenus, febri permolesta implicitus, adesse ipse non poterat, ex eaque febri paucis post diebus est mortuus, vir ad bella gerenda atque rempublicam armis illustrandam, si ei vita suppeditavisset, plane natus. Cuius postea matri auri libra annua in victum a senatu constituta; duabus autem sororibus, alterae dos auri librae viginti, alterae in sacrarum virginum collegium ternae librae.

37   Postea cum rex Salernum ac nonnulla alia vi, nonnulla condicionibus oppida municipiaque recepisset, aliqua etiam sponte ad illum sua rediissent, Ursinos, Vitellios, qui ex Gallorum erant partibus, fugavisset planeque dissipavisset, ipse autem, si qui reliqui essent in eius regno Galli, ab iis nihil sibi magnopere verendum existimaret, Graecos equites, quorum opera egregia et fideli fuerat

reach Pozzuoli and take ship for the crossing to France in safety. When they had given the king hostages as pledges of this understanding, they desired to have the Venetian ambassador, whom they had learned was with Ferrandino, employed by the king as guarantor in the name of the Republic that the agreement would be carried out.

With these conditions written down and signed, the French 36 commander promised the king that if 100 gold pounds were loaned him so he could give the army the pay he owed them, he would hand over the town and leave in three days. The offer accepted, the king ordered 50 pounds to be paid him at once. The remaining 50 he undertook to have his paymaster pay out to the Swiss soldiers, to whom they were owed and whom he wanted to take the oath of allegiance in his presence. Released by the French, the Swiss were happy to be subject to the king, and they passed over into his service. As the French were leaving after the town was handed over, the king added to their number the Venetian general, along with the stradiots and the rest of the Italian light cavalry, to see to it that they suffered no harm en route. Contarini, in the grip of a very severe fever, was not able to be present in person, and he died of the fever a few days later, a man clearly born to fight war and add military luster to the Republic had he lived longer. The Senate later gave his mother an annual grant of a gold pound to live on, and to one of his sisters 20 pounds as dowry, to the other 3 pounds to enter a convent.

Later the king took back Salerno and other towns and commu- 37 nities, some by force, others after coming to terms, others again returning to him of their own free will. He also routed and altogether shattered the forces of the Orsini and Vitelli, who had taken the French side, and came to believe if there were any Frenchmen left in his kingdom, he had nothing much to fear from them. He then first of all discharged the stradiots, by whom he had been excellently and loyally served, so as to reduce his ex-

usus, quo minus sumpti faceret, primos omnium missos fecit. Paucis post diebus, imperatori valetudine temptato omni cum exercitu abeundi facultas data. Metaurensium autem et Pisaurensium principes Alexandrique filium, quibus stipendium a foederatis pendebatur, Prosperumque Columnam, cum sua quemque manu, navesque longas reipublicae decem, onerarias Hispanae classis quamplures, tum Federicum patruum, qui praeesset, Caietam, quod Galli oppidum communierant, misit. Atque a Malchione triremes duae Salernitanorum principi, sedibus patriis pulso, quibus ille in Galliam Provinciam transmitteret, petente Ferdinando traditae. Acceperat etiam in urbe a senatu Ferdinandus mutuas auri libras sexaginta. Iisdem diebus Vestini legatos de deditione ad senatum miserunt, neque sunt recepti. Cumque in Calabris Ferdinandi navem onerariam Galli qui illis in locis erant, pace facta, Neapolim appulsuri conscendissent nautaeque cursum eo dirigerent, illi nautis comprehensis navem alio convertere coeperunt; sed cum, magna coorta tempestate, malo infracto antennae concidissent, nautis ad gubernaculum revocatis, Neapolitano portu capto, omnes in vincula coniecti sunt.

38   Ferdinandus autem cum graviter ex intestinis in Vesuvio laboraret, episcopum Theani, quem habebat in custodia, securi uti percuterent suis imperavit; addubitansque eius rei ministros sese aegro dicto audientes non fuisse, episcopi caput in cubiculum ad se afferri iussit; quo inspecto quievit. Pauloque post Neapolim allatus, urgente vi morbi Nonis Octobribus excessit e vita; cuius locum Federicus, eo ipso die una cum Malchione Caieta Neapolim approperans, a regni principibus suffectus tenuit. Is, regiis acceptis insignibus, primum omnium Salernitanorum principi abitum par-

penses. A few days later the captain-general, beset by ill health, was given permission to leave with his whole army. The king despatched to Gaeta, a town whose fortifications the French had strengthened, the duke of Urbino, the lord of Pesaro, and Pope Alexander's son,[9] all of them on the League's payroll, and also Prospero Colonna, each commander with his own force. He also sent there 10 of the Republic's galleys, and a great many merchant ships of the Spanish fleet, with his uncle Federico to take charge of them. At Ferrandino's request two galleys were handed over by Melchiorre Trevisan to the prince of Salerno,[10] who had been driven from his ancestral estates, to take him to Provence. Ferrandino had also received in Venice a loan of 60 gold pounds from the Senate. In the same period the people of Vieste sent spokesmen to the Senate to discuss their surrender, but the Senate would not receive them. In Calabria, after the peace was signed, the Frenchmen in those parts boarded one of Ferrandino's merchant vessels on the pretext of wanting to land at Naples, and the sailors set their course in that direction, but the French seized them and began to steer the ship in another direction. A great storm arose, however, in which the mast was shattered and the yard-arms collapsed. The sailors were called back to the rudder, and when they made the port of Naples, all the French were thrown into jail.

While he was seriously indisposed with an intestinal ailment   38 at Vesuvius, Ferrandino ordered his men to behead the bishop of Teano, whom he had in custody. Doubting that his henchmen would obey his order while he was ill, he told them to bring the head of the bishop to him in his bedchamber, and when he had seen it, he calmed down. A little later, as the disease tightened its grip, he was taken to Naples and passed away on 7 October. In the company of Melchiorre Trevisan, Federico rushed from Gaeta to Naples that very day and took his place, being appointed Ferrandino's successor by the princes of the Kingdom. On receiv-

anti auctor, ne discederet, fuit, regni praefectura, qui magistratus habetur amplissimus, ei tradita filiaque sua illius desponsa filio. Reliquos deinde viros principes, qui cum Ferdinando dissidebant, prope omnes sibi amicos certis condicionibus atque muneribus reddidit. Nondum autem iis confectis rebus, dum reginas Federicus inviseret, unam quae patris, alteram quae fratris filii uxor fuerat, Bissinianorum principis, qui una cum plerisque in procubiculo regem operiebatur, famulus gladio districto erum percussit, geminatis ter ictibus, interficere illum cupiens; comprehensus, quaestione habita dixit id efficere quod fecisset se in animo annos tredecim habuisse, propterea quod princeps suam olim sororem violavisset; antea patrandi facinoris occasionem idoneam sibi nullam datam; tunc rem ad exitum perducere vel certo vitae suae periculo voluisse.

39   Paucis post diebus Federicus, Malchione omni cum classe dimisso, suum Caietam exercitum adduxit; ac parte suburbiorum et montis capta, tormenta muralia ad portum conversa collocavit, ut naves quas habebant Galli collabefaceret atque deprimeret. Quod quidem illi veriti ea se condicione dediderunt, si rex eos suis cum rebus omnibus mari discedere permitteret. Itaque tribus onerariis conscensis navibus, oppido tradito, non multis ante brumam diebus sunt profecti. Accidit autem ut navis ea in qua erat Caietae magistratus cum militibus trecentis, magno adverso impellente vento, Terracinae iniecta litori, cum vectoribus perierit.

40   Tarentini vero, qui, ad eam diem Gallorum fidem secuti, in magna rerum omnium inopia magnisque in difficultatibus versabantur, Caesare Ferdinandi fratre notho et terrestribus obsidente oppidum copiis, et mari navibus longis tribus commeatus importari

ing the royal insignia, his first action was to propose that the prince of Salerno should not leave the realm, as he was preparing to do. Instead, he made him Prefect of the Kingdom, considered to be the most important office, and gave his own daughter to the prince's son in marriage. Then by means of certain offers and gifts, he made almost all the other magnates, who had been at odds with Ferrandino, well disposed toward him. But before these matters were settled, while Federico was visiting the queens (one his father's wife, the other his nephew's), a servant of the prince of Bisignano, who was awaiting the king in the antechamber along with many others, drew out a dagger and dealt his master three blows, meaning to kill him. When he was arrested and interrogated, he said that he had had it in mind to do what he had done for 13 years, because the prince had once raped his sister. No good opportunity to commit the crime had presented itself to him before, and he had wanted to finish the business off at that point, even at the certain risk of his life.

A few days later, after letting Trevisan go with the entire fleet, 39 Federico led his army to Gaeta. He seized part of the outlying districts and the mountain, then turned his siege artillery on the harbor so as to shatter and sink whatever ships the French had. Fearful of this outcome, the French surrendered on condition that the king allowed them to depart by sea with all their gear. And so, boarding three merchant ships, they handed over the town and set out a few days before the winter solstice. It happened that the ship which was carrying the governor of Gaeta, as well as 300 infantry, was pushed by a great wind in the opposite direction and driven onto the coast at Terracina, foundering with all its crew.

The people of Taranto had up to that point remained loyal to 40 the French, but they were now destitute and experiencing considerable difficulties, since Ferrandino's illegitimate brother Cesare was laying siege to the town with his land forces and had three galleys to prevent supplies reaching them by sea. Their plight was

prohibente, praesertim quod, si quid antea in villis aut frumenti aut pabuli circa oppidum fuerat, eo ne hostes potirentur, tectis incensis corruperant ipsi, Ferdinandi morte cognita, concilio coacto quid agendum sibi esset inter se quaerebant. Ea re longis disceptationibus agitata, ac tribus dictis sententiis, una ut Federico, altera ut regi Turcarum, tertia ut Venetae reipublicae oppidum traderent, legem tandem magno studio tulerunt, ut senatus fidei et pietati sese committerent. Itaque insigni reipublicae sublato, litteras ad Aloisium Lauredanum, praefectum Monopolitanorum, dederunt, orantes uti se reciperet. Litterae Aloisii ea de re ad senatum perlatae, alteroque post eas litteras die legati Tarentinorum cum eisdem mandatis Venetias advecti, eius rei exspectatione civitatem erexerunt. Atque illis quidem hospitium publice datum est.

41   Patres vocati complures dies sententiis dicendis consumpserunt; quarum pars non esse Tarentinos recipiendos, propterea quod in foedere caput erat ne dediticios, rege non permittente, civitas acciperet, pars recipiendos censebant, ne, obstinatis in Neapolitanos reges animis, Tarentini regi Turcarum sese dederent; quod si fieret, non illis modo nationibus Federicoque in primis, sed toti etiam Italiae perniciosum futurum; nullum senatui cum Federico foedus, Ferdinando mortuo; quod tamen si esset, praestare id uno in capite[4] neglegi quam permittere oppidum, natura munitissimum atque ad exercitus in Italiam transportandos classesque continendas opportunissimum, inimico Italis omnibus regi atque bellicosissimo attribui. Vicere demum quae, neutra earum probata, Tarentum civem Venetum mitti oportere sententiae censuerunt, qui auctoritate reipublicae Federico civitatem conciliaret commeatumque sufficeret. Itaque Andreas Zancanius senatorum suffragiis

particularly acute because they had burned down the buildings and destroyed any grain or foodstuffs in the farms around the town to stop the enemy getting it. When they heard that Ferrandino had died, they held a meeting to discuss the best course of action. After lengthy arguments on the matter, three views emerged: first, that they should surrender the town to Federico, second, to the Turkish sultan, or third, to the Republic of Venice. In the end they resolved with enthusiasm to entrust themselves to the protection and mercy of the Senate. And so, raising the flag of the Republic, they sent a letter to Alvise Loredan, the governor of Monopoli, asking him to receive them. Loredan's letter to the Senate on this matter and the arrival of Taranto's ambassadors with the same instructions a day later aroused great excitement among the citizens. The ambassadors were put up at public expense.

The senators in assembly spent several days giving their views. 41 Some spoke against accepting the Tarantines, since there was a clause in the treaty forbidding the city to receive people who had surrendered unless the king granted permission. Others thought they should be received, in case with their hearts hardened against the kings of Naples, the Tarantines surrendered to the sultan; and if that happened, it would bring ruin not just on those peoples, and Federico in particular, but on Italy as a whole. With Ferrandino dead, there was no treaty in force between the Senate and Federico, and even if there were, it would be better for it to be disregarded in a single particular than to allow the town to be given over to a ruler who was the enemy of all Italians and bellicose in the extreme — a town that was very well fortified by nature, and excellently suited for the transport of armies to Italy and sheltering fleets. In the end, though, neither of these positions prevailed, but rather the view that they should send a Venetian citizen to Taranto to use the authority of the Republic to reconcile the city to Federico and supply it with provisions. Andrea Zancani

legatus est ad Tarentinos lectus. Atque is antequam navem conscenderet, Alexandri atque Hispaniae regum legati itemque Ludovici principem et patres adierunt eosque ne se in causam Tarentinorum insinuarent neve quid agerent monuerunt. Quorum
intellecta voluntate, ne laborem cum invidia patres sumerent,
Andreas senatus consulto retentus neque postea missus est.

42   Atque illis diebus Ludovici ad Alexandrum scriptas litteras
Ursini prope Urbem interceperant, quibus litteris Ludovicus ab
Alexandro petebat uti patres commonefaceret a Tarentinis recipiendis abstinerent, neve eos augere suas opes suamque potentiam,
nimium quantum iam auctam, permitteret. Eas illi senatui litteras
miserunt, ut quo esset in ipsos animo Ludovicus patres inspicerent, qui, tantis a republica tamque illustribus affectus beneficiis, a
suis tamen moribus non recederet. Zancanio retento patres, quod
cum Tarentinorum civitate illo misso facere decreverant, id cum
eorum legatis ipsimet sunt aggressi, ut illos Federico per eius legatum conciliarent; quod quidem perfecerunt, sponsoresque Tarentinis fuerunt regem illos in eum quo antea erant statum restitutu-
rum, neque quidquam, propterea quod a regibus Neapolitanis
descivissent, civitati succensurum. Quibus constitutis rebus, Georgium Francum, senatus scribam, una cum legatis revertentibus Tarentum miserunt earum rerum firmandarum causa; annusque insequens iam inierat. Illi autem, intellecta oratorum suorum litteris
de sese regi pacandis senatus voluntate, pridie quam is Tarentum
appelleret, aliquanto minus bonis condicionibus quam illae erant
de quibus transegerat senatus, se Federico dediderunt. Eum exitum Tarentinorum obfirmatio habuit.

was accordingly chosen as envoy to the Tarantines by vote of the senators. Before he could take ship, ambassadors of Pope Alexander and the Spanish sovereigns, and of Ludovico too, approached the doge and the senators and warned them not to involve themselves in the affairs of the Tarantines or take any action in the matter. Once their wishes became known, Andrea was stopped from going by senatorial decree, nor was he sent later, in case the Senate took on a laborious task which attracted nothing but resentment.

At around that time the Orsini intercepted near Rome a letter   42
of Ludovico il Moro to the pope, in which he asked Alexander to impress upon the senators that they should refrain from taking the Tarantines under their protection, and not to permit them to further increase their already excessive wealth and power. The Orsini sent the letter on to the Senate so that the senators might judge Ludovico's attitude toward them, a man who had received from the Republic such great and signal benefits, yet was still not deviating from his settled habits. Zancani having been prevented from going, the senators themselves took on the task they had resolved to carry out with the city of Taranto by his despatch, that is, to reconcile the envoys of Taranto with Federico through his own ambassador. This indeed they accomplished, and gave guarantees to the Tarantines that the king would restore to them the status they had before, and that he would show not the slightest anger at the city for having rebelled against the kings of Naples. This business settled, they sent Giorgio Franco, a secretary of the Senate, to Taranto with the returning ambassadors to confirm the agreement, the new year having already begun. When the Tarantines learned   1497
the Senate's decision about making peace with the king from a letter of their spokesmen, they surrendered to Federico on the day before he landed at Taranto, on terms somewhat less favorable than those on which the Senate had deliberated. So the obduracy of the Tarantines came to an end.

43   Iamque in urbe, advenarum contagione invectioneque siderum, morbus peratrox initium acceperat, is qui est Gallicus appellatus, quo genitalibus ante omnia plerumque vitiatis, corpus doloribus afficiebatur, deinde pustulae maculaeque prodibant, cum in membris reliquis, tum magnopere in capite facieque; ac saepe tumores et tamquam tubera, primum subdura, post etiam saniosa exoriebantur. Itaque multi, diu vexati membrorum prope omnium doloribus deformatique tuberculis et ulceribus, ut vix agnoscerentur, miserabiliter interibant; neque quorum medicamentorum pestilentia indigeret nova insolensque sciri poterat. Quamobrem, annos complures omnibus in reipublicae municipiis et finibus licenter pervagata, magnum hominum numerum absumpsit, foedavit multo maximum. Sed quoniam eo de morbo Fracastoriani libri tres, heroicis versibus multa cum dignitate venustateque conscripti, vulgo in manibus habentur, nihil nos quidem attinet haec scribentes commorari, praesertim quod eius acerbitas et vis, multo nunc iam remissior tolerabiliorque facta, vel inventis ad ea mala perfugiis opibusque, vel caelo minus in dies saeviente, plane deferbuit.

44   Verum ad Pisanum bellum, de quo superius dicere coepimus, revertamur; quod tamen ipsum impeditum magis, et diuturnum variumque, tum[5] impensae plurimae atque multiplicis, quam usui aut gloriae civitati fuit—quamquam eius quidem rei culpam omnem Ludovici aemulatio atque perfidia sustinuit; quae tamen culpa, uno ab illo fonte derivata, paulo post in ipsius caput redundavit. Magnum enim hostem nactus, cum respublica, saepius ab illo lacessita et prodita, hominis infidelissimi atque arrogantissimi societatem semel renuisset, regno expulsus, deinde etiam captus, turpissima in custodia vitam reliquit. Adductis Pisas reipublicae auxiliis equitatus gravioris leviorisque armaturae per Ludovici

Due to infection from foreigners and the influence of the stars,   43
that terrible ailment called the "French disease" now began to appear at Venice. It generally afflicts the genitals first of all, and the
body is wracked with pain, then boils and blotches break out,
chiefly on the head and face but also on other limbs. Tumors and,
as it were, lumps appear, at first somewhat hard, later full of blood
and pus as well. Thus many people met a miserable end after long
torments in almost every limb, and so disfigured by protuberances
and ulcers as to be scarcely recognizable. It was impossible to
know what medicines were needed against this new and unprecedented pestilence. For this reason, having spread freely for quite a
few years in all the towns and territories of the Republic, it carried
off a great number of people, but left a very great many more disfigured. But since Fracastoro's three books on the disease, written
in hexameter verse with much dignity and charm, are widely available,[11] I do not need to dwell on describing it here, especially since
its virulence and strength have already become much milder and
more bearable, and have definitely abated, whether through the
discovery of protective measures and remedies against the complaint or because heaven's rage has lessened as the days wear on.

But let us return to the Pisan war, which we began an account   44
of above.[12] The war, it must be said, was more of a burden to the
Republic—long drawn-out, with fluctuating fortunes, and hugely
expensive as it was—than to its advantage or renown,[13] though
the entire blame for this state of affairs was laid at the door of
Ludovico's ambition and faithlessness. But the blame soon enough
redounded on his own head, from which alone it had flowed.
When once the Republic, provoked and repeatedly betrayed by
him, renounced its alliance with this most untrustworthy and arrogant of men, he acquired a great enemy: Ludovico was driven
from his realm, then actually taken captive, and ended his life in
shameful imprisonment. The Republic's forces of heavy and light
cavalry were taken to Pisa through Ludovico's territory, who had

fines, qui et ipse suos equites, multo tamen pauciores, eodem miserat, tum per Lucensium, quos suscepti a tribus maximis Italiae
populis communi consilio belli fama compulerat, nihil ut eis esse
negandum existimarent, conscripti Pisis reipublicae pecunia milites plus mille, quos ex Umbria et Piceno et Corsica praedae atque
stipendii spes evocaverat, ad eos qui Genua venerant milites
adiunguntur. Itaque spei bonae plena civitas, suis sociorumque copiis, ad vicum qui Pisanus appellatur eratque in ipsius potestate,
hostium equitatum caede facta in fugam vertit, captis compluribus. Milites, qui tunc ab equitibus tria milia passus aberant, cum
suis praesto esse non possent, quod inter se equitesque interposi-
tum hostem videbant, eius adventu non exspectato, raptim temereque, quo cuique visum est, fuga comparata sibimet consulue-
runt.

45   Paucis autem post diebus eodem ex municipio emissos pabula-
tores hostium est manus parva ex insidiis consecuta; ad quos cum
ii qui erant in municipio, equites cataphracti sexaginta, leviter ar-
mati centum, milites minus trecenti, auxilio accurrissent, reliqui se
hostes ostenderunt impetumque in eos fecerunt, equites utriusque
armaturae quingenti quinquaginta, milites ad duo milia; illi se
paulatim referentes ad eius loci pontem constiterunt, fortiterque
pugnantes, cum aliquot ex suis amisissent, aliquot etiam capti essent, se tamen loco non movebant vulneraque et caedes inferebant;
quo in certamine Franciscus Siccus, hostium praefectus, accepto
vulnere proelio excessit pauloque post est mortuus. Eo cedente
finis est pugnae factus. Atque illa quidem in pugna Veneti cum ad
Lucium Malvetium Bononiensem, Ludovici legatum, qui non
longe aberat, misissent, uti sibi auxilio confestim veniret, prandere
se prius velle respondit. Is, quod ex eiusmodi ludibrio responsi,
nec allato celeriter auxilio, omnium se vocibus culpari sentiebat,

himself sent his cavalry there (in much smaller numbers, however), and then through the territory of Lucca — talk of a war undertaken in concert by the three greatest powers of Italy had obliged the Lucchesi to believe that they had to grant their every request. More than 1,000 infantry were recruited at Pisa at the Republic's expense, attracted out of Umbria, the Marches, and Corsica in hope of plunder and pay, and they joined up with the soldiers who had come from Genoa. The Pisan citizenry was consequently full of optimism, and with their own and the allied troops they put the enemy cavalry to flight at Vicopisano, a town they controlled, with much slaughter and many captives taken. The Florentine infantry were then three miles away from the cavalry. Seeing from the enemy lying between them and the cavalry that they could not support their comrades, they did not wait for the enemy to arrive but looked after themselves, taking flight in haste and disarray in whatever direction each thought best.

A few days later, foragers sent out from Vicopisano were ambushed and pursued by a small band of the enemy. When the forces in the town ran to their aid (60 heavy cavalry, 100 light, fewer than 300 infantry), the rest of the enemy, numbering 550 cavalry of both sorts and about 2,000 infantry, revealed themselves and fell upon them. The former gradually drew back and made a stand at the local bridge, putting up a brave fight. Although they lost some men killed or captured, they nevertheless stood their ground, and inflicted injuries and fatalities on the enemy. In the struggle the Florentine captain Francesco Secco was wounded and quit the battlefield, dying a little later. Upon his withdrawal, the battle came to an end. In the course of that battle the Venetians had sent word to Ludovico's captain Lucio Malvezzi of Bologna, who was not far off, that he should come to their assistance at once, but he answered that he wanted to have lunch first. When he sensed that he was being universally condemned for the flippancy of his answer and for his failure to bring speedy assis-

honoris sui causa Pontem Sacci, castellum Florentinorum, noctu adortus scalisque ad murum positis cepit, cum tamen eo in castello esset Antonii Martiani filius adolescens cum equitibus cataphractis sexaginta, quorum pars in Lucii potestatem venit. Atque illud quidem castellum Florentini, decimo post die quam est captum, iisdem prope artibus recuperaverunt, e vestigioque diruerunt. Ita utrisque haec atque consimilia multa conantibus, aliquot menses abierunt, cum utri eorum superiores in bello essent constaret satis nulli.

46   Interim, cum Pisani commeatus inopia propter anni tempus laborarent idque patribus significavissent, senatus, ad suum statim hominem qui erat Genuae traiecta pecunia, imperavit uti frumenta coemeret Pisasque transmitteret. Qui cum senatui celeritate adhibita paruisset, annona sublevata reipublicae munere civitatem recreavit. Senatus ubi ea manu quam Pisas miserat quamque ibi atque Genuae conscripserat, aestatis parte iam praeterita, parum se proficere animadvertit, quingentos equites Graecos Iustiniano Mauroceno praefecto Pisas mittendos decrevit. Is ante medium Quintilem mensem omni cum equitatu eo se contulit.

47   Tum autem, quod erat iam antea in Alexandri et Ludovici et reipublicae militia Ioannes Bentivolus, pro sua parte misso ad illum stipendio, senatus, cum etiam Alexander misisset, uti se ad Pisanum bellum compararet imperavit; simul ab Ludovico petiit, suam Ioanni partem itidem mitteret. Id ille negare cum non posset, se facturum recepit neque misit tamen. Quin etiam ne ulla condicione proposita proficisceretur clam ab eo impetrasse illum nemo non credidit; nam Ioannes multa cottidie causari, multa temere ab senatu petere, denique diem de die ducere, ut quilibet scire posset illudi senatum callidis et propinquis ab hominibus, Ludovico et Ioanne. Duxerat autem Hannibal, Ioannis filius, in

tance, to salvage his honor he made a night march to the Florentine castle of Ponsacco and took it with siege-ladders placed
against the walls, despite the presence in the fortress of the young
son of Antonio da Marsciano[14] with 60 heavy cavalry, some of
whom Lucio captured. But ten days after it was taken the Florentines recovered the castle in very much the same manner, and at
once destroyed it. These and many similar ventures on both sides
continued for several months, with nobody sure which of them
had the upper hand in the war.

Meanwhile, the people of Pisa were suffering from lack of sup-   46
plies owing to the time of the year, and conveyed this to the senators. The Senate immediately sent a transfer of money to their
agent in Genoa and told him to buy grain and send it to Pisa. He
carried out the Senate's orders with all speed, and revived the city's
spirits by easing the food supply. When the Senate observed that
with part of the summer gone it was making little headway with
the force it had sent to Pisa and the one raised there and at
Genoa, it resolved to send 500 stradiots to Pisa under the command of Giustiniano Morosini. Morosini took himself there with
his entire cavalry by the middle of July.

At that time Giovanni Bentivoglio was already in the joint ser-   47
vice of Alexander, Ludovico, and the Republic. The Senate sent
him its share of his pay, Alexander having already sent his share,
and ordered him to get ready for war at Pisa, at the same time asking Ludovico to send Bentivoglio his share too. Since Ludovico
could not well refuse, he promised to do so, but still failed to send
the money. Everyone in fact believed that Ludovico had secretly
prevailed upon Giovanni Bentivoglio not to set out on any terms
that might be offered him, for he made constant excuses and any
number of random requests to the Senate. In short, he was drag-
ging things out from day to day so that it became obvious to ev-
erybody that the Senate was being made a laughing-stock by that
crafty pair Ludovico and Giovanni, who were related by marriage

matrimonium unam ex Herculis Atestini filiis notham; altera, ut
ante dictum est, Ludovico nupserat. Itaque eam affinitatem etiam
animis ad improbitatem mutuis paribusque conglutinabant. Qua
in mora illud accidit, ut Hercules eam equitum militumque manum quam tuendo regno habere consueverat prope omnem cum
praefectis dimitteret. Missi e vestigio Florentiam militatum abierunt, ne cui dubium fieret qua haec mente quove consilio essent
instituta.

48   Sed et illud senatus consultum factum est, ut praefectis tribus
qui erant Pisis equitum numerus augeretur; Iacoboque Tarsiae,
qui Ravennae erat, pecunia subministraretur ad milites in Faventi-
nis finibus conscribendos mille, quibuscum Pisas accederet, ceteris
quoque militibus qui reipublicae stipendium mererent eo bello im-
peraturus. Tum missi Pisas praefecti equitum, cum sua quisque
turma, quattuor.

49   Iis imperatis rebus ac prope etiam confectis, Helvetii quadrin-
genti, quos Ludovicus Pisas miserat, domum discesserunt, cum dicerent sibi stipendium non subministrari. Reliquae deinde Ludovici copiae praefectique paucorum dierum spatio singillatim
abeuntes idem fecerunt, Lucio excepto, qui quidem, consilia cete-
rorum cognoscendi atque impediendi belli causa, cum paucis equitibus remansit. Ita quod initio de communi sociorum sententia
Ludovicus sumpserat, ut Pisas una cum reliquis tueretur, id pri-
vato consilio reiecit, furtim in medii fervore belli sese subtrahens.
Sed antequam Helvetii et reliquae Ludovici copiae discessissent,
propterea quod multo plus oneris et vastitatis civitati quam aut
praesidii aut emolumenti afferebant, videbaturque id unum Lucio
deliberatum esse, ut Pisanos conterendo et maleficiis everteret, civitas ad patres misit, sese ulterius Ludovici auxilia perpeti sustine-

(Annibale, Giovanni's son, had married an illegitimate daughter of Ercole d'Este; another daughter, as previously mentioned, had married Ludovico).[15] So it was that their kindred spirits, each bent on mischief in equal measure, likewise cemented their relationship. In the course of this inactivity, it happened that Ercole d'Este paid off almost all of the cavalry and infantry force with which he had always defended his realm. Those that he let go immediately went away to fight for Florence, just in case anyone was in doubt as to the intent and purpose of his actions.

The Senate also decreed that the number of cavalry under the   48
three captains who were at Pisa should be increased, and that money should be given to Giacomo da Tarsia, presently at Ravenna, for recruiting 1,000 infantry in the territory of Faenza. He was to go to Pisa with them, and also take command of all the other foot soldiers serving the Republic in the war. Four cavalry captains, each with his own company, were then sent to Pisa.

These orders had been given and almost put into effect when   49
the 400 Swiss soldiers that Ludovico had sent to Pisa left for home, saying that they had not been paid. The rest of Ludovico's troops and captains followed course one by one over the next few days, with the exception of Lucio Malvezzi, who remained with a few cavalry to learn what plans the others were making and to hold up the war. So what Ludovico had undertaken to do at the outset in line with the common purpose of the League, namely, to defend Pisa alongside the others, he rejected for his own private reasons, slipping away furtively amid the heat of war. But the Swiss and Ludovico's other troops brought the city more affliction and devastation than protection or benefit. On that account, and also because it seemed that Malvezzi's only object was to ruin the Pisans by exhausting their resources and inflicting malicious damage on them, before they departed, the city had sent word to the senators that they could not endure or support Ludovico's troops any longer. They had decided and resolved to put themselves un-

reque non posse; velle ac decrevisse uni senatui se addicere vexil-
laque reipublicae sustollere; rogare ut eorum voluntate id sibi
facere liceret. Patres Pisanis collaudatis, quod eo erga rempublicam
studio, ea mente essent, aliud posse tempus accidere dixerunt, cum
id et illi tuto facere, et ipsi eis permittere uti facerent iure possent;
nunc vero illud curarent, ut liberi per eorum fidem essent, qui pepigerunt se in eo suas partes omni diligentia praestaturos; bo-
noque animo eos esse iussos dimiserunt.

50   Naves interea reipublicae longae sex, Neapoli in Liguriam atque
in Galliam Provinciam missae, cum nihil earum rerum quarum
causa ierant reperissent, conversae ad eas naves Florentinorum in-
sectandas a quibus, ne frumenta neve reliqui commeatus supportari Pisas possent, magnum impedimentum afferebatur, plurimo
usui ea in re fuerunt. Quibus quidem navibus aliae naves longae
complures additae eundem sane usum atque operam reipublicae
praestiterunt, hostium navibus commeatibusque qui Triturritam
invehebantur, deinde in eorum castra comportabantur, saepe disiectis fugatisque, saepe captis. Neque tunc terrestres reipublicae
copiae in cessatione fuerunt, sed et castella hostium aliquot sunt
ab iis capta, et legatus eorum Petrus Capo interfectus, et proelia
nonnulla secundiora facta. Quo etiam tempore Pisani Librafactae
castellum ipsorum, quod ab eisdem Gallis qui arcem Pisanam res-
tituerant etiam nunc obtinebatur, auri libris triginta praefecto traditis, magna hostium invidia recuperaverunt. Omnibus autem ex
utilitatibus, quas quidem classis exercitusque reipublicae in medium eius belli contulit, eae crebriores neque postremae fuerunt
quae ab Graecis sunt equitibus profectae. Nam et praedae saepe
ingentes abactae ab illis sunt, et plurimi commeatus intercepti, et
hostium turbata eorum audacia atque celeritate consilia; quodque
magis mirum videbatur, castella quoque ab iis nonnulla capta, caedes vero pluribus locis factae, ut laudari et bene de republica meriti
existimari iure possent.

der the protection of the Senate alone and to raise the Republic's flag, and they asked to do this with their agreement. The senators praised the Pisans for their zeal and general attitude toward the Republic, but said that while there might come a time when it was both safe for the Pisans to do so and right for the Senate itself to allow them to do so, they should see only to this, that they achieved their freedom by trusting in the good faith of the senators, who had pledged that they would fulfill their part in the matter to the utmost of their abilities. And bidding them be of good cheer, they dismissed the envoys.

Meanwhile, the six galleys of the Republic that had been sent 50 from Naples to Liguria and Provence had not found what they were looking for,[16] and turned back to attack the Florentine ships that were largely blocking the supply of grain and other provisions to Pisa, and to great effect. Many more galleys were added to these ships and they proved to be equally useful to the Republic on the frequent occasions that they routed or captured the enemy ships and supplies that were being taken to Livorno and from there to their camp. Nor were the Republic's land forces inactive at that time: they took some enemy fortresses, killed the Florentine commander Piero Capponi, and fought a number of successful battles. At the same time, to the enemy's great indignation, the Pisans recovered their fortress of Librafatta, which was still held by the French who had given back the citadel of Pisa, by handing over to the French captain 30 gold pounds. But of all the advances contributed by the Venetian fleet and army to the common war effort, the most frequent and impressive were those made by the stradiots. They often took massive amounts of booty and intercepted much of the enemy's supplies, throwing their plans into confusion by their boldness and speed. And, more surprisingly, they managed to capture a number of fortresses too, and in many places caused carnage, so that they came in for deserved praise for their services to the Republic.

51   Dum haec ad Pisas geruntur, e Gallia Transalpina nuntii venerunt: ab rege Carolo reditum in Italiam magno studio comparari,
ipsum paucis diebus ad Lugdunum fore, in via quidem certe iam
esse. Quamobrem Ludovicus a senatu quaesivit, velletne, si Carolus urgeat, sibi exercitum et auxilia mittere; nam se promeritum ne
quam sui curam respublica sumeret probe intelligebat. Senatus ei
respondit: tametsi Pisano bello implicata civitas esset, cui bello
quanto studio quantisque impensis opus sit sciret ipse omnium
optime, tamen se in eo tuendo non defuturum. Simul Marcum
Beatianum ad Helvetios misit, qui eis ab republica stipendium
polliceretur, ne ad Carolum se converterent. Pauloque post, cum
Triultius, Gallorum manum secum ducens, traiectis Alpibus
Astam venisset, Ludovicus ad senatum misit: videri sibi optimum
esse Maximilianum regem suo et Alexandri et reipublicae stipendio in Italiam accersiri, ut sit qui regem Carolum et auctoritate sua
deterrere ne Alpes traiciat, et, si traiecerit, suis et sociorum opibus
et copiis comprimere facile possit; eiusque se rei iam apud illum
initia et fundamenta iecisse per legatos suos, a qua, ut videtur, non
abhorreat.

52   Ea agitata re de Alexandri et Hispaniae regum legati sententia
celeriter a patribus, sextodecimo Kalendas Iunias senatus decrevit
Maximilianum accersiri oportere; cui sint[6] in trium mensium stipendia (tot enim menses satis fore) a republica quadringentae auri
atque octoginta librae, a Ludovico alterae totidem, ab Alexandro
parte dimidia pauciores; ducatque is Helvetiorum secum militum
quattuor milia, quibus ipse stipendium numeret singulis mensibus
libras auri centum viginti. Ea cum lege mandatisque, Franciscum
Foscarum legatum senatus ad illum misit. Quae quidem lex eo fes-

While this was unfolding at Pisa, news came from France that 51
King Charles was busying himself with preparations to return to
Italy. He would himself be at Lyon within a few days, and was
doubtless already on his way. Ludovico therefore asked the Senate
whether it would be prepared to send him an army and reinforcements if Charles should begin to threaten him, for he was perfectly aware that he had not deserved the slightest consideration
on the part of the Republic. The Senate responded that although
the city was involved in the Pisan war — and Ludovico knew as
well as anyone how much effort and expense was needed for
that — they would nevertheless not fail to defend him. At the same
time they sent Marco Beazzano to the Swiss to promise to engage
them for the Republic, so that they would not switch to Charles'
side. A little later, when Giangiacomo Trivulzio had crossed the
Alps at the head of the French forces and reached Asti, Ludovico
sent word to the Senate: he thought the best course would be to
summon King Maximilian to Italy at the expense of himself, Alexander, and the Republic, so as to have someone who might well
have enough influence to deter Charles from crossing the Alps or,
if he did, to stop him with his and the allies' troops and resources.
He said that he had already laid the beginnings and foundations
of this scheme through his envoys at the king's court, and it
seemed the king was not averse to the idea.

After a quick discussion of the matter in the light of the pope's 52
views and those of the ambassador of the Spanish sovereigns, the
Senate resolved on 17 May to invite Maximilian to Italy, with his
pay for three months (it seemed that would be enough) fixed at
480 gold pounds from the Republic, a similar sum from Ludovico
and half as much from Alexander. He was to bring 4,000 Swiss
soldiers and pay them 120 gold pounds a month. The Senate sent
their envoy Francesco Foscari to him with the decree and those instructions. Indeed the decree was passed in some haste because a
letter had reached the Senate saying that the Swiss had announced

tinantius est lata, quod litterae ad senatum venerant: Helvetiis, qui
se profitebantur nihil eorum quae vellet Carolus esse facturos, nisi
prius reliqua quae debeat quaeque permagna sint eis persolvat, iam
ab rege quingentas auri libras esse curatas; quod tamen, ut postea
cognitum est, falsum fuit. Beatianus ad Helvetios missus effecit ut
tres eorum pagi reipublicae sacramentum dicerent, stipendiumque
eis dedit.

53   Maximilianus, accepta a patribus pecunia, in fines regni sui venit, Comensem agrum versus. Eum Ludovicus, cum uxore Beatrice obviam profectus, excepit; pransique una venatum secum
duxerunt. Qua commotus fama, Aloisius, dux Genabensium,
Astam oppidum communivit, veritus Maximilianum eo primum
omnium suas copias adducturum. Ille autem, ut Philippo filio,
Belgarum regi, ad se venienti sui conveniendi potestatem faceret,
etiam interius in Alpes reversus, suspicionem multis attulit sese
amplius in Italiam non venturum. Atque illis ipsis diebus Henri-
cus Britanniae rex inter foederatos est receptus; missique ad Maximilianum legati duo, Antonius Grimanus, Marcus Antonius Maurocenus, qui venientem exciperent.

54   Maximilianus, convento filio rediens Comum, quo ei praesto
Ludovicus fuit, deinde in agrum Mediolanensem ad Vigevenum
venit. Ibi cum esset, litteras ad Pisanos dedit: velle se suum hominem, qui eis consuleret civitatemque regeret, eo mittere. Civitas ad
ea respondit: unum se ab eius initio belli semper optavisse diligen-
tissimeque curavisse, ut in libertate, qua permultos annos carue-
rant quamque dii eis reddiderant, permanerent; si eius praefectum
recipiant, contrariam rem suis studiis facturos sibique ipsos dominum imposituros; se vero non consiliorum indigere, sed auxilii.
Itaque, cum paulo post Maximilianus illum ipsum praefectum

that they would carry out none of Charles' wishes unless he first paid out the remainder of the considerable sum he owed them, and that Charles had already paid them 500 gold pounds on that account. But they later learned that the report was false. When he reached Switzerland, Beazzano managed to get three of the cantons to take the oath of allegiance to the Republic, and he gave them their pay.

After receiving the money from the senators, Maximilian went   53 to the borders of his realm adjacent to the district of Como. Ludovico went to meet him with his wife Beatrice and made him welcome, and after lunch together they took him hunting with them. Disturbed by this report, Louis, the Duke of Orleans, strengthened the defenses of Asti for fear that Maximilian would lead his troops there first. But in order to give his son Philip, Duke of Burgundy, the chance to join him on his arrival, Maximilian actually turned back into the Alps, fostering in many people the suspicion that he would not proceed further into Italy. At just that time, King Henry [VII] of England was brought into the League. Two ambassadors were sent to Maximilian, Antonio Grimani and Marcantonio Morosini, to welcome him on his arrival.

After meeting his son, Maximilian returned to Como, where   54 Ludovico attended him, and then went to Vigevano in the neighborhood of Milan. While he was there, he sent a letter to the people of Pisa to say he was ready to send one of his men there to advise them and take over the governance of the city. To this the city replied that, from the outset of the war, the one thing they had always wanted and fought for with all their tenacity was to hold on to the freedom which they had gone without for so many years, and which God had restored to them. If they were to accept his governor, they would be acting contrary to their own wishes and imposing a master on themselves. What they really lacked was not advice but help. And so, when Maximilian actually sent them the

ad eos misisset, non est receptus. Interim, cum de adventu Caroli rumor nuntiique refrixissent, Ludovici suasu, qui omnino nihil eorum quae impedire paulum modo possent, ne Pisae sub reipublicae dicionem redigerentur, praetermittebat, senatu non abnuente Maximilianus statuit Pisas accedere, ut ei bello finem imponeret. Itaque Dertonam est profectus cum equitibus quos secum duxerat trecentis, militibus Helvetiis duobus milibus, equitibus Ludovici mille.

55   Dertonae res huiusmodi accidit. Legatis Florentinorum duobus, qui ad Maximilianum venerant, in via forte obviis legati Veneti salutem dixerunt; illi eis ne verbum quidem unum reddiderunt, sed illiberali contumacia ire perrexerunt. Postridie autem eius diei iterum obvii, cum de via legatis reipublicae non cederent arrogantiusque in eos cum suo comitatu prope conglobarentur, Maurocenus, cui quidem praeclara atque mirifica faciei dignitas cum vasta membrorum magnitudine inerat, alterum illorum ita reppulit ut in luto provolveretur, "Disce cedere maioribus" pronuntians. A Dertona Genuam Maximilianus profectus arcem oppidi sibi tradi postulavit. Ea non tradita, postridie eius diei oppido egressus in suburbio paranda classe complures se dies continuit.

56   Nonis autem Octobribus omni cum sua copia conscendens navibus longis reipublicae octo, Genuensium duabus, onerariis item decem, quas Genuae armari atque instrui curaverat, adversa tempestate, quod in onerariis tunc erat, paulisper est iactatus; post a Dominico Maripetro, praefecto classis Venetae, receptus, cum dies aliquot in mari portubusque consumpsisset, Arni fluminis ostium[7] ingressus, navicula cum eodem praefecto prioreque legato reipublicae (nam recentiores affecti valetudine domum abierant) Pisas appulit. Ibi, explorato loci situ, concilio legatorum et praefectorum et civitatis coacto, Triturritae arcem, quae mari undique alluitur et

governor shortly afterwards, they would not accept him. The talk and reports of Charles' arrival had died down, and in the meantime, at the urging of Ludovico (who overlooked nothing that could help even a little to stop Pisa being brought under Venetian rule), and with the acquiescence of the Senate, Maximilian decided to go to Pisa and put an end to the war. And so he left for Tortona with the 300 cavalry that he had brought with him, 2,000 Swiss soldiers, and 1,000 of Ludovico's cavalry.

At Tortona the following incident occurred. Meeting by chance 55 on the street two Florentine ambassadors who had come to Maximilian, the Venetian ambassadors greeted them, but got not a word in return as the Florentines continued on their way in an ill-bred and haughty manner. Meeting again the next day, they would not give way to the Venetian ambassadors, but practically jostled them with their retinue in an arrogant manner. Morosini, who had a face of remarkable dignity and was very strongly built, cried, "Learn to give way to your betters!" and gave one of them such a push that he fell over in the mud. As he reached Genoa from Tortona, Maximilian asked to be given the Genoese citadel. When his request was refused, he left the town the next day and spent a number of days in the outskirts preparing his fleet.

On 7 October, he put to sea with his entire force on eight Ve- 56 netian galleys, two Genoese, and ten cargo-vessels as well, which he had had armed and fitted out at Genoa. He was tossed about a bit by adverse weather, being at that point in the cargo-ships. Afterwards, he was welcomed by Domenico Malipiero, the captain of the Venetian fleet, and spent some days at sea and in harbor before entering the mouth of the Arno in a small ship in the company of the same Malipiero and a former proveditor of the Republic[17] (the more recent ones had been taken ill and had gone home), and landing at Pisa. Having explored the lay of the land there and held a meeting of the proveditors and captains with the citizenry, he decided to attack the fortress of Livorno. This is

ponte sublicio litori coniungebatur eratque hostibus opportunissima, quod ea una omnes maritimi Pisanorum conatus et rei frumentariae administratio magnopere impediebantur, oppugnare instituit. Itaque, legatis reipublicae qui exercitui praeerant iussis in diversas partes equitatum mittere, ut hostes aliis in rebus occupati morarentur, milites Helvetios trecentos, e navibus cum tormentis et praefectis suis principibus egressos, occupare eum collem, qui e regione arcis est, imperat aediculamque in colle positam capere, ne auxilia iis qui in vico atque in arce sint, quod erat illac transeundum, ab hostibus submitti possint. Qua re animadversa, Triturritani portis emissi animo aediculae praeripiendae in collem evolant. Proelium committitur caedesque utrimque fit. Tum praefectus classis milites e navibus remigesque auxilio laborantibus submittit; ab iis hostes repelluntur, ipsi et Helvetii fugatis hostibus ad naves revertuntur. Hostes postea eam aediculam diruerunt.

57   Interim naves aliquot e longinquo visae sunt eo cursum tendere; ad quas suis cum triremibus praefectus, ut unde aut cur venirent scire posset et, si hostiles essent, ipse eas adoriretur, statuit accedere; naves enim onerariae, quod ventus erat adversus, commovere se non poterant. Maximilianus, eius consilio comprobato, triremes et ipse conscendit. Cum ad naves praefectus appropinquasset, quae quidem erant sex omnesque Gallicae ac plenae commeatus et armatorum militum, a legatis Florentinis Caroli permissu in Gallia Provincia conscriptorum, eas aggredi non est ausus; quarum una erat amphorarum supra mille ducentarum capax, reliquae plus minus quadringentarum. Itaque, sine molestia cursum tenentes, ad Triturritam iactis ancoris constiterunt. Sequebatur magno eas intervallo navis una reliqua longa, verum non ita velox remigioque habilis ut triremes sunt, sed altior latiorque ac magno ad bellum

washed by the sea on all sides and connected to the shore by a wooden bridge, and had very great advantages for an enemy, because it could by itself largely block all Pisa's maritime enterprises and grain supplies. The proveditors in charge of the army were told to send out cavalry in a number of directions so that the enemy would be hampered by being distracted with other matters. Then he ordered 300 Swiss soldiers, who had disembarked with their artillery and officers, to occupy the hill facing the fortress and to take the small church on the hill, so that the enemy could not send reinforcements to its men in the village and the fortress, since they had to pass that way to get to them. When they noticed what was going on, the people of Livorno streamed out through the gates and rushed to the hill with the intention of seizing the church first. Battle was joined and slaughter ensued on both sides. The captain of the fleet then sent infantry and rowers from the ships to help the hard-pressed Swiss fighters. They pushed back the enemy and returned with the Swiss to the ships after putting the enemy to flight. The enemy later demolished the church.

Meanwhile some far-off ships were seen sailing in their direction. To learn where they were coming from and why, and attack them if they proved to be hostile, the captain decided to approach them with his galleys — as the wind was against them, the merchantmen were not able to move. Maximilian approved the plan and went on board one of the galleys himself. The ships were six in number, all French and full of provisions and armed infantry that the Florentine commissioners had raised in Provence with Charles' permission. When the captain drew near the ships, he did not dare to attack. One of them had a capacity of more than 1,200 barrels, the others of about 400. Holding their course undisturbed, then, they dropped anchor and moored at Livorno. They were followed at a great distance by another ship, a warship, but not as swift and easily rowed as galleys are, being taller and broader and built for battle, its capacity about 600 barrels. The

57

usui, amphorarum circiter sexcentarum; ad quam praefectus omnibus cum triremibus contendens eamque assecutus, ubi se qui in navi erant milites septuaginta velle defendere coeperunt, tormentis aëneis pilas ferreas in eos magni ponderis emitti e triremibus imperavit. Quorum terrifico strepitu audito conspectisque ignibus, Maximilianus sua cum triremi abiit. Eum aliae quattuor triremes sunt subsecutae. Praefectus cum reliquis, in navem Gallicam facto impetu, eam cepit; qua in navi erat frumenti magnus numerus. Id navis hostium maior, quae in portu iam erat, conspicata, vento paulisper converso sublatis ancoris, ut auxilio sociae navi esset, vela ad naves Venetas fecit; sed praefectus navem captam remulco breviorem in aquam abstraxit, quam illa terra tacta assequi non potuit.

58   Venerat interim Pisas Hannibal Bentivolus patris loco cum equitibus septingentis et militibus ducentis; eum Lucius veritus, quod erat ex adversa factione, abiit neque postea Pisis fuit. Is igitur Hannibal copiaeque reliquae Venetorum omnes cum legatis instructo exercitu sese ad Triturritam contulerunt. In itinere castellum unum vi ceperunt; alia se duo sponte dediderunt. Exercitus castris positis ubi arcem obsidere ac concutere tormentis coepit, ii sunt imbres consecuti, ut Maximilianus obsidionem reliquerit. Itaque suis cum equitibus quingentis, militibus mille trecentis, ad Vicum Pisanum profectus est; inde, prope subiratior seque deceptum dictitans, nullo loco commoratus Ticinum pauloque post suum in regnum rediit.

59   At domi, ut more institutoque maiorum civibus aedium suarum incendio damna perpessis publice subministraretur, quo facilius amissa restituerent, decemviri legem tulerunt, ut Petri Molini filiis auri libras viginti, Hieronymo et Marino Albertis quindecim,

captain made for it with all his galleys and caught up with it. When the 70 soldiers in the vessel showed they were ready to defend themselves, the captain ordered the galleys to fire heavy iron cannonballs from the bronze artillery against them. Hearing their terrifying blast and seeing the fire, Maximilian left the scene with his galley, followed by four others. With the remaining galleys, the captain made an assault on the French ship and captured it; there was a great quantity of grain in the vessel. Seeing this, a larger enemy ship already in port raised anchor when the wind veered round a little, and made sail for the Venetian ships to bring help to its companion vessel. But the Venetian captain dragged the captured ship into shallower water with a tow-rope, where the other vessel, touching bottom, could not follow.

Meanwhile Annibale Bentivoglio had come to Pisa to replace his father, with 700 cavalry and 200 foot soldiers. Lucio Malvezzi was afraid of him because Annibale belonged to the opposing faction,[18] so he left and did not return to Pisa again. The army was drawn up in battle array and Annibale marched to Livorno with the rest of the Venetian troops and their proveditors. On the march they took one fortress by force and two others voluntarily surrendered. The army pitched camp and began to lay siege to the fortress, pounding it with artillery, but such a deluge of rain followed that Maximilian abandoned the siege. And so with his 500 cavalry and 1,300 foot soldiers, he left for Vicopisano. In some anger, and declaring he had been deceived, he left there for Pavia without stopping on the way, and a little later returned to his own kingdom.

On the home front, to make public assistance available to citizens who had suffered financially when their houses burned down and to make it easier for them to make good their losses, in line with ancient custom and practice, the Council of Ten passed a law that the Salt Office[19] should award 20 gold pounds to the sons of Pietro Molin and 15 to Girolamo and Marino Alberti, whose

quibus utrisque aedes ad Cassiani et Apollinaris conflagraverant; Andreae Ripae, cui suburbium in Muriano, alteras totidem; Veneriis, quibus domum cum taberna mercium Indicarum maxime celebri ad Bartholomaei ignis absumpserat, auri libras triginta, quinquevirum sale procurando magistratus daret. Neque multo post, onerariis navibus duabus naufragio amissis, Philippo Bernardo, Aloisio Contareno, quorum illae fuerant naves, auri librae sexaginta aequis partibus, decemvirum item lege ab eodem magistratu sunt curari iussae, ea condicione, si navem alteram eorum uterque fabricandam reciperet.

60   Florentini ea re elati, quod Maximilianus, a quo sibi magnopere timuerant, infecto negotio discesserat, castella complura quae a Pisanis tenebantur aggressi, partim vi, partim se dedentia recuperaverunt. Legati Veneti exercitu distributo, Pisanum ad Vicum et Cassinam et Butrium et Libraefactae municipia se in hiberna contulerunt. Graeci equites centum, ut commeatus inopiam sublevarent, quod illis diebus naves Gallicae quattuor Venetorum naves duas frumentarias Pisas convehentes interceperant, hiemandi causa Ravennam profecti sunt, insequente anno inito. Aliquot etiam, eorum qui remanserant, ad hostes ob stipendia non soluta transierunt.

61   Quibus etiam diebus, Faventiae arcis praefecto aegerrime ferente oppidum a reipublicae legato ita regi, ut sibi, quod antea consueverat, magistratus creandi, pecuniam publicam avertendi, quidquid collibuisset patrandi facultas non esset, novasque res cum sui similibus moliente, ut legati ius et maiestas impediretur, puero etiam delenito et in suas partes traducto, senatus ea intelligens litteras ad legatum dedit, quibus litteris legatus iubebatur Hestori puero civitate adhibita denuntiare: senatum non ambitionis aut dominationis causa civem suum Faventiam misisse, sed

houses at San Cassiano and Sant'Apollinare had burned down; the same sum to Andrea da Ripa, whose suburban property in Murano had burned down; and 30 gold pounds to the Venier family, whose house with a famous spice-shop at San Bartolomeo had been consumed by fire. Not long afterwards, following the shipwreck of two merchant vessels, 60 gold pounds equally divided were ordered, again by decree of the Ten, to be paid by the same office to Filippo Bernardo and Luigi Contarini, the owners of the ships, on condition that each of them promised to build another ship.

The Florentines were elated at the fact that Maximilian, of 60 whom they had been much afraid, had left without accomplishing his task. They attacked a good many fortresses held by the Pisans and recovered some by force, some by voluntary surrender. The Venetian proveditors divided their army and took them to winter quarters in the towns of Vicopisano, Cascina, Buti, and Librafatta. At about that time four French ships intercepted two grain-ships bound for Pisa, and in order to alleviate the shortage of supplies, 100 stradiots left to spend the winter in Ravenna at the beginning of the following year. Some of those who stayed behind actually 1497 went over to the enemy because they had not been paid.

Also at this time, the castellan of the fortress of Faenza had 61 become very vexed that the town was now administered by the Venetian proveditor in such a way that he could no longer, as he had been used to doing, appoint officials or divert public funds or do whatever he liked, and he was hatching a plot with like-minded men with the intention of weakening the proveditor's rights and authority, even winning over the boy Astorre and getting him on their side.[20] When the Senate learned of this, they sent the proveditor a letter in which he was told to make a public declaration to Astorre and the assembled citizenry: the Senate had not sent its citizen to Faenza out of ambition or a desire to dominate. In the first place they had with their troops crushed Faenza's ene-

cum prius otii et quietis cupiditate eius hostes, qui illum regno
prope deiecerant, suis auxiliis repressisset, postea, et civium precibus et ipsius periculo permotum, constanti eius diuturnoque rogatu id fecisse, ut esset et qui oppidanis ius aequabiliter diceret, et
quem eius inimici propter rempublicam vererentur, ne is cottidie
ob aetatis imbecillitatem et hostium audaciam suo de regno periclitari cogeretur, illum etiam in suam militiam scripsisse, stipendio
iuvisse ornatumque esse voluisse, dignitate auxisse, sua benevolen-
tia pietateque fovisse; atque haec illum ab senatu omnia sine ullo
faenore tamquam a patre filium impetravisse, annumque integrum
his reipublicae muneribus et liberalitate usum fuisse; nunc vero,
quando non modo nulla gratia tantis officiis referatur, sed etiam
legati iurisdictio impediatur, reipublicae auctoritas labefactetur,
velle senatum et legato iubere ut statim decederet; fatuum porro
eum esse qui alteri suo cum dispendio beneficium dat, quod ipse
cui datur invitus accipiat. Iis litteris palam a legato recitatis, puer
rogare illum lacrimans obtestansque coepit ne decederet, multique
idem optimates frustra fecerunt; nam legatus nihilo sequius dece-
dens domum rediit.

62   Inter haec Carolus, Iuliano Genuae ac Savonis ei deditionem
pollicente, Alexandriae Dertonaeque Triultio, modo ipse reditum
in Italiam apparet, Lugdunum venit. Quibus intellectis rebus, foe-
derati trium milium militum numerum in Liguria celeriter con-
scripserunt eosque per arces oppidorum et castella distribuerunt;
et Ioannem Aloisium Fliscum, adversae factionis hominem magna
auctoritate, qui tum Genua exulabat resque novas moliebatur, civitati restitutum, communi stipendio ei tradito, ut quiesceret effecerunt. Crebrescente vero iterum fama Carolum ad Lugdunum mag-   •

mies, who had almost driven Astorre from his realm, and had later been moved by the entreaties of the citizens and by his own perilous situation to bring it about, at Faenza's long-standing and often repeated request, that there was someone to administer justice equitably for the inhabitants, and to inspire fear in her enemies out of respect for the Republic. And so that he would not be obliged to live in daily fear of losing his realm from the weakness of youth and the boldness of his enemies, Venice had even enrolled him in her military, helped him with pay and sought to promote his honor, had enhanced his position, had fostered him with her goodwill and mercy.[21] And all this he had obtained from the Senate without any expense on his part, as a son does from a father. For an entire year he had enjoyed these generous gifts of the Republic. Not only was no gratitude shown for such services, however, but the proveditor's administration of justice was actually being hindered and the Republic's authority was being weakened, so it was now the desire and order of the Senate to the proveditor that he should leave at once. It was a foolish man indeed who to his cost did another a good turn which the beneficiary was unwilling to accept. When the proveditor had read aloud this letter in public, with tears and entreaties the boy started begging him not to go, and many of the leading citizens did likewise, but in vain, for the proveditor departed all the same and returned home.

While this was going on, Charles went to Lyon, with Cardinal 62 Giuliano della Rovere promising him the surrender of Genoa and Savona, and Trivulzio that of Alessandria and Tortona, as long as he made preparations for his return to Italy. When this became known, the League swiftly raised 3,000 infantry in Liguria and distributed them among the citadels of the towns and the castles. Gianluigi Fieschi, a man of great influence who belonged to the dissident faction at Genoa, was at that time an exile from the city and was attempting to foment a revolution, but the allies managed to restore him to his city by means of a joint payment to him not

nos exercitus cogere, senatus decrevit ut trecenti equites
cataphracti Ludovici auxilio mitterentur, principisque collegium
civem legeret, qui eis quaestor et legatus esset. Patres Vincentium
Valerium legerunt. Pauloque post equites levis armaturae alteri totidem Mediolanum sunt a senatu missi. Triultius, cum eo quem et
secum e Gallia transalpina ducere et in Salassis ac Helvetiis cogere
potuit exercitu, in Ludovici fines ingressus, castella quinque haud
paulum opportuna communitaque perceleriter cepit, expulso
Ioanne Francisco Severinate, Ludovici praefecto, qui ne primum
quidem hostium impetum sustinuit. Alia ex parte cum militibus
sex milibus Asta Iulianus profectus Savonem versus, praemissis
qui eam civitatem pollicitationibus incitarent, cum nihil eo studio
profecisset, itinere non intermisso illo venit atque in colle apud oppidum castra posuit.

63   Iamque Pisis Savonem senatus iussu venerat classis praefectus
cum triremibus reipublicae septem, onerariis navibus Federici regis
quattuor; ad quas utrasque Genuenses duas eiusdem generis addiderant. Itaque Lucius et Severinas legati, quos eodem Ludovicus
miserat sua cum manu et cum equitibus Graecis militibusque
quos ex hibernis et Pisano agro Genuam contendere senatus iusserat, adiunctis classiariis, proelio cum Iuliani copiis commisso, eas
reppulerunt. Iis repulsis submotisque (retro enim cesserant), Novium oppidum tormentis positis ut se dederet compulerunt.
Classis autem praefectus, ea litora percurrens, naves magnas par-
vasque complures commeatu onustas, qui e Provincia cum Iuliano,
quem quidem iam Galli oram illam tenere confidebant, tum Florentinis afferebatur, naviculasque longas militares aliquot paucis
diebus cepit.

to make any trouble. But as talk grew again of Charles gathering great armies near Lyon, the Senate decreed that 300 heavy cavalry should be sent to help Ludovico, and that the doge's Council should choose a citizen to be their paymaster and proveditor. The Signoria chose Vincenzo Valier. A little later, another 300 light cavalry were sent by the Senate to Milan. Trivulzio entered Ludovico's territory with an army which he had partly brought with him from France and partly collected at Saluzzo and in Switzerland. He very swiftly took five well-fortified and strategically placed fortresses, driving out Ludovico's commander Gianfrancesco da Sanseverino, who buckled under the very first enemy attack. Elsewhere Cardinal Giuliano set out from Asti toward Savona with 6,000 infantry, sending men ahead to offer the city assurances and encourage its defection. But making no progress with this plan, without breaking his journey he marched to Savona and pitched camp on a hill near the town.

At the Senate's order the captain of the fleet had already come 63 from Pisa to Savona with seven galleys of the Republic and four merchantmen of King Federico, to which the Genoese had added two of each. Ludovico had sent the Milanese commissioners Lucio Malvezzi and Sanseverino to Savona with his own force and the stradiots and foot soldiers that the Senate had ordered to march from their winter quarters in the district of Pisa to Genoa. Reinforced by marines from the fleet, they joined battle with Giuliano's troops and drove them back. Once they had been repulsed and had left the scene following their retreat, the legates brought up siege-artillery and forced the town of Novi Ligure to surrender. Besides that, in the course of sailing along the coast the captain of the fleet captured in the space of a few days some small naval galleys and a good many ships great and small, loaded with provisions that were being brought from Provence for Giuliano (who the French were sure now controlled the coastline) as well as for the Florentines.

64   Triultii autem rebus successibusque cognitis, senatus decrevit ut Nicolaus Ursinus, cui omnium reipublicae copiarum praefectura decreta erat, Bernardinus Montonius Mediolanum celeriter contenderent imperatorque Franciscus se compararet ut, si opus esset, ipse quoque eo proficisceretur. Legati etiam ad bellum Gallicum lecti, Nicolaus Fuscarenus, Andreas Zancanius, ire celeriter sunt iussi. Tum centuriones militum tribunique delectibus conscribendis, quibus uterentur, ad plura loca missi. Ubi Ursinus una cum altero legato Mediolanum venit (nam Zancanius in itinere ad Cremam luxato pede restitit), Ludovicus edici frequenti foro iussit: quae legati Veneti iussissent, mandavissent, iis velle iubere se ita omnes homines audientes esse, uti si ea ipsemet imperavisset. Triultio vero, cui, antequam exercitus reipublicae illuc accessisset, omnia secundiora fuerant, Ursino et Montonio reliquisque praefectis et tribunis militum suas ei copias opponentibus, primo ad Castellatium, quod municipium tormentis concutere instituerat, mille et quingentis Gallis ab equitatu reipublicae levis armaturae male habitis, non leve detrimentum est illatum. Deinde, cum proelio decertare non auderet, paulatim sese retrahens et castella Ludovici capta deserens, apud Astam octo milia passus castra posuit et communivit, ante tamen Bergomascio Ludovici castello de via ei obvio, propterea quod se dedere noluerat, vi capto, interfectisque ad unum qui in eo erant omnibus. Ex Veneto etiam et Ludovici exercitu equites et milites Montis Alti municipium, quod a Novaria tria milia passuum abest, expugnaverunt simulque diripuerunt atque incenderunt.

65   Savone autem et Genua recte firmatis, cum Pisani commeatus inopia conflictarentur, propterea quod classis reipublicae ab eorum litoribus afuerat, Florentini suis navibus frumenta in oppidum supportari prohibuerant, pauculosque se dies sustinere posse ulter-

When the activities and successes of Trivulzio became known   64
to them, the Senate resolved that Niccolò Orsini (who had been
given overall charge of all the Republic's troops) and Bernardino
Fortebraccio da Montone should march swiftly to Milan, and
that their general Francesco Gonzaga should prepare to go there
as well if need be. Niccolò Foscarini and Andrea Zancani were
also appointed proveditors for the war in Lombardy, and were told
to get there with all haste. Officers and captains were then sent to
a number of places to levy troops for their use. When Orsini
reached Milan in the company of the second proveditor (Zancani
had broken his journey at Crema because of a sprained ankle),
Ludovico had a proclamation read out in a busy square: he desired
and commanded that whatever the Venetian proveditors ordered
or instructed should be obeyed by everyone just as if he had himself given the orders. Everything had been in Trivulzio's favor before the Venetian army arrived there, but with Orsini, da Montone
and the rest of the officers and captains ranged against his forces,
he suffered no small losses—in the first place at Castellazzo, a
town he had decided to subject to artillery bombardment, where
1,500 French were roughly handled by the Republic's light cavalry.
Then, not daring to engage in pitched battle, Trivulzio gradually
withdrew and abandoned the fortresses of Ludovico that he had
taken. He pitched his camp and secured its defenses eight miles
from Asti, but not before he had taken by force Ludovico's castle
at Bergamasco, which was on his way, and killed every last person
in it because it had refused to surrender. Horse and foot soldiers
from the Venetian and Milanese armies also stormed the town of
Montalto Pavese, three miles from Novara, and at once plundered
and burned it.

Savona and Genoa were now well secured, but the Pisans were   65
struggling with a lack of provisions, because the Venetian fleet was
a long way from their shores and the Florentine ships had prevented grain being brought into the town. The Pisans having

ius significavissent, reipublicae classis praefecto cum triremibus
quinque, navigiis minutis frumentariis, quibus erat praesidio, supra quinquaginta e Portu Veneris Pisas revertenti, ex omni sua copia Florentini fortissimo quoque milite navibus imposito, Triturrita solventes, occurrerunt. Naves erant eorum sex: quattuor
biremes, una et ipsa longa sed triremibus multo vastior atque pro-
cerior, oneraria magna alia, militibus amplius sexcentis, tormentorum atque missilium omni genere instructissimae. Ex iis ad impediendas frumentarias, ne Arni fluminis ostium ingredi possent,
biremes miserunt; reliquae duae magnae, ut in triremes impetum
facerent, remis velisque propellebantur.

66   Id praefectus conspicatus, triremem unam cui maxime confidebat commeatui praesidio reliquit; ipse cum reliquis provectus, tametsi periculosum esse intelligebat cum tam magnis navibus
confligere, tamen, propterea quod videbat omnem eius belli fortunam in eo commeatu supportando consistere, ad eas conversus, citatis remigibus suae navis proram in longae hostium latus magno
animo imprimit. Conflictu mutuo ambae naves concutiuntur, et
hostes manum ferream in praefecti navem iaciunt eamque retinent.
Itaque omni telorum genere comminus acerrime utrimque pugna-
tur; sed de superiore loco hostium milites tela in Venetos adigen-
tes facile eos vulnerabant; tum pilas piceas igne succenso in triremem iaciebant, quae res magnum incommodum praefecto attulit,
transtris compluribus et maiore velo igne combustis; ut qui
proximi pugnarent milites remigesque perterrerentur atque animos
virtutemque remitterent. Verum tamen et reliquae aderant, ut
quaeque poterat, triremes et utramque navem hostium virtute magis atque artificio gubernandi celeritateque remorum quam viribus

made it known that they could hold out for no more than a few days, the Venetian captain of the fleet was returning from Portovenere to Pisa with 5 galleys and more than 50 small grain-ships under his protection, when he was met by the Florentines, who had set sail from Livorno after putting on board the very best troops of their entire force. Their ships were six in number, four small galleys and a warship (but a warship much larger and longer than the galleys), and another large merchantman,[22] all supplied with more than 600 soldiers and all manner of artillery and ammunition. Of these they sent the small galleys to prevent the grain-ships from entering the mouth of the Arno; the other two large ships were put under oar and sail to attack the Venetian galleys.

Seeing this, the captain of the fleet left behind his most trusted 66 galley to guard the supply convoy. Although he realized that it was risky to engage such large ships, he nevertheless saw that the whole outcome of the war depended upon bringing in the provisions, and himself sailed forth with the remaining galleys. He turned toward the Florentine ships, and driving on his oarsmen with great spirit he rammed the prow of his ship into the side of the enemy warship. Both vessels shuddered with the impact as they crashed against one another, while the enemy cast a grappling hook onto the captain's ship and held it fast. Hand-to-hand fighting ensued, extremely fierce on both sides and with weapons of every sort, but the enemy soldiers could launch their missiles at the Venetians from higher up and so found them easy to injure. Then they began to throw balls of burning pitch onto the galley, something which was a great setback for the captain when a large number of thwarts and the mainsail itself caught fire. Those soldiers and rowers fighting closest at hand became very frightened, and their spirit and courage deserted them. Yet the other galleys were present to help as best they could and they assailed both the enemy ships, more with courage and skill in steering and quick row-

et facultate lacessebant; et modo hac, modo illac concitatae infere-
bantur. At navis magna hostium pilas ferreas creberrimas tormentis in triremes iaciebat et, si qua ei appropinquasset, saxa et tela insuper e carchesiis iaculabatur.

67   Pugnatum est acriter ab utrisque continenter horas ferme quattuor, cum interea navigia commeatum convehentia unius triremis
praesidio, quae biremes quattuor fortissime pugnando reppulerat,
ostium Arni fluminis capiunt, uno tantummodo navigio amisso,
quod tamen sponte ad Triturritam vela converterat. Praefectus id
quod unum maxime cupiebat assecutus, ut commeatum in tuto
sisteret, navibus hostium, magno et ipsis detrimento illato, vento
adspirante se subtrahentibus, interfectis suae navis hominibus per-
multis, vulneratis centum viginti, ex reliquis navibus non paucis
desideratis, vulneratis parte plurima, hostes discedentes Triturri-
tamque conversos reliquit.

68   Terrestri autem itinere dum reipublicae milites et Graeci equites Pisa missi reverterentur, Cevae oppidi, quod est supra Savonem atque in Gallorum partibus a regulis indigenis obtinebatur,
fines ingressi, eos percurrere coeperunt. Ea intellecta re oppidani
permoti, cum militibus, quos habebant complures, armis captis ad
eos contenderunt; quos illi excipientes universos fuderunt, complures occiderunt, captivos ducentos fecerunt; deinde ulterius progressi cohortatique inter se, in oppidi suburbia bipartito irrumpen-
tes, praeda et caede facta, duabus ex partibus ignem intulerunt.

69   Atque ea prope omnia tametsi ex Ludovici usu et reipublicae
voluntate maxime tunc quidem cecidissent, tamen propterea quod
illis ipsis diebus nuntii crebriores sunt allati Carolum omnino aut
ipsum in Italiam venturum aut magnos exercitus missurum, senatus decrevit ut imperator cum equitibus octingentis ad exercitum

ing than with strength and power, launching a furious attack on this side and on that. But the artillery of the enemy's big ship was firing cannonballs thick and fast onto the galleys, and if any of them got close, rocks and javelins were hurled down from the mastheads above.[23]

Fighting raged fiercely and without pause on both sides for almost four hours. In the meantime, protected by the single galley, which had driven back four small ones in a brave fight, the vessels carrying the supplies gained the mouth of the Arno. Only one vessel was lost, though that had of its own volition changed course for Livorno. The captain of the fleet had achieved the thing he most desired, to bring the provisions in safely. He left the enemy ships alone as they departed toward Livorno, withdrawing on a favorable wind after suffering extensive damage. For himself, a great many of the men on his ship had been killed, and 120 of them wounded. Not a few of the other ships were lost, and most of them had been damaged. 67

As the Republic's foot soldiers and stradiots sent from Pisa were returning overland, they entered the lands of Ceva, a town above Savona under the rule of local lords who sided with the French, and they began to pass through it. The inhabitants were greatly disturbed when this came to their attention, and seizing arms they hastened to meet them with the soldiers that they had in large quantities. Coming upon them, the Venetians put them all to flight, killing a good many and taking 200 prisoners. As they proceeded further, egging one another on, they burst into the outskirts of the town on two fronts, and with pillage and slaughter set it aflame on both sides. 68

Although almost all these events, at that stage especially, had fallen out to Ludovico's advantage and the Republic's satisfaction, there were nevertheless increasingly strong rumors at the time that Charles was either coming to Italy in person or would be sending a great army. The Senate accordingly resolved that the captain-gen- 69

contenderet, copiaeque reipublicae omnes ad Padi ripas sese sisterent. Delecti etiam centuriones decem, militibus Brixiae conscribendis mille, ad exercitumque adducendis. Ex Rhaetis quoque trium milium militum numerus pusilla pecunia conscriptorum adventare dictus est, ut Brixiae solidum stipendium acciperet.

70   Ea per populos opinione de Carolo timoreque crebrescente, Tristanus Saornianus e Fori Iulii principibus, Hieronymi frater, homo reipublicae amantissimus, Bernardum Bembum patrem meum, decemvirum magistrum, adit. Proponit habere se necessarium sibi hominem Epirotam, callidum et ingenio peracri, nihil omnino ut sit quod ei non mandari recte possit; huic esse cum propinquo suo, quem Carolus Gallorum rex cubiculi ministrum habeat, magnam perque veterem benevolentiam; audere illum in Galliam proficisci et vel propinquo persuadere ut veneno, quod secum allaturus est, regem tollat, vel, illo de ea re celato, ipsum per se regem tollere, si decemviri velint Epirotae illi tantae rei praemium aliquod statuere; sperare se atque confidere brevi negotium ab eo confectum iri. Bembus, tametsi sciret ea flagitia a magistratibus repelli, more tamen institutoque maiorum re cum reliquis decemvirum magistris communicata atque ab ipsis ad collegium perlata, Tristano ad se vocato, de collegii sententia respondit: eiusmodi contra hostes insidiis ad eam diem numquam usam rempublicam fuisse, cum saepenumero potuerit; neque nunc velle incipere; magis deos immortales quam humanas opes vereri; porro vinci ab suamet nequitia illos qui per scelus alios vincere perque nefas parant.

eral should take 800 horse and go to the army with all haste, and that all the Venetian forces should be drawn up on the banks of the Po. Ten officers were also chosen to raise 1,000 infantry at Brescia and take them to the army. It was said too that a body of 3,000 infantry had been recruited at small cost in the Tyrol and was on the point of arriving at Brescia to get their full pay.

As the rumors and fears about Charles grew among the popu- 70 lace, Tristano Savorgnan, one of the leading men of Friuli, the brother of Girolamo and a man utterly devoted to the Republic, approached my father Bernardo Bembo, one of the Heads of the Council of Ten. He mentioned that he had a friend in Albania, a shrewd man with a very sharp mind who could be given any task with complete confidence. This man had for a very long time been on close terms with a relative of his who served in the bedchamber of King Charles. The Albanian ventured that he would leave for France and persuade his relative to do away with the king with poison that he would take with him, or, alternatively, that he would conceal the matter from his relative and kill the king himself, if the Council of Ten was prepared to offer him some reward for a deed of such moment. Savorgnan hoped and believed that the Albanian could bring the business to a quick conclusion. Although Bembo knew that such crimes were repellent to the magistrates, in accordance with ancestral custom and usage he nevertheless communicated the matter to the other Heads of the Ten, and they reported it to the Council. Summoning Tristano to him, Bembo gave him the Council's decision, to the effect that the Republic had never used such schemes against its enemies, although it could often have done so, and was not about to start now. They feared Almighty God more than they feared the power of men, and, apart from that, those that planned to topple others through crime and sin were themselves brought low by their own wickedness.

LIBER QUARTUS

1   Iis in Italia rebus administratis, Caroli et Hispaniae regum legati,
qui quidem reges, ad saltum Pyrenaeum exercitibus missis, bellum
inter se gerebant, sex mensium indutias in Aquitania faciunt; quibus uterque rex indutiis non ab altero modo ipsorum sed a sociis
etiam et foederatis bello lacessendis abstineat. Quamobrem Carolus, ubi id ei nuntiatum est, ad Triultium mittit, imperans ne
quam Ludovici rebus indutiarum tempore turbam aut molestiam
inferat. Ea intellecta re, senatus suas et ipse copias domum revo-
cat. Ita qua ex parte quoque tempore maximi tumultus exspectabantur, subitum otium est adlatum. Eas ob res senatus Dominicum Trivisanum, Antonium Bolduum ad Hispaniae reges legavit,
qui procurarent uti ex indutiis semestribus diuturna pax fieret.

2   Quibus profectis Antonius, eloquentia plane singulari et praes-
tanti vir ingenio, in itinere adversa valetudine interceptus, Genuae
interiit. Eius morte audita, senatus consultum factum est: cum
Antonius Bolduus Andr. f. ex equestri ordine, nullum laborem pro
republica refugiens, legatione ad reges Hispaniae suscepta, in itinere mortem obierit, senatui placere ut Gabrieli Bolduo, eius filio,
primo quoque tempore in fano Patavino sacerdotium attribuatur,
quo se fratresque suos alere commodius atque honestius possit.
Idque paulo post sacerdotium ab Alexandro senatu petente Gabrieli est attributum.

3   Miserant illi quidem reges superioribus mensibus ad senatum
per Franciscum Capellum legatum, qui ex Hispania domum redierat, Fortunatarum insularum unius regem dono medius fidius non

BOOK IV

Following these events in Italy, the ambassadors of Charles and   1497
the Spanish sovereigns, who had sent armies to the area of the
Pyrenees in their war on one another, declared a six-month truce
in Gascony. By the terms of the truce both monarchs were to refrain from waging war not only on one another but on their
friends and allies as well. As soon as this was reported to Charles,
he sent Trivulzio an order not to cause Ludovico any disturbance
or trouble during the period of the truce. When they learned of
this, the Senate too called its forces home. So a sudden calm was
introduced from the very quarter and at the very time that most
trouble was anticipated. On that account the Senate sent
Domenico Trevisan and Antonio Boldù as ambassadors to the
Spanish sovereigns to see to it that the six-month truce turned
into a lasting peace.

After they had set out, Antonio, a man of great eloquence and   2
singular intellect, was taken ill on the journey, and he died at
Genoa. On hearing the news of his death the Senate passed a decree: since Antonio di Andrea Boldù of the order of knights had
shunned no labor on the Republic's behalf and had undertaken an
embassy to the sovereigns of Spain, but met his death en route, it
was the Senate's wish that his son Gabriele Boldù should be assigned a canonry in the cathedral of Padua at the earliest opportunity,[1] so that he might support himself and his brothers in a more
honorable and appropriate way. At the Senate's petition the office
was assigned to Gabriele by Pope Alexander shortly afterwards.

A few months earlier Francesco Capello, the ambassador to the   3
Spanish sovereigns, had returned home from Spain, and the sovereigns sent with him the king of one of the Islands of the Blessed as
a gift to the Senate. And it was indeed a gift not to be scorned,

spernendo, quando ea porro elementi ora solidi, quae in oceano
Atlantico est circiter decies centena milia passus a continenti meridiem versus, multis ante patres nostros saeculis ignorata, eorum
indagatione ac diligentia tota tum demum reperta et colonis magistratibusque missis in potestatem redacta, orbi terrarum adiungi-
tur. Eum regem publice Patavii[1] enutriri senatus iussit.

4   Eodem fere tempore patres certiores facti Franciscum imperatorem, stipendio reipublicae non confecto, cum rege Carolo agere ut
se in suam militiam recipiat, illum ad urbem accersitum, ubi
morbo ne venire posset impediri se respondit, decemvirum decreto
missum fecerunt. Is auri libras ducentas stipendiorum nomine
ante tempus acceptorum reipublicae debebat; salis autem crediti
neque dum soluti, centum. Accidit tamen ut eo ipso missionis die
infrequenti comitatu Franciscus Venetias appelleret, dictitans se a
Ludovico eiusque genero Galeatio in fraudem ob invidiam coniec-
tum, qui litteras ab eo conscriptas finxissent, ad patresque misissent, quas ipse numquam scripserit. Eius rei satis magnum argu-
mentum esse quod ipse in eorum potestatem venerit. Quod si alia
etiam pignora patres postulent, arces se sui regni suosque liberos
reipublicae traditurum, modo sibi purgandi iure criminis facultas
ne intercludatur. Neque tamen ut sententiam patres mutarent impetrare potuit. Qui ad eum tertio post die miserunt, moram in
urbe diutius ne traheret. Is etiam, quo ab urbe discessit die, Ioannem fratrem ad patres misit; quibus se ab eo conveniri non est visum. Post haec dum indutiarum Aquitanicarum tempus labitur,
Hercules ad urbem venit, principem et patres salutatum roga-
tumque ut Ferdinandum filium suum in equitatu reipublicae vel-

since that stretch of solid land, found in the Atlantic about 1,000 miles south of the continent, had been unknown for many centuries before our fathers' day and now forms an addition to the world.[2] It was only at that time that it was at last discovered by the sovereigns' painstaking explorations and brought under their dominion with the despatch of colonists and magistrates. The Senate ordered that the king should be kept in Padua at public expense.

At about the same time, the senators were informed that their   4 captain-general Francesco Gonzaga was negotiating with King Charles to enter his service before he had completed his contract with the Republic. They summoned him to Venice and when he replied that he was too ill to come, they dismissed him by decree of the Ten. He owed the Republic 200 gold pounds on account of pay received in advance, and 100 on account of salt consigned and not yet paid for. It happened, however, that on the very day of his dismissal Francesco landed at Venice with a sparse retinue, declaring that owing to a grudge he had been the victim of a fraud on the part of Ludovico and his son-in-law Galeazzo da Sanseverino: they had forged the letter supposed to be from him, which he had never written, and sent it to the senators. He said that the fact that he had put himself in their power was sufficient proof of the truth of his assertion, but if the senators required further guarantees, he would hand over the fortresses of his realm and his children to the Republic, as long as he was not deprived of a proper opportunity to clear himself of the charge. But he was not able to prevail upon the senators to change their mind, and two days later they sent word to him that he should tarry no longer in the city. On the day he left Venice, Francesco actually sent his brother Giovanni to the senators, but they did not think it advisable to receive him. After that, while the period of the truce in Gascony was running out, Ercole d'Este came to Venice to pay his respects to the doge and senators and to ask them to agree to take his son

lent esse. Quod quidem ei patres liberaliter concesserunt, equitibus cataphractis alendis centum stipendio adulescenti per senatum
attributo.

5   Quod autem ad Pisanum bellum attinet (ut eodem saepius revertamur), is quidem annus et pro parte insequens nihil prope
quod magnopere memoratu dignum esset habuerunt. Missi ad
Florentinos per Triturritam commeatus in tam magnis navibus, ut
eas aggredi naves reipublicae non sint ausae. Capti ab eorum exercitu milites Veneti centum et exuti armis. Conscripti ab eisdem
equites levis armaturae tercentum, qui sagittis contra Graecos uterentur; atque ii eorum impetus ad modum represserunt. Ob id ab
senatu equites ferreis cum fistulis ad exercitum missi, et item
Graeci submissi. Cataphracti quoque equites conscripti novi, dilapsis veteribus. Qui Pisarum portas custodiebant, iis addita ab senatu stipendia, ut studiosiores suo in munere obeundo essent;
missa etiam ad senatum Ludovici nova legatio, quae ad componen-
das Pisanorum cum Florentinis controversias patres hortaretur:
praestare eos Florentinis attribui quam bellum diutius alere; omnia in Italia pacis et quietis plena momento temporis futura, si
Pisae restituantur; ut non tam commutata illius tempore aut even-
tibus consilia viderentur — quid enim tum novi? — quam semper
illum id unum spectasse palam fieret, ne respublica eo municipio
potiretur. Sed nihil plane ultra; aliis vero de rebus perpauca.

6   Navis reipublicae longa, ex earum genere quae ad mercaturam
proficiscuntur, more institutoque maiorum convehendis iis hominibus qui, aut voto suscepto aut religione permoti, Christi Dei filii
sepulcrum quod est Hierosolymis adire atque invisere cupiunt, in
Syriam quotannis stato tempore mitti solita, cum ad Maleam iter
faceret, in Turcarum regis classem Arige praefecto incidit. Ea erat

Ferrante into the Republic's cavalry. The senators generously granted his request, and allotted the young man pay for the upkeep of 100 heavy cavalry.

Now as regards the Pisan war (to return once again to the subject), nothing specially worth recording happened in this year and part of the next. Supplies were sent to the Florentines by way of Livorno in vessels so large that the Venetian ships did not dare to attack them. A hundred Venetian soldiers were taken captive by the Florentine army and disarmed. The Florentines also recruited 300 light cavalry as archers against the stradiots, and these men considerably hampered the stradiot attacks. For that reason the Senate despatched cavalry armed with guns to the army, and stradiots were likewise sent in support. Fresh heavy cavalry were also recruited, the former cavalry having disbanded. The garrisons of the gates of Pisa received additional pay from the Senate to induce them to take extra care in the performance of their duties. Ludovico also sent a new embassy to the Senate to urge the senators to settle the quarrel of the Pisans with the Florentines. It would be better, they said, to make them over to the Florentines than to support the war any longer. The whole of Italy would have peace and quiet in a moment if Pisa were given back. From all of which it appeared not so much that Ludovico's strategy had changed over time or in the light of events — for what had changed at that point? — but that he had only ever had one end in view, as was now obvious, that Pisa should not fall into the hands of the Republic. But apart from that, there is nothing else to record, and very little about anything else.

By ancient custom and practice, a Venetian galley of the sort used in commerce was usually sent to Syria at a fixed time each year to convey people wanting to visit the Holy Sepulchre of Christ, the Son of God, at Jerusalem in performance of a vow or with some religious motivation. When the ship was on course toward Cape Malea, it happened upon a squadron of the Turkish

navium onerariarum duarum, triremium item duarum, biremium quinque. Quarum biremes duae ad navem reipublicae praemissae vela demittere iusserunt. Mos est nauticus eiusmodi, ut qui plus aut viribus aut dignitate pollent velint ut quae sibi occurrerint naves velificationem intermittant antennasque demittant, cum honoris sui causa, tum ut, si quid ab illis quaerere aut petere velint, possint. Id qui nolunt facere, ius est bello cogere ut faciant. Saepeque accidit ut ea de causa pugnae maximae existerent plurimorumque hominum caedes consequerentur.

7   Aloisius Georgius (is enim erat navis Venetae praefectus) classem esse illam piratarum existimans, antennis non demissis cursum tenuit. Quod ubi Turcae conspexerunt, ab utroque illum latere suis triremibus cinxerunt et sagittarum magnam vim in eum mittere coeperunt. Id cum parum proficeret, navibus suis omnibus illum expugnare contenderunt. Eo in certamine Turcae navis Venetae scalam saepe conscenderunt aliisque a partibus in navem prosilierunt; saepe ignem iniecerunt, quo et plutei combusti, et praefecti cenaculum ipsa in puppi et maiora vela conflagraverunt. Sed tanta remigum et nautarum atque imprimis advenarum virtus fuit ut, cum ab hora diei sexta usque ad quartam decimam pugnavissent, Turcae receptui canentes, et signo pacificationis sublato, priores pugnam desinerent, Arigesque, missis ad Aloisium ex suis qui salutem illi dicerent magnumque atque fortem virum esse testarentur, pacem benevolentiamque cum illo iniit. Missi quadraginta milites ex iis quos Ianizaros appellant suis in navibus interfectos esse Aloisio significaverunt. Ex Veneta interierunt quinque, vulnerati complures; in his praefectus, quattuor vulneribus acceptis, neque tamen periit.

8   In Punicis etiam litoribus Bernardus Ciconia, eiusdem generis navibus a republica praefectus, Perucam piratam ingenio magis

sultan under the command of one Ariges, consisting of two merchantmen, two large galleys, and five small ones. Two of the small galleys were sent up to the Venetian ship and ordered it to lower its sails. Nautical custom holds that those in more powerful or important ships will have boats that encounter them stop sailing and lower their sailyards, not only as a mark of respect but also so that they can question them or ask for something if they so wish. Those who refuse can be lawfully compelled to do so by force. It often happens that this leads to great battles taking place, and consequent slaughter on a large scale.

Alvise Zorzi, the captain of the Venetian ship, held his course 7 without lowering his yards in the belief that it was a pirate fleet. When the Turks saw this, their large galleys hemmed him in on both sides and began to rain great volleys of arrows down on him. Not making much headway with this, they made to storm his vessel with all their ships. In the struggle the Turks several times climbed the scaling-ladder of the Venetian ship and leapt onto the ship from the other side. They frequently hurled in firebrands, causing the rowing benches[3] to catch fire, while the captain's own cabin on the poop and the mainsails were consumed by flames. But such was the valor of the oarsmen and sailors, and above all of the passengers, that when they had fought from six in the morning to two in the afternoon, the Turks sounded the retreat and raising the flag of peace, stopped fighting first. Ariges sent some men to offer his respects to Alvise and proclaim that he was a great and brave man, and so they ended on peaceful and amicable terms. The envoys indicated to Alvise that 400 soldiers (the so-called janissaries) had been killed on their ships. On the Venetian ship five died, and many were wounded. Among them was the captain, but though he was wounded four times, he did not perish.

On the Mediterranean coast of Africa, Bernardo Cicogna 8 (whom the Republic had put in charge of ships of the same merchantman class) won a victory over the pirate Peruca, more by

quam viribus expugnavit. Erat uterque ad Tuneta in portu; atque ille, navem onerariam permagnam habens, ut exirent Veneti expectabat, illos in mari aggressurus; seque id conaturum palam antea prae se tulerat, multa minaciter oblocutus. Interim Dalmatae, qui sub imperio reipublicae degebant, navem non magnam eundem in portum adducunt. Id ut est Ciconiae nuntiatum, nocte ex suis navibus homines complures in illam imponit navesque aptari ad pugnam imperat. Ea re, tametsi furtim fiebat, tamen a piratis animadversa, confestim Peruca, relictis ob celeritatem ancoris, e portu sese eripit. Ciconia illum cum triremibus sequitur; tranquillitateque oborta, remigum labore assecutus oppugnansque comminus, ubi propter navis altitudinem nihil ferme virtute militum proficit et suos facile vulnerari de superiore loco videt, fabros in navis scapham iubet descendere, eosque suae puppis pluteis armamentisque contegens, ex piratae navi stuppas inter tigna constipatas paulum sub aqua extrahere imperat. Ea re hostibus imprudentibus effecta, implenteque se navi aqua, Peruca illi deditur.

9   Nostro autem in mari Andreas Lauredanus, navis onerariae bellicae a senatu praefectus, magna vir virtute, cum intellexisset a Crotoniatis Petrum Cantabrum piratam recipi, qui reipublicae hominibus damna intulisset, eumque ad Oricellam esse cum navibus longis quattuor, secum naviculas quas appellant gripos, quae commeatum advexerant, duas ducens eo proficiscitur; iactisque procul ancoris noctem opperiens, in suae navis scaphis duabus atque in gripis milites trecentos imposuit, imperans ut ante lucem egressi turrim ipso in litore, qua in turri esse Cantabrum intellexerat, circumfunderentur, ne is effugere posset, eamque expugnare conaren-

out-thinking him than by brute force. Both men were in port at Tunis, and Peruca, with a very large cargo-vessel, was waiting for the Venetians to leave so that he could attack them on the open sea — something he had openly boasted he would attempt to do beforehand, with many threats and insults. Meanwhile Dalmatians who lived under Venetian rule brought a ship of no great size into the same port. When Cicogna learned of it, he transferred a large number of his men from their ships to the Dalmatian vessel during the night, and ordered it to be made ready for battle. Although this was done in secret, it was nonetheless observed by the pirates, and Peruca rushed out of the harbor, leaving his anchors behind for greater speed. Cicogna followed with his galleys and as the sea was becalmed, caught up with him by dint of the oarsmen's efforts. He engaged the enemy in hand-to-hand fighting, but owing to the height of the other ship, the courage of his soldiers was of little avail. Seeing his men easily wounded from above, he told carpenters to board the ship's skiff and hiding them with the breastworks and tackle of his poop, told them to take out the tow fitted between the planks of the pirate ship a little below the water line. This was done without the enemy noticing it, and with his ship filling with water, Peruca surrendered to Cicogna.

Andrea Loredan, a man of great courage, had been put in 9 charge of an armed merchantman in the Adriatic by the Senate. He learned that the pirate Pedro Navarro, who had caused Venetians much harm, had been taken in by the people of Crotone and was at Roccella with four warships.[4] Taking with him two of the smaller craft called *grippi* which had brought their provisions, he made for Roccella, and dropped anchor some way off as he waited for nightfall. Then he put 300 soldiers on two skiffs and on the *grippi*, telling them to land before dawn. They were to surround a tower on the shore where he had been told Navarro was, so as to prevent his escape, and attempt to take it. But because the journey

tur. Missi, quod iter erat longius, orto iam sole in litus descende-
runt.

10   Cantaber ubi naves advenientes e longinquo vidit, coactis non
suis modo, sed eius etiam loci copiis equitatus et peditatus quas
Antonius Centilius, cuius erat in potestate castellum, ut ei praesidio essent ad illum statim miserat, in eos impetum fecit. Veneti
cum sex horas continenter pugnavissent, interfectis compluribus,
vulneratis octoginta Cantabroque ipso, omnes in fugam coniecerunt. Fugientes loci castellum recipiens texit. Turri deinde expu-
gnata, quique in ea erant propugnatoribus novem reste suspensis,
castellum capere sunt aggressi. Biduo in ea oppugnatione
consumpto cum acerrime castellum defenderetur, murorum parte
deiecta, vastato agro, tormentis hostium abductis, uno suorum
tantummodo amisso, vulneratis perpaucis, piratae classem incenderunt ad navemque redierunt.

11   Superiori vero aestate Ioannes Corvinus, Matthiae regis Pannoniae filius, per suum legatum senatui significavit cupere sese
perpetuo amoris et benevolentiae vinculo cum republica coniungi,
itaque petere ut in civitatem et ius comitiorum reciperetur. Quamobrem maioribus in comitiis civitas et ius comitiorum ei datum.

12   Armenii quoque, qui Venetias venerant, tabellas testamentarias,
Ziani principis tempore ab homine Armenio confectas, aedis
Marciae procuratoribus ostenderunt; quibus tabellis domum in
urbe demortui pecunia emere procuratores iubebantur; quam quidem domum Armenii ad urbem venientes incolerent; eamque postea domum cum sacello emptam ad Iuliani fuisse in laternarum
via, quae tunc a procuratoribus locetur; itaque illam ipsam domum sibi restitui ex testamento petierunt. A procuratoribus intellecta eorum postulatione domus est Armeniis restituta atque ab iis

was rather longer than anticipated, the expedition did not disembark on the shore until after sunrise.

Navarro saw the ships arriving from a long way off, and gathering his own men as well as local forces of cavalry and foot soldiers (which had been instantly sent for his protection by Antonio Centelles, whose castle it was), he launched an attack on them. After fighting continuously for six hours, the Venetians put them all to flight, with many killed and 80 wounded, including Navarro himself. The castle of Roccella took the fugitives in and gave them cover. Then after the tower on the coast was taken, and the nine defenders in it hanged, the Venetians turned to taking the castle. They spent two days on the assault, but the castle was very fiercely defended, and so with part of the walls destroyed, the countryside laid waste, the enemy's artillery carried off, and with the loss of only one man and very few wounded, the Venetians set fire to the pirate fleet and returned to their ship.

In the previous summer [of 1497] Joannes, the son of Matthias Corvinus, King of Hungary, let the Senate know through his ambassador that he desired to be united with the Republic in a perpetual bond of love and goodwill, and he accordingly sought to be admitted to Venetian citizenship and the status of a noble, both of which were granted him in the Great Council.

There were also Armenians who came to Venice and showed the Procurators of St. Mark's a will made by one of their countrymen in the time of Doge Ziani.[5] Under the terms of the will the Procurators were instructed to purchase a house in the city with a bequest from the deceased, where Armenians coming to the city might live. The house and a chapel had subsequently been purchased near San Zulian in the Calle delle Lanterne,[6] but it was then rented out by the Procurators. The Armenians therefore sought to have the house restored to them in accordance with the will. Once they learned of the request, the Procurators returned the house to them, and they started to live there. The Armenians

incoli coepta. Ipsi a civitate comiter et liberaliter accepti, gens tam
longinqua, urbi amico spectaculo fuerunt.

13   Vere autem insequentis anni iam medio Ludovicus, regni ac dominationis ingenio et natura cupidissimus eiusque rei magnopere
impatiens, quod videbat Pisarum civitatem multo reipublicae ami-
ciorem esse magisque tribuere quam illius vel benivolentiae vel
fidei, Lucam oppidum suam in potestatem redigere malis artibus
est conatus; quo facilius vel Pisas, si qua posset, occuparet ipse
suasque faceret, vel reipublicae occupare illas cupienti firmius ob-
sisteret, municipio omnem ad copiam opportunissimo et vicinitate
coniunctissimo suae dicioni adiecto, ad seque traducto. Itaque
compositis quas intendebat ei municipio insidiis, ire se Genuam
simulat, ut Lucenses imparatos aggredi, tamquam alio properans,
improviso possit. Sed in itinere dum esset, detecta proditione oppidani se communiunt. Potiundi oppidi occasione amissa, Ludovicus, ne simulasse videretur, Genuam profectus est; ibique dies aliquot commoratus domum rediit.

14   Senatus, iis Ludovici artibus cognitis, cum in se plane uno positam omnem eius belli rationem et constitutam videret, Graecos
equites trecentos, qui in agro Patavino hiemaverant, Pisas mittere
prioribusque addere decrevit; militumque numerum duum milium
statim imperare, qui Pisas mitterentur; tum legatum exercitui le-
gere, qui Iustiniano domum redire postulanti succederet. Lectus
Thomas Zenus viae se dedit. Quae intelligens Ludovicus palam,
ut etiam reipublicae legatus exaudierit, "ea quidem senatus

themselves were graciously and generously welcomed by the citizenry: hailing from so far away, they made an agreeable sight for the city.

Now Ludovico was by nature and inclination bent on rule and 13 dominance. He bridled at seeing the city of Pisa better disposed toward the Republic and setting more store by her than on his own goodwill and good faith. By the middle of the following spring, in consequence, he made an attempt to seize control of the 1498 town of Lucca by his unprincipled schemes, with a view either to facilitating his occupation of Pisa and making it his, if it could be done, or to providing stiffer opposition to the Republic in her own desire to occupy it, by adding to his dominion and bringing over to his side a town that was rich in resources of all kinds and through its proximity much involved with Pisa. Having laid his trap for Lucca, he made as if to go to Genoa, so that by giving the impression of hurrying off somewhere else, he could make a surprise attack on the unprepared people of Lucca. But while he was on his way, his treachery was uncovered and the townspeople took steps to defend themselves. Having lost the opportunity of taking the town, Ludovico left for Genoa anyway, in case he should be seen to have been only pretending, and after a stay of a few days, returned home.

When Ludovico's tricks became known, the Senate realized 14 that the whole burden and conduct of the war had devolved on them alone. They resolved to send to Pisa 300 stradiots who had spent the winter in the district of Padua, and to add them to those already there, and to have a troop of 2,000 foot soldiers sent to Pisa at once; also, to select a proveditor for the army to succeed Giustinian, who was asking to return home. Tommaso Zen was chosen and took to the road. When he learned of this, Ludovico said openly, so that even the Republic's ambassador heard him, "I see what those Senate decrees are aiming at. The senators want to

consulta," inquit, "quo spectent, video. Volunt enim patres Pisis potiri, sed eos eventus frustrabitur; numquam enim potientur."

15   Inter haec Carolus Galliae rex moritur. Itaque accidit ut, cum Marcus Lipomanus, reipublicae legatus, ab Ludovico peteret uti Zeno, cum Graecis equitibus Pisas eunti, iter ad Apuanos Ligures pateret, Ludovicus nihil responderit; tum ipsi, in Ludovici fines progresso, itineris facultas permissa non fuerit. Senatus, iis de rebus certior factus reputansque id quod erat, Ludovicum nihil sibi amplius a Carolo timentem, propter quod reipublicae indigeret, spiritus sumpsisse, neque quidquam praeterea in Pisani belli administratione reipublicae concessurum illum existimans, ad Herculem misit, ut equitibus et legato reipublicae per Mutinae Regiique Lepidi fines iter daret; qui quidem dedit.

16   Ludovicus autem ea re cognita, tum e Gallia certior factus Aloisium ducem Genabensium, qui in Galliae regnum Carolo successerat, quem Galli Ludovicum appellabant, iam ad bellum in sese animum et cogitationem adiecisse, senatui significavit nihil se de itinere legato reipublicae negavisse; illum potius perperam ipsius verba interpretatum; suos fines omni tempore senatus exercitibus patuisse, neque umquam occlusos fore. Quam ob rem Zenus ipse per Ludovici fines, quod iter erat commodius, Pisas venit, cum tamen equites, Pado iam traiecto, per Herculis fines antea misisset. Florentini, qui omnino saepe a Graecis equitibus male habiti eos pessime oderant; edictum proposuerunt, ne quis ex eis captivus duceretur, sed captus interficeretur. Ea intellecta re, legatus Venetus edici contra iussit: idem sui milites facerent, neque ulli omnino ex hostium numero parcerent, sed omnes peraeque interficerent.

take possession of Pisa, but they will find themselves frustrated by events, for they will never lay their hands on it."

In the midst of all this, King Charles of France died. And it 15 so happened that when the Republic's ambassador Marco Lippomano asked Ludovico's permission for Zen and the stradiots to march by way of Pontremoli on their way to Pisa, Ludovico made no reply. Permission to continue was then withheld, when Zen had already proceeded into Ludovico's territory. On being informed of this turn of events, the Senate supposed (as was in fact the case) that since Ludovico now had nothing to fear from Charles for which he would need the Republic, he had recovered his spirits. What was more, in the belief that he would make no concessions to the Republic in the matter of the war with Pisa, they sent word to Ercole d'Este, asking him to permit the Venetian proveditor and cavalry to march through the territory of Modena and Reggio, to which Ercole acceded.

But when Ludovico heard of it, and further learning from 16 France that Aloisius, Duke of Orleans (whom the French called Louis),[7] had succeeded Charles as king of France and had already fixed his heart and mind on war against him, he intimated to the Senate that he had not refused the Venetian envoy anything with regard to his journey, but the envoy, rather, had misunderstood his words. His lands were open to the Senate's armies at any time, nor would they ever be closed. Consequently, Zen himself went to Pisa by way of Ludovico's territory, the more convenient route, although he had earlier sent his cavalry through Ercole's lands, since they had already crossed the Po. The Florentines had a perfect hatred of the stradiots, having often been roughly treated by them, and now published an edict that none of them should be taken captive, but were to be killed as soon as they were taken. Learning of this, the Venetian proveditor had a counter-edict issued, to the effect that his soldiers would do the same: they would not spare a single man of the enemy force, but would kill them all without

Statimque in eorum fines Graecos equites ducens, excursione introrsus facta, quoscumque in agris reperit interfecit. Qua re cognita Florentini, edicto publice rescisso, ad morem belli pristinum
redierunt. Pauloque post Butrium magno impetu aggressi, scalisque ad murum positis, repulsi sunt a propugnatoribus, detrimento parvo accepto.

17   Sed non parvo illis detrimento ea quae subsecuta est clades fuit.
Iacobus Savornianus, turmae equitum reipublicae praefectus, adolescens impiger, cum suis equitibus centum, Graecis quater centum in hostium fines Populoniam versus e castris praedabundus
proficiscitur; multisque milibus passuum confectis, ad castellum[2]
(quo in castello halumen proximis e securis erutum incredibili
dominorum lucro plurimarum nationum usui conficitur) accedens,
oppidanos ad illum repellendum egressos fugat; aedificia, quae pro
portis sunt, incendit; alias in partes incursione facta atque in ea biduo consumpto, magna cum pecudum et armentorum praeda dum
revertitur, hostes, de ea re certiores facti, omnibus copiis ad ea loca
quae per illum iter facturum putabant contenderunt.

18   Alia ex parte Zenus legatus, ob Iacobi longiorem moram veritus ne hostes intellecta re in itinere illum aggrediantur, cum reliquo exercitu obviam Iacobo proficiscitur, praemisso tubicine,[3] qui
eum de suo adventu certiorem faciat. Hostes Iacobum nacti impetum in eum faciunt. Interim tubicen celeritate usus de legati adventu eum admonet. Ille id intelligens hostium modo impressio-
nem lente sustinere, etiam cedere interdum, deinde pugnam
paulisper redintegrare. Id ubi aliquamdiu facit, legatus advenit.
Hostes pugnantes a tergo repente aggreditur. Tum Iacobus Grae-
cique clamore sublato acerrime in eos invehuntur. Quod ubi hostes
viderunt, omnes perterriti fugere contenderunt. Interfecti ex iis

distinction. He at once led the stradiots to the Florentine border and making a sortie inside, slew anyone he found in the country-side. When they heard of it, the Florentines publicly rescinded their edict and returned to their former rules of engagement. A little later they launched a great assault on Buti and brought up siege-ladders to the wall, but they were repelled by its defenders, though they came to little harm.

But no small harm was caused them by the defeat that fol- 17 lowed. Giacomo Savorgnan, a lively youth and captain of a troop of Venetian cavalry, left camp to plunder enemy territory around Piombino with 100 horse and 400 stradiots. After many miles he came to a castle where alum extracted from nearby mines was pre-pared for use around the world, to its owners' vast profit.[8] The in-habitants came out to repel him but he put them to flight, set fire to the buildings in front of the gates, and spent two days making raids elsewhere before returning with considerable spoils of sheep and cattle. When the enemy got wind of it, they took all their men and hurried to the places that they thought he would have to pass through.

Elsewhere, during Giacomo's lengthy absence the proveditor 18 Zen grew fearful that the enemy had grasped the situation and would attack him as he returned, so he went to meet him with the rest of the army, sending a trumpeter on ahead to inform him of his arrival. The enemy caught up with Giacomo and launched an attack on him. Meanwhile the trumpeter made all speed and ad-vised him of the proveditor's arrival. Apprised of this, Giacomo calmly absorbed the enemy onslaught, even yielding ground from time to time, then renewing the fight for a short while. When he had been carrying on like this for some time, the proveditor ar-rived, and suddenly attacked the enemy from behind as they were engaged in the fight. Then Giacomo and the stradiots raised a shout and launched a fierce onslaught against them. When the en-emy saw this, they all hastened to flee in terror. More than 200 of

plus ducenti. Capti ex praefectis Ranutii Martiani frater Gallusque
is qui ob virtutem bellator magnus appellabatur, aliique complures; ex equitibus centum septuaginta, ex militibus quingenti; signa
militaria quinque relata. Ranutius ipse, toti exercitui praefectus,
equo amisso fugiens, vix aegreque se in proximum oppidum
contulit. Reliqui aut idem in oppidum aut in montes atque silvas
fugientes se abdiderunt.

19   Florentini, clade accepta, Paulo Vitellio, qui priore stipendio
confecto ad gentiles suos, quibuscum Alexander bellum gerebat, in
Romanum agrum se contulerat, imperium totius belli deferunt;
Vitellotio eius fratri praefecturam equitum tradunt. Ii cum equitibus trecentis in eorum castra percelериter veniunt. Caterina, Forum Livii et Forum Cornelii obtinens, Ludovici fratris filia notha,
mulier vidua, milites quater mille suis in oppidis atque finibus imperat, magna celeritate adhibita. Eos, quod nulla suberat causa cur
imperarentur, Ludovici iussu cogi omnes homines existimaverunt,
ut illos auxilio Florentinis mitteret. Ludovicus ipse Franciscum
Mantuanorum principem, quem respublica missum fecerat, imperatorem suis copiis deligit sub Maximiliani copiarum nomine.

20   Iis intellectis rebus senatus consultum fit: ut equitum praefecti
aliquot Ravennam mittantur; ut Vincentius Naldius Faventinus,
magna in oppidi finibus auctoritate, homines montanos cogat reipublicae pecunia, numero ad mille; ut Antonius Ordelafius Foroli-
viensis, cuius pater eius oppidi regnum obtinuerat, quemque ipsum respublica complures in urbe annos enutrierat, Ravennam
proficiscatur, bellum Caterinae, ni quiescat, suorum factione
reique publicae opibus illaturus; ut Ferdinandus Herculis filius,

them were slain. Of the officers, the brother of Ranuccio da Marsciano was taken captive, and the Frenchman who was called the "Great Warrior" on account of his courage, and many others. Of the cavalry 170 were taken, of the infantry 500, and five battle standards were won from them. Ranuccio himself, the captain of the whole army, took to flight when he lost his horse, and with great difficulty just made it to the nearest town.[9] The rest of them fled and went into hiding, either in the same town or in the mountains and forests.

Following this defeat, the Florentines gave the direction of the entire war to Paolo Vitelli, who on completing his earlier *condotta* had made his way to his people in the country around Rome, with whom Pope Alexander was at war. His brother Vitellozzo was given a cavalry command. The pair of them, with 300 horse, reached the Florentine camp very quickly. Caterina Sforza, the widowed ruler of Forlì and Imola and the illegitimate daughter of Ludovico's brother, very speedily raised 4,000 foot soldiers in her towns and territory. Since there was no reason for the levy, everyone supposed that the troops were being collected at Ludovico's behest, so that he could send them to help the Florentines. Ludovico himself chose as captain-general of his forces Francesco Gonzaga, the Marquis of Mantua, who had been discharged by Venice, though he was nominally elected the commander of Maximilian's forces. 19

On learning of this, the Senate passed a decree that a number of cavalry captains should be sent to Ravenna; that Vincenzo Naldi of Faenza, a person of great weight in the territory of that town, should raise about 1,000 men from the mountains at the Republic's expense; that Antonio Ordelaffi of Forlì, whose father had ruled the town and whom the Republic had for many years raised in Venice, should proceed to Ravenna, and if Caterina made any trouble, make war on her with the aid of his supporters and Venetian backing; that Ferrante, the son of Ercole d'Este, whom 20

quem senatus in suam militiam adlegerat, et Ioannes Ripa, equitum praefectus, iter Pisas e vestigio suscipiant; ut Nicolaus Ursinus Bernardinusque Montonius ad Ollii fluminis ripas sese confe-
rant.

21   Post haec, propterea quod Ludovici legatus, eo senatus consulto
intellecto, inter patres dixerat res quas vellent alias cogitarent,
unum modo, Pisas se tueri posse, ne cogitarent neve in animum
induceret, adhibitis foederatorum legatis, Barbadicus princeps eis
ostendit, quod bellum respublica in Florentinos Pisis tuendis sus-
cepisset, factum sociis quidem omnibus consentientibus, Ludovico
autem magnopere hortante ac belli aequam partem in sese reci-
piente. Quantas eo bello impensas senatus fecerit, quantos exercitus eo miserit, aluerit, quot triremes naves, ignorare prorsus neminem. Maximilianum in Italiam adduxisse quidem et reliquos, sed
unius Ludovici causa, ut esset qui illum ab Carolo, bellum ei primum omnium parante, pari auctoritate tueretur. Eos tamen sumptus omnes unum prope senatum sustinuisse largiterque Maximiliano suppeditavisse. Annos esse elapsos duos, ex quo bellum
initium habuerit. Nunc autem, cum eo res perducta sit, ut, si
quam Pisarum civitati fidem Ludovicus dedit etiam praestet, illa
suam libertatem facile retineat, eum non modo suas domum copias reduxisse, sed hostes etiam Pisanorum fovere milite, pecunia,
consilio, rebus omnibus; ut, qua ipse perfidia volens libensque in
Pisanos utitur, velit alios cogere ut eandem perfidiam vel inviti
exerceant. Is quoniam senatui animus non est, scire eum cupere
quid sibi his rebus Ludovicus postulet. Nam si pacem agere desti-
nat, pacis ei senatum auctorem fore, dum in fide quam Pisanis

the Senate had taken into its service, and the cavalry captain Giovanni dalla Ripa should at once leave for Pisa; and that Niccolò Orsini and Bernardino da Montone should proceed to the banks of the Oglio.

When Ludovico's ambassador learned of this decree of the Sen- 21 ate, he said before the senators that they might think whatever they liked on other matters, but on this one thing they should not suppose—or even entertain the possibility—that they would be able to defend Pisa. At that, Doge Barbarigo summoned the ambassadors of the League and pointed out to them that the war waged by the Republic against Florence for the protection of Pisa had been made with the consent of all the allies, and indeed with much encouragement from Ludovico, who had undertaken to do his fair share in the war. There was absolutely no one who was unaware how great the expenses were that the Senate had incurred in the war, or the size of the armies or the numbers of galleys it had despatched and maintained there. It was true that Maximilian had been brought into Italy by the others as well, but only for Ludovico's sake: it was so that there would be someone of equal standing to defend him from Charles, who was preparing to make war on Ludovico before anything else. Those expenses, however, had been borne by the Senate almost alone, and Maximilian had in large measure been supported by them. Two years had gone by since the start of the war. Now, when the situation had reached a point where Pisa could hold on to her liberty without difficulty if Ludovico would only stand by the assurances he had made to the city, he had not only marched his troops home, but was even sending her enemies help in the form of soldiers, money, advice, and everything else, so that he meant to force others against their wishes to practice the same treachery as he was using against the Pisans of his own free will. Since the Senate was not minded to do so, they wanted to know what Ludovico was looking to get out of such behavior. If it was peace he wanted, the Senate would bring

dedit maneat. Sin bellum gerere mavult, bellum ei per senatum non defuturum. Earum duarum rerum, pacis bellique, utra ei magis cordi est, eius eligendae sese potestatem illi facere. Ipsos autem legatos non tam suae orationis testes habuisse, quam ut, si quid durius Ludovico acciderit, sciant memoriaque teneant iure id meritoque accidisse.

22 Ea oratione habita, legatus Ludovici tempus se dixit sumere, dum quid ad illa responderi Ludovicus velit scire possit; neque tamen dubitare se iam nunc quin auri libras quindecies milies Ludovicus habeat, quibus Florentini tamquam suis eo bello uti possint. Paucisque post diebus litterae sunt ab Ludovico ad patres datae: mirari sese quam ob causam ea senatus mandata nuntiari sibi iussisset, qui quidem non socius modo atque amicus, sed plane filius reipublicae semper fuerit. Aequissimum sibi videri, quam pecuniam Pisis tuendis civitas erogarit, eam pecuniam senatui restitui. Itaque si velint, cum reliquis foederatis rationem patres ineant, quonam id quidem modo agi commode conficique possit; se nihil eius impediturum.

23 Iisdem diebus decemviri Petro et Hieronymo et Aloisio Bragadenis, Andreae filiis, propterea quod ii Nicolaum Georgium, rationibus publicis praefectum, in eius aedibus dum alloquerentur, verbis arrogantioribus interiectis minis fuerant usi, ius comitiorum et magistratuum adipiscendorum facultatem annos decem interdixerunt; qui quidem ante id tempus nequeant restitui, nisi omnibus collegii sententiis ea lege absolvantur. Idem postea in Vincentio Barbaro servatum, quod is Dominico Lamberto magistratus pacis scribae maledixerit.

24 Florentini aestate ineunte, per Caterinam perque Ludovicum, qui eis pecuniam mutuo dederat, confirmati novisque aucti copiis,

him peace, as long as he stood by the undertakings he had given to Pisa. If he preferred to make war, the Senate would see to it that he would have war. The Senate gave him the opportunity of choosing which of the two, peace or war, was more to his taste. They had had the ambassadors there, not so much to bear witness to the doge's speech, as to have them realize and bear in mind that if anything untoward happened to Ludovico, it would be no more than his just deserts.

After this speech had been delivered, Ludovico's ambassador 22 said that he needed time to find out what Ludovico might wish to say in reply. But he could assure them there and then that Ludovico had 15,000 gold pounds which the Florentines could use as their own in the war. A few days later, the senators received a letter from Ludovico. He wondered what had caused the Senate to have those instructions sent him when he had always been not only an ally and friend but a veritable son of the Republic. It seemed to him the fairest course that the money that Venice had paid out on the defense of Pisa should be returned to the Senate. If they wished, then, the senators could come to an arrangement with the rest of the League as to the most convenient method of bringing this about. He would not stand in their way.

In the same period, Pietro, Girolamo, and Alvise Bragadin, the 23 sons of Andrea, were barred by the Ten from sitting on the Great Council and holding office for ten years, because they had used insulting language mingled with threats in talking to Niccolò Zorzi, the commissioner of public accounts, at his home. They could not be reinstated before that time unless absolved from the decree by the votes of the entire Council of Ten. The same punishment was later meted out to Vincenzo Barbaro for abuse of Domenico Lamberti, secretary for the Magistracy of the Peace.[10]

The Florentines were reinforced and strengthened by new 24 troops obtained from Caterina Sforza, and from Ludovico, who had lent them the money. With the coming of spring, they killed

militum reipublicae non magnum numerum, qui Lunam, ut eorum locorum dominis praesidio essent, ab legato missi fuerant,
caede facta in fugam verterunt. Deinde, tametsi senatus cum Petro
Duodo, altero legato Pisas profecto, equitatum qui sagittis utebatur eodem misisset, tamen apud Cassinam, magna caligine oborta
ita ut conspici non possent, maximam copiarum omnium partem
fuderunt, Ioanne Gradonico, qui eis praeerat, interfecto, captis
compluribus. Reliqui Savornianus Tarsiasque, qui erant Cassinae,
veriti ne interciperentur, tormentis abductis sese Pisas contulerunt, atque ad muros castris positis constiterunt.

25   Iis intellectis rebus, senatus exercitu restaurando Guidum
Ubaldum Metaurensium ducem suam in militiam adscivit; cui sti-
pendium esset in equites cataphractos ducentos, levis armaturae
centum, auri librae annuae centum septuaginta. Petrum autem
Marcellum legatum declaravit, qui Urbinum accurreret, ut Guido
Ubaldo praesto esset, militesque mille in eius finibus conscriberet.
Tum, quod Petrus Medices patribus significaverat, quoniam
Ursini propinqui sui pacem cum Alexandro fecissent, si ei pecunia
in stipendium subministretur, illos se omnes quocumque opus esset adducturum, senatus ea de causa Petro Medici pecuniam decrevit, equitesque Graecos, qui aestiva in agro Taurisano habebant
quique tum e Graecia venerant, in Flaminiam mittendos censuit,
ut alio itinere Pisas contenderent. Nam per Ludovici fines unum
modo militem aut omnino nuntium eo patres mittere non poterant, quando is et itinera clauserat et omnes tabellarios excutiebat
atque intercipiebat, ne senatus certior illis de rebus fieret.

26   Itaque nihil iam novi Pisis adferebatur, compluresque dies magna earum rerum ignoratio senatum tenuit. Emanavit tamen hoc:
Florentinos cum Genuensibus Ludovico procurante foedus per-
cussisse; quo ex foedere Genuenses litora Florentinorum ab reipublicae classibus tuta reddere tenerentur. Neque multo post eorum
magistratus Marco Beatiano, quem antea senatus Genuam mis-

and put to flight a small body of Venetian soldiers which had been sent by the proveditor to Luni to defend the local rulers. Despite the fact that the Senate had sent mounted archers to Pisa, with Pietro Duodo as a second proveditor, the Florentines then routed the largest part of the entire army at Cascina, after a great fog had arisen that rendered them invisible, killing the commander Giovanni Gradenigo and taking many prisoners. The others who were at Cascina, Savorgnan and Giacomo da Tarsia, grew afraid that they might be cut off and withdrew their artillery and went to Pisa, where they pitched camp and took up position in front of the walls.

When they heard the news, the Senate took into service 25 Guidobaldo, Duke of Urbino, to rebuild the army. His pay was to be 170 gold pounds a year for 200 heavy cavalry and 100 light. Pietro Marcello was appointed proveditor to go at once to Urbino to assist Guidobaldo, and to raise 1,000 infantry in his territory. Since his Orsini relatives had made peace with Alexander, Piero de' Medici then intimated to the Senate that he would lead them all wherever they were needed, if he was paid for it. The Senate accordingly allotted Piero funds for this purpose, and decided that the stradiots in summer quarters in the countryside of Treviso and those who had just come from Greece should be sent to Romagna, so that they could make haste to Pisa by a different route — the senators were not able to send so much as a single soldier or even a messenger through Ludovico's territory, since he had blocked the routes and was searching and intercepting all couriers, so as to keep the Senate in the dark about what was happening.

There was therefore no news now coming out of Pisa, and for 26 many days the Senate was in complete ignorance of events there. It did however emerge that at Ludovico's instance the Florentines had struck a treaty with the Genoese, by which the Genoese were to protect the Florentine coast from the Venetian fleets. Not long afterwards, the Genoese authorities gave notice in harsh terms to

erat, asperioribus verbis denuntiavit se numquam passuros ut in
reipublicae imperium Pisae redigantur. Cui Beatianus respondit:
minus iniuste eos et Ludovicum facturos, si semel iniurii in rempublicam fierent, foederum et societatis quam diis hominibusque
testibus sanxissent laesae atque violatae nomine; nunc illos dupli-
citer peccare atque delinquere, semel in eo quod infidelitate se pol-
luunt, iterum autem propterea, quia rempublicam ambitionis insi-
mulant; quae profecto numquam Pisas sui iuris facere concupivit,
sed tantum libertati restituere, quemadmodum se facturam una
cum ipsis initio spopondisset.

27   His igitur atque aliis unius Ludovici artibus (numquam enim
quiescebat) cum suum magnopere Florentini exercitum autumni
mensibus amplificavissent, reipublicae autem copiae multis essent
partibus attenuatae, Paulo imperatore Butrium aggressi, per deditionem oppidum capiunt. Eo tamen ita capto, omnibus tormentorum magistris, ne amplius exercere artem possent, manus dexteras
praeciderunt suaque cuiusque collo appensa eos dimiserunt. Quorum pars ad urbem veniens sese patribus commendavit. Patres,
quoad viverent, stipendium singulis cum vacatione omnium munerum tribuerunt. Illi, manibus ferreis fabrefactis, se ad artem redi-
turos et reipublicae usui futuros suasque iniurias, si Pisas remit-
tantur, vindicaturos, fidem senatui fecerunt.

28   Auxit patrum curam exercitus instaurandi Butrium captum.
Itaque Baliones, familiam Perusinam magnopere militarem, antiqua necessitudine cum Ursina Romanorum gente consociatam
atque coniunctam, equites cataphractos centum quinquaginta pol-
licentem, senatus conduxit, qui per suos fines et Senarum agrum
Pisas proficiscerentur. Eo tempore Petrus Medices cum se viae

Marco Beazzano, whom the Senate had previously sent there, that they would never allow Pisa to be brought under the dominion of the Republic. To whom Beazzano replied that they and Ludovico would behave with less injustice if they were doing the Republic but a single injury, in violating and dishonoring the treaties and alliances that they had ratified before God and men. But now they were committing a double offence and were doubly at fault, once in degrading themselves by their perfidy, and a second time in accusing the Republic of self-interest. Venice had never desired to make Pisa her subject but merely to restore her to liberty, just as she had promised to do in concert with them at the outset.

All these schemes, and others too, derived from Ludovico 27 alone, for he was never at rest, and it was thanks to them that the Florentines considerably increased their army in the autumn, while the Republic's forces were attenuated on many fronts. The Florentines under Paolo Vitelli attacked Buti and took the town's surrender. Though it was taken in this way, all the gunners had their right hands cut off so that they would no longer be able to practice their profession, and with each man's hand hung from his neck they were sent away. Some of them came to Venice and implored the Senate's protection. The senators allotted all of them a pension for as long as they lived, with exemption from all taxes. They gave their word to the Senate that once they had artificial iron hands, they would return to their trade and make themselves useful to the Republic and, if sent back to Pisa, would avenge their injuries.

The capture of Buti increased the senators' concern for rebuild- 28 ing the army. The Senate therefore hired the Baglioni, a notable military family of Perugia, associated and allied with the Orsini clan of Rome by ancient ties of friendship, who promised to contribute 150 heavy cavalry. They were to proceed to Pisa through their own territory and the lands of Siena. At that point Piero de' Medici was ready to take to the road and make a speedy incursion

dare vellet, ut in fines Florentinorum contenderet, in febrim incidens substitit. Interim Paulus omni cum exercitu ad Pisanum Vicum castra posuit oppugnandi oppidi causa. Quod cum plures dies tormentis percussisset atque ad muros milites adduxissset, saepe cum clade repulsus, oppidanis acerrime propugnantibus, tandem oppidum per deditionem capit.

29   Eius oppugnationis tempore accidit ut Veneti quoque castellum Pisanorum, in hostium potestatem redactum, in quo erant milites ducenti quinquaginta, noctu aggressi uno impetu expugnaverint. Quo successu incitati paulo post ad castellum Pisano Vico proximum item noctu cum accessissent, re per exploratores significata repulsi a propugnatoribus, tum in reditu ab hostibus intercepti magnam cladem acceperunt. Vico capto et clade accepta, senatus censuit uti Perusiae milites conscriberentur, numero ad duo milia; et quod Senarum civitas per suos fines iter reipublicae copiis non dabat, Petrum Medicem Guidumque Ubaldum in Flaminiam vocavit, ut per Faventinorum fines in hostium agrum irrumperent. Ea enim de causa cum ad eos Iacobum Venerium legatum misisset, civitas concilio convocato reipublicae copias sententiis prope omnibus recipiendas censuerat. Itaque etiam Hestori puero paenitentia ducto, quod se per suos malis artibus a republica distrahi permisisset, pristinum senatus locum gratiae restituit, cum reliquis stipendii veteris novo stipendio tradito.

30   Hostes interea Pisanum Vicum, quem quidem murorum parte magna tormentis nudaverant, restituunt. Veneti se in Pisarum suburbiis vallo cinxerunt. Librafactae autem in colle, qui e regione oppidi est, castello excitato classiariisque septuaginta cum tormentis introductis, munierunt. Quae tamen eis cura studiumque haud

into Florentine territory, but he came down with a fever and called a halt. Meanwhile Paolo Vitelli and his entire army pitched camp at Vicopisano with a view to attacking the town. Though he pounded it with artillery for several days and led his infantry up to the walls, he was repeatedly repelled and took casualties as the inhabitants defended themselves with great ferocity, but in the end he took the town by surrender.

During the course of this attack it happened that the Venetians 29 also made a night attack on a Pisan fortress that had come into enemy hands, where there were 250 soldiers, and they took it in a single assault. Inspired by this success, a little later they turned to a castle close to Vicopisano, again at night, but were found out by scouts and driven back by the defenders. On their return they were caught by the enemy and suffered a great defeat. With the loss of Vicopisano and the infliction of this defeat, the Senate decided to recruit 2,000 or so soldiers at Perugia. Since the city of Siena would not allow Venetian forces passage through their lands, they summoned Piero de' Medici and Guidobaldo to Romagna so that they could invade enemy territory through that of Faenza (when they had sent Giacomo Venier as envoy to Faenza on the matter, the city had convened its council and decided almost unanimously to accept the Republic's troops). On that account the Senate even restored the boy Astorre Manfredi to his former favored status, since he had repented of having permitted his people to alienate him from the Republic by their wicked plots. He was given a new stipend, added to what remained of the old.

Meanwhile the enemy rebuilt Vicopisano, whose walls had been 30 largely destroyed by their artillery. The Venetians erected a palisade around themselves in the outskirts of Pisa, and constructed defenses on a hill opposite the town of Librafatta by building a fort and equipping it with 70 marines and artillery — not that their painstaking efforts did them much good against the stratagems of

multum contra Pauli artes profuit. Nam cum illi, Librafacta[4] copiis omnibus profecto diesque complures castellum oppugnanti, parum usui cetera fuissent, cuniculis partem muri sustulit, submissisque per ruinas militibus, non tamen sine caede, castello est potitus. Eo capto, Librafacta,[5] iam et ipsum tormentis murorum parte nudatum, tridui spatio ad deliberationem sumpto se dedidit.

31   Rebus apud Pisas in adversum reipublicae labentibus, et Paulo nihil eorum quae ex usu esse possent praetermittente, senatus decrevit ut Guidus Ubaldus, Petrus Medices per Faventinorum fines Maratam Crispinumque, municipia natura magis quam artificio communita, quae prima eo latere in hostium sunt finibus, aggrederentur, ut illis expugnatis aditus in agrum Florentinorum eis pateret. Itaque tormenta ad muros deiciendos Ravennam patres miserunt, quae eo supportarentur, Ioannemque Paulum Gradonicum et in Ubaldi exercitu quaestorem et Graecis equitibus quos ei praesto esse iusserant praefectum legerunt. Iulianus autem Medices, Petri frater, cum Faventiam prior venisset, Maratam profectus ab oppidanis libentissimis recipitur. Laurentii enim recordatione, magni clarissimique viri eorumque municipio amicissimi, qui civitatis principatum multos annos obtinuerat, permoveri sese dixerunt, ut quam benivolentiam patri, si viveret, se debere sentiebant, filio praestarent. Maratae arx, summo in colle posita, militibus referta sese tenuit.

32   Interim Bartholomaeus Livianus, ex Ursina Romanorum gente, in Medicum partibus, homo paratissimus, Faventiam et ipse cum equitatus parte praemissus, milites centum quinquaginta, quos in Ferrariensium finibus Caterina scripserat atque ad se venire iusserat, in itinere aggressus omnes cepit armisque exuit. Petrus medio

Paolo Vitelli. He went to Librafatta with his entire army and attacked the fort for many days on end, but other measures proving of little use, he made a stretch of the walls collapse by burrowing tunnels underneath. He sent his men in through the ruins, and despite taking some casualties, gained possession of the fort. With the fort taken, and Librafatta itself also now stripped of part of its walls by the Florentine artillery, the town surrendered to him after taking three days to consider the matter.

With matters at Pisa going against the Republic, and Paolo   31
Vitelli letting nothing slip that could be turned to his advantage, the Senate decided that Guidobaldo and Piero de' Medici should attack Marradi and Crespino del Lamone by way of the territory of Faenza. These towns, fortified more by nature than by human handiwork, were the first beyond the border with the enemy, and if they were conquered, the way into the Florentine countryside would be clear. The senators therefore sent siege-artillery to Ravenna for transport there, and they appointed Giampaolo Gradenigo paymaster in Guidobaldo's army as well as captain of the stradiots which they had ordered to support him. But Piero's brother Giuliano de' Medici arrived in Faenza before him and set out for Marradi, where he was made very welcome by the inhabitants. They said they were much moved at the memory of Lorenzo de' Medici, for many years the head of state, and a great and famous man who had looked with favor on their community, so that the goodwill they felt they would owe to his father if he were alive, they offered instead to the son. But the fortress of Marradi on top of the hill was full of Florentine soldiers and held out.

Meanwhile Bartolomeo d'Alviano, a follower of the Orsini of   32
Rome and a Medici supporter, a man of action, had himself gone on ahead to Faenza with part of the cavalry. On the way he attacked 150 infantry that Caterina Sforza had raised in the territory of Ferrara and ordered to come to her, and he captured and disarmed them all. Having left Guidobaldo behind midway between

inter Maratam Faventiamque spatio, ne commeatus intercludi eis posset, Guido Ubaldo relicto, suis cum equitibus militibusque mille iugum quod Maratae arci imminet capit; tormentisque in eo iugo positis, muros deicere aggreditur. Iis, vallo portae diruto, legatus qui in arce erat, sibi veritus ac domum clam recurrens, eius capiendae occasionem hostibus utique dedisset, si eius fuga cognosci potuisset. Ille vero, ad arcem defendendam, quae maximo momento ipsorum rebus esset, civitatem incitans, maioris etiam praesidii celeriter eodem submittendi causam praebuit. Qua re effectum est ut, tametsi in ea oppugnatione complures dies exercitus reipublicae consumpsisset, arx tamen capi non potuerit, quoad Ioanne Francisco Severinate Gaspareque eius fratre cum exercitu ab Ludovico Forum Livii missis, ut una cum Florentinorum coniuncti copiis in Ubaldum impetum facerent, Petrus et Iulianus, oppugnationem relinquere coacti, sese Ubaldo adiunxerunt. Baliones tardius profecti Ravennae constiterunt.

33   Itaque cum in magna consiliorum inopia patres versarentur, Paulo modis omnibus Pisanas res urgente, novo exercitu reipublicae nihil proficiente, Franciscus Mantuanus senatui se obtulit, si ei pristinum locum gratiae restituat, illi praesto celeriter futurum veteremque suam fidem magno cum reipublicae usu tam dubiis temporibus praestaturum. Re a patribus agitata, decemviri, priore iudicio in Franciscum rescisso ac lege missionis antiquata, senatui permiserunt uti de eo, quod sibi e republica videretur esse, id statueret. Eo cognito decemvirum decreto, Franciscus equites levis armaturae septuaginta quos ad Caterinam miserat statim revocavit et Ravennae iussit esse reipublicae obtemperaturos; et Ioannem

Marradi and Faenza so that their lines of supply could not be cut, Piero de' Medici with his own cavalry and 1,000 foot soldiers took the ridge which overlooks the fortress of Marradi, and placing his artillery there, began to knock down the walls. After the defenceworks of the gate had been destroyed, the Florentine commissioner in the fortress began to fear for his own safety and made off home in haste and in secret, something that would certainly have given his enemy an opportunity of taking it if they had been able to find out about it. But he stirred Florence to defend the citadel, which was of the greatest importance for their cause, and induced them to send an even stronger garrison there with all speed. So it came about that, though the Venetian army spent many days on that action, it was impossible to take the fortress before Piero and Giuliano were forced to abandon the attack and join Guidobaldo, since Ludovico had sent Gianfrancesco Sanseverino and his brother Gaspare to Forlì with an army to link up with the Florentine forces and attack the latter. The Baglioni, having set out too late, came to a halt at Ravenna.

The senators were now almost bereft of ideas, with Paolo 33 Vitelli pressing the Pisans hard in all sorts of ways, and the army of the Republic making no headway. At this point Francesco Gonzaga of Mantua offered his services to the Senate, saying that, if he was restored to his former position of favor, he would at once come to their aid and demonstrate his old loyalty, to the Republic's great profit at such a critical time. After discussion of the matter by the senators, the Ten rescinded its earlier judgment on Francesco and revoked his discharge,[11] allowing the Senate to decide in his case whatever they thought was in the best interests of the Republic. When he learned of the decree of the Ten, Francesco immediately recalled the 70 light cavalry that he had sent to Caterina, and ordered them to place themselves at the service of the Republic at Ravenna. He sent his brother Giovanni to

fratrem ad urbem misit actum patribus gratias, tum ut militiae condicionem a senatu acciperet.

34   Senatus Francisco equites cataphractos ducentos quinquaginta, Ioanni centum attribuit; qui si numerus in tempore expleri ab illis non posset, binos equites sagittarios unius cataphracti loco uterque eorum conficeret; statuitque ut ex reliquo equitatu reipublicae tot ad hos cum praefectis adiungerentur, ut essent omnes octingenti quos Franciscus secum adduceret; itemque ut milites ter mille magistratus Taurisani, Vicetini, Veronenses, Brixiani, Bergomates celeriter conscriberent, qui Francisco traderentur, ut Pisas, vel invitis iis per quorum fines iter esset faciendum, pervenire posset; legatumque ei Nicolaum Fuscarenum declaravit. Senatus consulto accepto, Franciscus e vestigio ad urbem venit, principisque pedibus prope advolutus tempus dixit sibi exoptatissimum venisse, ut fidem studiumque in illum suum, atque amorem erga rempublicam quem a puero susceptum constantissime semper coluisset, improborum eorundemque invidorum hominum maledictis offusum et interpellatum senatui probaret. Patres ei libras auri centum in stipendii partem numerari statim iusserunt; quibus decem dono datae adiungerentur.

35   Iis Pisas rebus celeriter perlatis, civitas animos iam prope infractos confirmavit spemque cepit fore ut hostes non diutissimam ex recenti victoria laetitiam essent habituri, seseque ad omnem oppugnationem sustinendam, dum auxilia instituta adducerentur, comparavit. Neque tamen ea porro fama deterreri Ioannes Bentivolus satis potuit, ut per suos vellet fines exercitui reipublicae senatu postulante iter dare, quod diceret sibi apertissime Ludovicum denuntiavisse, si id faceret, exules se Bononiam reducturum atque illum principatu oppidoque eiecturum; tanta tamque atrox in rem-

Venice to offer thanks to the senators, and to receive from the Senate the terms of his military service.

The Senate assigned Francesco 250 heavy cavalry and 100 to 34 Giovanni. If they could not fill the quota in time, each of them could recruit two mounted crossbowmen in place of one heavy-armed cavalryman. It further decided that to these should be added from the rest of the Venetian cavalry as many as would, with their officers, make up a total of 800 horse for Francesco to take with him, and also that the authorities at Treviso, Vicenza, Verona, Brescia, and Bergamo should quickly recruit 3,000 foot soldiers to be given to him, so that he could reach Pisa even against opposition from those whose territory had to be traversed. Niccolò Foscarini was announced as his proveditor. On receipt of the Senate's decree, Francesco went at once to Venice, and virtually falling at the doge's feet, said that this was the moment he had been longing for, when he could demonstrate to the Senate the loyalty and devotion he had for the doge and his love for the Republic, which he had conceived in boyhood and had steadfastly cultivated ever since, though it had been obscured and obstructed by the calumnies of the wicked and envious. The senators ordered that he should be given 100 gold pounds at once as part of his pay, to which they added a present of 10 pounds.

This news soon reached Pisa and revived the city's spirits, by 35 this point almost utterly crushed, and gave them reason to hope that the enemy's recent victory would bring them no lasting pleasure. They set themselves to weather any assault of the enemy until the promised reinforcements arrived. The report of those reinforcements, however, did not concern Giovanni Bentivoglio so much as to make him permit the Venetian army passage through his territory when the Senate requested it: he said that Ludovico had quite openly told him that if he did so, he would restore the exiles to Bologna and expel him from his town and his realm — so bitter and intense was Ludovico's rivalry with the Republic, so

publicam aemulatio, tam aversa a bonis moribus cupiditas eius mentem atque animum occupaverat.

36   Sed fuit ea plaga levior; vel enim vi contendere Ioannes noluisset, vel copiis multo maioribus exercituque firmiore per Faventinos in hostiles iri fines atque irrumpi potuisset. Illa gravis, quod statim Franciscum a suscepti cura muneris novis pollicitationibus Ludovicus avertit. Misso enim ab senatu Mantuam legato, cum ad profectionem suscipiendam admoneretur, quod reliquae copiae iam convenissent, nolle se dixit proficisci, propterea quod ab Ludovico meliores ei condiciones proponerentur; quibus quidem condicionibus se addixisset, quoniam patres quo se nomine appellarent nihildum deliberavissent. Itaque libras auri nonaginta, ex centum quas in urbe acceperat, Nicolao restituit; decem quae essent reliquae se dixit reipublicae militibus adnumeravisse.

37   Condiciones autem erant huiusmodi: Maximilianus bello in Italia gerendo suis illum copiis imperatorem declaraverat, Ludovicus item suis, Florentini praefectum ipsorum loco. Equitatus utriusque muneris magnus ei numerus ab singulis attributus. Itaque nummi etiam eo nomine missi, sed a Ludovico tantum. Maximilianus enim suam modo unius auctoritatem in commune proponebat; pecuniae nihil conferebat. Florentini, propter belli diuturnitatem, quas adferrent non habebant. Additum etiam condicionibus ut, si bellum in reipublicae finibus geratur, quidquid agri, quidquid oppidorum in regum Mantuanorum dicione aliquando fuisset, quod nunc Veneti possideant, id omne Francisco restitueretur. Quibus intellectis rebus, legatus a senatu iussus domum rediit. Neque multo post Ioannes, Francisci frater, se ad

distant from morality the passion that had gripped his heart and mind.

But this was not the heaviest blow, for either Giovanni would 36 not have been prepared to use force, or a much greater number of troops and a stronger army would have been able to pass through the territory of Faenza and invade the enemy's lands that way.[12] The real blow was that Francesco was immediately diverted from attending to the duties he had taken on by fresh promises from Ludovico. The proveditor was sent to Mantua by the Senate, and when he told Francesco to get under way because the rest of the force was already assembled, Francesco said he was unwilling to leave because he had been offered better terms by Ludovico. And he had in fact committed himself to those terms, since the senators had not as yet had any debate as to what title to give him. He therefore returned to Niccolò Foscarini 90 of the 100 gold pounds which he had received in Venice. The remaining 10 he said he had paid out to the troops of the Republic.

Now the terms of his engagement were as follows: Maximilian 37 had declared him captain-general of his forces for wars fought in Italy, Ludovico likewise for his forces, and the Florentines declared him their commander, taking the place of their own commanders. Each of them assigned him a great number of cavalry, both heavy and light. And so he was also sent cash on this account, but only by Ludovico, for Maximilian had lent the common cause only his personal authority, and he contributed no funds. Owing to the length of the war, the Florentines had no money to give. There was an additional clause that if war was waged in the territory of the Republic, any land or towns that had once been subject to the marquises of Mantua but were now Venetian possessions should all be restored to Francesco. On learning this, the proveditor returned home by order of the Senate. Shortly afterwards, Francesco Gonzaga's brother Giovanni went to Venice and

urbem contulit velleque reipublicae stipendium facere patribus confirmavit. Patres eum missum fecerunt.

38   Verum enimvero cum antea de Francisco restituendo patres agerent, senatus decrevit uti is exercitus qui Marata se receperat Antonium Ordelafium in Fori Livii regnum induceret, expulsa Caterina, quae Florentinis auxilia in rempublicam miserat. Id cum propter municipum in feminam impudicam et crudelem odium, tum pro Antonii factione posse ad exitum perduci patres existimaverunt. Sed provisis ad eam oppugnationem iis rebus, quarum rerum exercitus indigeret, nova occasio patribus oblata senatum a sententia removit.

39   Est in Apennino Metaurensium proximum finibus castellum Sollianum; cuius castelli ager ad Florentinorum fines pertingit. Id castellum Rambertus Malatesta obtinebat. Is igitur Rambertus, ad Petrum Medicem veniens, ei ostendit posse Venetos per fines suos in hostium, qui sibi finitimi essent, agrum atque vicos penetrare, nullo prohibente. Facillimum esse docet, propterea quod nemo id cogitet, nemo vereatur, hostes eo ab latere imparatos adoriri magnumque iis terrorem incutere, magnam perniciem inferre, antequam occurri ab eis possit. Cupere sese in reipublicae fidem recipi. Non sine reipublicae usu futurum demonstrat, si recipiatur. Medices, explorato ab eo itinere reliquisque rebus cognitis, ad urbem celeriter venit patribusque rem denuntiat. Patres Rambertum in reipublicae fidem recipiunt, stipe annua quinis auri libris ei constituta.

40   Reverso in castra Medice reliquisque rebus a legato ducibusque constitutis, Livianus, cui quidem et item Carolo Ursino, Virginii filio, senatus praefecturam equitum tradiderat, ad eam rem temp-

confirmed to the Senate that he wished to serve the Republic, but the senators dismissed him.

But at the same time, in earlier discussions of renewing   38
Francesco's hire, the Senate had decided that the army which had retreated from Marradi should install Antonio Ordelaffi as lord of Forlì and drive out Caterina Sforza, who had sent the Florentines reinforcements against the Republic. The senators thought they could bring this about not only because of the citizens' hatred of a shameless and cruel woman, but also in view of the support Ordelaffi had there. But after making all the arrangements needed by the army for the assault, a new opportunity presented itself which caused the Senate to change its mind.

Near the borders of the territory of the Montefeltro in the   39
Apennines, there is a castle called Sogliano, the country around it stretching to the Florentine border. The lord of the castle was Ramberto Malatesta. Ramberto went to Piero de' Medici and showed him how the Venetians could get to the neighboring lands and villages of the enemy through his territory, with no one to stand in their way. He told him that, because no one contemplated it and no one feared it, it would be very easy to take the enemy un- awares from his side, and to strike great terror into them and wreak great destruction upon them, before a counter-attack could be made. He said he wished to be taken under the Republic's pro- tection, and if he were, he showed that it would not be without profit for the Republic. Having learned the route from the man and acquainted himself with the other circumstances, Piero went quickly to Venice and informed the Senate of the matter. The sen- ators took Ramberto under the Republic's protection, awarding him an annual payment of five gold pounds.

After Piero de' Medici returned to his camp and the rest of the   40
arrangements were made by the proveditor and the captains, Bartolomeo d'Alviano, to whom the Senate had entrusted com- mand of the cavalry alongside Carlo di Virginio Orsini, was cho-

tandam deligitur. Is itaque Livianus castris, quae in Foroliviensi erant, magno silentio profectus cum equitibus levis armaturae ducentis quinquaginta, militibus octingentis, per Cesenae agrum et Solliani fines, noctu itinere confecto, ante lucem ad fanum Camaldulense, quod est in valle angusta magnis montibus circumdata, dum sacerdotes nocturnas preces facerent, pervenit, vocatisque qui portas aperirent, esse se reipublicae Florentinae milites qui ad imperatorem mitterentur,[6] patefactis portis, fano capto et, quoniam arcis vicem turri praealta parietibusque solidis praebeat, praesidio in eo collocato ac refectis cibo potuque militibus, Bibienam oppidum eadem usus celeritate contendit; praemissisque paucis equitibus Leonis nomen, antiqua eorum appellatione, conclamantibus (ea est enim significatio Florentinae civitatis, quae voce accipitur et redditur) magistratum itemque arcis praefectum ad speciem imperatoris iussu ad se vocatos retinuit oppidumque cepit; statimque ad Marcellum, qui rem ei nuntiarent atque ut ocissime cum reliquo exercitu subsequi contenderet hortarentur, misit.

41   Legatus Carolum Ursinum et Baliones, qui ad eum aliquando tandem venerant, auxilio ad Livianum iussit praecurrere. Ille interim, aliud ad castellum profectus, eo capto Popium venit, celebre municipium et sibi iam exemplo Bibienensium cavens. Quod quidem ad municipium, insidiis cognitis, Florentini milites ducentos cum legato et stipendio miserant. Sed eos Livianus ex itinere congressus fudit, interfectis captisque compluribus; parumque abfuit quin legatus caperetur stipendiumque interciperetur. Popio deinde per imperatorem Paulum militibus sexcentis intromissis confirmato, Carolus Balionesque adveniunt.

42   Guidus Ubaldus recenso exercitu, in quo erat Hannibal Bentivolus, a senatu in reipublicae militiam separatim antea sublectus,

sen to make the attempt. Taking 250 light cavalry and 800 foot
soldiers, d'Alviano accordingly left his camp in the area of Forlì
with the minimum of noise, and marched by night through the
district of Cesena and the territory of Sogliano. He arrived at the
abbey of Camaldoli, which is in a narrow valley surrounded by
high mountains, while the monks were at matins, and summoning
people to open the gates, he said that they were soldiers of the
Florentine Republic who were being sent to their general. When
the gates were opened, he took the monastery and, since it was as
good as a fortress with its high tower and solid walls, he left a garrison in it. His soldiers refreshed with food and drink, he made
for the town of Bibbiena at the same swift pace. He sent on ahead
a few cavalry shouting the word "Lion,"[13] their ancient call (this
being the Florentine password), and summoning the magistrate
and the officer in charge of the fortress, ostensibly at the command
of the general, he took them prisoner and captured the town.
D'Alviano immediately sent men to inform the proveditor Pietro
Marcello of the event and to urge him to hurry and follow him
with the rest of the army as quickly as possible.

The proveditor ordered Carlo Orsini and the Baglioni, who had   41
at long last finally reached him, to press on ahead to bring assistance to d'Alviano. The latter, meanwhile, left for another fortress,
which he took, and then came to Poppi, a populous town and now
on its guard after the example of Bibbiena. Indeed, once the ruse
became known, the Florentines had sent 200 soldiers to the town
with a commissioner and pay. But d'Alviano met them on the way
and put them to flight, with many killed and captured. He actually came very close to capturing the commissioner and intercepting the payroll. The captain-general Paolo Vitelli next reinforced Poppi by putting in 600 foot soldiers, and then Carlo
Orsini and the Baglioni arrived.

After reviewing his army, which included Annibale Bentivoglio,   42
whom the Senate had previously drafted separately into Venetian

itineri se dedit. Livianus auxilio submisso castella hostium quattuor, quorum in uno erant milites ducenti, Popio circumfusa vi cepit. Venerat autem Popium cum militibus ducentis etiam Populoniam obtinens. Guidus Ubaldus eo in itinere tardior quam cogitaverat fuit, propterea quod milites ad duo milia singillatim fugientes eum reliquerant, Hannibale furtim, ut id facerent, per suos cohortante sub non dati in tempore stipendii querela. Eius enim fugae initium, ab iis qui cum illo venerant factum, legatus postea quaerendo reperit; tum illos ipsos qui aufugerant prope omnes ex Bononiensibus fuisse cognovit. Quin etiam Hannibalis equites clam se cottidie castris atque turmis subtrahebant. Iamque Gaspar Severinas, cum equitibus a Ludovico missus, ad ea loca pervenerat Ranutiusque una cum illo Martianus, cui ut Venetis occurreret Florentini mandaverant. Etiam librae auri centum, Florentiam a Ludovico missae, magno eis usui ad celeritatem, cuius res magnopere indigebat, adhibendam fuerunt. Livianus aliud castellum cepit, vulnere in facie accepto, ac diripuit. Atque illis ipsis diebus (hiems autem iam advenerat) milites ter mille, qui Francisco attribui debuerant, Ravennam sunt ut ad Marcellum contenderent missi.

43   Dum haec sic administrantur, Paulus, ad Pisas castris positis, verberare muros tormentis coepit. Id cum parum propter murorum firmitudinem processisset, crates in latitudinem quoquoversus pedum denum, in altitudinem senum, inter se coniunctas noctu muris admovit; terraque iniecta milites uti murum suffoderent tecti cratibus imperavit. Pisani autem, cum in muro consistendi propter tela multitudinemque hostium potestas esset nulli, fossam intra muros latam atque altam duxerunt castellisque munierunt. Paulus turrim oppidi muro coniunctam deicit. Ea deiecta per rui-

service, Guidobaldo set out on the march. Now reinforced, Bartolomeo d'Alviano took by force of arms four enemy forts around Poppi, in one of which were 200 infantry. The lord of Piombino had arrived at Poppi, also bringing 200 soldiers.[14] The march took Guidobaldo longer than he had anticipated, because some 2,000 soldiers had deserted one by one and abandoned him, with Annibale having his men secretly egg them on under the pretext that their money was not being paid on time. On inquiry, the proveditor later discovered that the desertion started with those who had come with Annibale, and he learned that the men who had fled were almost all from Bologna. Indeed, Annibale's cavalry were quietly abandoning their camp and companies on a daily basis. Gaspare da Sanseverino, sent by Ludovico with cavalry, had already arrived in the area, and with him Ranuccio da Marsciano, whom the Florentines had ordered to engage the Venetians. The 100 gold pounds sent Florence by Ludovico was also a considerable help in their making good speed, as the situation required. D'Alviano took another fortress, receiving a wound to the face, and sacked it. And just at that time, with winter now setting in, 3,000 foot soldiers, whom it had been intended to assign to Francesco Gonzaga, were sent to Ravenna to proceed to Pietro Marcello with all speed.

While all this was going on, Paolo Vitelli pitched camp near 43 Pisa and began to pound the walls with an artillery barrage. Little headway was made owing to the strength of the walls, so he joined together wicker hurdles measuring ten feet square and six feet high, and set them against the walls at night. Earth was piled on top, and then Paolo told his soldiers to undermine the wall under cover of the hurdles. Since no one was able to stay on the wall owing to the missiles and the great numbers of the enemy, the Pisans for their part dug a wide and deep trench inside the walls and strengthened it with guardposts. Paolo brought down a bastion attached to the town walls, and as soon as it fell, ordered the soldiers

nas militibus introire iussis, ubi fossam esse obiectam et Pisanos in aggere circumiectos hostes opperiri, ut in fossa telis atque ignibus eos conficerent, et magnum irrumpentibus instare periculum cognovit, receptui cani iussit. Paucisque post diebus, in hostium captis ab se castellis praesidio relicto, castra movit, ut in Clusentinos saltus contra Medices Livianumque contenderet.

44   Pisanis obsidione liberatis, Graeci equites portis emissi castellum Calcem, deiecto Pauli praesidio expugnatum, diripuerunt. Classis praefectus, qui Pauli obsidionem una cum reliquis sustinuerat, cum classiariis egressus, eosdem Graecos equites secum ducens, castellum ad Pontem Stagni, ei appositum itinere quod Triturrita Pisas ducit magna ipsum opportunitate, tormentis concussum ad deditionem compulit agrumque Pisanum, eo ab latere satis patentem, ad sementes faciendas civitati colonisque restituit. Neque multo post iidem Graeci equites, quod intellexerant in Populoniae fines Clusentinos homines, ut primum exercitus reipublicae ad ea loca venerit, sua quae potuerant armenta compulisse, eo celeriter profecti ingentem inde praedam abduxerunt. Deinde Volaterranum percurrentes agrum, praeda onusti Pisas redierunt.

45   Paucis autem post diebus Tarsias, una cum Valerio quaestore et praefectis militum equitumque Pisis egressus, itinere in fines hostium medio fere inter Pisas Florentiamque spatio ad castellum Montopolim noctu confecto, oppugnare portas coepit. Eae cum ab oppidanis, qui clamoribus interea exciti undique convenerant, portae defenderentur, Tarsias ad aliam castelli partem, quae, quod ab eo latere nihil timebatur, propugnatoribus vacua tum quidem

to enter through the ruins, but he found that the trench had been put in their way and that the Pisans were ranged on the bank awaiting the enemy in order to finish them off in the trench with arrows and firebrands. Recognizing the great danger that threatened the attackers, he ordered the retreat to be sounded. A few days later, leaving garrisons in the enemy fortresses he had taken, he struck camp in order to march into the Casentino valleys against the Medici and Bartolomeo d'Alviano.

Once the Pisans were freed of the siege, the stradiots were let 44 out through the gates, and they captured and sacked the castle of Calci after driving out Paolo's garrison. The captain of the fleet,[15] who had endured Paolo Vitelli's siege along with the rest, came out of the city with his marines, taking the stradiots with him, and after pounding it with his artillery, forced the surrender of the fortress at Ponte dello Stagno, very strategically placed for him on the route that leads from Livorno to Pisa. The Pisan countryside, in those parts very extensive, he gave back to the city and its farmers so that they could sow their seed. Not long afterwards the same stradiots learned that when the Venetian army first came to their district, the men of the Casentino had driven all of their flocks that they could into the territory of Piombino, so they made a quick incursion and came away with a vast amount of plunder. With a speedy passage through the lands of Volterra, they then returned to Pisa loaded with booty.

A few days later Giacomo da Tarsia left Pisa in company with 45 the paymaster Valier and the infantry and cavalry captains. They marched by night into enemy territory to the castle of Montopoli, about half way between Pisa and Florence, and launched an assault on its gates. The townsfolk, roused by the shouting while this was going on, gathered together from all sides and defended the gates. Tarsia now silently and quickly sent infantry to another part of the castle, which was at that point bare of defenders, since they feared no attack on that side. The boldest and lightest of the

erat, milites tacite atque celeriter misit. Horum audacissimi atque levissimi murum per hastas sublevati conscenderunt aliosque ut conscenderent adiuverunt. Intromissi portas aperuerunt. Ita oppidum captum ac direptum est, nuptiarum apparatu, quas erant illo die oppidani celebraturi, praedae militum atque direptui addito.

46   Ubaldus cum ad fanum Camaldulense pervenisset, quod quidem fanum, eiecto Liviani praesidio, eius regionis homines recuperaverant, proelio aggressus portas irrumpere non potuit. Itaque discedens Popiumque versus ducens, Graecos equites ut praecurrerent dimisit. Ii milites hostium centum, qui molas frumentarias Popianorum muris propugnaculisque communitas tormentis circumdispositis custodiebant, aquola traiecta in fugam verterunt; quorum maior pars tum caesa, tum capta, tormentaque incensis aedificiis abducta. Id Populoniam obtinens cum intellexisset, ne intercluderetur Popio relicto discessit. Ubaldus, Bibienam profectus, tormenta quibus Popianorum muros deiceret, a senatu missa, expectare constituerat. Sed ea propter nives, quarum magna vis itinera impeditissima reddiderat, adduci non potuerunt, exceptis levioribus minoribusque aliquot; quae tamen ipsa vix aegreque sunt perducta. Quibuscum nihilo secius Livianus castellum Orniam obsidens, cui castello milites erant ducenti praesidio, brevi spatio cepit. Eo[7] digressus ad castellum Qualianum castra posuit. Oppidani casu Orniensium permoti se celeriter dediderunt. Itaque duobus captis castellis, cum pluviae continentes omnia itinera illuvie foedavissent, Bibienam rediit. Taedet me eius belli leviora consectari. Quis enim legat sine fastidio singula, praesertim si ad rerum exitus, ut plerumque fit, tantummodo properet? Sed mihi facile veniam omnes homines daturos puto, cum scierint illud me

infantry were lifted up on their spears and scaled the wall, and they helped the others to climb up. Those who got inside opened the gates. And so the town was taken and given over to plunder, the paraphernalia of a wedding which the inhabitants had been going to celebrate on that day being added to the soldiers' loot and spoils.

When Guidobaldo arrived at the abbey of Camaldoli, which 46 the people of those parts had recovered after expelling d'Alviano's garrison, he attacked it but was unable to break through the gates. Guidobaldo therefore left and led his troops away towards Poppi, sending his stradiots off to run ahead. They crossed a little stream and put to flight 100 enemy soldiers watching over the mills of the people of Poppi, which were protected by walls and other defenses and had artillery deployed about them. The majority of them were killed or taken prisoner, the buildings were put to the torch and the artillery taken away. When the lord of Piombino heard of it, he abandoned Poppi and went away, for fear that he might be cut off. Guidobaldo, arrived at Bibbiena, decided to wait for the artillery sent by the Senate so he could knock down the walls. But a great snowfall rendered the roads almost impassable and the artillery could not get through, except for a few of the smaller and lighter pieces, and even they were brought in with great difficulty. D'Alviano nevertheless used them to lay siege to the castle of Ornia, which had a garrison of 200 infantry, and he took it in short order. He left Ornia and pitched camp at the castle of Quagliano.[16] The inhabitants, mindful of what had happened to the people of Ornia, quickly surrendered. And so, though constant rain had turned the roads to mud, he returned to Bibbiena with two fortresses taken. It is tiresome for me to go through the minor points of the war. Who can read every last detail without aversion, especially if, as in most cases, the reader is only looking to reach the conclusions as soon as may be? But I think that people will readily forgive me when they realize that my chief aim in

assequi hoc scribendi labore vel cum primis cupere, ne cui videar publice gesta meorum civium, quae nihil habeant dignitatis, silentio dissimulavisse.

47   Hostibus post haec propter Pauli adventum ad sese (iam enim is in Clusentinos fines venerat) magnopere confirmatis, in Veneto exercitu de ducendo bello ducibus diversa sentientibus, senatus anni exitu decrevit uti Ubaldus cum parte copiarum legatoque Bibienae in hibernis se contineret, reliquam Livianus partem ad Averniam hibernorum causa deduceret. Is abest vicus a Bibiena septem milia passuum, monti vastae crepidinis impositus, Francisci in deorum numerum recepti mora atque domicilio celeber. Tum ut militum duo milia in Ubaldi finibus conscriberentur ad eosque mitterentur praesidii hibernorum causa, eodem senatus consulto constitutum. Liviano etiam, propterea quod equites illius octoginta, Orniae praesidio relicti, ab hostibus furtim introductis capti fuerant, pecunia est amissis sarciendis a senatu dono tradita. Ante autem quam haec ita fierent, Ramberti suasu, qui diceret, si sibi exercitus tribuatur, in Vallem Stagni sibi finitimam, quae in Florentinis esset finibus, se irrupturum, qua capta priorem ad exercitum et commeatus supportari et copiae submitti facile possent, Brixia equites cum praefectis septem evocatos, Ioannem Paulum Gradonicum, cum Graecis quibus praeerat equitibus et militum non magno numero Ravenna profectum, senatus eo mittendos censuit. Ii, Ramberto duce usi vallemque ingressi, castellis hostium quattuor captis, aliud castellum, quod erat communitius, tormentis levioribus adorti, Cyriacum praefectum, virum fortem cum militibus sexcentis egressum, proelio commisso in fugam coniecerunt; Turcam centurionem cum plerisque occiderunt castellumque ceperunt. Neque tamen is exercitus propter nives impeditaque itinera ulli praeterea usui reipublicae fuit. Gradonicus

this historical labor is to avoid the appearance of passing over in silence the public deeds of my fellow citizens, as if they had no importance.

The enemy was greatly strengthened after this by the arrival of 47 Paolo Vitelli, who had now come into the Casentino, while the leaders of the Venetian army had differing views about how the war should be conducted. At the end of the year, the Senate decided that Guidobaldo should remain in winter quarters at Bibbiena with part of his forces and the proveditor, and d'Alviano would take the rest to La Verna for the winter. This village is seven miles from Bibbiena, perched on a hill with a massive cliff and famous for the visit and domicile there of St. Francis.[17] The same Senate decree then provided for the recruitment of 2,000 infantry in Guidobaldo's territory, who were to be sent to them as a guard for the winter quarters. D'Alviano had had 80 cavalry left at Ornia as garrison captured when the enemy was secretly let in, and the Senate consequently gave him a sum of money to make good his losses. But before these instructions could be put into effect, Ramberto Malatesta urged the Senate to assign him an army so that he could invade the nearby Valle dello Stagno, which was in Florentine territory. Taking the valley would make it easier to supply provisions and send troops to the existing army. So the Senate agreed to send him cavalry units summoned from Brescia with their seven officers, and Giampaolo Gradenigo, who was to leave Ravenna with the stradiots he commanded and a modest number of foot soldiers. Under Ramberto's guidance these troops entered the valley, took four enemy fortresses and attacked another better fortified one with light artillery. Their brave commander Ciriaco came out of the castle with 600 soldiers and engaged in battle, but he was put to flight, and most of their men, including a Turkish officer, were killed, and the castle taken. This army, however, was of no further use to the Republic on account of the roads

etiam adversa valetudine implicitus Ravennam, deinde ad urbem rediit.

48   Anno autem insequente vix inito, ex Caroli Ursini turma complures, qui nondum in hiberna convenerant, sunt cum castello in quo erant capti. Captus etiam a Gaspare Severinate legati scriba Marcelli, ex Ubaldi finibus cum stipendio et commeatu et militibus quatercentis, Graecis equitibus ducentis Bibienam sese conferens; in quos quidem Severinas difficillimis in iugis de superiore loco impetum fecerat. Pauloque post cum equites circiter quingenti, a Guido Ubaldo in eius fines propter commeatus inopiam missi, per angusta loca iter facerent, ab hostibus intercepti sunt magnumque iis detrimentum est illatum; quorum plerique, fuga capta, itinerum ignoratione in manus hostium, montanorum hominum, pervenerunt.

49   His acceptis incommodis senatus Nicolaum Ursinum, paulo ante ab se stipendio auctum, cum equitibus gravioris leviorisque armaturae octingentis, militibus quot contrahi et conscribi possent, commeatu quem oporteat, Bibienam submittendum Ubaldi auxilio censuit. Eius quoque uxor per sese et milites et commeatus, quod ad virum mitteret, comparavit. Sed is valetudine temptatus ab hostium ducibus cum peteret uti medico ad se venienti iter darent, nihil impetravit. Sibi autem paulo post, morbo ingravescente, domum redire cupienti, uti darent impetravit. Itaque cum paucis suum in regnum discessit.

50   Ad haec intentis patribus cum nuntiis esset crebrioribus allatum, a Turcarum rege classem non spernendam comparari, Andream Zancanium senatus legatum ad illum misit. Causa mittendi fuit quod timebat Baiasetem in rempublicam cum aliis de causis incensum, tum propterea quod Nicolaus Pisaurus classis

being blocked by snow. Gradenigo also suffered a bout of illness, and he returned to Ravenna, and then to Venice.

With the following year scarcely begun, a good many men of 48
Carlo Orsini's company, who had not yet gone into winter quar- 1499
ters, were captured along with the castle where they were. Also
captured, by Gaspare da Sanseverino, was the secretary of the
proveditor Marcello as he made his way from Guidobaldo's territory to Bibbiena with the payroll, provisions, and 400 infantry
and 200 stradiots. Sanseverino had attacked them from higher
ground as they traveled through an extremely difficult pass. A little later, about 500 cavalry had been despatched by Guidobaldo to
his own territory because provisions for them were lacking. They
were making their way through a narrow defile when they were
caught by the enemy and suffered terrible losses. Most of them
took to flight and owing to their unfamiliarity with the roads fell
into the hands of the enemy, who were men of the mountains.

On hearing of these setbacks, the Senate decided that Niccolò 49
Orsini, whose pay they had recently increased, should be sent to
Bibbiena to assist Guidobaldo with 800 cavalry, heavy and light, as
many foot soldiers as they could find and recruit, and all necessary
provisions. Guidobaldo's wife also procured infantry and provisions to send to her husband on her own account.[18] But when
Guidobaldo suffered a bout of ill health and asked the enemy
commanders to allow a doctor to come to him, his request was
turned down. A little later, however, as the illness got worse and
he wanted to return home, they did grant him passage. And so he
departed into his own lands with a few of his men.

The Senate was preoccupied with these matters when it was re- 50
ported to them by increasing numbers of messengers that a considerable fleet was being got ready by the Turkish sultan. The Senate sent Andrea Zancani as ambassador to the sultan, the reason
for sending him being that they feared that Bayazid had decided to
make war on Venice: he was incensed at the Republic for a num-

legatus navem onerariam unius ex regis ducibus, quos illi Bassas
appellant, aestatis exitu in Aegaeo depresserat, bellum facere Venetis instituisse.

51   Ea res autem sic acciderat. Dum Nicolaus apud Mitylenem
cum triremibus quattuor iter faceret et navi onerariae bellicae militibus, tormentis, reliquisque rebus omnibus ad pugnandum idoneis instructissimae, amphorarum plus trecentarum, quam vento
ferri viderat, appropinquavisset, vela uti demitterent vectores admonuit. Illi autem non vela modo non demiserunt sed, pilis ferreis
tormentis emissis, Nicolae praefectum interfecerunt, ac nonnullos
ex remigibus, sagittis celeriter coniectis, vulneraverunt. Quod ubi
fieri Nicolaus vidit, arma suis uti caperent imperavit atque, in navem Thraciam impetu facto, eam expugnavit cumque omnibus qui
pugnae superfuerant depressit. Erant ea in navi homines circiter
ducenti quinquaginta.

52   Zancanius Byzantium profectus magnum quidem classis apparatum institutum cognovit; a rege tamen, nullo ostenso in rempublicam offensi animi indicio, liberaliter est acceptus. Qui cum reipublicae bellum facere decrevisset, existimans, propterea quod ei
Ludovicus receperat eodem se tempore bellum in Gallia reipublicae illaturum, hostibus eo ab latere occupatis omnia sibi prospere atque feliciter cessura, ut magis Venetos eluderet, foedus quidem cum Zancanio renovavit; sed foederis capita Latinis scripta
litteris ei dedit. Est autem in eorum legibus ut, quae suae linguae
verbis scripta non sunt, ea praestari non sit necesse. Erat tum Byzantii civis Venetus, Andreas Grittus, qui mercaturam ea in urbe
annos complures exercuerat, vir faciei elegantia corporisque pul-
chritudine, qua inter Venetos suae tempestatis omnes facile prae-
stitit, et morum gravitate ac liberalitate insignis eique nationi apprime atque magnopere carus. Is, quod omnia Turcarum instituta
callebat, ea de re Zancanium admonuit atque, uti foedus verbis

ber of reasons, but chiefly because Niccolò Pesaro, the proveditor of the fleet, had at the end of the previous summer [1498] sunk in the Aegean a merchant ship of one of the sultan's commanders (known to them as "pashas").

Things had fallen out in this fashion. Niccolò was sailing near 51 Mytilene with four galleys when he approached a military cargo ship which he had seen sailing by. It was amply equipped with soldiers, artillery, and other fighting gear, with a capacity of more than 300 barrels. He signalled those on board to lower their sails, but not only did they fail to do so, they started firing their cannon, killing Niccolò's captain and wounding some of the rowers too with a thick hail of arrows. When Niccolò saw what was happening, he ordered his men to take up their arms. Turning on the Turkish vessel, he destroyed it and sank it with all the survivors of the fight aboard. There were about 250 men on that ship.

When Zancani arrived in Constantinople, he learned that great 52 preparations were indeed being laid for a fleet. He was hospitably received by the sultan, however, with no obvious indication that he was angry with the Republic. The sultan had in fact decided to make war on the Republic, and judged that as Ludovico had promised him he would wage war on Venice in Lombardy at the same time, everything would turn out well for him, with the enemy occupied on that front. In order to carry the deception of the Venetians further, he renewed the treaty of alliance with Zancani, but the clauses of the treaty he gave him were written in Latin. Now there is a provision in their law that what is not written in their own language need not be fulfilled. There was a Venetian citizen in Constantinople at the time, Andrea Gritti, who had been engaged in commerce in the city for many years. He was a man of elegant appearance and handsome physique, more so than any other Venetian of his day, notable for his dignified and generous character, and extremely well liked by the Turks. Since he knew all about their customs, he warned Zancani about this circumstance,

Thraciis conscriptum haberet, pro sua in patriam caritate illum est
hortatus. Zancanius re temptata cum nihil efficere potuisset, cum
foedere Latinis scripto litteris ad urbem rediit; neve nihil videretur
attulisse, id quod ab Gritto ea de re Byzantii accepisset senatui re-
ticuit.

53   Ea foederis tam propensa renovatio magis etiam suspensos patres fecerat, existimantes ea de causa regem sua consilia suppres-
sisse, ut eos imparatos atque inermes adoriretur; praesertim quod
missae ad illum a Ludovico atque a Florentinis communi consensu
paulo ante legationes, multa de senatu questae, nihil eorum quae
regis animum in rempublicam inflammare possent praetermise-
runt. Quamobrem ut muniti ad omnes casus essent, senatus decrevit uti naves onerariae bellicae tres confestim ornarentur eisque
praefectus legeretur; lectusque est Aloisius Marcellus, uti navis
item oneraria magna, quam Sebastianus Marcellus aedificari sibi
curaverat quaeque Naupliae tunc erat, armaretur classique adiun-
geretur; litteraeque ad illum publice datae, ut Corcyram navem adduceret; uti naves triremes triginta deducerentur; quarum navium
decem ipsa in urbe, totidem Cretae, sex in Apulia, quattuor in Illyrico magistratus Veneti remigibus atque militibus instruerent.
Pauloque post decem aliae triginta prioribus sunt additae.

54   At Aloisio rege Galliae salutato, uti supra dictum est, legati
sunt ad eum ire iussi tres gratulatum reipublicae nomine: Antonius Lauredanus, Nicolaus Michaeles, Hieronymus Georgius.
Missae deinde ab senatu regi dono aquilae in Creta insula captae
sexaginta, ex earum genere quibus in aucupio reges uti consueve-
runt, pellesque pretiosiores canis ab summo inter nigrum colorem
conspersae ducentae. Quae ille munera vultu laetissimo accepit
egitque de iis senatui gratias apud legatos, cum iam ii ad illum pervenissent. Sed ea dum ad regem legatio proficiscitur, Triultius, qui

and out of patriotic feeling, urged him to have the treaty written in Turkish. Zancani tried to have this done, but his efforts met with no success, and he returned to Venice with the treaty written in Latin. So that he should not appear to have come back empty-handed, he kept from the Senate what Gritti had told him at Constantinople.[19]

The readiness with which the treaty had been renewed made 53 the senators even more suspicious. They reckoned that the sultan had concealed his plans only so he could attack them unarmed and unawares, especially since Ludovico and the Florentines had recently sent him embassies with a common aim. They had made many complaints about the Senate to him, overlooking nothing that could inflame the sultan's mind against the Republic. To strengthen their position against all eventualities, they accordingly decided to have three military merchantmen fitted out at once, and a proveditor set over them. Luigi Marcello was chosen, so that the large cargo-vessel then at Nauplia, which Sebastiano Marcello had had built for himself, could also be armed and join the fleet. An official letter was sent to him to have him bring the ship to Corfu, and to assemble 30 galleys, of which the Venetian authorities would fit out with oarsmen and soldiers 10 in Venice itself, 10 in Crete, 6 in Apulia, and 4 in Dalmatia. A little later 10 others were added to the original 30.

After Louis was acclaimed king of France, as mentioned 54 above,[20] three ambassadors were ordered to go and congratulate him on behalf of the Republic, Antonio Loredan, Niccolò Michiel, and Girolamo Zorzi. The Senate then sent the king a gift of 60 eagles caught on Crete, the sort used by kings for hunting,[21] and 200 precious furs, their black surface spotted with white.[22] He received these gifts very gladly and offered the Senate his thanks for them before the ambassadors, who had now arrived. But while the embassy was on its way to the king, Giangiacomo Trivulzio (who had remained at Asti with his cavalry) took the

se Astae cum equitatu continuerat, Bretolam oppidum, quod quidem illis in finibus fratres duo in Ludovici fidem recepti obtinebant, capit. Ludovicus per legatum ea de re certiores patres facit
eorumque consilium exquirit. Patres molesta sibi esse quae intellexissent legato responderunt; belli enim initium sese factum vi-
dere; ita se tamen Ludovici prudentia confidere, ut omnibus illum
incommodis remedia celeriter adhibiturum esse non dubitent;
praesertim cum is tantum auri possideat, quantum paulo ante ipsemet eius legatus exploratum sibi esse palam dixerit.

55   Legatis in Galliam profectis rex proposuit constitutum sibi esse
Mediolani regnum, quod sibi hereditatis iure deberetur, ab Ludovico armis repetere; cupere se rempublicam eius belli sociam habere. Illi se ad senatum ea de re litteras daturos dixerunt eique
quod senatus iussisset renuntiaturos. Illis autem in litteris legati
adscripserunt nihil praetermittere Ludovicum per amicos regios
orando, pollicendo, ut se in regis amicitiam insinuet. Patres, re
complures dies agitata, tametsi viderent periculosum esse maximum amplissimumque regem sibi finitimum in Italiam adducere,
tamen, propterea quod existimabant neminem eo in regno perni-
ciosiorem civitati esse posse quam is erat quem permultos annos
habuissent, verebanturque, si regis amicitiam repudiarent, ne se is
cum Ludovico in reipublicae fraudem coniungeret, quam certe societatem Ludovicus nullis non condicionibus esset accepturus, ut
bellum ab se averteret, ei rei animum adhibuerunt. Accedebat ad
superiores causas etiam haec, quod nonnihil recentes ac perpetuae
in rempublicam Ludovici contumeliae, oblata prope a diis immortalibus facultate, civium animos ad vindictam expetendam incita-
bant. Nonnullos etiam augendi fines imperii cupiditas, iusto prae-

town of Brettola,[23] a possession of two local brothers who were subjects of Ludovico. Ludovico informed the senators about this through an ambassador and asked for their counsel. The senators replied to the ambassador that they were troubled by what they had learned, for they saw that war had begun. But they had complete confidence in Ludovico's good sense and did not doubt that he would soon find solutions to all his difficulties, especially since he had such quantities of gold as his ambassador had openly told them he was sure he had.

When the ambassadors arrived in France, the king mentioned 55 that he had decided to take back the duchy of Milan from Ludovico by force of arms, since he owned it by right of inheritance, and he wanted to have the Republic as his ally in the war. They said that they would send a letter on the matter to the Senate and report back to him what the Senate's instructions were. But in the letter the ambassadors added that Ludovico was letting slip no opportunity of insinuating himself into the king's friendship with appeals and promises put to him by the king's friends. The senators discussed the affair for many days and although they saw the danger in having such a great and powerful king come to Italy as their neighbor, they nevertheless thought they could have no one in the duchy who would be more harmful to Venice than the man they had actually had for many years. They were afraid, too, that if they spurned the king's friendship, he would ally himself with Ludovico to the Republic's peril, an alliance that Ludovico would surely accept under any conditions to divert the war away from himself. Such were the considerations they mulled over. Added to all of which was the fact that Ludovico's recent and continued affronts to the Republic were stirring the hearts of the citizens to seek revenge, for which this seemed a heaven-sent opportunity. Some were also inflamed with a desire to extend the boundaries of empire, especially with just title and just cause, tak-

sertim nomine iustisque de causis, incendebat, ut sunt plerumque
homines natura proclinati ad ea propaganda quae possident.

56   Itaque litteras ad legatos dant: regi respondeant se cum eo
consensuros bellumque una suscepturos atque gesturos; modo is
ipsorum dicionem tutam ab se atque tectam velit esse. Ab legatis
quaerenti regi quanam id ratione vellent fieri, quodve saeptum suis
finibus aut propugnaculum exposcerent, responderunt, si Cremo-
nam oppidum reipublicae concesserit, cum eo agro finibusque omnibus qui citra flumen Abduam sint, tutos se fore existimaturos.
Tum rex concessurum quidem se reipublicae eam quam peterent
ex Ludovici regno partem recepit, quam quidem sciret esse totius
regni optimam atque opulentissimam, Lecco tantummodo excepto, de quo nulli cedere statuerat (id est municipium in laeva
Abduae e lacu Lario exeuntis ripa); petere autem et ipsum pro iis
rebus ab republica equites in id bellum septies mille, milites sex
mille, auri libras mille; ea sibi datum iri si polliceantur, foedus se
cum illis initurum.

57   His intellectis regis postulatis, senatus legatis rescripsit sese
milites equitesque, quot rex peteret, in commune adducturos; de
pecunia nihil polliceri, cum propterea quod tribus gerendis nullo
interiecto temporis spatio bellis, Gallico, Neapolitano, Pisano,
grandem pecuniam insumpsissent, tum etiam quia in id quod ab
Turcarum rege in praesentia bellum reipublicae immineat, cuius
rei fama certioribus in dies nuntiis iam percrebuerat, ad classem
comparandam satis superque civitas muneris atque oneris esset ha-
bitura. Ea rex cum intellexisset, in alium diem re dilata, ubi ea dies
venit, pecuniam nisi dent, nihil se de foedere acturum legatis re-
nuntiavit. Id ea causa fiebat, quod erant nonnulli magna apud il-

ing into account the general and natural inclination of men to enlarge their possessions.

They therefore sent a letter to the ambassadors to reply to the   56
king that they were of one mind with him, and would join him in
undertaking and prosecuting the war provided that he agreed to
secure and protect their dominions. When the king asked them on
what basis they wanted this done, and what sort of barrier or defense they were after for their territory, they replied that they
would regard themselves as secure if he ceded Cremona to the Republic, with its hinterland and all the territory east of the river
Adda. The king then undertook to give Venice the portion of
Ludovico's duchy that they were seeking, which he knew to be the
best and richest part of the entire state, except for Lecco (a town
on the east bank of the Adda as it flows out of Lake Como), on
which he was resolved to make no concession to anyone. But in return for that, he asked from the Republic for his part 7,000 cavalry and 6,000 infantry for the war, and 1,000 gold pounds. If
they promised to give him these things, he would enter into alliance with them.

On learning of the king's demands, the Senate wrote back to its   57
ambassadors that they would bring to their joint enterprise all the
infantry and cavalry the king was seeking, but that they could
make no promise about the money; and this not just because they
had used up large sums in fighting three wars in uninterrupted
succession, the French, the Neapolitan, and the Pisan, but also because the city was going to have to shoulder quite enough in the
way of burdens and obligations in preparing a fleet for the war
with which they were threatened by the sultan of Turkey, talk of
which had of late greatly increased and on which they had ever
more accurate reports by the day. When the king heard this, he
put the matter off to another day. When that day came, he told
the ambassadors that unless the money was forthcoming, he
would do nothing with regard to the treaty. This came about for

lum Galli homines auctoritate, qui Ludovici rebus favebant. Ii cum palam regi obsistere ne bellum susciperet non auderent, existimarent autem Venetos ad condicionem dandae regi pecuniae non descensuros, in eo illum ut perseveraret hortabantur. Nonnulli etiam fingi a Venetis quae de rege Thracio nuntiarent dictitabant. Accidit autem ut, dum haec agitarentur, litterae ab Rhodiorum magistratu ad regem venerint, quibus rex litteris certior fiebat Baiasetem classem ingentem comparare atque in ea cura dies atque noctes versari, ut quam posset maximam atque ornatissimam educeret. Ea intellecta re, Venetos nihil fingere ubi rex vidit, quinto Idus Februarias, nulla pecuniae mentione habita, iis quibus dictum est legibus foedus in omne tempus cum legatis percussit, ea etiam condicione foederi addita, ut si, quo rex tempore in Italiam transmitteret, bello Thracio respublica impediretur, ad auxilia ei danda non teneretur.

58   Icto foedere — quae quidem res longe alium, ac sibi Ludovicus persuaserat, exitum habuit (is enim, cum quis ei suorum consensuros cum rege Galliae Venetos contra illum diceret, "bono es animo," inquiebat, "numquam id senatus decernet; numquam Veneti maiorem se finitimum sibi regem statuent esse; itaque in rempublicam quos volo meo iure ludos facio, eius rei non dubius quin me malit, ita ut sum, quam regem Galliae mei regni dominum") — sed foedere concelebrato, Ludovicus saepe se ipse accusans, qui numquam id in animum potuerit inducere, Ioannem Franciscum Severinatem, quem quidem ad Pisanum bellum bona cum manu Florentinorum auxilio mittere statuerat, retinuit, ut Astam versus, ubi iam Triultium copias cogere nuntiabatur, eum mitteret.

the following reason: there were some Frenchmen of great influence with him who favored Ludovico's interests. While they did not dare to offer open opposition to the king's embarking on the war, they also thought that the Venetians would never stoop to the requirement to give him the money, so they urged him to persevere in asking for it. Some even insinuated that the Venetians were inventing what they were saying in public about the Turkish sultan. But it so happened that while these discussions were going on, a letter came to the king from the Grand Master of Rhodes[24] in which he informed him that Bayazid was putting together a huge fleet and was occupied with it night and day, intending to lead out the largest and best equipped fleet that he could. Once the king realized, on receipt of this intelligence, that the Venetians were not making things up, without mentioning the money he struck a perpetual treaty with the ambassadors on 9 February.[25] The league was made on the terms mentioned above, with the addition of a clause stating that if the Republic was involved in war with the Turks when the king descended into Italy, it would not be required to render him assistance.

The upshot of this business was very different from what 58 Ludovico had persuaded himself would happen: whenever one of his men said to him that the Venetians were going to conspire with the king of France against him, he used to say, "Don't worry, the Senate will never opt for that course. The Venetians will never agree to have a ruler greater than themselves as their neighbor. I can play any games I want with Venice at my pleasure, being quite sure that she prefers me, such as I am, to the king of France as lord of my realm." When the treaty was celebrated, Ludovico often criticized himself for never conceiving that it could happen, and he kept back Gianfrancesco da Sanseverino (whom he had intended to send to the Pisan war with a quantity of men to help the Florentines) so that he could send him towards Asti, where it was being reported that Trivulzio was collecting forces.

59   Interea cum in fines Guidi Ubaldi Nicolaus cum eo de quo diximus exercitu pervenisset, neque propter nives difficiliaque itinera et hostium copias, per angustos montium aditus et castella distributas, Bibienam se conferre satis posse tuto confideret, civitas vero, defessa stipendiis in id bellum erogandis, surdior ad tributi vocem fieret, praesertim bello Gallico alia stipendia, alias impensas iam deposcente, senatus Herculi, qui se reipublicae pridem obtulerat, si vellet, se cum Florentinis curaturum uti bellum pro eius dignitate componeretur, aures tandem praebuit permisitque ut ea de re agere inciperet. Ille primo per Bernardum Bembum, patrem meum, qui Ferrariae prodominum gerebat, deinde per suos quos in urbe interpretes habebat ad fallendum idoneos, sat bonis condicionibus propositis, effecit ut senatus, existimans illum de condicionibus fidem servaturum, cum de iis ipsis patres omnibus in sermonibus et collocutionibus antea egissent atque inter ipsos Herculemque convenisset, potestatem ei faceret de Pisano bello, quemadmodum sibi videretur, ita statuendi.

60   Potestate ab utrisque tradita, Hercules cum legatione quam ad illum Florentini miserant cumque Ludovici legato ad urbem venit. In urbe cum esset, tres ei cives principis collegium attribuit, qui ei praesto essent, si quid petere aut cognoscere vellet, atque ad principem et patres renuntiarent. Scripto autem neque dum prolato iudicio, cum se id Hercules patribus ostensurum esse diceret, ut, si quid aboleri aut commutari vellent, liceret, Georgius Cornelius, unus ex principis collegio, patres est hortatus: afferri ad se libellos iuberent atque inspicerent, ne ignaris ipsis quid Hercules iudicaturus esset sententia proferretur. Sed is, reprehensus a patribus —

Meanwhile Niccolò Orsini arrived in Guidobaldo's lands with   59
the army I mentioned above,[26] but because of the snows and the
difficulty of the roads, as well as the enemy forces stationed in the
mountain passes and castles, he was not confident that he could
make his way to Bibbiena in safety. On the other hand, the city
had wearied of paying the costs of the war and was becoming increasingly deaf to the word "taxes," especially now that the war in
Lombardy required further payrolling and expense. In this situation, the Senate at length lent an ear to Ercole d'Este, who had
long since offered his services to Venice, saying that if the Republic wished, he would arrange with the Florentines a settlement of
the war that would be honorable to her. And so the Senate allowed him to begin negotiations on the matter. Ercole proposed
sufficiently attractive terms, initially through my father Bernardo
Bembo, at that time *visdomino* of Ferrara, and then through his
own agents in Venice, men practiced in the arts of deception, for
the Senate to grant him authority to arbitrate on the Pisan war as
he thought best. They believed he would stick to the terms he had
proposed, since the senators had previously discussed them in all
their talks and deliberations with him, and agreement had been
reached between themselves and Ercole.

Both sides having handed over this power of arbitration, Ercole   60
came to Venice with the embassy the Florentines had sent him
and Ludovico's ambassador. While he was in the city, the Doge's
Council assigned him three citizens to assist him, if need be, with
any questions or points of information, and to report back to the
doge and the senators. After his judgment had been written, but
not yet published, Ercole said that he would show it to the senators so that they could have an opportunity to delete or change
anything if they wished. Giorgio Corner, a member of the Doge's
Council, told the senators that they should have the document
brought in and look at it, so that the judgment would not be
published without them knowing what Ercole had decided. But

qui dicerent non esse aequum, data Herculi per senatum potestate suo arbitrio iudicandi, nunc ei leges velle imponere si quae scripserit sint improbaturi; si non sint, frustra inspici quae non improbentur — conticuit.

61   Hercules octavo Iduum Aprilium sententiam tulit ut, remissis atque abolitis quaecumque in Florentinos quoquo modo Pisani detrimenta eo bello intulissent, Pisae restituerentur; ut reipublicae auri libras mille octingentas Florentini darent annis duodecim expensi nomine; multis capitibus ad speciem Pisanae rei meliorem in statum atque formam redigendae quam antea fuisset summae iudicii additis, re autem quibus ad pristinam servitutis condicionem temporis momento Pisae reciderent. Biduo post, Hercules salutatis patribus — quorum nemo fuit qui eum non invitus et non maesto vultu viderit, vel etiam qui non de eo magnopere sit questus, quod fidem quam reipublicae dederat, tantis praesertim de rebus, non praestitisset — mediam per urbem verbis contumacibus et sibilis a populo explosus, domum rediit. Senatus Ferdinandum, Herculis filium, et Bentivolos patrem et filium, et Baliones, et Marcum Martinengium, quo exercitus praefecto Pisis usus fuerat, qui se omnes neque strenue nec amanter eo bello gesserant, missos fecit. Guidum Ubaldum autem, qui valetudine curata se ad patres salutandos invisendosque contulerat, praefectura equitum et stipendio confirmato, in reipublicae fidem recepit.

62   Aloisius Galliae rex, Ludovico bellum illaturus, ex eorum numero quos consulere singulis de rebus consueverat legatos Venetos facit. Ipse legationem ad senatum mittit. Ad bellum equites eius generis mille octingentos quorum singuli more Gallico equos[8] sex secum ducerent, militum numerum decem milium habere instituit. Triultium suis exercitibus in Italia praeficit. Veneti, ubi foedus

Corner fell silent when he was rebuked by the senators, who said
that once Ercole had been given the power of independent adjudication, it was unfair to seek to impose conditions on him if they
were going to object to what he wrote; if they were not, it was a
waste of time to inspect what they did not disapprove.

On 6 April[27] Ercole delivered his judgment that Pisa should be   61
restored to Florence, with any damage the Pisans had in any way
caused the Florentines during the war being waived and cancelled;
the Florentines were to give Venice 1,800 gold pounds over twelve
years on account of her expenses; many sections were added to the
body of the judgment which gave the impression of giving Pisa
better political conditions and arrangements than it had had before, whereas in reality they instantly returned the city to its former state of servitude. Two days later Ercole took his leave of the
senators — there was not one of them that did not look upon him
with aversion and a black expression, and bitter complaints were
actually voiced that he had not lived up to the pledge he had made
the Republic, on a matter of such importance too — and he went
back home, booed through the city by the insults and catcalls of
the populace. The Senate discharged Ercole's son Ferrante, and
the Bentivoglio, father and son, and the Baglioni, and Marco
Martinengo, employed by them as commander of the army at
Pisa, all of whom had acted neither vigorously nor loyally in the
war. On the other hand, Guidobaldo, recovered now from his illness, had come to see the senators and pay his respects, and was
taken under the protection of the Republic, with his cavalry captaincy and pay confirmed.

As he prepared to make war on Ludovico, King Louis of France   62
made the Venetian ambassadors part of the group he regularly
consulted at every turn. He himself sent an embassy to the Senate.
For the war, he decided to take 1,800 cavalry, of the French type
where each took six horses with him,[28] and a force of 10,000 foot
soldiers. He put Trivulzio at the head of his armies in Italy. When

cum rege ictum ab legatis intellexerunt, sacris in aede Marcia so-
lemni ritu factis, foro apparatissimo verba foederis in vulgus pro-
nuntiari pro suggestu voluerunt. Ea dum pronuntiantur, ventus
coortus vexillum reipublicae templi turriculis implicuit, vexilli
parte abscissa. Quod quidem postea ex eventu rerum portenti loco
civitas habuit. Neque multo post alios regi legatos Marcum Georgium, Benedictum Trivisanum senatus creavit, prioribusque legatis, cum hi ad regem pervenissent, domum est reditionis facultas
data. Rex aestate media, suis in Italiam copiis praemissis, Lugdunum venit. Senatus, exercitu et ipse comparato, Melchionem Trivisanum, Marcum Antonium Maurocenum legatos exercitui su-
blegit. Alteroque ex duobus legatis quos ad urbem rex miserat una
cum illis ad exercitum reipublicae profecturo, ut rebus omnibus in-
teresset, equus pro eius dignitate ac tentorium et ferrea corporis
tegumenta cum auri libris duabus a senatu dono data.

63 Inter haec Federicus rex Neapolis per suum legatum patribus
significavit velle se equites quingentos Ludovici auxilio Mediolanum mittere. Patres neque eum illa copia Ludovico profuturum,
cui longe firmioribus praesidiis ad salutem opus esset, et se ea re
inferri sibi magnam ab eo iniuriam existimaturos, regi rescribere
legatum iusserunt: nullos plane homines maiora in Ludovicum be-
neficia contulisse quam sese, pro quibus ille rebus gratiam una tantum semper re, maleficiis contumeliisque alia super aliam inferendis, reipublicae rettulisset. Venisse nunc tempus ut deos iratos
habeat quos fefellit; rectius itaque eum facturum, si quieverit. Pauloque post Ludovicus ipse, si quo pacto Venetos placare posset, legatum ad senatum misit. Sed is cum Ferrariam appulisset, Hercu-

they learned that their ambassadors had concluded the treaty, the Venetians celebrated mass in St. Mark's and then desired to have the words of the treaty read out to the crowd from the tribune in the Square, solemnly decorated for the occasion. While the text was being read out, a wind blew up and entangled the standard of Venice in the pinnacles of the basilica, tearing away part of the flag. This was later taken as an ill omen by the citizenry in the light of subsequent events. Not long afterwards, the Senate appointed new ambassadors to the king, Marco Zorzi and Benedetto Trevisan, and the previous ambassadors were given permission to return home when Zorzi and Trevisan reached the king. Sending his troops on ahead into Italy, the king arrived in Lyon at midsummer. The Senate, which had put together its own army, chose as replacement proveditors in the field Melchiorre Trevisan and Marcantonio Morosini. As one of the two ambassadors that the king had sent to the city was about to leave with them for the Venetian army, so as to take a full part in the action, the Senate made him a gift of a horse befitting his rank, a tent and a suit of armor, along with two gold pounds.

Meanwhile King Federico of Naples sent word to the senators 63 through his ambassador that he wished to send 500 cavalry to Milan in aid of Ludovico. The senators told the ambassador to write back to the king that such a force would be of no help to Ludovico, since he required far stronger defenses than that to be safe, and that they would regard him as inflicting a great wrong on them if he did so. Certainly nobody had given Ludovico better service than they had, for which the only thanks the Republic had received was to have injuries and insults heaped on her one after another. The time had now come when Ludovico must face as an enemy the God he had deceived, and the king would therefore do better to do nothing. Shortly thereafter, Ludovico himself sent an ambassador to the Senate, to see if he could somehow placate the Venetians. When the ambassador arrived at Ferrara, Ercole d'Este

les suum hominem ad patres cum Ludovici litteris praemisit petiitque ut Ludovici legato ad eos veniendi potestatem facerent. In Ludovici litteris erat scriptum se magnis utilibusque de rebus suo et Ascanii fratris sui nomine legatum ad eos mittere; petere a patribus ut reciperetur mandataque cognoscerent. Patres lectis litteris Herculis internuntio iusserunt uti statim urbe discederet, litterasque Ludovici legato regio legendas dederunt.

64 Triultius, ad quem quidem regis duces duo cum equitum duobus milibus accesserant, in Ludovici regnum ingressus municipia complura partim vi cepit, partim ad deditionem compulit. Deinde Novium profectus, quod quidem municipium Ludovicus, septingentis militibus intromissis, communierat, tormentis ad murum positis atque uno tempore omnium ferreis emissis pilis, oppidanos ita terruit ut confestim se dederent. Milites in arcem recepti cum se ad propugnationem comparavissent, tantus Gallorum militum impetus et tormentorum reliquarumque rerum apparatus tam subitus tamque ardens fuit, ut quinque horarum spatio arcem expugnaverint militesque Ludovici omnes ad unum interfecerint. Quo successu ad celeritatem usus, Triultius paucis diebus castella numero ad viginti Tortonamque oppidum cepit. Iis rebus cognitis, Antonius Maria Severinas, Galeatii frater, qui una cum illo Alexandriae praeerat, Ticinum rediit neque ab oppidanis est receptus.

65 Veneti, ubi a Triultio belli factum initium cognoverunt, exercitu equitum amplius septem milium, militum supra sex milium coacto, Ollioque flumine cum parte copiarum Liviano duce transmisso, plura uno die municipia per deditionem capiunt. Reliquaque ad priorem exercitus partem adiuncta parte, parvo temporis spatio vicis castellisque quae cis Abduam flumen sunt compluribus in deditionem acceptis, Caravagium, quod est eius reg-

sent a man to the Senate with Ludovico's letter, asking them to grant him permission to approach them. Ludovico's letter announced that he was sending them an ambassador in his own name and that of his brother Ascanio, to discuss matters of great importance and advantage to them. He asked the senators to receive him and hear the mission he had been entrusted with. Having read Ludovico's letter, the senators told Ercole's messenger to leave the city at once, and gave the letter to the French king's ambassador to read.

Trivulzio, who had been joined by two of Louis' captains with 2,000 horse, entered Ludovico's dominions and took several towns, some by force of arms, some by compelling them to surrender. He then left for Novi Ligure, a town which Ludovico had strengthened with 700 infantry, positioned his artillery at the walls and fired a broadside of cannonballs, at once terrifying the inhabitants into surrender. The soldiers retreated into the fort and prepared to defend it, but the onslaught of the French infantry and the suddenness and ferocity of their array of artillery and other materiel was such that in the space of five hours they stormed the fort and killed every last man of Ludovico's soldiers. Turning this success to quick account, within a few days Trivulzio took about 20 castles and the town of Tortona. When this became known, Galeazzo's brother Antonio Maria da Sanseverino, who shared the command of Alessandria with him, returned to Pavia, but the inhabitants would not admit him.

When the Venetians learned that Trivulzio had embarked on the war, they collected an army of more than 7,000 cavalry and over 6,000 foot soldiers. Some of their forces crossed the river Oglio under the command of d'Alviano and took the surrender of several towns in a single day. When the rest joined the forces earlier in the field, many villages and castles east of the Adda were taken by surrender in short order, and the army marched on to Caravaggio, the principal town of the region. The proveditors sent

ionis caput, exercitum adducunt. Legati ad oppidanos miserunt: se si oppugnari sinerent, sese oppidum militibus tradituros. Ea nocte nullum est responsum datum. Itaque stationibus militum ad oppidi fossas dispositis, legati ut muros mane quaterent se comparabant. Oppidani autem prima luce ad legatos venerunt seque eis dediderunt, arce excepta, quae ab ipsis non tenebatur; eamque fuisse causam dixerunt, cur non se legatis e vestigio permisissent, quod arcem quoque tradere voluissent. Legatis introductis missisque ad praefectum arcis internuntiis, postridie eius diei arx deditur, legato Ludovici, qui in ea erat, militibusque omnibus abeundi potestate impetrata, oppidanis postulantibus. Hoc idem Sonzinates fecerunt. Sed arcis praefectus, misso ad legatos internuntio, velle se arcem tradere sponte pollicitus, quae quidem esset tormentis rebusque omnibus munitissima, ab eis petiit ut sibi civitatem et ius comitiorum darent. Illi eius rei facultatem se habere nullam cum respondissent litterasque ad senatum daturos recepissent, praefectus, se in eo reipublicae fidei velle permittere ne qua propterea mora legatis fieret liberaliter pronuntians, arcem tradidit.

66   Iisdem diebus parte altera Triultio Alexandriam tormentis oppugnante, Galeatius, Ludovici gener, qui oppidum defendebat, cum paucis clam noctu egressus, Mediolanum abiit. Qua intellecta re, complures eius equites militesque oppido aufugerunt. Itaque mane Galli ab oppidanis introducti oppidum capiunt. Placentini, missis ad Triultium legatis, itemque Ticinenses sese ei dediderunt. Mediolani autem, militibus Ludovici stipendium postulantibus, cum eos Ludovicus ad quaestorem suum reiecisset, ille vero moram interponere ei rei vellet, milites, multis illatis vulneribus, quaestorem prope interfecerunt. Civitatis principes, veriti ne dirip-

word to the townspeople that if they allowed themselves to be attacked, the proveditors would give the town over to the soldiery. No response came that night. The proveditors therefore disposed detachments of soldiers around the town moats and prepared to breach the walls in the morning. But at dawn the inhabitants came to them and surrendered, except for the citadel, which was not under their control. They said that this was the reason why they had not surrendered to the proveditors straightaway, because they had wanted to hand over the citadel as well. When the proveditors had been let in and messengers sent to the commander of the citadel, the fortress surrendered the next day, with permission to leave granted to Ludovico's commissioner, who was there, and all the soldiers, at the inhabitants' request. The people of Soncino did the same. The captain of the citadel there sent a messenger to the proveditors, promising that he was ready to hand over the citadel, which was well fortified with artillery and the rest, of his own free will, but he asked them to give him Venetian citizenship and noble status. When they replied that they had no authority to do so, but undertook to send a letter to the Senate, the captain nobly declared that in that matter he was ready to trust in the good faith of the Republic, so that the proveditors would suffer no delay on that account, and he handed over the citadel.

Elsewhere in the same period, when Trivulzio launched an artillery attack on Alessandria, its defender, Ludovico's son-in-law Galeazzo da Sanseverino, secretly departed by night with a few of his men and went off to Milan. When this became generally known, a good many of his cavalry and infantry fled the town. And so in the morning the French were let in by the inhabitants and took the town. Piacenza surrendered after sending a deputation to Trivulzio, and Pavia too. At Milan, Ludovico's soldiers were demanding their pay and were referred by him to his paymaster. When the latter proposed delaying payment, he was severely injured by the soldiers and almost killed. The leading citi-

erentur, simul quod novis rebus studebant, agrestes homines in oppidum adduxerunt seseque munierunt. Quibus rebus cognitis Ludovicus, incitatae plebis studia omniumque plane hominum in se invidiam pertimescens, liberos et concubinam (nam uxor mortem obierat) et Ascanium Cardinalem fratrem Federicumque Severinatem, item Cardinalem, Galeatii fratrem, oppido eductos Comum misit. Oppidani ubi Ludovicum suis rebus diffidere ipsum intellexerunt, concilio civitatis coacto, quattuor ex principibus legerunt, qui rebus omnibus praeessent. Ii, ad Ludovicum profecti, velle se oppidum regi tradere dixerunt; eius autem rei causam ipsum dedisse, qui liberos et familiam emiserit. Ludovicus, intellecta civitatis voluntate, stipendio equitibus levis armaturae quingentis dato, postridie eius diei una cum Galeatio genero equitibusque paulo plus ducentis discessit, cum reliqui stipe accepta eius imperio se subtraxissent, arcemque, artificio atque immani mole murorum omnibusque idoneis ad obsidionem sustinendam rebus, tum militum duobus milibus apprime communitam, Bernardino Curtio, uni ex suis maxime intimis, cui supra ceteros confidebat, quemque ipse a parvulo aluerat, commendavit, cum eam tradere Ascanio fratri custodiendam, qui se illi obtulerat, noluisset. Triultius quatriduo post a Mediolanensibus magna hominum gratulatione in oppidum receptus est; reliquaque oppida quae supererant ei se confestim dediderunt.

67   Venetis Cremonae appropinquantibus, civitas legatos obviam misit, qui tempus ad deditionem peterent. Quo tempore, missis ad Triultium interpretibus, ubi se principes civitatis in ea regni parte quae ad rempublicam ex foedere spectabat esse intellexerunt, omni

zens, afraid that they would be plundered and at the same time keen to see a change of regime, brought the country population into town and took steps to defend themselves. When Ludovico learned of this, he became very much afraid of the passions of the common people once they were roused, and of the universal hostility of the population toward himself. He had his children and concubine (his wife being dead), his brother Cardinal Ascanio, and Federico da Sanseverino, Galeazzo's brother, another cardinal, brought out of the town and sent to Como. When the inhabitants realized that Ludovico himself had no confidence in his regime, they called a council of the citizenry and chose four of the nobles to take overall charge of the situation. These men went to Ludovico and told him that they wanted to hand the town over to the king. He had brought this about himself when he sent his children and family away. Grasping the mood of the city, Ludovico gave 500 light cavalry their pay, and on the following day departed with his son-in-law Galeazzo and a little more than 200 cavalry, the rest having left his command on receipt of their money. The fortress was well defended by its artful construction, the huge bulk of its walls, and all the necessities for withstanding a siege, above all by its garrison of 2,000 soldiers. Ludovico entrusted it to Bernardino da Corte, one of his most intimate friends, the one he trusted above all others, whom he himself had supported from his earliest boyhood—he had refused to hand it over to his brother Ascanio, who had offered to defend it for him. Four days later Trivulzio was welcomed into the city by the Milanese amid general rejoicing, and the other towns that were holding out at once surrendered to him.

As the Venetians approached Cremona, the city sent ambassa- 67 dors to meet them, to ask for more time to surrender. They had at that time sent representatives to Trivulzio, and as soon as the Cremonese nobles realized that they were in the part of the duchy which fell to the Republic under the treaty, they proceeded to the

cum senatu et sacerdotibus atque pontifice ad portas progressi, legatos una cum ducibus accersitos sub tentoriolo sacro in oppidum introduxerunt, postulantesque ut tributis a Ludovico vel impositis novis vel adauctis acerbissime veteribus civitatem levarent, impetraverunt. Erat in oppido arx perquam munita difficilisque captu, si qua alia. Eam Petrus Antonius Battalio a Ludovico acceptam custodiebat. Legati postridie eius diei, qui arcem reipublicae nomine ab illo peterent, miserunt. A praefecto interpretibus ultro citroque missis, cum ei libras auri ducentas quinquaginta legati partim dedissent, partim se daturos recepissent, civitatem et ius comitiorum ipsi patrique eius posterisque eorum una cum domo urbana et fundo et villa in agro Veronensi senatus permissu donavissent; arce sunt potiti. Eodemque fere die Triultius, auri libris item ducenties quinquagies Curtio numeratis, concessaque Ludovici et Galeatii supellectili sane regia quae in ea erat, Mediolani arcem, de qua diximus, tenuit. Ita is cui fides ab sese data rata atque sancta numquam fuisset neminem habuit suorum qui ei fidem quam dederat, cum id facere nullo negotio posset, tam duro eius tempore pauculos modo dies praestaret.

68   Cremona in reipublicae potestatem redacta, magistratus, qui ius dicerent, Dominicus Trivisanus, Nicolaus Fuscarenus eo missi; oratoresque adlecti duo, ad priores alios qui adhuc in urbe praestolabantur, Nicolaus Michaeles, Benedictus Iustinianus; Mediolanumque una omnes ire iussi, ibi regem excepturi eique reipublicae nomine novo de regno gratulaturi. Quos quidem postea rex, Mediolanum cum venisset, nam tum quidem esse in Alpibus dicebatur, perhonorifice tractavit, apud seque habuit. Eorum tres, quorum in numero erat Antonius Lauredanus, qui ex Gallia cum rege

gates with their entire senate, their priests and bishop, and bringing together the proveditors and captains under a ceremonial canopy, led them into the town. They requested to be exempted from Ludovico's taxes, both the new ones imposed by him and the old ones that he had cruelly increased, and their request was granted. The town had a fortress that was extremely well fortified and as difficult to capture as any ever was. It was defended by Pietro Antonio Battaglione, who had received it from Ludovico. On the next day, the proveditors sent men to ask him for the fortress in the name of the Republic. After the negotiators had gone back and forth to the captain several times, and the Venetians had awarded him 250 gold pounds, some of it given outright, some of it promised to him, and with the Senate's permission granted citizenship and noble status to him, his father and his descendants, together with a house in Venice and an estate and villa in the countryside of Verona, they took possession of the fortress. And on virtually the same day, Trivulzio, paying out another 250 gold pounds to da Corte, and granting him the royal trappings and accoutrements of Ludovico and Galeazzo that were in it, took control of the fortress of Milan of which I spoke above. And so Ludovico Sforza, whose own word had never been reliable and inviolate, in his hour of need had not one follower who would keep his word to him for just a few days, even when he could easily have done so.

With Cremona brought under the sway of the Republic, magis-   68
trates were sent there to administer justice, Domenico Trevisan and Niccolò Foscarini, and two ambassadors, Niccolò Michiel and Benedetto Giustinian, were added to the previous ones who were still waiting in the city. All four were told to go to Milan together, there to welcome the king and congratulate him on his new realm in the name of the Republic. When Louis arrived in Milan (for at that time he was said to be in the Alps), he subsequently treated these men with every mark of respect and kept them about his person. Three of them, including Antonio Loredan, who had

venerat, suo functi munere domum redierunt. Petierat, ab legatis reipublicae qui in Gallia transalpina foedus cum rege percusserant, Ludovicus Lucemburgius, regis propinquus, ut, cum ad urbem rediissent, sibi a patribus civitatem et ius comitiorum impetrarent. Itaque eius postulatis intellectis, civitas utrumque munus Ludovico est elargita. Eadem liberalitas in Hannibalem Angusciolum, qui arcem Sonzinatium reipublicae legatis tradiderat, et Marsilium eius fratrem collata; annuusque insuper proventus utrique dono additus. Victor quoque Martinengius Brixianus, unus ex principibus civitatis, Ioannesque Maria eius frater ob eorum egregia in rempublicam officia civitatem et ius comitiorum paucis post diebus sunt adepti.

69   Ludovicus, in Raetos profectus ut exercitum cogeret ad Gallos repellendos (id enim fama vulgaverat), Helvetiis Lepontiisque temptatis, nihil efficere quod ex usu esset potuit. Rex, adhibitis legatis qui Mediolani erant omnibus, velle se Federico regi bellum inferre pronuntiavit, ut regnum Neapolitanum, quod paulo antea Caroli fuisset, suam in potestatem redigeret. Cui statim Hispaniae regum legatus, "Ego vero," inquit, "bellum tibi a meis regibus denuntio, si id aggredi statueris. Non enim sunt passuri ut propinquum suum regno quis eiciat." Rex de eo se cogitaturum respondit. Deinde duos cum menses Mediolani fuisset, Genuensium civitatem certis condicionibus in fidem recepisset, Triultium, cui etiam Vigevenum in Ticinensi agro, oppidum regiis aedibus atque ad venationes opportunum, dono dederat, una cum altero ex suis ducibus novi regni rebus omnibus praefecisset, in ulteriorem Galliam rediit.

come from France with the king, returned home after fulfilling their mission. The Venetian ambassadors who had struck the treaty in France with the king were requested by his relative, Louis of Luxembourg, to ask the Senate to grant him citizenship and noble status when they arrived in Venice. When they learned of Louis' wishes, the state bestowed both favors on him. The same liberality was shown to Annibale Anguissola, who had surrendered the fortress of Soncino to the Venetian proveditors, and to his brother Marsilio, and both were given an annual pension besides. A few days later, Vittore Martinengo, one of the leading citizens of Brescia, and his brother Gian Maria also acquired citizenship and noble status for distinguished service to the Republic.

According to rumor, Ludovico left for the Tyrol to collect an 69 army to drive the French out, but despite working on the men of Ticino and Graubünden he got nothing of any use from them. The king summoned all the ambassadors who were at Milan and declared that he wished to make war on King Federico, in order to bring the Kingdom of Naples, which had a little earlier belonged to Charles, under his sway. The ambassador of the Spanish monarchs immediately said to him, "Then in the name of my sovereigns I declare war on you, if you are set on doing this. They will never allow anyone to expel their kinsman from the Kingdom." The king replied that he would think about it. He spent two months in Milan, during which he took the city of Genoa under his protection on certain conditions, and having made Trivulzio a present of Vigevano in the district of Pavia, a town of royal residences and good for hunting, put him in overall charge of running his new realm alongside another of his captains. After that, Louis returned to France.

Note on the Text and Translation

❧❧❧

The Latin text of Bembo's *Historia Veneta* was first published in 1551, four years after his death, in both Venice and Paris; the Italian version appeared in 1552. There were subsequent Latin editions in 1722 (Leiden) and, in editions of his *Opera*, in 1556 (Basel), 1567 (Basel), and 1611 (Strasbourg). Both versions are included in parallel columns in the edition of his *Opera* of 1729 (Venice). Both versions were subjected to censorship by the Council of Ten and the *Riformatori* in Padua before the initial publication, causing excisions, rewriting, and additions in a few places. The manuscript of the Latin version has remained lost, but Bembo's original of the Italian version was finally published at Venice in 1790, enabling a comparison with the censored version and the archival record of the deliberations of the Ten about the passages that were altered (see the studies by Teza and Lagomaggiore cited in the Bibliography). These changes are indicated in the Notes to the Translation. It should be noted that Bembo's vernacular was altered in the original printing, mostly in passages that were being changed for their content, but in some other passages as well, so that his particular stylistic preferences for the *volgare* are not always observed. I have consulted both versions in preparing my own English version.

The text presented in this volume is not a critical edition, but a working edition to serve as a basis for the translation. It is based upon the edition of Venice, 1551, incorporating the Errata (which stop in Book IX), with additional minor corrections from the edition of Venice, 1729. The latter are indicated in the *Notes to the Text*. The first edition is not divided into paragraphs (except by capitalizing the first word of some sentences); the divisions of the later edition have mostly been retained, and others added. Capitalization and punctuation have been modernized, as has been Bembo's orthography, with the exception of proper names. In the case of the latter Bembo's spelling is given in the Latin text but the modern English or Italian form of the name in the translation.

ABBREVIATIONS

A   Petri Bembi cardinalis historiae Venetae libri XII. Venice:
       Manutius, 1551.

B   Della historia vinitiana di M. Pietro Bembo cardinale volgarmente
       scritta libri XII. Venice: Gualtero Scotto, 1552.

C   Opere del Cardinale Pietro Bembo, ora per la prima volta tutte in
       un corpo unite. Venice: Francesco Hertzhauser, 1729.

D   Bembo, Pietro, Della istoria viniziana di M. Pietro Bembo,
       cardinale, da lui volgarizzata, libri dodici, ora par la prima volta
       secondo l'originale pubblicati. Ed. Jacopo Morelli. Venice: A.
       Zatta, 1790.

Notes to the Text

☙§?❧

BOOK I

1. operae *A*, opera *C*
2. victoria *A, corrected in C*
3. Vicentia *AC*
4. *thus AC; one should perhaps read* sanandae civitati
5. *thus AC; one should perhaps read* animadverterunt

BOOK II

1. aliquod *A, corrected in C*
2. *thus AC; one should perhaps read* existimabat
3. Calendas *AC*
4. Entimilium *A*, Intemelium vel Albium Intemelium, nunc vintimilia *A (Errata)*
5. ei *A, corrected in C*
6. *thus AC: one should perhaps read* quattuor

BOOK III

1. puten *A, corrected in C*
2. Hydruntem mallem *A (Errata)*
3. *I should prefer* <cum> eodem equitum numero
4. in *omitted in C*
5. cum *AC*
6. sit *AC*
7. hostium *A, corrected in C*

BOOK IV

1. Patavio *AC*
2. Castellum *A*, castellum *C*
3. tibicine *AC*

4. Librafactae *AC*
5. Librafactae *AC*
6. *A verb of speaking is to be understood, implied by the idea of command in* vocatisque qui portas aperirent.
7. *thus AC: one should perhaps read* Ab eo
8. equites *AC: cf. BD* cavalli

Notes to the Translation

ॐ॥ॐ

1. On 30 January 1516, Navagero was the first to whom the Council of Ten entrusted the official task of writing a history of Venice, and he was also named keeper of the library of Cardinal Bessarion; see Cochrane, *Historians*, pp. 227–28.

2. Bembo usually refers to Venice as the Republic, hereafter capitalized and referred to by a feminine pronoun. He also refers to Venice as "the city" (hereafter translated as Venice) and uses the proper noun only (with some exceptions in the later books) when "the city" might be read as Rome.

3. Sabellico had in 1485 presented to the doge and Senate his 33 books *Rerum Venetarum ab urbe condita* ("of Venetian history from the foundation of the city"); see Gilbert, "Biondo, Sabellico," pp. 280–81.

4. 1482–84.

5. I.e., Austrian; see 5 below.

6. Not identified; both vernacular versions (*B* and *D*) have Monte Membraio; the source is actually Lago di Resia/Reschensee in the Alpi Venoste / Oetztal Alps.

7. *Provveditori in Campo* were patricians elected by the Senate who accompanied the captain-general in war (M. E. Mallett and J. R. Hale, *The Military Organization of a Renaissance State: Venice c. 1400 to 1617* [Cambridge, 1984], pp. 168–80).

8. This phrase is omitted in *D* and was presumably added by the censors.

9. noble status: lit., the right of the Great Council, i.e. (honorary) membership in it.

10. According to Marin Sanudo, *Le vite dei dogi (1474–1494)*, vol. 2 (Padua, 2001), p. 571 (f. 294r), the German combatant was "Conte Zuanne di Norimberg".

11. B and D have *Buerna & Lodrone*. Moerna is a village about 40 km north-east of Brescia; the *Licates* of the Latin text were an Alpine tribe, far to the north, mentioned in Pliny, *Natural History* 3.137, but apparently taken by Bembo as located at Lodrone, some 10 km north-west of Moerna.

12. According to Frederic C. Lane and Reinhold C. Mueller, *Money and Banking in Medieval and Renaissance Venice*, vol. 1 (Baltimore and London, 1985), p. 148, all state obligations are given in a money of account based upon the *grosso*, and a *lira di grossi a oro* = 10 ducats; but Bembo's figures are regularly in *librae auri* (*libbre d'oro* in the vernacular version), each apparently equal to about 100 ducats. This term has been retained in the translation as "gold pounds."

13. Bembo refers sometimes to the *patres*, sometimes to the *senatus*, in recording decisions and decrees; a consistent distinction seems impossible to maintain, and *patres* will usually be translated here as "the senators", sometimes as "the Signoria" (technically the doge, his Council, and the Heads of the Forty). The term *senator(es)* is reserved for the senator(s) as individual(s). Only rarely are they addressed as *patres conscripti* in the ancient Roman rhetorical mode.

14. I.e., the Piazzetta.

15. Dorothea of Brandenburg, Queen of Denmark, went on pilgrimages to Rome in 1475 and 1488.

16. Actually, Alfonso; same error initially in Marin Sanudo (above, n. 10), p. 599 (f. 306v).

17. I.e., aqua regia.

18. The ceremonial barge of the Doge.

19. Lit., Greek cavalry; originally Albanian, special light cavalry.

20. See Sanudo, *Le vite*, p. 595 (f. 304v).

21. Lit., a bireme, Ital. *fusta*.

22. *Sestiaria*; Bembo later uses the medieval Latin term *staria* (Ital. *staio*). All are derived from Lat. *sextarius*.

23. I.e. the campanile in Piazza San Marco and that of S. Maria Gloriosa dei Frari. See Sanudo, *Le vite*, p. 619 (f. 315v).

24. The Franciscan convent of S. Maria dei Miracoli: this was the date of the consecration of the church and presumably the first investiture of its nuns.

25. Ivan Cernovich ruled Montenegro from 1461 till his death in 1490, his son Zorzi (as Sanudo calls him; Duradj in Slavonic) marrying Isabetta Erizzo in the latter year.

26. Lit., iron tubes.

27. Zaccaria Barbaro was a Procurator of St. Mark's.

28. Of the plague (*plebeius morbus*) in A; in B and D, of a tumor. Ermolao died in July 1493.

29. *Quarantie* or Courts of Forty; see Robert Finlay, *Politics in Renaissance Venice* (New Brunswick, NJ, 1980), pp. 68–73; to the *Quarantia civile vecchia* (now for civil cases within Venice), and the *Quarantia criminal* (for criminal cases), was added the *civile nuova* (for civil cases outside the city).

30. I.e., to the Court of the Forty.

31. See Finlay, *Politics*, p. 202; he says this invention remained in use until 1797, but with a tripartite division rather than a separate box for undecideds.

32. See n. 29 above. Each of the three *Quarantie* or Colleges of Forty would elect a Head for each of the four two-month periods which made up a session of their being in office.

33. I.e., the *Pien Collegio*, consisting of the Signoria (the doge and his six councillors and the three Heads of the Forty), and the sixteen *savi* or "wise men."

34. Text unclear; in BD "parties and dances of the most select women and of the children of leading men."

BOOK II

1. Bembo had written "the minds of the French are extremely changeable," as in D; revised by the censors, as in B; see Teza, p. 78.

2. Boldù and Bollani were two of the three *Avogadori di Comun*, powerful public prosecutors who served for a year.

3. *BD* have Candia (the Venetian name for Crete) for Canea (Chania), omitting "a town on Crete."

4. Ferrante's son Alfonso II of Naples married Ippolita Sforza, sister of Duke Galeazzo, whose son Duke Giangaleazzo married Ippolita's daughter Isabella of Naples, his first cousin. Giangaleazzo was therefore the son-in-law of Ferrante's son Alfonso (and Ippolita at once his mother-in-law and aunt).

5. Lit., the Roman Republic, Bembo's usual term for the Church of Rome and the Papal State.

6. "Round ships"; see Frederic C. Lane, *Venetian Ships and Shipbuilders in the Renaissance* (Baltimore, 1934); a merchant ship or merchantman, two-masted lateener.

7. Skradin and Klis in Croatia.

8. The illegitimate son of Duke Galeazzo Sforza, elder half-brother of Duke Giangaleazzo, nephew of Ludovico il Moro.

9. And later pope, Leo X, reigned 1513–21.

10. Guillaume Briçonnet, 1451–1514.

11. Actually to Flanders (so in *BD*); they are the Galleys of Flanders.

12. Alfonso d'Avalos.

13. The Castel dell'Ovo (see above, 2.23).

14. I.e., between Spain, Maximilian, Ludovico and the pope.

15. He means *Paolo* Fregoso, cardinal, archbishop of Genoa, three times doge, and brigand (he seems to be the "Paulus" mentioned in 56 below).

16. Now Sazan, the only island of Albania, opposite Brindisi across the Straits of Otranto.

17. As condottiere.

18. Thus begins the account of the Battle of Fornovo; see John S. C. Bridge, *A History of France from the Death of Louis XI*, vol. 2 (Oxford, 1924), pp. 243–66; Charles Oman, *A History of the Art of War in the Sixteenth Century* (London, 1937), pp. 105–14.

19. Lit., opposed doing this, i.e. attacking.

20. The description of the artillery and the route is omitted in *B*.

21. 30 June in Bembo's Latin and vernacular versions.

22. Specified as "precious books from the holy chapel, a plaque inlaid with gems and deserving of reverence for its sacred relics, and rings loaded with jewels" in Alessandro Benedetti's *Diaria de bello Carolino* (Venice, 1496), perhaps Bembo's source.

23. The Banco di San Giorgio.

24. The Latin says that Gonzaga "should be called *imperator* very widely," rendered by Bembo in the Italian as "che fosse chiamato Capitan Generale." Yet we have already learned that he received this title earlier in the year (40, "imperator dictus est" / "Capitano general fatto"), and Bembo's point is unclear.

25. 2,000 ducats, according to Mallett and Hale, *Military Organization*, p. 196.

26. Mallett and Hale *ibid*. give the figure as 500 ducats. Bernardino died in 1531 at the age of 90.

27. 1,000 ducats, *ibid*.

28. Probably an error for four gold pounds; *BD* read 400 gold pounds; according to Mallett and Hale (*loc. cit.*), the daughters of Farnese and Corso were given allowances of 400 ducats a year each.

29. Understand "many men *who had survived the battle* and the children and brothers of many others *who had not*," as in *BD*.

BOOK III

1. See 2.28.

2. Bembo says "our ancestors," as representing senatorial discussion and not his own ostensibly objective viewpoint.

3. 7 October 1495; see 2.63.

4. Brother of Ludovico il Moro.

5. See 1.33.

6. Piero was the son of Lorenzo de' Medici and Clarice Orsini (cf. 2.18).

7. Unidentified. *BD* have "alla Foglia"; perhaps Foggia is meant.

8. Onorato Caetani.

9. Guidobaldo da Montefeltro, Giovanni Sforza, and Cesare Borgia.

10. Antonello da Sanseverino.

11. See Girolamo Fracastoro (1478–1553), *Syphilis sive de morbo gallico*, 1521, published Verona, 1530; Bembo's comments on the work: *Avertimenti nella Siphili di Hieronimo Fracastoro*, ed. F. Pellegrini, in G. Fracastoro, *Scritti inediti* (Verona, 1955), pp. 35–61 (cited by Dionisotti, see Introduction above, n. 4).

12. See §§11–15, 23–25 above.

13. In *D* Bembo added, "and would to God it had not been such a disgrace to her"; excised by the censors in *B*, see Teza, pp. 79–80.

14. Ludovico da Marsciano, this at the end of May 1496.

15. See 1.64.

16. See §32 above.

17. *BD* refer to the former as a proveditor and the latter as an ambassador.

18. The Malvezzi and Bentivoglio were on opposite sides in their native Bologna, but there was also personal enmity between Annibale and Lucio.

19. Lit., the magistracy of the Board of Five for the Administration of Salt.

20. The young lord of Faenza, Astorre Manfredi. See §19 above.

21. *B* has no phrase corresponding to "with her goodwill and mercy."

22. I.e., four *fuste*, one *galeone*, and one "round ship."

23. This last sentence is omitted in *D* and may thus have been added by the censors. *B* does not translate the unusual phrase *e carchesiis*, "from the mastheads."

BOOK FOUR

1. The information that the *sacerdotium* ("priesthood") was specifically a canonry derives from Bembo's Italian translation.

2. The Isles of the Blessed lay in classical mythology in the far west of the Ocean sea, in later times identified with the Madeira or Canary islands. Bembo in 6.3 explicitly identifies them with the latter.

3. *B* translates *plutei* as "benches," *D* as "tables," and in both versions *praefecti cenaculum ipsa in puppi*, here "the captain's own cabin on the poop" is "the cover of the poop."

4. Roccella Ionica in Calabria, a feud of the Marquis of Crotone, Antonio Centelles, mentioned below. (Roccella is actually on the Ionian sea coast, but Bembo regards the Ionian as part of the Adriatic, *nostrum mare* above, as opposed to the more general Mediterranean of the previous section.) The Venetian captain is elsewhere given as Domenico Malipiero.

5. Sebastiano Ziani was doge 1172–78.

6. The street of the lanterns, now the Calle degli Armeni.

7. Louis XII; Bembo's distinction between Aloisius and Ludovicus, possible in the vernacular as Luigi (or Alvise for Venetians) and Lodovico, is not practicable in English; he continues to call the new king of France Aloisius, as he had when he was duke of Orleans, partly to distinguish him from Ludovico, the duke of Milan.

8. If the fortress is actually named Castellum (capitalized in *A*), there is a Castelnuovo (di Val di Cecina) NE of Piombino, in the Colline Metallifere. According to Guicciardini (4.2), this was in the Maremma di Volterra, and the ensuing battle was in the Valle di San Regolo.

9. "Nearby castle" in *BD*.

10. The Cinque della Pace.

11. Bembo's original phrase was apparently stronger, as *D* reads "the annulling of his contract was cut off," and was changed to this by the censors, as in *B*, despite the vote of the Ten to keep it; see Teza, p. 80.

12. That is, Bentivoglio might not have resisted the passage of the Venetian army through Bolognese territory with physical force, or the Venetians could send a larger force than they had intended through the neighboring Faventino.

13. *B* has "Marzocco, Marzocco" (the lion symbol of Florence), but *D* has "Leone, Leone."

14. Jacopo d'Appiano, fighting for the Florentines, this in November 1498.

15. Domenico Malipiero.

16. Both fortresses unidentified; Chiesa di Ornina is a place-name close to Castel Focognano, south and west of Poppi and Bibbiena.

17. Lit., "Francis, received into the number of the gods." Francis received the stigmata there.

18. Elisabetta Gonzaga.

19. *D* adds "to such an extent did he, a man of the utmost inconstancy and vanity, allow himself to be hindered by his ambition"; excised by the censors, as in *B*; see Teza, pp. 80–81.

20. See above, §16.

21. That is, falcons, *falconi* in the Italian.

22. That is, sables, *gibellini* (i.e., *zibellini*) in the Italian.

23. Unidentified, possibly Bertola in the province of Asti; the place is called a castle in *BD*.

24. The Frenchman Pierre d'Aubusson, defender of Rhodes against the Turks in the siege of 1480.

25. January in *BD*.

26. See above, §49.

27. 8 April in *BD*.

28. Reading *equos* for *equites*; *BD* interpret as *cavalli*.

Bibliography

᠀᠀᠀

EDITIONS

Historiae Venetae libri XII. Venice: Sons of Aldus Manutius, 1551.

Rerum Venetarum historiae libri XII. Paris: Michael Vascosanus, 1551.

Quaecunque usquam prodierunt opera, in unum corpus collecta et ad postremam autoris recognitionem diligentissime elaborata, vol. 1. Basel: M. Isingrin, 1556.

Quaecunque usquam prodierunt opera, in unum corpus collecta, et nunc demum ab C. Augustino Curione, cum optimis exemplaribus collata, et diligentissime castigata, vol. 1. Basel: Thomas Guarinus, 1567.

Omnia quaecunque usquam prodierunt opera: in unum corpus collecta cum optimis exemplaribus collata, et diligentissime castigata, vol. 1. Strasbourg: Lazarus Zetzner, 1609–52.

Historiae venetae libri XII. Editio novissima, cum optimis exemplaribus collata, accuratissime castigata, atque indice copiosissimo adaucta. Leiden: P. Vander Aa, 1722. In J. G. Graevius, *Thesaurus antiquitatum et historiarum Italiae*, vol. 5, pt. 1.

Opere del Cardinale Pietro Bembo, ora per la prima volta tutte in un corpo unite, vol. 1. Venice: Francesco Hertzhauser, 1729.

ITALIAN TRANSLATIONS

Della historia vinitiana di M. Pietro Bembo cardinale volgarmente scritta libri XII. Venice: Gualtero Scotto, 1552.

Della historia vinitiana di Pietro Bembo cardinale volgarmente scritta libri XII; Aggiuntavi di nuovo la tavola delle cose piu notabili, coi nomi di tutti i principi, patriarchi, cardinali vinitiani fino al serenissimo Luigi Mocenigo, per M. Alemanio Fino. Venice: Giordano Ziletti, 1570. The text is a reissue of the previous edition.

Istorie veneziane latinamente scritte da Pietro cardinale Bembo. In vol. 2 of *Degli istorici delle cose veneziane, i quali hanno scritto per pubblico decreto.* [Edited by Apostolo Zeno.] 10 vols. Venice: Lovisa, 1718–22.

The edition of Venice, 1729, as in the previous section.

Pietro Bembo, *Istoria Veneziana*. Venice: A. Savioli, 1747.

Della istoria viniziana di M. Pietro Bembo, cardinale, da lui volgarizzata, libri dodici, ora par la prima volta secondo l'originale pubblicati, ed. Jacopo Morelli. Venice: A. Zatta, 1790.

Pietro Bembo, *Opere*, vols. 3–4. Milan: Società tipografica dei classici italiani, 1809. (Edizione dei classici italiani, 57–58.)

MODERN STUDIES

Cochrane, Eric. *Historians and Historiography in the Italian Renaissance*. Chicago, 1981.

Cozzi, Gaetano. "Cultura politica e religione nella 'pubblica storiografia' veneziana del '500." *Bolletino dell'Istituto di storia della società e dello Stato Veneziano* 5–6 (1963–64): 215–96.

Dionisotti, Carlo. "Bembo, Pietro." *Dizionario biografico degli italiani* 8 (1966): 133–151.

——. *Scritti sul Bembo*, ed. Claudio Vela. Turin, 2002.

Elwert, W. Theodore, "Pietro Bembo e la vita letteraria del suo tempo." In *La civiltà veneziana del '500*, pp. 127–176. Florence, 1958.

Gilbert, Felix. "Biondo, Sabellico, and the Beginnings of Venetian Official Historiography." In *Florilegium Historiale: Essays presented to Wallace K. Ferguson*, pp. 275–93. Toronto, 1971.

Lagomaggiore, Carlo. *L'Istoria Viniziana di M. Pietro Bembo*. Estratto dal *Nuovo archivio veneto* 7–9 (1904–1907). Venice, 1905.

Monfasani, John. "The Ciceronian Controversy." *Cambridge History of Literary Criticism*, vol. 3 (1999): 355–401, esp. 397–99.

Pertusi, Agostino, ed. *La storiografia veneziana fino al secolo XVI: Aspetti e problemi*. Florence, 1970.

Santoro, Mario. *Pietro Bembo*. Naples, 1937.

Teza, E. "Correzioni alla Istoria veneziana di Pietro Bembo proposte dal Consiglio dei Dieci nel 1548." *Annali delle università toscane* 18 (1888): 75–93.

Index

🔊🔊🔊

Publication of this volume has been made possible by

The Myron and Sheila Gilmore Publication Fund at I Tatti
The Robert Lehman Endowment Fund
The Jean-François Malle Scholarly Programs and Publications Fund
The Andrew W. Mellon Scholarly Publications Fund
The Craig and Barbara Smyth Fund
for Scholarly Programs and Publications
The Lila Wallace–Reader's Digest Endowment Fund
The Malcolm Wiener Fund for Scholarly Programs and Publications